Amritasya Putrah

Advance Praise

'Kanchan Banerjee's *Amritasya Putrah: Children of the Rishis and Immortals* is an excellent introduction to Hindu Dharma and its foundations. Its arguments are based on original textual sources, and it presents the story of how its history is being reclaimed from old neo-colonialist narratives.'

Dr Subhash Kak, Regents Professor,
Oklahoma State University, USA

'With this book, Kanchan Banerjee articulates an important perspective that has become increasingly prominent as the twenty-first century has unfolded: a perspective that challenges the dominant Western narratives about India (that is, Bharat). With India's economic and political rise on the world scene, it is a perspective that can no longer be ignored.'

Jeffery D. Long, professor of religion and Asian studies,
Elizabethtown College, USA

'In *Amritasya Putrah*, Kanchan Banerjee discusses samskriti, culture, divinity, Hindu system, dharmic systems, etc. The discussions, juxtaposed with narrations from primary sources, lend themselves to deeper analyses and reflections. The reader can draw his inferences. He also takes a deep dive into the concept of nationhood, nationalism, Hindutva, Hinduism, freedom, Manuvad, secular, etc., in more analytical ways. The contrasts he provides with the Western approach and his arguments strongly counter many narratives that tend to undermine our foundations. *Amritsya Putrah* is a treatise on Bharatiya civilization, which will be useful for learners searching for a deeper understanding of our philosophical and cultural foundation. It gives plenty of references that will be useful for anyone interested in digging deeper into their subject of interest.'

Dr G. Ramesh, professor (retd.),
Indian Institute of Management Bangalore,
director, Niti School of Public Policy and Leadership,
and a former member of Indian Economic Service

Amritasya Putrah

Children of the Rishis and Immortals

Kanchan Banerjee

ink | OCCAM

ISBN: 978-93-6547-950-8

First published in India 2025
This edition published 2025

BluOne Ink Pvt. Ltd
A-76, 2nd Floor, Sector 136, Noida
Uttar Pradesh 201301
www.bluone.ink
publisher@bluone.ink

Kali and Occam are imprints of BluOne Ink

ink | OCCAM

To

Pujya Gurudev Srijukta Jagadish Chandra Sanyal

Contents

Acknowledgements xi
Foreword by Prof. Arvind Sharma xii
Foreword by Dr David Frawley xv
Preface xix
Introduction by Sean Bradrick xxvii

Chapter 1: 'Amritasya Putrah': The Children of the Rishis and the Immortals 1
Chapter 2: Bharat and India 22
Chapter 3: Bharatiya Civilization or Sabhyata 39
Chapter 4: Religion and Dharma 50
Chapter 5: Samskriti and Culture 74
Chapter 6: Divinity in Vedic and Hindu System 113
Chapter 7: The Hindu Dharmic System 166
Chapter 8: Bengal's Contribution to Modern Patriotism and Nationalism 196
Chapter 9: Hindutva 242
Chapter 10: Nationalism: Meaning and Scope of Freedom 263
Chapter 11: Misperceptions about the Hindu Dharmic System 287
Chapter12: Dharma Is the Future 307

Notes 359
About the Author 385

Acknowledgments

I am indebted to the renowned Vedic scholar Shri Vamadeva Shastri, aka Dr David Frawley, for his constant inspiration and guidance for this and other work.

I am also grateful to my wife, Haimanti, and our children, without whom this book could not have been completed.

Foreword

Prof. Arvind Sharma[1]

We live in times that are as fascinating as they are challenging. There is an old Chinese saying, often interpreted as a curse, that wishes upon the recipient to live in 'interesting times'. Whether these times are seen as a curse or a blessing, it is undeniable that we are living in interesting times.

Our era has become even more intriguing since 2014, when a Hindu nationalist party gained power at the Centre in India. This development has had numerous implications, one of which is that Hindus no longer feel apologetic about expressing their identity in public. As a result, Hindus have been participating more fully in the intellectual life of India.

This book is evidence of that shift. It reflects the author's desire, as a layperson, to explore and understand his own tradition more deeply. Within its pages, the author addresses almost all the challenges facing the tradition, covering topics ranging from Hinduphobia to artificial intelligence. The book provides an accessible introduction to the various issues confronting the tradition, offering an informed Hindu perspective.

By writing this book, the author has made our times even more interesting.

---

1 Professor at School of Religious Studies, McGill University, Canada.

Foreword

Dr David Frawley[1]

Kanchan Banerjee has produced a well-referenced and in-depth study of India and Hindu Dharma, otherwise referred to in the West as Hinduism, tracing its great civilization from its origin to the present day. He addresses the challenges, difficulties, and dangers that have emerged over time and continue to pose threats for the future. Yet, he also offers a remarkable vision and insight that transcend these issues, providing a deeper understanding of India, Hinduism, and our place as a species in a greater self-aware universe that remains a mystery to us.

Banerjee highlights how the Vedic rishi and dharma traditions have laid the foundation for the Hindu worldview and the great civilization of India, or Bharat. Yet, we are all children of the ancient seers who have left us a legacy of immortality to discover and realize. Our origins as a species lie in the cosmic mind, not merely in physical or social evolution or external technological progress.

In India, the rishi tradition of the ancient sages has survived, persisted, and renewed itself to this day, despite long periods of

1 Dr David Frawley, aka Pandit Vamadeva Shastri, is a Vedacharya and one of the world's leading exponents of Vedic knowledge, integrating an interdisciplinary approach. He founded the American Institute of Vedic Studies, which serves as a platform for his work, offering online resources alongside his numerous published writings. He has authored over forty books on the Vedas, yoga, and Ayurveda.

foreign rule marked by destruction. This culminated in the British colonial era, which sought to dismantle the country's cultural and educational traditions. The British, as part of modern Western civilization, failed to grasp the deeper vision of Bharat, just as they failed to inspire a spiritual aspiration for humanity beyond a materialistic and physical worldview.

Banerjee's book clarifies the true concepts, ideals, and universal perceptions underlying the Hindu worldview. He argues that understanding it requires a radically different approach from modern civilizational theories and contemporary assertions. This demands knowledge of key Sanskrit terms central to Hindu thought, rather than reducing it to the framework of Western religious faith or scientific empiricism. He carefully examines and skilfully counters the distortions that persist in educational, academia, and the media, exposing their cultural and political biases that perpetuate long-standing misunderstanding of Hinduism. These distortions are part of broader civilizational challenges facing humanity, which, despite technological advancements, continues to grapple with deep divisions, social conflicts, and emerging wars. While modern technology benefits us in many ways, it also poses risks, particularly when weaponized—an imminent threat we must confront.

With depth and precision, Banerjee unfolds the great wisdom and inspiration that Bharat has given to the world, particularly through its Vedic, Vedantic, and yoga traditions, which continue to expand globally despite persistent media stereotypes against Hindus. He also draws attention to the rich traditions of Bengal, which played a pivotal role in Indian's independence movement. He highlights the contributions of Raja Ram Mohan Roy, Sri Aurobindo, Rabindranath Tagore, and Swami Vivekananda, aligning himself with this philosophical legacy. Banerjee's work is a much-needed renewal of Bengali's dharmic tradition, crucial not only for Bengal and India but for the entire world. He offers key insights to revive the Bengali dharmic identity and, more broadly, that of Bharat—an identity that had been systematically undermined by ruling political parties; first, the Congress party, followed by decades of communist rule, and now the current ruling establishments, have all sought to subvert Bengal's Bharatiya identity for 'vote bank' politics.

I have known Kanchan for over three decades and have engaged in extensive discussions with him on the issues affecting Bharat, both personally and in various forums. His book is not only just a philosophical and cultural analysis but also a connection to the past and a new visionary approach to the future—not as a mere intellectual exercise, but as a blueprint for action.

Such works are vital to counter the ongoing misrepresentations and diminishing portrayals of India and its dharmic civilization. Banerjee's lucid approach dismantles these distortions, offering a true understanding that enables us to rise once more as children of immortality and build a new civilization—not on material power, but on a yogic vision. His remarkable book exemplifies the emerging scholarship of India today, and we eagerly anticipate his continued guidance and future contributions.

Preface

My fascination with Indian history started in my early years. The initial spark was ignited by the stark contrast between the lessons imparted in our classrooms and the broader historical narratives that permeated the urban environments during the early years of India's independence. This incongruity piqued my curiosity, compelling me to embark on an extensive journey of reading and research, delving into both India's historical tapestry and its contemporary reality.

Subsequently, my move to the United States provided a unique vantage point from which to compare the ancient Indian civilization with its modern American counterpart. I found myself pondering the remarkable prosperity of the latter, despite its relatively short history. My readings revealed that India, too, had once enjoyed a period of great prosperity, leading me to question the factors that precipitated its decline. Driven by this inquiry, I commenced a comprehensive study and analysis of all pertinent aspects of this subject. As my research progressed, my understanding of the complex interplay of sociopolitical and economic issues deepened, forming the bedrock of my previous work, *The Crash of a Civilization*. The book meticulously traced the historical events and developments that culminated in the Bharat we know today, acknowledging the confluence of both external and internal factors that shaped its destiny. This present volume, the second instalment in this series, extends an invitation to readers to transcend the confines of the past and engage with the present, while looking towards the future. It endeavours to provide answers to the questions posed in my earlier work and to seek viable solutions to the multifaceted challenges confronting this civilization. The ultimate aspiration is to recover and re-establish the profound depth and richness of the Bharatiya civilization, drawing upon its historical legacy. The key to this resurgence lies in the transformative process of collective and individual soul-searching, self-discovery, and enlightenment.

Many readers and friends expressed their reservation with the use of the word 'crash' in the title of my previous book, arguing that it conveyed an unduly negative message, whereas India remains a vibrant and resilient nation. To these concerns, I respond by drawing an analogy to a vehicle: even a severely damaged car can be repaired and restored. Thus, the 'crash' I speak of is not merely a physical event but also a virtual, real, and metaphorical phenomenon. Over the last 1,200 years, Bharat, as a civilization, has experienced an immeasurable loss of wealth. Furthermore, the people of Bharat have endured the loss of significant portions of their ancestral lands, including Afghanistan, Pakistan, and Bangladesh, alongside the erosion of a cultural heritage of the highest order. Bharat's rich heritage has suffered profound blows, both spiritually and culturally. We have witnessed the depletion of a substantial portion of the Bharatiya artistic and architectural legacy, and perhaps more significantly, the dilution of the very essence of what it means to be Bharatiya, the collective identity of a people whose ancestry stretches back millennia.

Following the publication of *The Crash of a Civilization*, I was frequently asked about the path forward. Even Prime Minister Narendra Modi said, 'So the crash has happened, what is the way to recover?' This book attempts to provide a thoughtful response to this critical inquiry.

Bharat envisions its ascent to the status of a developed nation within the next 25 years. However, a fundamental question arises: Is the construction of infrastructure synonymous with 'development'? What about the need to nurture the deeply rooted relationship between nature and culture, and their vital connection to humanity? We are confronted with the alarming reality of mass extinction, exacerbated by human-induced global warming. To be sure, I don't feel comfortable with the conventional understanding of 'development'. Instead, I find myself drawn to the holistic Bharatiya concept of *vikas*, which encompasses the harmonious and symbiotic relationships between nature, animals, individuals, diverse groups, and the myriad cultures within and beyond the nation's borders. This book champions the enduring relevance of the wisdom gleaned from the rishis.

Imagine a young person who comprehends and acknowledges the reality of climate change. Such an individual would naturally develop a deep concern for the earth and embrace the principles of sustainable living. This concern would manifest in a desire to reduce energy and fossil fuel consumption, among other things. Moreover, they would come to understand that by adhering to the principles of sustainability, they are not only safeguarding the planet but also enhancing their own well-being. Regrettably, the average individual tends to perceive personal welfare as distinct from global welfare. Therefore, it is important to forge a connection between the sustainability of the earth and society and the sustainability of the self. This connection can be established by drawing upon our ancient teachings and discourses, which resonate with the ideals of global sustenance and welfare.

Was it this profound understanding that propelled Bharat to its former heights of success? Are there other critical factors? Indeed, India was a knowledge-based society, fostering an environment of intellectual freedom that encouraged research in all domains, both spiritual and material. Free-thinking Indians introduced a multitude of groundbreaking concepts across various disciplines in the sciences and arts. Subsequently, the rishis and scientists generously shared their accumulated knowledge with all. However, with the onset of invasions from the West, we suffered the loss of numerous universities and centres of learning, effectively stifling free thought and confining intellectuals to rigid, hidebound ideologies.

Every Bharatiya must actively participate in the pursuit of prosperity. However, should this pursuit come at the expense of our civilizational harmony? Should we forsake our own cherished philosophy of '*sarve bhavantu sukhina*' (let everybody be happy)? The answer is a resounding no.

Instead, we must endeavour to cultivate a deep understanding of the core traits that define Bharatiya civilization, much like we strive to identify the attributes necessary for success in our respective professions. Certain characteristics are indispensable for success; for instance, an entrepreneur must possess not only product and marketing expertise but also a willingness to embrace risk. Civilizations, too, are subject to the ebb and flow of fortune, vulnerable to both internal and external forces. As Will Durant observed, 'It is a discouraging tale, for its evident moral is that civilization is a precarious thing, whose delicate complex of order and liberty, culture and peace may at any time be overthrown by barbarians invading from without or multiplying within.'[1]

Throughout history, there have been those who have sought to consume, exploit, and destroy societies, cultures, and civilizations. Notable examples include Chenghiz Khan, Mahmud of Ghazni, Aurangzeb, Hitler, Stalin, Churchill, and Mao. However, for every exploiter, there exists a protector and sustainer of civilization—figures like Ram, Krishna, Mahavir, Buddha, and Shivaji, among countless others. We owe our present existence to their tireless efforts in fostering and nurturing our culture. It appears that contemporary society has become overly focused on material prosperity, with families prioritizing self-advancement, emphasizing larger cars or houses, elite education for their children, and overseas opportunities. We have lost sight of our civilizational identity and our collective purpose. The 'nationalists' reiterate the slogan 'Bharat will be the Vishwa Guru', the teacher of the world, the guide to

1 Will Durant, *The Story of Civilization* Part 1, XVI, New York: Simon and Schuster, 1954, p. 459.

peace and harmony. However, it is said that the world belongs to the *veer*, the heroes—'*veer bhogya vasundhara*', or simply stated, 'the brave shall inherit the earth'. If we lack the power to protect and propagate our ideas, if we are not prosperous, we cannot effectively preach either. It appears that we are currently deficient in both the capacity to protect and the ability to propagate. We could reclaim Bharat's position as the Vishwa Guru by returning to a knowledge-based society, as in our past. Bharat could once again foster an environment of free research, both spiritual and material, leading to a resurgence of awareness in natural mathematics, material science, yoga, dharma, and ayurveda—a nation of free thinkers capable of conducting experiments and disseminating knowledge to scientists, policymakers, leaders in various fields, and the public.

It is easy to proclaim 'गर्व से कहो हुम हिन्दु है' (*garv se kaho hum Hindu hein*), that is, 'say proudly I'm a Hindu', but to truly embody the principles of Hinduism is a far more complex undertaking. Integrity in thought and action, a relentless pursuit of truth, and unwavering commitment to truthfulness are sorely lacking in contemporary society. Admittedly, pride is the initial and most crucial step; identity is essential, but it will only acquire significance if our actions resonate with our words. As Swami Vivekananda eloquently stated, 'Upon us depends whether the name Hindu will stand for everything that is glorious, everything that is spiritual, or whether it will remain a name of opprobrium, one designating the downtrodden, the worthless, the heathen. If at present the word Hindu means anything bad, never mind, by our action, let us be ready to show that this is the highest word that any language can invent.'[1]

One of the central goals of this book is to foster a comprehensive understanding of the term 'Hindu' and the concept of 'Hindutva',

---

1 Swami Vivekananda, 'The common bases of Hinduism,' Lectures from Colombo to Almora, *The Complete Works of Swami Vivekananda*, Vol. 3, https://www.ramakrishnavivekananda.info/vivekananda/volume_3/lectures_from_colombo_to_almora/the_common_bases_of_hinduism.htm

and subsequently, to strive to live in accordance with the all-encompassing principles, morals, and duties that promote a harmonious yet progressive world. A progressive world demands an evolution of the mind, the people, society, and civilization, transcending the animalistic tendencies to embrace the human, and ultimately, the divine. This encompasses the principles of unwavering resistance to the *danavs* (monsters), intolerance of *danavic* actions, the unwavering support of *manavata* (humanism), and the pursuit of *devatva* (divinity) for every soul—the hallmarks of Bharatiya civilization. Truth, dharma, pluralism, innovation, and excellence are the defining characteristics of this civilization.

It is imperative that society, in its entirety, transcends the debilitating influences of selfishness, cowardice, and a deficiency in integrity. My sincere hope is that this book will serve as an inspiration to a wide spectrum of individuals, particularly those in positions of leadership across various domains, including politics, business, spirituality, and social work. The land that once nurtured the wisdom of Ram, Krishna, Mahavir, Buddha, Nanak, Vikramaditya, and Chanakya has strayed from its intended path. Now is the opportune moment for self-introspection, wherein we collectively redefine the very purpose of human existence and realign our actions towards this renewed understanding for the betterment of our people and the world at large.

It is essential that Bharatiyas liberate themselves from certain limiting terms imposed by Western civilization, such as 'religion' and 'secularism'. These concepts, widely employed today, demand a thorough re-evaluation and contextualization. They represent mere fragments of the comprehensive ideas and ideals embedded within the Bharatiya worldview. Therefore, let the new generation of Bharatiyas, and indeed, people across the globe, redirect their focus towards the pursuit of truth and freedom, transcending the constraints of rigid 'isms'. We must forge ahead. As demonstrated in my previous work, *The Crash of a Civilization*, a deep understanding and awareness of Bharatiya history can illuminate the path towards a more prosperous future, provided we glean wisdom from past experiences. This present volume, *Amritasya Putrah: Children of the Rishis and Immortals*, serves a dual purpose: first, to identify the inherent weaknesses and afflictions that plague our society and nation, and second, to illuminate the civilizational strengths that enabled us to attain historical heights and endure formidable aggressions. The tools, processes, and strategies necessary to redirect our nation's course can be derived from the vast repository of millennia-old wisdom accessible to us. This book, in essence, is a collective effort to embark on a journey of self-discovery, both for the nation and its people.

While the focus of this discourse may appear to be 'Hindu', it is crucial to clarify that there is no 'other'. All individuals residing in Bharat, who are citizens of Bharat and hold reverence for its land and civilization, may identify themselves by various appellations, such as Bharatiya, Indian, or Hindustani. The term 'Hindu' encapsulates the rich cultural heritage and ethos that have evolved within this land over millennia. Historically, outsiders have used 'Hindu' to denote the people of Bharat. The confluence of historical conflicts with external forces and ideologies has contributed to the development of a diverse and multifaceted society. India has consistently tried to extend a welcoming hand to people and ideas from beyond its borders, while simultaneously resisting their forceful or deceptive imposition. Therefore, all those who demonstrate respect for Bharat's history, culture, and heritage are integral members of the Bharatiya family, irrespective of their religious practices, attire, culinary preferences, or festival celebrations, provided there is no conflict with fundamental Bharatiya principles.

It is important to note a crucial distinction: the three non-Indic terms 'religion', 'God' (or 'god'), and 'philosophy' do not precisely correspond to the Bharatiya concepts of dharma, ishwar, and darshan. During the colonial period, Bharatiya masters and scholars were compelled to utilize these Western terms to convey the essence of these profound concepts to their English-speaking audiences. Similarly, the term 'Hinduism' is often used as a substitute for 'Hindu' or 'Sanatan Dharma'. Therefore, it is my sincere hope that readers will not be misled by these linguistic discrepancies. The current era presents a unique opportunity for Hindus to educate the global community about the authentic meanings of these terms, employing the original Sanskrit words, for the collective benefit of humanity.

This book emphasizes the profound imperative to 'know thyself'. For you are the children of immortals, as proclaimed in a sacred verse from *Svetasvatara Upanishad* (Chapter 2, Verse 5):

युजे वां ब्रह्म पूर्व्यं नमोभिर्विश्लोक एतु पथ्येव सूरेः।
शृण्वन्तु विश्वे अमृतस्य पुत्रा आ ये धामानि दिव्यानि तस्थुः॥

yuje vāṁ brahma pūrvyaṁ namobhirviśloka etu pathyeva sūreḥ |
śṛṇvantu viśve amṛtasya putrā ā ye dhāmāni divyāni tasthuḥ ||

Following only in the footsteps of the wise, I merge you both in the ancient Brahman by continued meditation. May the Glorious One manifest Himself! May the sons of Immortal Bliss hearken to me—even they who occupy celestial regions.

Introduction

Sean Bradrick[1]

In *Amritasya Putrah: Children of the Rishis and Immortals*, Kanchan Banerjee presents a deeply researched, well-annotated, and logically compelling exploration of Shastrik, sociological, philosophical, linguistic, historical, and psychological perspectives. He does so without imposing his views, instead allowing the reader to engage with the material on their own terms. This book is truth on paper—an authentic and rigorous examination of crucial topics for Hindus, India, and her cultural realm, and indeed for the broader democracies of the world.

Some books have changed the world for the better. Many others could have, had they been widely read. There are books that possess that potential to free humanity from its delusions and performative pretentions. Banerjee has offered such a book—an elegant, eloquent, yet accessible work. This may well be his magnum opus, and it is certainly among the most significant books I have read on these vital subjects. It has the power to awaken the Hindu mind, liberating it from imitation and freeing it from congregational, colonial, and Abrahamic influences.

This text could ignite a revolutionary awakening among Hindus, breaking the largely invisible noose of evangelism and

1 Sean Bradrick, author of *A Hindu's Guide to Advocacy and Activism: Fighting the Narrative War*, is an American poet and an adoptee of Sanatana Dharma. Based in Omaha, Nebraska (USA), he is also a yoga teacher and Ayurvedic counsellor.

colonial or Catholic exploitation and oppression. I say 'largely invisible' not because these oppressive forces cannot be seen—they most certainly can—but because they remain unnoticed by many Hindus who, unknowingly, have chosen wilful ignorance. This is akin to the phenomenon of Native or Indigenous Americans who, gazing upon the sea's vast expanse, could not initially comprehend the Spanish ships on the horizon. Read this book, and you will see the 'hidden ships'.

This book is essential in an age of spiritual darkness, where even Hindu Dharma risks being reduced to mere 'religion' and religiosity. This is precisely what the Mullahs and Padris want Hindus to do. A thousand years ago, the indigenous people of Bharat were forced into the games of competitive religion—play or perish. The compulsion to compete with lesser opponents, though unfortunate, remains a lingering necessity. However, when we view Hindu Dharma as Sanatana, Adi, and Vishva Dharma, such competition is revealed as an absurdity. After all, as Swami Vivekananda proclaimed, Hindus—and indeed all people—are 'amritasya putrah', that is, 'heirs of immortal bliss'. This is a concept uniquely and proudly intrinsic to Hindu Dharma.

Is Hinduism primarily a religion? To suggest so, in my view, is an affront to the purity of dharma. Religion, as historically and conventionally understood, is a Western construct. Perhaps when Rudyard Kipling wrote, 'Oh, East is East, and West is West, and never the twain shall meet', he was reflecting on the stark contrast between religious dogma and the dharmic traditions of Bharat. Christian supremacists and radical Islamists have long sought to demean Hinduism, often by distorting its deities into demonic figures. We must not allow them to define Sanatana Dharma in terms of mere religion.

In Banerjee's book, we find a thoughtful, profound, and precise exploration of modern Hinduism, ancient Hinduism, and Sanatana Dharma. Not every Hindu is a *dharmi*, and not every *dharmi* is a

Hindu. We do not live in an ideal age, nor an ideal world. Hindu identity is crucial, but without integrity, knowledge, clarity, and discernment, it risks backfiring. *Sanatani* is what we all are—or were—before being exposed to a world of artifice and greed.

Sanatan Dharma is the boundless, eternal truth of the universe. It is not a thing, place, or accolade. It is not something one can leave or join, nor is it bound by dogma. It is not religion. Hindu Dharma is an expansive, pluralistic, multicultural, philosophical, and practical path to the divine, rooted in natural law. More than that, it is a journey towards the realization of one's own divine self. In that sense, Hinduism represents the religious aspect of Sanatana Dharma—a contemporary yet still limited worldview of its vast essence. Neither Hinduism nor Sanatana Dharma is confined to a single belief system, a set of commandments, or a man-made faith. *Amritasya Putrah: Children of the Rishis and Immortals* delves into these themes with clarity and depth.

For centuries, the Catholic Church and colonialism have gaslit pagan and indigenous peoples worldwide. This book can serve as an awakening for indigenous communities who have been blindsided to the authenticity of their own heritage. There is no longer any need to conform to Western religious figures who attempt to confine Vedic Hindu Dharma within an Abrahamic framework. The persistent gaslighting of indigenous cultures by Christian leaders only highlights their narrow understanding, which remains a hinderance to true freedom and democracy. As many economists predict, modern India is poised to surpass the United States in GDP by 2030. Now, Indians must reclaim their dharma. Sanatana Dharma does not need saving—it simply needs to be remembered.

The greatness of Sanatana Dharma was beyond the comprehension of Abrahamic traditions, so they reduced it to 'Hinduism' and, inevitably, added an '-ism'. The systems of *jati* and *varna* were once righteous, but colonialists interjected their 'master and servant' mentality to create what is now appropriately termed the 'British caste system' in India. Their strategy was to make the indigenous people despise or forget their own heritage. Now, thanks to works like this, those truths are being rediscovered—framed in Hindu and Vedic discourse rather than colonial narratives. We are emerging from our spiritual, cultural, and intellectual amnesia, guided by scholars and dharmic seekers who have awakened with clarity and purpose.

Sanatana Dharma represents the world's oldest, continuously practised, indigenous spiritual, and philosophical tradition—one that prioritizes inner knowledge over external belief and is founded on universal truths and natural law. These truths have been recorded in our scriptures for millennia. The wisdom of the Vedas was revealed by the ancient rishis, nagas, and yogis, who observed nature and consciousness, including the profound state of *samadhi* or super consciousness.

Sanatana Dharma is also an intellectual and multicultural tradition, encompassing sophisticated schools of philosophy, medicine, psychology, architecture, astronomy, metaphysics, mathematics, and the arts. In this light, Hindutva, or Hinduness, holds immense potential to heal a fractured world—not just in metaphysical or transcendental matters but in social, economic, and political domains as well. Banerjee's book covers these subjects with scholarly depth and radiant authenticity. His style is precise yet poetic, never cold or dry. It is evident that this book is a labour of love, imbued with dharmic intent and unwavering commitment. Reading it, one will grasp the true meaning of knowledge, inspiration, and *Satyamev Jayate*. It is revolutionary.

CHAPTER 1

'Amritasya Putrah': The Children of the Rishis and the Immortals

If we follow the progression of dignity as a concept, from its theological origins through its philosophical evolution to its sought-after position as a constitutional right, it makes for an interesting study. However, before examining dignity in the present-day context, we must first understand the concept and essence of human dignity and human rights, which find their roots in the age-old Vedas and Upanishads. Within Bharatiya civilization, human dignity is encapsulated in the phrase '*Amritasya Putrah Vayam*', which means, 'We are the children of immortal, all-pervading, almighty divine supreme'. The divine *ātman* resides in us all; hence, we are the children of immortality. This is how our ancient texts introduce humanity.

One note to the readers: as the Constitution of India refers to the nation as 'India, that is Bharat' in the English version and 'भारत, अर्थात् इंडिया' ('Bharat, that means India') in the Hindi version, I will be using both India and Bharat, as well as Indian and Bharatiya, interchangeably throughout this book.

Scholars often quote Plato's teaching, 'Know thyself'. This ancient Greek aphorism, *gnōthi seautón*, resonates strongly with Sanskrit and Indian linguistic traditions. You don't have to be a linguist to sense its familiarity if you know Sanskrit or some Indian languages: *gnothi* aligns with the Sanskrit *janoti*, meaning 'to know'.

The English word 'knowledge' itself bears close ties with Sanskrit *jnana* or *gyan*. Meanwhile, *seautoú* derives from *sé* (you) and *autos* (self). The term *autós* echoes the Sanskrit *atma* or *atman*. Thus, *seautoú* denotes something related to the self, making *gnōthi seautón* translate to 'know thyself' or 'know yourself'.

As we know, many European languages share a close association with Sanskrit or derive roots from it. Philosophers like Plato and Socrates were likely aware of India and the scholarship emanating from Bharat during their time. It is highly probable that these ideas were transmitted via trade routes by merchants and scholars. The Sanskrit phrase *atmanam viddhi* (know the *ātman*) is also well-known and bears a striking resemblance to *gnōthi seautón* (know thyself). However, for the Upanishadic rishis, the concept of 'thee' (which refers to the individual or the self) carried much deeper connotations, centred on the profound idea of the *ātman*.

The *Katha Upanishad* (1.3.3) offers a penetrating definition of the *ātman* and its relationship to our self-existence:

आत्मानँ रथितं विद्धि शरीरँ रथमेव तु ।
बुद्धिं तु सारथिं विद्धि मनः प्रग्रहमेव च ॥

ātmānamँrathitaṃ viddhi śarīramँrathameva tu ।
buddhiṃ tu sārathiṃ viddhi manaḥ pragrahameva ca ॥

(Know the *ātman* to be the master of the chariot; the body is the chariot; the intellect, the charioteer; and the mind itself the reins.)

So, Who Is an *Amritasya Putrah?*

Amritasya putrah is one who understands and follows the path to self-realization, possessing तत्रामृतंस्य चेतंनं—the awakening of consciousness to immortality.

अरँ कृण्वन्तु वेदिं समग्निमिन्धतां पुरः ।
तत्रामृतंस्य चेतंनं यज्ञं तें तनवावहै ॥

araṃ kṛṇvantu vediṃ sam agnim indhatām puraḥ |
tatrāmṛtasya cetanaṃ yajñaṃ te tanavāvahai ||

(Let the priests decorate the altar; let them kindle the fire to the east; and then let us both consummate the sacrifice, the inspirer of immortal [wisdom])
—*Rigveda* (1.170.4)

A person with this awakening is a child of the rishis.

The *Shvetashvatara Upanishad* teaches that humans are not inherently sinful and can achieve immortality through their actions. Thus, *amritasya putrah*—the child of immortality—embodies this potential. To realize this, one must embrace knowledge and see the universe as unified, as one. The path to enlightenment, Brahma (the all-encompassing), and dharma (sustainability) is one of self-awareness and wisdom. Regardless of their location in the world, the modern *amritasya putrah* must return to their roots of knowledge, self-actualization, and self-realization, ultimately discovering the self.

*****

It is a fact that Bharat has never conquered any nation. However, its knowledge, *samskriti*, and technologies have reached most corners of the globe since ancient times. While the now-discredited 'Aryan Invasion Theory (AIT)' suggested that outsider Aryans made the subcontinent 'civilized', studies over the past few decades prove that it was the people of Bharat, dating back to the Saraswati–Indus Valley civilization, who were spreading their knowledge and engaging in global trade.

Swami Vivekananda said, 'The debt which the world owes to our Motherland is immense. Taking country with country, there is not one race on this earth to which the world owes so much as to the patient Hindu, the mild Hindu.'

'The mild Hindu' is sometimes used as an expression of reproach, but if ever a reproach concealed a profound truth, it is in the term 'the mild Hindu'. He has always been the 'blessed child of God' (*amritasya putrah*).[1]

> Here activity prevailed when even Greece did not exist, when Rome was not thought of, when the very fathers of the modern Europeans lived in the forests and painted themselves blue. Even earlier, when history has no record, and tradition dares not peer into the gloom of that intense past, even from then until now, ideas after ideas have marched out from her, but every word has been spoken with a blessing behind it and peace before it. We, of all nations of the world, have never been a conquering race, and that blessing is on our head, and therefore we live.[2]

For the last 150 years, Swami Vivekananda's assertions have yet to be fully understood. Much of India's global footprint has been obscured by time and forces that failed to recognize its extraordinary contributions to mathematics and science, grammar and language, health sciences, astronomy, architecture, and the inner sciences, such as yoga. This is evident in the occasional discovery of Bharatiya icons and murtis in various parts of the world, including Russia and Italy.[3]

Imprints of India are clearly evident in present-day Southeast Asia. India reached these regions without invasion, colonization, or imperial intent. Hu Shih (1891–1962), a Chinese diplomat, literary scholar, philosopher, and politician, stated: 'India conquered and dominated China culturally for 20 centuries without ever having to send a single soldier across her border.'[4] Alternatively, he is quoted as saying: 'Rather than sending soldiers, India sent a few missionaries to conquer China culturally.'[5]

What about the West? The early Christian expeditions, which decimated indigenous and pagan cultures in the West, also obliterated evidence of India's presence, particularly in Europe. Later, Islamic invaders destroyed much of the remaining traces of India's influence in Persia, other Middle Eastern countries, and especially Afghanistan.

Since India's independence, the history taught in textbooks has often been 'sponsored', presenting a narrative that glorified the

Mughal period as if it was India's only significant era. However, today's aware Bharatiyas are questioning these perspectives. Tragically, much of Bharat's ancient past remains hidden, unexplored, and overshadowed by Islamic/Mughal and colonialist narratives, as well as refurbished building structures.

After Independence, history textbooks continued to emphasize the medieval past, while the ancient past received less attention and was frequently undermined. The full splendour of Bharat is yet to be uncovered. As Arthur Llewellyn Basham's book, *The Wonder that Was India*, it is almost as if no wonder remains. Now, aware Bharatiyas are gradually piecing together the fragments of their history, presenting a more complete picture and challenging contentious theories, such as the Aryan invasion.

We hope that Swamiji's following assertions will soon be fully appreciated by both average Indians and global citizens:

> Civilisations have arisen in other parts of the world. In ancient times and in modern times, great ideas have emanated from strong and great races. In ancient and modern times, wonderful ideas have been carried forward from one race to another. In ancient and in modern times, seeds of great truth and power have been cast abroad by the advancing tides of national life; but mark you, my friends, it has been always with the blast of war trumpets and with the march of embattled cohorts. Each idea had to be soaked in a deluge of blood. Each idea had to wade through the blood of millions of our fellow-beings. Each word of power had to be followed by the groans of millions, by the wails of orphans, by the tears of widows. This, in the main, other nations have taught; but India has for thousands of years peacefully existed.[6]

The Hindu and Hinduism

Over 1.2 billion people worldwide identify as Hindus. Sanskrit, one of the world's oldest languages, is the mother of numerous Indian and European languages. Yet, in any of the hundreds of

Indian languages, including Sanskrit, the word 'Hindu' does not appear to denote a people or their culture. Swami Vivekananda wrote, 'In old times, [the term Hindu] simply meant people who lived on the other side of the Indus River.'[7]

Many Hindu enthusiasts claim the term 'Hindu' is used in various ancient texts. However, these claims remain inconclusive. Punjab, the 'land of five rivers' (Pancha-ab), along with its adjacent regions containing two additional rivers, was referred to as Sapta Sindhu (seven water bodies) in the Vedas. In the ancient Persian text *Zend Avesta*, dating around 6th century BCE, it was called Hapta Hindu. According to scholar Prof. Arvind Sharma, an inscription from the same period, attributed to King Darius I, referred to India as Hi[n]dush or H-n-d-w-y.[8] The term *Hindush* evolved into *Hidūš* because the nasal 'n' before consonants was omitted in the Old Persian script.

Some scholars have cited the *Chachnama*, an Arabic historical text, which purportedly used the word *hinduvan* to denote Hindus or Indians,[9] though this claim remains unverified by the author.

The ancient Iranians, or Persians, shared close ties with India and appear to have coined the term 'Hindu' several thousand years ago to describe the people of the Indian subcontinent.[10] In the *Zend Avesta,* the term 'Hindu' was used as a geographic marker rather than a demographic or religious one. Over time, the people came to be called Hindus, and the land became known as 'Hindustan'—primarily by Middle-Eastern invaders. The suffix '-stan' is derived from the Sanskrit word 'sthan', meaning place or land.

The Sindhu River, which flows from India into modern-day Pakistan, was once a massive waterbody, akin to an ocean. The Persians, seeking a term related to this river, named those living beyond it. Since Avestan Iranian and Sanskrit are cognate languages, the linguistic rule where the Sanskrit 'S' becomes 'H' in Iran led to Sindhu becoming Hindu.[11]

The British scholar of comparative religion, Gavin Flood, suggested that the term 'Hindu' was originally a 'Persian geographical term for the people who lived beyond the river Indus'.[12] Prof. Sharma further noted that the 7th-century CE Chinese traveller Xuan Zang used the term 'In-tu', which may have been a corrupt form of Hindu.[13]

The Europeans, particularly the Greeks, dropped the 'S' from Sindhu, referring to the river as Indus, the people as 'Indoos', and the land as 'India'. The Arabs called it 'Al-Hind', and later, Muslim rulers and travellers referred to it as 'Hindustan'.[14]

Is there anything wrong with identifying with the word 'Hindu'? Much like our personal names, which are given to us by others at birth, we carry forwards identities associated with those names. Unless a name has undesirable connotations, we rarely feel the need to change it—and in this case, the term's origin traces back to Sindhu.

Interestingly, 'Saptaha' (a week or seven days in Sanskrit) is pronounced as 'haptah' in several Indian languages. Meanwhile, the people of Sindh province of Pakistan are still referred to as 'Sindhu' or 'Sindhi', and their language is also called Sindhi.

When we extend this Hindu identity, it could be argued that all people living in 'Bharatvarsh' are, in a broader sense, ethnically and culturally Hindu. This is irrespective of differences in religious beliefs, ethnicity, race, or practices. Over millennia, various races and groups came to this subcontinent and became an integral part of its civilization.

As Nobel laureate poet Rabindranath said:

হে মোর চিত্ত,পূণ্য তীর্থে
জাগো রে ধীরে—
এই ভারতের মহামানবের
সাগরতীরে।

Hey mor chitto, punya tirthe
Jago re dhire—
Ei Bharater mahamanaber
Sagartire.

(O my heart, in this sacred pilgrimage,
Awaken slowly—
On this shore of the great souls of Bharat.)

Here I stand, I spread my two hands
And I bow down to the Divine in humans in obeisance
With heartfelt delights, in lofty rhythm
For Him I sing rhymes in prayer.
These mountains, so sanctified with sacred meditation,
These grasslands, so washed with chanting rivers
Here! O only here! Find the sacred earth every time
Around this shore of great people of Bharat.

Who may know it at all
For whose beckoning call
From where had come
Streams of humans in tides vigor,
To end up mingling with the ocean
Here the Aryans, also the Non-Aryans
The Chinese along with the Dravidians-
The Shakas and the Huns,
The Pathans and the Moghuls
Mingled in one body in a perfect union.
—'He Mor Chitto, Punya Tirthe', *Gitanjali*, Rabindranath Tagore

Early Christian Missionary Activities in India Concerning Hindu Phraseology

If 'Hindu' represents both a geographical and ethnic identity, you might wonder how the terms 'Hinduism' and 'Hindu religion' came into being. To understand this, we must look at the interaction between Christians and Hindus, particularly during the early British period in India. It was through the lens of British colonizers that the world became more familiar with Bharatiya traditions, and to some extent, this perspective continues to shape how Hindu traditions are viewed today. To explore the history of these terms, we need to revisit key figures from Bharat's European colonial period as they played a significant role in shaping the concept of 'religion' within the Indian and Hindu contexts. While this is not an exhaustive list, understanding their backgrounds and contributions is crucial to comprehending the current state of our nation.

William Jones (1746–94) was an Indologist and scholar who inspired many British employees of the East India Company (EIC) in the 18th century to explore India's historical past. Although he propagated the now-discredited AIT, his meticulous work shed significant light on the antiquity of Indian history. Jones served as the chief justice of the Supreme Court of India in Calcutta.

Charles Grant (1746–1823) was a British soldier turned Christian missionary who played a pivotal role in establishing missionary and evangelical work in India. A study of Grant's letters reveals that he used the term 'Hinduism' thirty years before Raja Ram Mohan Roy.

William Carey (1761–1834) was an English missionary and Baptist minister who founded the Serampore College and University, the first degree-awarding university in British India, in 1818.[15] In his book *An Enquiry into the Obligations of Christians to Use Means for the Conversion of the Heathens* (1792), Carey reflected the contemporary view of India's traditions, referring to them as 'heathenism'. According to a dictionary definition, 'heathenism' referred to the 'belief or practice of heathens; idolatry and barbaric morals or behaviour; barbarism'.

John Thomas (1757–1801) was a founding member of the Baptist Missionary Society and accompanied William Carey to India in 1793. Trained as a doctor at Westminster Hospital, London, Thomas faced financial difficulties and decided to take a position as a surgeon on one of EIC ships. With the help of Charles Grant, he began a missionary enterprise in Bengal, where he learned

Bengali and translated Hindu scriptures into the language. He also studied Sanskrit.[16]

William Wilberforce (1759–1833) was a British politician and evangelist, and a founding member of the Church Mission Society. He was a vocal critic of the EIC and its rule in India, accusing it of 'hypocrisy and racial prejudice'. He used the 1793 and 1813 renewals of the EIC's charter to promote the 'religious improvement' of Indians, a euphemism for conversion to Christianity. According to Wilberforce, Christianity was 'sublime, pure and beneficent', while he described Hinduism as 'mean, licentious and cruel'.[17] His successful lobbying, along with that of others, led to changes in the EIC Charter, which allowed evangelists to enter India for the purpose of preaching Christianity and carrying out conversion work.[18]

Zachary Macaulay (1768–1838) was a Scottish statistician and one of the founders of London University. Known for his work in ending the slave trade, his worldview was shaped by the concept of the 'white man's burden', which held that it was the duty of the West to 'Christianize and improve the world'. He was the father of Thomas B. Macaulay.

Claudius Buchanan (1766–1815) was a Scottish theologian, an ordained Church of England minister, and an evangelical missionary for the Church Missionary Society. Buchanan played a significant role in introducing the Jagannath tradition and other Hindu practices to Western audiences in the early 19th century. He referred to Jagannath as 'Juggernaut' and used the term 'Hindoo' in his letters from India. According to Michael J. Altman, a professor of Religious Studies, Buchanan presented Hinduism through the lens of 'Juggernaut' as a 'bloody, violent, superstitious and backward religious system' that needed to be eradicated and replaced by the Christian gospel.[19]

Alexander Duff (1777–1851) was a Christian missionary in India who greatly influenced the development of higher education during the British period. As the first overseas missionary of the Church of Scotland to India, he played a pivotal role in founding the General Assembly's Institution in Calcutta in 1830, which is now known as Scottish Church College. Duff also contributed to the establishment of the University of Calcutta.

Thomas Babington Macaulay (1800–59) was a British historian and politician, best known for his division of the world into 'civilized nations' and 'barbarism', with Britain representing the pinnacle of civilization and India falling into the latter category. Macaulay is chiefly credited with introducing the Western education system in India. In the infamous 'Macaulay's Minute' or the 'Minute of Indian Education' (1835), he argued for replacing Persian, the official language of India's Muslim rulers, with English, making English the language of education in all schools. He wrote: 'It is, I believe, no exaggeration to say that all the historical information which has been collected from all the books written in the Sanskrit language is less valuable than what may be found in the most paltry abridgements used at preparatory schools in England.'[20] These actions, known as 'Macaulayism', led to the systematic destruction of India's ancient education and vocational systems, and, ultimately, its sciences and industries.[21]

Bishop Robert Caldwell (1814–91) was a Christian missionary from London who lived in southern India. He is known for his work *A Comparative Grammar of the Dravidian or South-Indian Family of Languages*. Caldwell argued that the so-called low-caste 'Chanar' people were not only Tamil speakers but also an 'indigenous Dravidian' group, ethnically and religiously distinct from their high-caste 'oppressors', the 'Brahmanical Aryans'. These speculative claims, which were far removed from the field of linguistics, aimed 'to develop a history which asserted that the indigenous Dravidians had been subdued and colonized by the Brahmanical Aryans'. However, the first edition of Caldwell's grammar was 'met with firm resistance' by the Chanar community, who 'did not like the idea of being divorced from Brahmanical civilization', the very division Caldwell sought to exploit.[22] Over time, Caldwell's work had a profound impact on the Tamil psyche, suggesting that the Tamil language had no connection to the so-called Aryan or Sanskritic culture of North India. The removal of Sanskrit words from Tamil aimed to create a systematic divide between the south and north of India, reinforcing the Aryan–Dravidian divide. This divide continues to be a significant point of contention, especially in southern India, where politicians and Christian missionaries have used it to convert Hindus in large numbers.

Harry Verrier Holman Elwin (1902–64) was a British-born Christian missionary who later became an anthropologist, ethnologist, and tribal activist. After joining the Indian National Congress, he grew close to Jawaharlal Nehru, who appointed him as an adviser on tribal affairs for northeastern India. Elwin was later made the anthropological adviser to the Government of North-East Frontier Agency (NEFA). He was sent to the northeastern states of India, where he worked closely with tribal communities, particularly in NEFA. Elwin is largely responsible for converting many tribals to Christianity in this region, contributing to the emergence of a Christian-majority region.

Friedrich Max Muller (1823–1900) was a German-born philologist, Orientalist, and Indologist. Muller, once a poor young man, secured a job with the British government and went on to produce a distorted translation of the Vedas and other ancient Indian scriptures, which served to foster negative perceptions of India's heritage and literature. Many Indians view him as both a figure of reverence and hatred. While much of his early work belittled Hinduism and Indian culture, over time, his views evolved, and by the end of his life, his attitude towards India's heritage had significantly changed, though the damage caused by his earlier works had already been done. For example, in 1860, he wrote:

> Max Muller called the Brahmanas 'a literature which for pedantry and downright absurdity can hardly be matched anywhere ...

> The general character of these works is marked by shallow and grandiloquence, by priestly conceit, and antiquarian pedantry ... These works deserve to be studied as the physician studies the twaddle of idiots, and the raving of madmen'.[23]

On 25 August 1866, Muller wrote to Chevalier Bunsen:

> India is much riper for Christianity than Rome or Greece were at the time of St. Paul. The rotten tree has for some time had artificial supports, because its fall would have been inconvenient for the Government. But if the Englishman comes to see that the tree must fall, sooner or later, then the thing is done ... I should like to lay down my life, or at least to lend my hand to bring about this struggle ... I do not at all like to go to India as a missionary, that makes one dependent on the Government. I should like to live for ten years quite quietly and learn the language, try to make friends, and then see whether I was fit to take part in a work, by means of which the old mischief of Indian priestcraft could be overthrown and the way opened for the entrance of simple Christian teaching.[24]

In a letter to his wife on 9 December 1866, he stated:

> The translation of the Veda will hereafter tell a great extent on the fate of India, and on the growth of millions of souls in that country. It is the root of their religion, and to show them what the root is, I feel sure, is the only way of uprooting all that has sprung from it during the last 3,000 years ... one ought to be up and doing what may be God's work.[25]

On 16 December 1868, he wrote in a letter to the duke of Argyll, 'India has been conquered once, but India must be conquered again, and that second conquest should be a conquest by education.'[26]

Despite his earlier views, Muller's later works, including his lecture series[27] and autobiography[28], suggest that by the end of his life, he had developed a genuine appreciation for Indian heritage, Sanskrit, and Vedic literature. In 1896, even Swami Vivekananda met Muller and praised him. This transformation in Muller's thought suggests a profound change in his views, often compared to the Ratnakar–Valmiki syndrome, which symbolizes a dramatic personal evolution from critic to admirer.

In his first lecture, Muller stated:

> You will now understand why I have chosen as the title of my lectures, 'What can India teach us?' True, there are many things which India has to learn from us; but there are other things, and, in one sense, very important things, which we too may learn from India.
>
> If I were to look over the whole world to find out the country most richly endowed with all the wealth, power, and beauty that nature can bestow—in some parts a very paradise on earth—I should point to India. If I were asked under what sky the human mind has most fully developed some of its choicest gifts, has most deeply pondered on the greatest problems of life, and has found solutions of some of them which well deserve the attention even of those who have studied Plato and Kant—I should point to India. And if I were to ask myself from what literature we, here in Europe, we who have been nurtured almost exclusively on the thoughts of Greeks and Romans, and of one Semitic race, the Jewish, may draw that corrective which is most wanted in order to make our inner life more perfect, more comprehensive, more universal, in fact more truly human, a life, not for this life only, but a transfigured and eternal life—again I should point to India.

He further said:

> [What] I feel convinced of, and hope to convince you of, is that Sanskrit literature, if studied only in a right spirit, is full of human interests, full of lessons which even Greek could never teach us, a subject worthy to occupy the leisure, and more than the leisure, of every Indian civil servant; and certainly the best means of making any young man who has to spend five-and-twenty years of his life in India, feel at home among the Indians, as a fellow-worker among fellow-workers, and not as an alien among aliens.

In his third lecture, Muller stated:

> That [Vedic and Buddhistic] literature opens to us a chapter in what has been called the Education of the Human Race, to which we can find no parallel anywhere else. Whoever cares for the historical growth of our language, that is, of our thoughts; whoever cares for the first intelligible development of religion and mythology; whoever cares for the first foundation of what in later times we call the sciences of astronomy, metronomy, grammar, and etymology; whoever cares for the first intimations of philosophical thought, for the first attempts at regulating family life, village life, and state life, as founded on religion, ceremonial, tradition and contract (samaya)—must in future pay the same attention to the literature of the Vedic period as to the literatures of Greece and Rome and Germany.

The evangelical missionary activities, which began with the mission of Charles Grant, continue to this day, with the ongoing mission to 'save' the Hindu 'heathens'. The 'white man's burden' remains in practice in many parts of India, particularly in the Northeast, Tamil Nadu, and many other states.

Introduction of the Terms 'Hinduism' and 'Hindu Religion'

Australian Professor A. Geoffrey Oddie observed:

> A feeling among some European observers that India's dominant religions were somehow different from that of other pagan nations gradually gained wider acceptance in the seventeenth and eighteenth centuries. This growing conviction that there was something distinctive in Hindu tradition which encouraged the formulation of the idea of 'the Hindu religion' or Hinduism. As a way of attempting to explore and understand non-Christian religious 'systems', the term Hinduism was then used increasingly as a category and concept, and as a label which has come to dominate how Indian, as well as Western, scholars think about Indian Religions.[29]

There are several million Jains, Buddhists, and Sikhs in India. While this book does not aim to delve into the intricate details of each of these traditions, it is important to note that they are all part of the dharmic system of Bharat. As mentioned earlier, the focus on the term 'Hindu' is not meant to exclude or neglect anyone; rather, it reflects the historical and cultural identity of Bharatiyas, rooted in the terms 'Sindhu' and 'Hindu', which have never referred to a 'religion' in the Western sense.

The purpose of this chapter is to highlight that the concepts of 'Hinduism' or the 'Hindu religion' are Western constructs imposed through Christian theological frameworks. Similarly, terms like Jainism, Buddhism, and Sikhism were classifications introduced by colonists. These traditions, despite their distinctions, are all integral to Bharat's cultural heritage, unified by shared principles of dharma, yoga, and karma. They emerge from the ancient yogic-Vedic tradition, which predates the concept of 'religion' as understood in Western discourse. Thus, the use of the term 'religion' for Bharatiya traditions is a misnomer and does not accurately reflect their essence or heritage.

For a long time, it has been suggested that Raja Ram Mohan Roy was the first to use the term 'Hinduism' in 1816–17. Below is an excerpt from Ram Mohan Roy's writings, addressed to British-educated Indians and British audiences:

> The whole body of the Hindoo Theology, Law, and Literature is contained in the [Vedas], which are affirmed to be coeval with the creation! […] In pursuance of my vindication, I have to the best of my abilities translated this hitherto unknown work, as well as an abridgment thereof, into the Hindoostanee and Bengalee languages, and distributed them, free of cost, among my own countrymen, as widely as circumstances have possibly allowed. The present is an endeavour to render an abridgment of the same into English, by which I expect to prove to my European friends that the superstitious practices which deform the Hindoo religion have nothing to do with the pure spirit of its dictates![30]

In his complete works, we find the usage of the following terms: Hindooism (pp. 102, 127, 252, 255, 277); Hindoo Religion (p. 92); Hindoo faith, theory, and practice of Hindooism (p. 102); Hindoo Theism (p. 123); Hindu Nation (p. 128) (not written by him); and Hindoo System (p. 250) (not written by him).

However, it is incorrect to claim that Ram Mohan Roy coined or introduced the term Hindooism or Hindu religion. He was not an Englishman to create a new English word. Someone before him must have already introduced these terms.

According to some accounts, William Jones coined the term 'Hinduism' to refer to 'the caste-discriminating principle of Varnashrama Dharma originated on the basis of Manu Dharma Śāstra' around 1794. However, no evidence has been found to support this notion. What we do find in the works of William Jones is the term 'Hindu' used eighty-two times (unlike 'Hindoo', which Charles Grant employed). Jones used expressions such as Hindu System[31], Hindu Nation (pp. 124, 181), Hindu Race (pp. 149, 154, 157, 409), Hindu Government (p. 182), and Hindu Theologians (p. 360). Notably, however, the term 'Hinduism' does not appear in his works.

Determining the actual origin of the term Hinduism is challenging. However, its earliest recorded usage predates William Jones. Charles Grant, who arrived in Calcutta in 1767 to join the EIC's military service, might be the first to coin or use the term. Initially, Grant was a critic of the company's corrupt practices, but later he became a missionary evangelist after some major personal tragedies. During this period, the EIC followed a policy of avoiding confrontations by tactically showing sympathy to local traditions and imposing a kind of ban on evangelical activities. Grant, driven by his vision of introducing Christianity to the natives, opposed the company's policy. To define Hindu traditions from a Christian theological perspective, he appears to have coined—or at least popularized—the term 'Hinduism'. This term would come to represent the perception and description of the Hindu system as understood by the Western and Christian world.

Grant firmly believed that Hindus were 'morally depraved' and sought to reform them by introducing the 'truth of Revelation and free them from the false religion'.

In his own words:

> I am not, as you may believe, for following the Mahomedan example of establishing opinions by sword; but I certainly am for helping these poor people whose [land] we enjoy, who are now in effect subjects of Britain, to recover the almost lost life of nature, and to become acquainted with the turn and excellence of Revelation, with the improvements and the rights of man.[32]

Grant advocated for the introduction of Christianity and Western education in India, laying the groundwork for the later efforts of Thomas Macaulay and Alexander Duff. Several Christian missionary schools were established, not only to educate the children of British officers but also the elite Indians. Grant campaigned to amend the EIC's Charter, which officially prohibited missionary activities. He referred to his missionary efforts as a 'social revolution' and argued that they would promote the well-being of the population while safeguarding the company's interests.

In 1787—thirty years before Ram Mohan Roy used the term—Grant wrote a letter to William Wilberforce, which included the following passage:

> The truth, as we presume to think, is that all objections to the extension of Christianity arise rather from Indisposition to the thing itself than any persuasion of its Impracticality. Some oppose it on the plea that Hindooism is a very good system, that is, that the few moral precepts which glimmer amongst an infinity of absurdities and enormities are a sufficient code for future happiness.[33]

From that point onward, instead of using terms such as the 'Hindu system', 'Hindu creed', and 'Hindu religion', Western theologians began to group the diverse traditions of India into one entity: the so-called Hindoosim or Hinduism. This new categorization placed Hinduism alongside Judaism, Christianity, Islam, and Paganism, effectively adding a new creed to the Western theological framework. The perceived heathenism and paganism of Indians, as viewed by Christians, now had a redefined identity under the term Hinduism.

Over time, the works of Grant and his contemporaries shaped and solidified British perceptions of India and its people, framing their understanding through the lens of these Western theological constructs.

The EIC Charter and Evangelism

Merchants from England needed official permission from the British Empire to conduct business in various parts of the world. In 1600, they formed a joint-stock company and received a royal charter from Queen Elizabeth I. The EIC easily obtained trade permissions and privileges from the Mughals, quickly becoming the de facto agent of the British Empire in India and other regions.

However, to curb the power of the EIC, the British government passed the 'Regulating Act' in 1773, which placed the company under the control of the British governor-general. Until then, Christian missionary work had been banned in India.[34]

The situation changed with the parliamentary acts of 1813, which ended the EIC's trade monopoly. Within a year, the company became a mere managing agency for the British government of India. As a renewal of the company's charter approached, Grant's writings were presented as a 'parliamentary paper' to support the removal of the missionary work ban. This effort, successfully led by Zachary Macaulay (the father of Thomas B. Macaulay) paved the way for the lifting of the ban. It was only after the 1857 Revolt and the War of Independence that the British government took full control of India and dissolved the EIC.[35]

After Charles Grant met John Thomas and presented his draft 'Proposals' in January 1787, Thomas made the following observations in a letter to his brother:[36]

> You must understand [that] there is a Mr. Grant here, a man of fortune and consequence, who has projected a mission of Gospel ministers to this country. The papers are drawn up and are now in my hands, [subject] to any alterations I may think necessary … but I stand as firm as a rock in mind and conscience, and I am too high in the favour and opinion of Mr. Grant. Mr. Grant proposes to send papers [informing] ministers of the Gospel in general about the opening in this country, and he also offers to entertain two missionaries at his own expense.[37]

In a letter to Thomas in 1790, Grant wrote:

> When early in 1786 a Proposal for a Mission was drawn up by others and myself, it was mentioned in it that one or two missionaries would be provided for. I happened to be the only person then in circumstance to afford such a provision, and I destined at least the missionaries for Goomalty. The advantages of such a situation are great and permanent. In case of converting any of the Natives, as soon as they renounce Hindooism, they must suffer a dreadful excommunication in civil life, unless they are under the immediate protection of the English. The converts may suffer persecution and death, living in heathen towns under heathen landlords. They are entirely in the power of the enemy.[38]

This document, known as the 'Proposal', was created in August 1787 by Grant and two other associates, including Thomas, with the aim of establishing a Protestant mission in Bengal and Bihar. It noted:

> We believe that this unique and important document has never been published, though it occupies a prominent place in the history of Christian Missions in India, and though it was really the bedrock on which the fabric of the Church Missionary Society was erected.
>
> The truth, as we presume to think, is that all objections to the extension of Christianity arise rather from Indisposition to the thing itself than any persuasion of its Impracticability. Some oppose it on the plea that Hindooism is a very good system, that is, that the few

> moral precepts which glimmer amongst an infinity of absurdities and enormities are a sufficient Code for future happiness. Others may oppose political Considerations, the danger of disturbing the present Order of things, and of introducing a Spirit destructive of that subjection and Subordination, which have made the Natives of Bengal so easy to govern.[39]

The letter from Charles Grant to the bishop of Calcutta, dated August 1817, reveals the following:

> The more general consequences of the adoption of this system then was that, instead of the Society's becoming the national organ for the introduction of Christianity in what was, at that time, properly British India, and maintaining the foreground, other English associations for the extension of the Gospel there sprung up, stimulated by a sense of duty resting' upon the nation as Christians, and as invested with the care of many millions of human beings sunk in the grossest pagan darkness.
>
> The society has thus lost the station it might, as I humbly conceive, most advantageously for itself, the Church, the nation, and the cause of the Gospel have occupied. I have troubled your Lordship with this detail, as the matter of it stands connected with the sentiments, I entertain respecting the attempts of different denominations of Christians to introduce the Gospel into India—a subject on which, in our relative situations, I deem it candid to explain myself to your Lordship. Although I would, on every account, have preferred the exertions of the Church of England in India, yet I could never ask whether any form of Christianity that held the essential doctrines of the Bible would not be better there than the gross superstitions of Hindooism.[40]

CHAPTER 2

Bharat and India

NeoCols (Neo-Colonists) argue that the idea of India did not exist before the British colonial era, or at least not until 1947. Realistically, had the British remained in India and succeeded in their plans—without figures like Sardar Vallabhbhai Patel and V.P. Menon—India might have resembled a jigsaw puzzle, with 565 pieces (princely states that could choose to join India, Pakistan, or remain independent). So, why blame the NeoCols only?

Some so-called nationalists too claim that India was 'born' on 15 August 1947, the day it supposedly gained freedom. Freedom from British rule? That might be true—the British rulers certainly left Indian soil that day. However, it was more a 'transfer of power' from the colonial rulers to their chosen representatives, mainly Indian Congress Party leaders.

But when, exactly, did India lose its freedom? Was it the 1757 Battle of Plassey? The establishment of Mughal rule in Delhi in 1542? Or perhaps the rise of the barbarian Slave dynasty after Mohammad Ghori's mercenary attacks in 1175? Alas, this is the confusing history Indians have been taught since 1947.

Yes, millions were indeed forcibly converted to a new creed—foreign to India's pluralistic tradition. Every such conversion has a deeply painful and tumultuous history: the daughters and sons of India were taken as spoils of war, and nearly every family silently carries a legacy of past trauma. The fact remains that these victims have accepted their reality. Their ancestors—and now, in many cases, their neighbours—have become enemies, fuelled by ambitious and vitriolic preachers. This animosity continues long after the country was divided along exclusive, monocultural lines. A question arises: Are these individuals epigenetically programmed forever, or is there hope for a future reset?

India was never truly unfree. The followers of the Bhagavad Gita were never fully conquered, though they may have endured periods of cruel subjugation under foreign powers. The foreign rules were but a small part of India's vast history, spanning thousands of years. However, alien forces and ideologies have psychologically ruled over the land and continue to exert their influence till today.

Have you heard the term 'Bharatavarsha' from the Mahabharata period, over 5,000 years ago? The famous utterance of Sri Krishna:

यदा यदा हि धर्मस्य ग्लानिर्भवति भारत।
अभ्युत्थानमधर्मस्य तदात्मानं सृजाम्यहम्॥
परित्राणाय साधूनां विनाशाय च दुष्कृताम् ।
धर्मसंस्थापनार्थाय सम्भवामि युगे युगे ॥

yadā yadā hi dharmasya glānir bhavati bhārata
abhyutthānam adharmasya tadātmānaṁ sṛijāmyaham
paritrāṇāya sādhūnāṁ vināśhāya cha duṣhkṛitām
dharma-sansthāpanārthāya sambhavāmi yuge yuge

(Whenever and wherever, there is a decline in Dharma,
O descendant of Bharata, at that time, I manifest Myself.
To protect the pious and to annihilate the wicked,
as well as to reestablish the principles of Dharma,
I, appear again and again, millennium after millennium.)
—Bhagavad Gita (4.7–4.8)

Or, for that matter, the name 'Hindustan', used by the Islamic invaders and rulers. Have you heard this daily bathing prayer of the Hindus, which can also be seen as a unity mantra?

गंगा च यमुने चैव गोदावरी सरस्वती |
नर्मदे सिंधु कावेरी जलेस्मिन संनिधिम कुरु ||

Gange Cha Yamune Chaiva Godavari Saraswati
Narmade Sindhu Kaveri Jalesmin Sannidhim Kuru.

(O rivers—Ganga, Yamuna, Godavari, Saraswati,
Narmada, Sindhu, and Kaveri—please sanctify the water
I am bathing in with your presence.)

Millions of Hindus around the world chant this prayer during their daily bath. All these rivers—Ganga, Yamuna, Godavari, Saraswati, Narmada, Sindhu, and Kaveri—are located across India, from north to south and west to east. Who composed this prayer? Was it a Greek pundit, an Arabic Sufi 'saint', or a British 'scholar'? In fact, it was a forgotten saint of India, and the prayer is so ancient that it is not recorded in history!

Before delving into the history of Bharat/India, let us take a moment to reflect on the importance of our ancient texts in determining the age of the land and its civilization.

The Vedas are the most ancient and meaningful human texts ever written. It is practically impossible to ascertain the exact date of the revelation or composition of the first Veda—the *Rigveda*. Its timeframe is believed to be somewhere between 10,000 and 20,000 years ago. Just as the term Hindu has evolved over time, Bharat was not initially the name of a country in ancient texts. However, the Bharata clan is frequently mentioned. One notable reference is the Battle of the Ten Kings (दाशराज्ञ युद्ध, Dāśarājñá Yuddhá) described in the *Rigveda*, (7.18.5–21). The king leading the Bharata clan in this battle was Sudas Paijavana.

Let's now review the Puranas. The eighteen major known Puranas have influenced millions of lives over millennia. These very texts provide detailed descriptions of Bharat's landmass, and they remain crucial in understanding the ancient geography and culture. While debates continue over the precise timeframe of their composition, many of these texts may have functioned as 'living documents', with additions (mostly) and omissions continued long after the original texts were scripted. Scholars such as Cornelia Dimmitt and J.A.B. Van Buitenen have supported this notion. They believed that the Puranas were akin to encyclopaedias, making it difficult to specify their authors and exact dates of composition.[1]

Hindus consider the Puranas as recordings of historical events, the *itihasa*, similar to the Ramayana and the Mahabharata. Among the most important of these is the *Vishnu Purana*. Many scholars agree that it is likely the oldest of the Puranas. However, the dating of the *Vishnu Purana*, along with that of other Puranas, remains a topic of debate in academic circles. While some academics have suggested that the *Vishnu Purana* dates to the 1st century CE,[2] many historians and Indologists place it somewhere between the 10th century BCE and the 1st century BCE. Horace Hayman Wilson, in 1864, proposed that the *Vishnu Purana* is rooted in Vedic literature and may have been written around the 1st millennium BCE.[3] In contrast, the controversial Indologist Wendy Doniger proposed a later date of 450 CE.[4]

Regarding the *Padma Purana*, another important text, some academics estimate its composition between the 4th and 15th centuries CE.[5] Others suggest that parts of the text may have originated between 750 to 1000 CE.[6] Asoke Chatterjee speculated that the text could have existed between the 3rd and 4th centuries CE but underwent significant revisions and expansions through the centuries, particularly in the second half of the 17th century.[7] Academics estimate that the *Bhagavata Purana* originated between 800–1000 BCE,[8] and it was composed to popularize the worship of Vishnu. According to the *Bhagavata Purana* itself, it was written at the onset of the Kali Yuga, which many researchers and experts, using astronomical calculations and archaeological evidence, estimate to have occurred around 3100 BCE.

The *Bhagavata Purana* mentions numerous *avataras* (incarnations) of Vishnu, with the ten most well-known as the *Dashavatara*.

However, the scriptures also reference twenty-three or twenty-four avataras.[9] According to this, the eighth avatar was King Rishava, the son of King Nābhi. In Jain tradition, Rishavadeva is considered the first among the lineage of twenty-four Tirthankaras. Rishavadeva is also known as Ikshvaku and Adinatha.[10] It is generally accepted that Avatar Rishava in the Purana and Tirthankar Rishavanatha or Rishabhadeva in Jain literature refer to the same figure.[11]

The *Srimad Bhagavata Purana* mentions: 'He [Rishava] begot a hundred sons that were exactly like him... . He [Bharata] had the best qualities, and it was because of him that this land by the people is called Bhârata-varsha.'[12] According to Dr S. Radhakrishnan[13], the *Yajurveda* mentions the names of three Jain Tirthankaras—Rishava, Ajitanath, and Arishtanemi—and the *Bhagavata Purana* supports the view that Rishava was the founder of the Jaina tradition. King Bharata, the son of Rishavanatha, is described as a *chakravartin* (the equivalent of an emperor) in Jain literature.

Various dynasties are associated with the Ramayana and the Mahabharata, the most notable being the Solar dynasty (Sūryavaṁśa), also known as the Ikshvaku Dynasty, founded by King Ikshvaku and linked to Sri Ram.[14] The Lunar dynasty (Chandravaṁśa) is associated with Sri Krishna. Of the twenty-four Tirthankaras, all except two belonged to the Ikshvaku Dynasty, with King Rishava (the founder) and King Bharata being part of the same lineage. A murti of King Bharata can be found in the prominent Jain pilgrimage site of Shravanbela Gola in Karnataka. Alternatively, King Bharata is also thought to be the son of King Dushyanta and Shakuntala, as described in the great epic Ramayana.[15]

The name 'Bharata' is often interpreted as follows: 'Bha' means light and knowledge while 'rata' means devoted. Thus, Bharata signifies 'devoted to light as opposed to darkness'.

The great epic, the Mahabharata, revolves around the landmass called Bhāratavarsha. India derives its names—Bhāratavarsha, Bhārata, and Bharata-bhumi—from King Bharata.[16]

Several Puranas also confirm this, including the *Vishnu Purana* (2.1.31), *Vayu Purana* (33.52), *Linga Purana* (1.47.23), *Brahmanda Purana* (14.5.62), *Agni Purana* (107.11–12), *Skanda Purana* (37.57), and *Markandaya Purana* (50.41). Let us delve into these Puranas to explore the naming and identity of the country.

The *Vishnu Purana* on King Bharata:

ऋषभो मरुदेव्याश्च ऋषभात भरतो भवेत्
भरताद भारतं वर्षं, भरतात सुमतिस्त्वभूत्

Risabho marudevyaasca rsabhaata bharato bhavet
bharataada bhaaratam varsam, bharataata sumatistvabhuut

(Rishabha was born to Marudevi, Bharata was born to
Rishabha, Bharatavarsha [India] arose from Bharata,
and Sumati arose from Bharata.)
—*Vishnu Purana* (2.1.31)

ततश्च भारतं वर्षमेतल्लोकेषुगीयते
भरताय यत: पित्रा दत्तं प्रतिष्ठिता वनम

atasca bhaaratam varsametalloke sugiiyate
bharataaya yatah pitraa dattam prati thitaa vanama

(This country has been known as Bharatavarsha since the
time the father entrusted the kingdom to the son Bharata,
and he himself went to the forest for ascetic practices.)
—*Vishnu Purana* (2.1.32)

The *Vishnu Purana* on the location of the country:

उत्तरं यत्समुद्रस्य हिमाद्रेश्चैव दक्षिणम् ।
वर्षं तद् भारतं नाम भारती यत्र संततिः ॥

uttaraṃ yatsamudrasya himādreścaiva dakṣiṇam
varṣaṃ tadbhārataṃ nāma bhāratī yatra santatiḥ

(The country [varṣam] that lies north of the ocean and south of the snowy mountains is called Bhāratam; there dwell the descendants of Bharata.)
—*Vishnu Purana* (2.3.1)

The *Vishnu Purana* further notes:
3.2.1: Maitreya says, 'O Sage! Now I wish to hear the description of the lineage of Priyavrata, who was the son of Swayambhu Manu.'
3.2.1: Rishabha had 100 sons, among whom Bharata was the eldest. When Rishabha grew old, he handed over the responsibility of his kingdom to his eldest son, Bharata, and retired to the forest for penance. Since that time, the landmass stretching from the snowy peaks of the Himalayas to the waves of the Indian Ocean has been called Bharatavarsha.
3.2.3: The landmass known as Bharatavarsha lies between the Himalayas and the ocean. It spans 9,000 yojanas and is inhabited by the descendants of Bharata. Bharatavarsha features seven native mountains: Mahendra, Malay, Sahaya, Shuktimaan, Rikshavan, Vindhya, and Pariyatra. The region is divided into nine divisions named: Indradweep, Kaseru, Taamraparn, Gamastimaan, Naagdweep, Soumya, Gandharva, Vaarun, and Yahadweep. Each of these divisions is surrounded by the sea and measures 1,000 yojanas. In the eastern part of Bharatavarsha live the Kiraatas, while the western part is home to the Yavanas. The central region is inhabited by Brahmins, Kshatriyas, Vaishyas, and Shudras, who engage in occupations suited to their respective classes.

To summarize the *Vishnu Purana*: 'The country north of the sea and south of the Himalayas is Bharata and her children are Bharati. A thousand yojanas from north to south, it has kiraatas in the east and yavanas in the west.'[17]

The *Padma Purana* offers a detailed account of some prominent holy places in Bharatavarsha.
2.3.1: Once, the sages requested Sutji to describe the most prominent places of pilgrimage in Bharatavarsha. Sutji began his narration by explaining the origin of creation and then transitioned

to the geographical characteristics of Bharatavarsha. Sutji said: There are seven prominent mountain ranges in Bharatavarsha—Mahendra, Malay, Sahaya, Shaktimaan, Rikshavan, Vindhya, and Pariyatra. Some of the key rivers that provide potable water to the inhabitants of Bharatavarsha include Ganga, Sindhu, Saraswati, Godavari, Narmada, Shatadru, Yamuna, Vipasha, Mahanadi, Vidisha, Varuna, and others.

The northern part of Bharatavarsha is home to several janapadas (kingdoms), such as Kuru, Panchal, Shalva, Matreya, Jaangal, Shoorsen, Pulind, Baudh, Chedi, Matsya, Bhoj, Sindhu, Utkal, Koshal, Madra, Kalinga, Kashi, Malav, Magadh, Videh, Anga, Banga, Saurashtra, Kekay, Kashmir, and Gandhar. Similarly, the southern part of Bharatavarsha comprises janapadas like Dravid, Keral, Prachya, Karnatak, Kuntal, Chol, Sauhrid, Kona, Korak, Kalad, Mushal, and Sutap.[18]

In Bharatavarsha, the people are referred to as either Bharatis or Bharatiyas. The Greeks referred to this land as India, a name later adopted by the British and other Europeans. It is likely that they preferred this name to avoid acknowledging Bharata's ancient history and heritage, thus, denying it due credit by not calling it Bharata or Bharati. The Constitution of independent India reflects this duality by stating, 'India, that is Bharat' (Article 1).

Bharatavarsha is perhaps the only continuous living civilization on Earth in this era, with a history spanning at least 20,000 years. All other civilizations have either perished or evolved so drastically that their connection to their original heritage has been entirely erased.

The *Agni Purana*, *Vishnu Purana*, *Bhagavata Purana*, and the Mahabharata all document the lineages of the Suryavanshi and Chandravanshi kings. Below is a brief summary of these records.

In the Svayambhuva Manvantara, the royal lineage begins with Svayambhu, whose son Priyavrata and his descendants rule the entire Earth. Among his descendants was Agnidhra, who was entrusted with the governance of the entire Jambudweepa, a region that can be mapped to present-day Eurasia.

The *Agni Purana* mentions the following:

जम्बुद्वीपेश्वरो राजा स चाग्नीध्रो महामतिः ।४०.३० ।

jambudviipesvaro raajaa sa caagniidhro mahaamatih

(The wise Agnidhra was the king of Jambudweepa.)

Agnidhra had nine sons, each of whom was given a portion of Jambudweepa to rule. The southernmost part of the land, located between the Himalayas to the north and the Sea to the south, was entrusted to his son Nabhi.

विभज्य नवधा तेभ्यो यथान्यायं ददौ पुनः ।
नाभेस्तु दक्षिणं वर्षं हिमाह्वं प्रददौ पिता ।४०.३१ ।

vibhajya navadhaa tebhyo yathaanyaayam dadau punah |
naabhestu daksinam varsam himaahvam pradadau pitaa ||

(By dividing the kingdom into nine parts, he gave the southern Varsha, Hima, named after the Himalayan Mountains to Nabhi.)

King Nabhi named this part of the land Ajanabha Varsha. He had a son named Rishabhdeva, who became the first Jain Tirthankara and one of the avatars of Narayana. Rishabhdeva eventually left the kingdom, and his son Bharata inherited Ajanabha Varsha.

ऋषभाद् भरतो जज्ञे वीरः पुत्रशताग्रजः ।
सोऽभिषिच्यर्षभः पुत्रं भरतं पृथिवीपतिः ।४०.३८ ।

rsabhaad bharato jajne viirah putrsataagrajah |
sobhisicyarsabhah putram bharatam prthiviipatih ||

(Rishabha gave birth to Bharata, who was the eldest amongst a hundred sons, and made him the king of his territory.)

Bharata was named after his father, Rishabha, and he named the land Bharatavarsha. The name holds significance not only because of its association with Bharata but also because all those born there are called Bharatas.

A Change of Wind

Joseph Rudyard Kipling, an English writer born in India, wrote his infamous poem:

> Wake up the White Man's burden—
> Send forth the best ye breed—
> Go, bind your sons to exile
> To serve your captives' need;
> To wait, in heavy harness,
> On fluttered folk and wild—
> Your new-caught sullen peoples,
> Half devil and half child.[19]

Was the goal of the colonizers to educate and 'save the souls' of the 'heathens'?

Merchants became colonizers, educators, and 'saviours of the souls'. It all began with Lord Macaulay, who sought to hide Indian contributions to world history and to erase human memory. In an effort to support his family and enhance their fortunes, he left his position as a member of Parliament and came to India. Determined to prove himself the right person for the job of serving his queen and bearing the 'white man's burden' to 'save the heathens', he wrote the *Memorandum on Indian Education*, which emphasized the 'inferiority of native Hindu culture and learning'.[20] He argued that by introducing English as the medium for higher education, a new class of people would emerge—'Indian in blood and colour, but English in taste, in opinions, in morals and in intellect'. This class, he believed, could then develop the tools necessary to transmit British learning in the vernacular languages of India. He claimed that Western learning was superior and could only be taught through the medium of English. Following his recommendations, the EIC stopped printing books in Arabic, Persian, and Sanskrit.

As a result of Macaulay's arguments, the English Education Act of 1835 was passed, supporting the teaching of a Western curriculum with English as the language of instruction, replacing Sanskrit and Persian. Furthermore, English was made the administrative language, and the higher law courts were to be conducted in English. This act established English as the language of communication for all administrative purposes, a practice that continues to this day.

John Strachey, a British civil servant in India, helped shape the narrative on India as early as 1880. The EIC had established a training school for British officers to be deployed in India—the British Military Seminary, or the East India Company Military Seminary, at Addiscombe, Surrey (1809 to 1861). Strachey completed his education there before entering the Bengal Civil Service in 1842. He later wrote in his book *India: Its Administration & Progress*: 'The first and most important thing to learn about India is that there is not and never was an India, or even any country of India, possessing, according to European ideas, any sort of unity, physical, political, social, or religious; no Indian nation, no "people of India" of which we hear so much.'[21]

The NeoCols continue to propagate this narrative to this day, seeking to negate India's past. I remember my grandfather telling us that some of his friends used to say that the British Raj was great, as it brought plenty of modernity to India, and they wished the British still ruled the country. This idea of Britain's contribution to India has fascinated many, as they were unaware of India's contributions to the global economy, science, and technology before the British arrived. Many of the British at that time were uneducated and poor, and they destroyed many indigenous systems, including education and industries, to serve their own needs.

A simple study of history reveals a very different story. Modern societies have yet to understand that 'one India' existed in a manner distinct from the nation-state model we define today. In addition to ancient Indian texts, numerous travellers from Greece and China documented their visits to India. Many came with the intent of learning or as part of a pilgrimage to the renowned Indian universities.

Scholars continue to debate the contents of a book called *Indica*, attributed to the 4th-century BCE ambassador Megasthenes, who served at Chandragupta Maurya's court in India. The original book is lost, but many Greek scholars have quoted fragments of it over the years. In 1845, the German Indologist Erwin Schwanbeck compiled and published available texts of *Indica* in Latin and Greek, with an English version released in 1877. According to the text reconstructed by the Scottish philologist J.W. McCrindle, Megasthenes's *Indica* describes India as follows:

> India, which is in shape quadrilateral, has its eastern as well as its western side bounded by the great sea, but on the northern side, it is divided by Mount Hemödos [Himalayas] from that part of Skythia which is inhabited by those Skythians who are called the Sakai, while the fourth or western side is bounded by the river called the Indus, which is perhaps the largest of all rivers in the world after the Nile. The extent of the whole country from east to West is said to be 28,000 stadia, and from north to south 32,000. Being thus of such vast extent, it seems well-nigh to embrace the whole of the northern tropic zone of the earth, and in fact, at the extreme point of India, the gnomon of the sun-dial may frequently be observed to cast no shadow, while the constellation of the Bear is by night invisible, and in the remotest parts even Arcturus disappears from view. Consistently with this, it is also stated that shadows there fall to the southward.[22]

During the 2nd century CE, the Greek mathematician, astronomer, and geographer Claudius Ptolemy lived under the Roman Empire's rule in Alexandria, Egypt. His work on geography and mapping of the world made him famous. He wrote:

> India within the river Ganges is bounded on the west by the Paropanisadai and Ara-khosia and Gedrosia along their eastern

> sides already indicated; on the north by Mount Imaos along the Sogdiaioi and the Sakai lying above it; on the east by the river Ganges; and on the south and again on the west by a portion of the Indian Ocean.
>
> Position of India beyond the Ganges: India beyond the Ganges is bounded on the West by the river Ganges; on the north by the parts of Skythia and Serike already described, on the east by the Sinai along the Meridian, which extends from the furthest limits of Serike to the Great Gulf, and also by this gulf itself, on the south by the Indian Ocean and part of the Green Sea, which stretches from the island of Menouthias in a line parallel to the equator, as far as the regions which lie opposite to the Great Gulf. India beyond the Ganges comprised with Ptolemy not only the great plain between that river and the Himalayas but also all south-eastern Asia, as far as the country of the Sinai [China].[23]

In the 1st century BCE (alternatively, in the 6th century CE), the astronomer Varahamihira wrote the *Brihat Samhita*, where the name 'Bharata Varsha' appears many times, providing minute details about almost every part of the Indian subcontinent, along with the boundaries of Bharata Varsha[24] at that time.

The 7th-century Chinese traveller Xuanzang (also known as (Heuen Sang) referred to the country beyond the Khyber Pass as 'Indu' or 'In-tu'.[25]

In the 16th century, the Mughal historian and scholar Abul Fazl, in his *Ain-I-Akbari*, wrote:

> The sea borders Hindustan on the east, west, and south. In the north, the great mountain ranges separate India from Turan, Iran, and China ... Intelligent men of the past have considered Kabul and Qandahar as the twin gates of Hindustan ... By guarding these two, Hindustan obtains peace from the alien [raider].[26]

It was in the colonizers' self-interest to assert that India was not a unified country and to take credit for 'uniting' or creating a nation called India. As for the Marxists, they take a very narrow view of history, seen solely through an economic lens. Civilization is multidimensional. Yes, there was no state called 'India', but Bharatavarsha was a civilizational unity, as attested in the previous paragraphs. It is a civilizational concept of a nation, not a political one. A state does not ensure unity, nor do shared ideals necessarily form a nation. Acceptance of diversity is a hallmark of Bharatiya civilization. Tolerance of all views and inclusiveness is a defining feature of mainstream thought here. Is it ignorance or ill intention that leads some to denigrate this civilization?

The historical tradition initiated by the British was undoubtedly motivated by their interests. It also reflected a lack of appreciation for a culture so different from their own that they did not have the vocabulary to understand it. This view was already facing challenges before Independence. Post-Independence, with shifting priorities and new currents becoming dominant, these perspectives were not challenged strongly enough, though research and writing continued. Ancient texts, epics, and later literature, such as the Puranas, were accepted as sources of history and studied accordingly. Slowly but surely, the nation is rising to reclaim its identity, which will emerge through a contestation of views.

Marxist history is a single-track narrative. The idea of history needs to be redefined. It should be rooted in the collective memories of people and societies, not the propaganda of some 'bard poets' or Marxists with an agenda. Consider how Hindus in the Ramayana, Mahabharata, and the Puranas wrote history. Even if the precise events may not be believed, the memories and lessons from the stories remain in the minds and hearts of the people. India must face the truth sooner than later, through genuine storytellers, not colonists, conquerors, or Marxists.

French historian Pierre Nora said:

> History, on the other hand, is the reconstruction, always problematic and incomplete, of what is no longer. Memory is a perpetually actual phenomenon, a bond tying us to the eternal

> present; history is a representation of the past ... Memory installs remembrance within the sacred; history, always prosaic, releases it again. Memory is blind to all but the group it binds—which is to say, as Maurice Halbwachs has said, there are as many memories as there are groups; memory is by nature multiple and yet specific; collective, plural, and yet individual. History, on the other hand, belongs to everyone and to no one, whence its claim to universal authority. Memory takes root in the concrete—in spaces, gestures, images, and objects; history binds itself strictly to temporal continuities, to progressions, and to relations between things. Memory is absolute, while history can only conceive the relative ... History is perpetually suspicious of memory, and its true mission is to suppress and destroy it.[27]

Bharat did not have the concept of 'history' as it is understood today. However, it did embrace the Greek idea of *historia*, meaning 'inquiry' or 'knowledge acquired by investigation', as well as *itihāsa*, which is derived from the Sanskrit phrase *iti ha āsa,* meaning 'so indeed it was'. The term 'Purana' means 'old memory'. While many societies honour and give great importance to 'oral history' and traditions today, some vested interest groups would deny this to the Bharatiyas, who possess the largest treasure of such histories.

You can now consider how each memory affects our epigenome, passing from generation to generation through the gotra of the rishis—the sages and seers revered for their perfection of life through yoga and sadhana, the pursuit of excellence in search of truth.

The concept of Bharatavarsha was more of a civilizational entity than a nation confined within borders and controlled by central rulers. Bharat was one interconnected land, continuously defining, redesigning, reconstructing, and reengineering itself, thus upholding its culture and heritage—Sanatana or 'ever renewed'. Bharat had many forms of government and governance, including democracy.

However, in a different way, the current concept of India never truly existed. India adopted the British parliamentary system, which was originally set up to rule over Indians, keep them under control, and exploit them to bring riches to Britain. Western philosophical and social values influenced the 'cocktail' that became the Indian Constitution. The entire system is founded on colonialism; will India ever escape the grip of this Neo-Colonialism?

India has faced an onslaught of outside influences. It is now time to sift through, recover all that is worthwhile—what was submerged—and reject what is undesirable—what does not sustain or propel the people forward.

The Shakti Peethas

The Puranic legend goes as follows: In the ancient era, the Creator Brahma performed a Yagna to please Shiva and Shakti for their help to create the universe. Shakti Devi helped him in this great venture. Afterward, Brahma's progeny Daksha, performed yajnas to obtain Shakti as his daughter. Shakti was born as the daughter of Daksha.

Daksha invited all the devatas and devis to a yajna, except Shiva and Sati. Though they had not received an invitation, Sati wished to attend her father's yajna. She tried to persuade Shiva to attend, but he declined and requested her not to go. Sati went to her father's yajna. Daksha did not offer the respect Sati deserved. It was not only an insult to Sati but also to Shiva. Sati was so anguished she immolated herself in the fire. The moment she immolated herself, Shiva knew. An enraged Shiva destroyed Daksha's yajna and then picked up the dead body of Sati and performed the 'Tandava', the celestial dance of destruction. The entire Devaloka was very worried and requested Vishnu's help. He brought his Sudarshan Chakra and cut Sati's body into many parts. These parts of Sati's body fell all over the world, and those that fell within the Indian Subcontinent are called the 'Shakti Peethas'. Some sources say there were 108 Shakti Peethas; however, the majority accept 51 Shakti Peethas, out of which 18 are called Maha (major) Shakti Peethas. Of which four are called Adi (original) Shakti Peethas, and those are: Bimala Temple, Puri (inside Jagannath Temple Complex), Odisha, Tara Tarini Temple, Berhampur, Odisha, Kamakhya Temple Guwahati, Assam and Dakshina Kalika, Kalighat Kali Temple, West Bengal.[28]

It is important to note that these Shakti Peethas are spread across the Indian subcontinent, from Kashmir to Tamil Nadu, Bengal to Assam, Meghalaya to Tripura, showing the unity of Bharatavarsha from a very ancient time. Additionally, some Shakti Peethas are located outside present-day India, in Bangladesh (six), Pakistan (two), Sri Lanka (two), and Tibet and Nepal (one each).

These primary sources for the Shakti Peethas are the *Vayu Purana* and the *Shiva Purana*, with contains over 1,00,000 verses. While no one can ascertain when these texts were composed, scholars like Klostermaier estimate that the oldest chapters in surviving manuscripts likely date back to the 10th to 11th centuries CE.[29] However, Hindus believe these texts to be much older, authored by Ved Vyasa, who also composed the Mahabharata over 5,000 years ago.

The existence and locations of the various Shakti Peethas, the twelve Jyotirlingas, and the Char Dhams provide a clear picture of Bharat's boundaries and the landmass of Bharatavarsha. This serves as clear proof that a united civilization and connected Bharat existed long before the British and the Muslims arrived in India.

CHAPTER 3

Bharatiya Civilization or Sabhyata

Imagine a time in history when hunter-gatherers were focused on survival. They wore basic clothes made from animal skins and subsisted on fruits, fish, deer, and other animals. By this point, they may have learned how to make fire. They witnessed thunderstorms, floods, earthquakes, and volcanic eruptions, and in their fear, they began to 'wish' (though not yet to pray) for protection from these natural calamities. From their primitive objects of fear and veneration, deities were born—manifested through the frightening or awe-inspiring events of nature. For many civilizations, including those in Europe and the Americas, this was the scene that could be painted on the mental canvas just a few hundred thousand years ago.

Yet one land on Earth moved beyond this phase long before others and began to do something different. They sought to uncover the secrets of nature. How could one overcome nature's wrath or accept her blessings? Their quest was for truth and for answers to the mysteries of the universe. This pursuit evolved into meditation. They devoted their lives to finding answers. Their goal was to conquer nature—not just externally but internally as well. They built homes, created language, and, most importantly, learned to manage inner nature—fear, greed, and the like—in order to focus inward and conserve energy, rather than looking solely outward.

A small rivulet winds through a deep forest in this picturesque land. The water breaks over small rocks in the riverbed, creating the music of nature. Birds sing, the sun shines, and its rays penetrate the dense forest, creating an aura of mystery. The people here could listen to the trees, speak with the rivers, and understand the language of the animals. They bowed in reverence to the mighty mountains—the Vindhyas and the Himalayas—and discovered the sacred abodes of the great *devatas* and *devis*.

They bathed in the rivers as if the waters were nectar, calling them names like Narmada, Sindhu, Ganga, Jamuna, Kaveri, Godavari, Brahmaputra, and many others that were beloved and sacred. For millennia, they bathed, performed puja, and protected these holy rivers. However, things began to deteriorate with the advent of foreign invasions, and today, their descendants no longer hesitate to pollute the once-sacred waters, forests, and mountains.

As human beings, our inherent tendency is to always desire more—to know more, to own more, to connect with more people. Ultimate networking! We belong to the infinite, and in that sense, we are infinite. Yet, we are never content with what we have; we always seek more. We also cry out, 'Not here, not here, somewhere else', rejecting what is real in search of the elusive. This yearning for truth and the infinite drove the Vedic rishis to expand the scope of their knowledge—by observing, focusing, and meditating constantly. They chanted the 'Pavamana Mantra', whose purpose is to 'purify'.

The mantra reads:

असतो मा सद्गमय ।
तमसो मा ज्योतिर्गमय ।
मृत्योर्माऽमृतं गमय ॥

asato mā sadgamaya,
tamaso mā jyotirgamaya,
mṛtyormā'mṛtaṃ gamaya.

(Lead me from the unreal to the real,
Lead me from darkness to light,
Lead me from death to immortality.)
—*Brhadaranyaka Upanishad* (1.3.28)

Our ancestors sought to transcend ignorance and lesser truths to attain higher truth, to progress from the dim light of limited knowledge to the brilliance of greater understanding, and to evolve from mortal beings to immortal ones. They were rishis, sages, who gifted us the wisdom of the Upanishads.

We know that Aristotle was regarded as one of the greatest 'pundits' of Western civilization at a certain point in history, yet much of his understanding of the universe was incorrect. However, Western thought was significantly enriched when philosophers such as Plato, Socrates, Pythagoras, and Archimedes came into contact with the 'Brahmins' and the rishis. Listen to what the French writer, philosopher, satirist, and historian Voltaire once said:

> I am convinced that everything has come down to us from the banks of the Ganges—astronomy, astrology, metempsychosis, etc. It is important to note that some 2,500 years ago, at least, Pythagoras went from Samos to the Ganges to learn geometry ... But he would certainly not have undertaken such a strange journey had the reputation of the Brahmins' science not been long established in Europe.[1]

The Arabs, too, learned extensively from the 'Hindoo Brahmins' and could not help but praise the contributions of Indian pundits. Yet, in the so-called 'history of civilization', India was rarely given its due. The 'experts' failed to recognize that India had a different worldview, which they couldn't identify, especially because the words were absent from their vocabulary. Since the authors of world history were too proud of their own cultures, they neglected and ignored all others. While Egypt, Mesopotamia, and even Persia were afforded much space, India's antiquity was largely overlooked.

What Is Civilization?

According to Alfred North Whitehead (1861–1947), British philosopher and mathematician, 'Simply speaking, it is the society, culture, and way of life of a particular geographical area … general definition of civilization: a civilized society is exhibiting the five qualities of Truth, beauty, adventure, art, peace.'[2]

The great American philosopher and historian Will Durant defined civilization as: 'Civilizations are the generations of the racial soul.' He also said:

> Civilization is not inherited; it has to be learned and earned by each generation anew; if the transmission should be interrupted for one century, civilization would die, and we should be savages again. It is not the race that makes the civilization, it is the civilization that makes the people: circumstances geographical, economic, and political create a culture, and the culture creates a human type.[3]

So, what is this Indic or Hindu *sabhyata* or civilization? As discussed earlier, the original name of the Indian subcontinent is Bharatavarsha, or Bharat, which literally means 'that which emanates light and is ever shining'. The quality of giving the light of knowledge is one that a Vishwa Guru (world teacher) must possess to become the benevolent teacher of the world.

I view Bharat as a diamond with innumerable facets. In this brief introduction to the idea of *Bhartiya sabhayata*, I will touch upon six key facets or unique pillars.

Rishi Sabhyata: Vision of the Past, Present, and Future

In case of India, the rishis had visions of various realities and truths of the universe; they were seeing it. We call them *drastas*—those with vision, the *rishis*. First, the Vedas were revealed to the rishis through their meditations. They were *mantra-drashtas*. Then came the Upanishads and other texts, and thus, the *sabhyata* expanded its scope and extent.

A rishi represents a *drasta*—a seer, a visionary. Yāska, an ancient grammarian and linguist from around the 5th century BCE, explained that '*drasta*' comes from '*drish*' (to see), and he cites 'Aupamanyava' to support his view.

Swami Vivekananda described *rishis* as *mantra-drashtas* or 'the seers with mental powers'. He said, 'The truth came to the *Rishis* of India—the Mantra-drashtâs, the seers of thought—and will come to all *Rishis* in the future, not to talkers, not to book-swallowers, not to scholars, not to philologists, but to seers of thought.'[4]

What is the *dristhti* or the vision of a *rishi*? What is the purpose of life to a *rishi*?

अरं कृण्वन्तु वेदिं समग्निमिन्धतां पुरः ।
तत्रामृतस्य चेतनं यज्ञं ते तनवावहै ॥

aram kṛṇvantu vedim sam agnim indhatām puraḥ
tatra amṛtasya cetanam yajñam te tanavā vahai

(Let them make the altar ready and let them set Agni ablaze in front. There, the awakening of consciousness to immortality. Let us extend for thee thy effective sacrifice.)
—*Rigveda* (1.170.4)

This verse essentially means that we are all 'the children of immortals'—that essentially means we are atmans and carriers of an immortal tradition, and to realize this, one must have the 'consciousness' of being immortal. This concept of immortality is a central theme in the Vedas and the Upanishads. The *Shvetashvatara Upanishad* (2.5) says:

युजे वां ब्रह्म पूर्व्यं नमोभिर्विश्लोक एतु पथ्येव सूरेः।
शृण्वन्तु विश्वे अमृतस्य पुत्रा आ ये धामानि दिव्यानि तस्थुः॥

yuje vāṃ brahma pūrvyaṃ namobhir vi śloka etu pathyeva sūreḥ,
śṛṇvanti viśve amṛtasya putrā ā ye dhāmāni diviyāni tasthuḥ.

(O senses and deities who favour them! Through salutations,
I unite myself with the eternal Brahman, who is your source.
Let this prayer sung by me, who follow the right path of the Sun,
go forth in all directions. May the children of the Immortal,
who occupy celestial positions, hear it!)

Therefore, every Bharatiya is the descendant of the *rishis* and the children of the immortals. This gives rise to the unique idea of *gotra* (गोत्र). *Gotra* is derived from गौः (go), meaning 'forward-moving', and त्रः (tra), meaning 'offspring'. So, literally, *gotra* means 'forward-moving descendants'. *Gotra* connects a person to the root of their ancestry, tracing back to a rishi—this practice is one of the most unique ways to trace one's lineage compared to the rest of the world's civilizations. Each gotra essentially represents a lineage back to the rishis. For example, Bharadwaj gotra is the lineage of Rishi Bharadwaj, genetic inheritors of the rishi.

Vedic Sabhyata: A Truth-Seeking Knowledge Society

The Vedas are not mere texts referred to as the Vedas; *veda* means knowledge, and *vidya* is the subject knowledge. India has been a society of knowledge for millennia. Truth-seeking and the discovery of knowledge form the foundation of civilization. Hence, the mantra:

सत्यमेव जयते नानृतं सत्येन पन्था विततो देवयानः ।
येनाक्रमन्त्यृषयो ह्याप्तकामाम्म् यत्र तत् सत्यस्य परमं निधानम्म् ॥

satyameva jayate nānṛtaṃ
satyena panthā vitato devayānaḥ
yenākramantyṛṣayo hyāptakāmā
yatra tat satyasyaa paramaṃ nidhānaam

(Truth alone triumphs, not falsehood.
Through Truth, the divine path is spread out,
by which the sages, whose desires have been completely fulfilled,
reach the supreme treasure of truth.)
—*Mundaka Upanishad* 3.1.6[5]

Truth is manifested in Devi Saraswati.

Dharmik Sabhyata: Sustainability and Sustenance Consciousness

Dharma represents sustainable principles and order, as well as sustainable actions or duties, leading to the sustainability of all aspects of life. The ultimate goal of dharma is to sustain and grant ultimate freedom to all. Dharma, however, is not synonymous with religion. As Swami Vivekananda stated, 'The word Dharma connotes "that on which everything rests". This concept is unique to Indian culture, and being many faceted cannot be expressed by any other word in any other language. Dharma is indeed the law of our being and therefore, it can be identified with God.'[6]

During the period of foreign domination in Bharat, the true meaning of dharma was forgotten. Today, in common parlance, it is equated with 'religion' and associated with various religious rituals, such as puja, archana, etc. The term 'ritual' stems from *riti* in Sanskrit, which means 'tradition or social norms and practices' and is rooted in *ṛta,* which denotes universal or divine laws and order—similar to the concept of dharma. The term *ritu* in Sanskrit refers to seasons and female menstruation, symbolizing nature's cycle and norm—its '*riti*'. Hindu rituals, therefore, are practices intended to align with *ṛta* and dharma. But, pujas, bhajans, mantras, dhyanas, and other rituals do not equate to dharma, though a part of them are, and importantly, they are not 'religion'.

Broadly speaking, yoga serves as a methodology to achieve *purusarthas* (artha, kama, and moksha) based on dharma. Hatha Yoga, for instance, consists of tools such as mantra, yantra, tantra, and, puja, all designed for self-empowerment in the pursuit of the *purusarathas* grounded in dharma. Similarly, bhajanas, archanas, and kirtanas contribute to physical, mental, and spiritual well-being as well as self-empowerment and the fulfillment of the self. These are methods and tools to align with dharma, but they are not dharma itself.

In Sri Shankaracharya's introduction to his *Commentary on the Gita*, he outlined a twofold concept of dharma, which has its roots in the teachings of Rishi Kanada, the founder of the Vaiseshika school of philosophy. He stated:

> The dharma taught in the Vedas is of two-fold nature, characterized by pravritti – outward action, and nivritti, inward contemplation (or power and tendency to detach), meant for the stability of the world, which is meant to ensure the true abhyudaya, freedom, material prosperity and socioeconomic welfare, and nihshreyasa, spiritual freedom and attainments of all beings.

Thus, the ideas of Vishnu (sustenance), Shakti (protection), Lakshmi (beauty and prosperity), and Shiva (renewal and regeneration) were discovered and revealed by the rishis.

Yogic Sabhyata: Connectedness and Unity

The three aspects outlined earlier, i.e., Rishi, Veda, and Dharma, established the fact that we are all interconnected through an eternal bond. 'Yog' means 'to unite, connect and add'. Connectedness with people to people, people to family, society and nation, people to nature, and people to entire creation. The essence of real connectedness is unity of 'yog'.

Mahayogi and rishi, Aurobindo said:

> Yoga stands essentially on the fact that in this world we are everywhere one, yet divided; one yet divided in our being, one with yet divided from our fellow creatures of all kinds, one with yet divided from infinite existence which we call God, Nature or Brahman. Yoga, generally, is the power which the soul in one body has of entering into effective relation with other souls, with parts of itself which are behind the waking consciousness, with forces of Nature and objects in Nature, with the Supreme Intelligence, Power and Bliss which governs the world either for the sake of that union in itself or for the purpose of increasing or modifying our manifest being, knowledge, faculty, force or delight. Any system which organises our inner being and our outer frame for these ends may be called a system of Yoga.[7]

अयं निजः परो वेति गणना लघुचेतसाम्।
उदारचरितानां तु वसुधैव कुटुम्बकम्॥

ayaṃ nijaḥ paro veti gaṇanā laghucetasām
udāracaritānāṃ tu vasudhaiva kuṭumbakam

(The small-minded say, this is mine, and that is his,
The wise believe the entire world is a family.)
—*Maha Upanishad* (6.71–6.73)

Thus, as part of society and societal good, we desire welfare and good for all.

सर्वेषां मङ्गलं भूयात् सर्वे सन्तु निरामयाः।
सर्वे भद्राणि पश्यन्तु मा कश्चिद्दुःखभाग् भवेत्॥

sarveṣāṁ maṅgalaṁ bhūyāt sarve santu nirāmayāḥ|
sarve bhadrāṇi paśyantu mā kaścidduḥkhabhāg bhavet||

(Let everyone be blessed with health and happiness.
May all see what is auspicious, and may no one experience sorrow.
The world is one large family, and this thought
is at the heart of this philosophy.)
—*Garuda Purana* (35.51)

Yog can, therefore, be defined more broadly as the various means, ways, and techniques employed to achieve the goals one pursues. It can be Bhakti, Gyan, Karma, and many other types of yog.

Sanskritik Sabhyata: Purifying, Cleansing, Renewal and Re-Invention, Re-Engineering

We often hear that change is the only constant. In this context, there are two key types of samskaras to consider. The first type refers to the imprints of our thoughts and actions, the seeds of karma, and their genetic lineage. These are the sixteen samskaras: subtle, invisible karmic imprints that shape our lives. In genetic terms, they resemble hidden switches in our DNA and mind, influencing both our inherited traits and epigenetic expression. The second type of samskara involves the process of cleansing, reorganizing, and renewing. These are the methods through which we purify and rejuvenate ourselves and our civilization.

For centuries, the people of Bharat had to adapt to new ways of life under hostile dominions. As Will Durant observed, 'It was not easy to be a Hindu' during the Islamic conquest, which he called the 'bloodiest in history'. Hindus survived, but in many ways, their culture became frozen in the past. They found shelter in Bhakti but lost the paths of Gyan marg (knowledge) and Karma marg (action).

Yet, this civilization is Sanatan. What does Sanatan mean? Eternal? Everlasting? The term 'Sanatan' literally means eternal or 'always residing'. It refers to something that is constantly renewed, reorganized, and re-engineered in the case of societal norms and, therefore, remains perpetually new.

Just as a river becomes stagnant when it loses its flow, allowing plankton to pollute its waters, society and civilization can also stagnate when they stop renewing themselves. The essential force of movement and renewal was severely damaged during the past 2,000 years, often referred to as the Kali Yuga or Dark Age in Bharatiya history. William Faulkner, the American writer and Nobel laureate, once said, 'Civilization begins with distillation.'[8]

Nevertheless, this is Bharatiya sabhyata—civilization. Its contributions to the world are immeasurable. From mathematics, astronomy, and chemistry to metallurgy, grammar, ayurveda, and yoga, the foundations of modern civilization are built on the knowledge and discoveries of the Hindus. Even many European languages trace their roots back to Sanskrit.

Mukti Sabhyata: Freedom, Liberty, Diversity, and Pluralism

A civilization that transcends the limitations of time and context is truly universal. This implies that its fundamental principle upholds absolute freedom of expression, practice, and way of life.

In this spirit, the civilization imparted the following mantra:

इन्द्रं मित्रं वरुणमग्निमाहुरथो दिव्यः स सुपर्णो गरुत्मान् ।
एकं सद्विप्रा बहुधा वदन्त्यग्निं यमं मातरिश्वानमाहुः ॥

Índraṃ mitrā́ṃ váruṇam agním āhur
átho divyáḥ sá suparṇó garútmān;
Ékaṃ sád víprā bahudhā́ vadanty agníṃ
yamáṃ mātaríśvānam āhuḥ.

(They called him Indra, Mitra, Varuṇa, Agni;
he is the divine Garuḍa, who has beautiful wings.
That which is One, the sages speak of as multifarious;
they called him Agni, Yama, Mātariśvan.)
—*Rigveda* (1.164.46)

People often ask why Indian civilization, once so great, is in such a sorry state today. While it is easy to point to invaders, alien forces, and other external factors, we must consider their real impact. When adharmic forces attacked civilization, institutions, and societies, something tragic occurred: society froze, ostracized itself, and focused solely on survival. The ideals of the civilization took a back seat, and compromises became necessary just to endure. The time is ripe to reorient society towards freedom of renewal and rejuvenation.

Here are thoughts of some great thinkers on civilization:

- Albert Einstein: 'Everything that is really great and inspiring is created by the individual who can labor in freedom.'[9]
- Arthur C. Clarke: 'Civilization will reach maturity only when it learns to value diversity of character and of ideas.'[10]
- Thomas Sowell: 'If you are not prepared to use force to defend civilization, then be prepared to accept barbarism.'[11]
- Nicolas Gomez Davila: 'Violence is not necessary to destroy a civilization. Each civilization dies from indifference toward the unique values which created it.'[12]

CHAPTER 4

Religion and Dharma

Once, legendary King Vikramaditya, famed for his wisdom and bravery, encountered a ghost named Betaal, who required the king to answer many of his questions after being freed from a tree. As Vikram carried Betaal's body, the ghost began to narrate a new story.

King Chandradeva was a just and noble ruler. One day, a neighbouring king threatened to attack him. To avoid war and protect his soldiers' lives, Chandradeva proposed a challenge: whoever won the battle would take over the other's kingdom. The neighbouring king agreed, but when Chandradeva emerged victorious, he chose not to take over the kingdom, sparing his opponent's life instead.

A few days later, while hunting in the forest, Chadradeva was suddenly attacked by a lion. A thief, who happened to be hiding nearby, saved the king's life. Expecting a reward, the thief was instead sentenced to death by Chndradeva.

Betaal then asked Vikram, 'Chandradeva spared the life of the king, his enemy, but hung the thief who saved him. Was the king's judgement just?'

Vikram responded, 'Chandradeva's judgement was correct. A king's primary duty is to safeguard the welfare of his kingdom. By forgiving the neighbouring king and executing the thief, he ensured the security of his kingdom and peace for his people.'

Betaal replied, 'You are right. But having broken your silence, I must now depart.' Betaal then flew back to his tree.

Religion

The word 'religion' is a relatively new addition to the English language. It did not appear in any ancient Abrahamic scriptures, including the Old and New Testaments, the Quran, or in any other language until recently. The concept of religion itself is also a modern development, originating as a limited-use Greco-Roman term in the 3rd and 4th centuries CE. Initially, it was a Western concept that later spread to other parts of the world. In its contemporary sense, the term was absent in both ancient and many modern cultures across various regions. It gained popularity around the 16th and 17th centuries, and terms like Hinduism, Judaism, and Buddhism began to take shape in the 18th and 19th centuries.

It is challenging to find a comparable term in other cultures. So, how does one apply the concept of religion to various cultures, particularly to Indian culture, which we are concerned with here?

Another commonly used term in this context is 'theology'. According to the Oxford Dictionary, it is defined as 'the study of the nature of God and religious belief' and 'religious beliefs and theory when systematically developed'. The word theology originates from the Greek *theologia,* where *theos* means 'deity' and *logia* means 'divine word or utterances'.[1]

Around 380 BCE, Plato used the word 'theology' in his work *The Republic* to mean 'discourse of God'.[2] The term first appeared in English around 1362.[3] The Greek term *theos* shares a relationship with the Sanskrit *deva*, meaning a divine entity, and also refers to 'heavenly, divine, terrestrial things of high excellence, exalted, shining ones'.[4] According to Monier-Willams in *A Sanskrit English Dictionary,* which etymologically and philologically lists Indo-European words, *deva* refers to 'one who wishes to excel, overcome' or the 'seeker of, master of or the best among'.[5]

The term *deva* is also connected to the Sanskrit root '*div*' (to shine) and *divya* meaning 'shining' or 'illuminating'.[6] Other related terms include *daiva* (due to *deva* or act of *deva*), *divas* (meaning day in English), and *divakar* (the Sanskrit name for the Sun). The Greek equivalent for divine is *dios* or *Zeus,* while in Latin it is *deus.*[7] In Persian, it is *daeva.*[8] *Deva* and *devata* are male expressions and representations of the divine and sacred, whereas *devi* or *devika* is the female counterpart.

But theology today refers to 'the subject and study related to God' and is closely connected to the term 'religion', which is used to understand and explain various belief systems.[9] This Western concept of theology is used in academia to define and describe a 'religion' (or non-religion) and serves as a lens through which different philosophical and cultural traditions are evaluated by categorizing them as religions. The case at hand is 'Hinduism' or the 'Hindu religion'.

In 1887, Scottish advocate and judge Adam Gifford, in his will, established the 'Gifford Lectures', an annual series aimed at promoting and diffusing the study of 'natural theology in the widest sense of the term, in other words, the knowledge of God'. The lectures from 1888, delivered by Max Mueller, were later compiled into a book called *Natural Religion.* Lecture 2 of this series included a definition of religion based on Mueller's interpretation from various sources. He noted:

> It is well known that Lactantius [a Christian author active from 250 CE to 325 CE] derived *religio* from *religare* to bind or hold back and he did so not simply as a philologist but as a theologian. 'We are born' he says 'under the condition that when born we should offer to God our justly due services should know Him only and follow Him only. We are tied to God and bound to Him [*religati*] by the bond of piety and from this has religion itself received its name and not as Cicero [Marcus Tullius Cicero, a Roman statesman and scholar who lived around 100 BCE] has interpreted it, from attention [a relegendo]'.[10]

Lucius Caecilius Firmianus Lactantius, an advisor to the first Christian Roman emperor Constantine I around 300 CE, played a key role in developing various religious policies for the empire. He also authored *Institutiones Divinae* (*The Divine Institutes*) to justify the eradication of 'pagan' cultures.

Mueller continued:

> Before we examine this etymology, it will be useful to give the etymology which Lactantius ascribes to Cicero and which he is bold enough to reject. Cicero says: 'Those who carefully took in hand all things pertaining to the worship of the gods were called *religiosi* from *relĕgere*—as neat people [*elegantes*] were so-called from *elegere* to pick out; likewise diligent people *diligentes* from *diligere* [to choose to value] and *intelligent* people from *intelligere* [to understand]; for in all these words there is the meaning of *legere* to gather to choose the same as in *religiosus*.'

Augustine of Hippo, known as Saint Augustine in the Christian world, was a theologian around 400 CE. Building on Lactanitus's *Divinae Institutions* (IV, 28), Augustine helped spread the concept of 'religion' to the world. This idea was also emphasized by Joseph Campbell and Tom Harpur. However, today, the world understands 'religion' quite differently.

Muller continued:

> Of later writers St. Augustin follows sometimes the one sometimes the other derivation as it suits his purpose; while among modern theologians it has actually been maintained that *religio* was descended from *religare* as well as from *relegere* so as to combine the meanings of both. From a purely philological point of view, it cannot be denied that *religio* might have sprung from *religare* quite as well as from *relegere*.
>
> The real objection to our deriving *religio* from *religare* is the fact that in classical Latin, *religare* is never used in the sense of binding or holding back. In that sense, we should have expected *obligatio* or possibly *obligio* but not *religio*. Cicero's etymology is therefore decidedly preferable as more in accordance with Latin idiom. *Relegere* would be the opposite of *neglegere* or *negligere* and as *neglegere* meant 'not to care' *relegere* would naturally have meant 'to care' 'to regard' 'to revere'. From a verse quoted by Nigidius Figulus from an ancient writer and preserved by Gellius (iv. 9) we learn that *religens* was actually used as opposed to *religiosus*. He said

> '*Religentem esse oportet religiosus ne fuas*' – it is right to be reverent but do not be religious, that is superstitious.[11]

Still, some people believe that the original meaning of the term 'religion' bears similarities to the concept of dharma.

In his book *The Meaning and End of Religion* (1962), Wilfred Cantwell Smith wrote: 'The idea of a "religion" by itself was a European and Western Construct. It was a concept derived from the Romans and further developed and influenced by Christianity and the ideas of the European Enlightenment.' The Romans thought of religion primarily in terms of ceremonies, customs, and traditions—actions to be performed. Early Christians, however, emphasized the importance of attitude and belief.

Today, according to the Merriam-Webster Dictionary, the definition of religion is:

- The service and worship of God or the supernatural
- Commitment or devotion to religious faith or observance
- A personal set or institutionalized system of religious attitudes, beliefs, and practices

The oldest Abrahamic tradition, Judaism, and the Jewish people did not have an equivalent word for 'religion' in Hebrew. They were historically known as Yehudah or Judah (an ancient kingdom). The word 'Judah' encompassed their 'otherworldly' rituals as well as their national, racial, or ethnic identities. The term 'Judaism' was introduced by the West, as the modern concept of 'religion' emerged during the 16th and 17th centuries. Similarly, just as the terms dharma and the Hindu dharmic system were renamed 'Hinduism', the Jewish people were given the term 'Judaism' to align their traditions with the concept that envisioned it as analogous to Christianity—an interpretation formalized only in the 19th century.

American professor Joseph Campbell, who studied the folklore of various cultures, concluded: 'Mythology is often thought of as other people's religions, and religion can be defined as misinterpreted mythology.'[12] The word 'myth' has its roots in the Sanksrit term '*mithya*',[13] which means 'false'. As a result, all mythologies are often perceived as mere stories of the past. Consequently, text like the Ramayana and Mahabharata are labelled as mythologies and, by that logic, are deemed non-historical and therefore false.

Today's framework for defining religion typically includes the following elements: a prophet or saviour, a holy book or scripture, a theology with defined dos and don'ts, personal and social practices, and set of celebrations and festivals. Through this theological lens, every culture in the world is evaluated based on this structure. However, Hindus remain outside this restrictive framework because the concept of dharma does not conform to it. Dharma is simultaneously open and well-defined. The Hindu dharmic system has no single prophet, no single holy book, and no singular scripture. And it applies to both the material and metaphysical spheres.

Understanding Dharma: Complex Interplay of Dharma, Society, and Science

As mentioned earlier, dharma bears little resemblance to the concept of religion. Let us take a few brief steps before delving into the profound meaning of dharma.

Democracy is a remarkable idea. A significant portion of the world has embraced it over the years, although a considerable section of the global population continues to resist it. As a concept, democracy stands head and shoulders above dictatorial and medieval systems of governance. Pluralism and the accommodation of diverse perspectives are its cornerstones, despite some notable limitations.

However, some binaries introduced by the West have further divided the world along secular and religious lines. These divisions have fuelled conflicts—between the state and religious institutions, between secular ethics and theology, and between laws intended for the common good and religious doctrines. It is no surprise, then, that previous centuries have witnessed widespread bloodshed as a result. Battle lines have been drawn, not necessarily over territorial disputes, but over ideological clashes involving worldviews, religious dogmas, and doctrines. The world has endured various violent movements, such as crusades, inquisitions, and jihads. Many ideologies have been pulled into the vortex of fascism and totalitarianism, often under the guise of development and progress. Neither the rule of the proletariat nor the pursuit of a classless society has significantly benefitted human civilization, and, regrettably, religions have further fragmented the world.

Secularists and atheists, capitalists and communists—all have revealed their limitations in one way or another. The fundamental flaw with these 'isms' is that they are 'belief systems'—composed of dreams, wishes, and imaginations—rather than grounded in the realities of nature, human behaviour and potential, society, and economics. These ideologies view the world through a narrow lens, constrained by their perspectives, and lack a well-rounded approach.

The scientific community propelled humanity to unprecedented heights over a century ago. Yet, in hindsight, this period appears akin to a 'dark age' in terms of its detachment from the science of the 'self'. The progress of humanity's inner sciences in the modern world has not kept pace with advancements in scientific and technological developments in the material realm.

Encouragingly, some scientists—following in the footsteps of great physicists like Werner Heisenberg and Eugene Wigner—are now confronting the fear of ostracization to tackle many unsolved riddles of existence. These riddles often dismissed as myths and superstitions, include phenomena like paranormal activities and psychic experiences, out-of-body occurrences, and past-life recollections. Gone are the days when efforts were largely aimed at disproving such phenomena rather than exploring their potential basis in empirical truth.

While secular ethics, such as the Golden Rule (the principle of treating others as one would want to be treated by them or

Do unto others as you would have them do unto you which was preached by the British Anglican theologians in the 17th century), and religion-based ethical systems have contributed positively in certain respects, they exhibit fundamental contradictions in how they have been adopted and practised on a broader scale.

All religions are referred to as 'belief systems', largely due to the emergence of rational consciousness following a long period of oppression in Europe. In many ways, scientific knowledge has rendered prophetic dictums redundant. Yet, while physicists can identify correlations with the fabric of creation, the concept of consciousness remains only partially integrated into science, particularly in the realm of quantum physics. Religions universally emphasize correlation and connectedness, often pointing to a common Creator as the unifying force. However, the growth of scientific and rational thought has successfully debunked several religious myths.

Despite these advancements, there remains a vast expanse of the unknown, the unseen, and the uncertain. It is human nature to seek solace in an unseen power, an unknown protector—much like a child finds comfort in its mother's lap. Even the most accomplished scientist, in their quest to unravel mysteries, may occasionally embrace a 'willing suspension of belief' in their search for an 'infallible' presence.

What Is Dharma?

Let us remind the reader that the *Katha Upanishad* warns us of the subtlety and complexity of dharma:

देवैरत्रापि विचिकित्सितं पुरा न हि सुविज्ञेयमणुरेष धर्मः

Devairatraapi vichikitsitam puraa na hi
suvijneyam anuh esha dharmah

(Even the devas were once perplexed by this; being subtle,
this essence of dharma is not easily comprehended.)[14]

In the Mahabharata (*Yaksha Prashna*), Yudhishthira stated:

धर्मस्य तत्त्वं निहितं गुहायां महाजनो येन गतः स पन्थाः

Dharmasya tattvam nihitam guhaayaam
mahaajano yena gatah sa panthak

(The essence of dharma is hidden, like a secret in a cave.
The path followed by great souls is the right one.)[15]

While the concept of dharma is indeed profound and intricate, patiently exploring its expressions and explanations from various sources can guide us towards some understanding.

Dharma is a Sanskrit term that literally means 'that which holds together' or 'sustains the natural order of things'. It encompassed universal principles, laws, duties, and righteousness that foster peace, harmony, and progress. Based on an understanding of dharma, one can define their *swadharma* (personal path) or 'religion' as one of the innumerable possible journeys towards individual material and spiritual aspirations.

धारणात् धर्म इत्याहुः धर्मों धारयति प्रजाः ।
यः स्यात् धारणसंयुक्तः स धर्म इति निश्चयः ॥

Dharanat dharmam ityahu dharmo dharayate praajah;
Yah svadharansamyuktah sa Dharma iti nischayah.

(The word dharma is derived from *dharana* [sustenance];
dharma sustains society. That which possesses the
capacity to uphold and sustain is indeed dharma.)[16]

The concept of dharma—encompassing orders, roles, duties, laws, personal and collective responsibilities—naturally leads us to the idea of karma. Karma represents the mental, physical, intellectual, and spiritual activities that uphold dharma, making the world both around us and within us sustainable. By aligning with dharma, individuals grow as enlightened beings, experiencing a profound sense of interconnectedness.

The ultimate aim of dharma is to free oneself from limitations and realize one's full or ultimate potential, equivalent to the infinite possibilities hidden within the cosmos or the supreme divine. It is about achieving the merger of micro and macro forces. A unique advantage of dharma is its adaptability, allowing individuals to reformulate and reinvent their goals and duties based on the prevailing context of time, space, and circumstances.

Hinduism is often erroneously interpreted as a religion. In truth, it is a grand system of yoga and dharma, where the material and the sacred are inseparable aspects of an all-encompassing, unified existence.

What are the definitions of dharma from various Hindu texts? Here are several descriptions of dharma to illustrate its deeper meaning. First, from the Ramayana:

धर्मो हि परमो लोके धर्मे सत्यं प्रतिष्ठितम् ।
धर्मसंश्रितमेतच्च पितुर्वचनमुत्तमम् ॥

Dharmo hi paramo loke Dharme satyam pratisthitam;
Dharmasamshritam etaccha piturvachanam uttamam.

(Dharma is supreme in the world, and the truth is based on dharma. This is sustained by dharma, and this is the highest command of the father.)[17]

The Ramayana[18] also discusses the effect of dharma:

धर्मादर्थः प्रभवति धर्मात् प्रभवते सुखम् ।
धर्मेण लभते सर्वं धर्मसारमिदं जगत् ॥

Dharmadartha prabhavate Dharmat prabhavate sukham;
Dharmena labhate sarvam Dharmasarvamidam jagaat.

(From dharma arises wealth; dharma is the source of happiness.
Through dharma we attain everything.
Dharma is the essence of the world.)

These verses highlight the centrality of dharma as the foundation of truth, prosperity, and harmony. Let us then ask ourselves a few serious questions:

- Do we wish to continue the endless debates that divide the world into secular and sacred, atheist and religious factions?
- Or should we look towards a vision of dharma that sustains, uplifts, harmonizes, integrates, and fosters evolution?

The current world order appears in dire need of resetting itself towards a universal order, guided by the principles of dharma. This would involve formulating new policies in all spheres of life—governance, education, technology, environment, health, ethics, and beyond. Such a shift could help eliminate artificial divisions and conflicts based solely on where one is born or the belief system they inherit.

Secularism, like communism, capitalism, or any other 'ism', is itself a belief system. A true embrace of dharma offers the possibility of transcending these divisions, fostering unity and progress rooted in the universal principles that connect humanity and nature.

Doesn't the world need to promote a paradigm shift—one that aligns with the forces and rules of nature, guided by science, and sets higher goals in life? For example, the idea of evolution from animal to man to divine could pave the way for a more peaceful, harmonious, and progressive world. Should we not adjust human ethics and behaviour to match the progress of science and technology?

The following section is a compilation of several ideas related to dharma, which will help us understand its deeper and broader meaning.

Sage Kanada, who is believed to have lived around 600 BCE, described dharma in his treatises on the *Vaisheshika Sutra* as:

यतोऽभ्युदयनिःश्रेयससिद्धिः स धर्मः ॥

yato'bhyudayaniḥśreyasasiddhiḥ sa dharmaḥ.

(Dharma is that through which a*bhyudayaa*
[general welfare and prosperity, benefaction] and
nihsreyasa [spiritual greatness] are attained.)[19]

Through the commentary of Sri Sankaracharya on the Bhagavad Gita, we discover:

द्विविधो हि वेदोक्तो धर्मः प्रव्र्‌तिलक्सनो निवृत्ति-लक्सनह च ।
जगतह स्थिती कारनम प्रानिनम अभ्युदय निश्रेयसा हेतुः ।

dvividho hi vedokto dharmah; pravrı́ttilaksano nivritti-laksanah ca;
jagatah sthiti karanam praninam abhyudaya nishreyasa hetuh.

(Twofold is the Vedic dharma: Of the nature of advancement
in the world of action and achievement [*pravrttilaksana*], and
withdrawal or turning inward into the world of Spirit and
Freedom [*nivrttilaksana*], both of which are necessary means and
counterparts of the world, leading directly to the attainment of
secular welfare and prosperity [a*bhyudaya*] and Spiritual Good
[*nihsreyasa*] for all beings.)[20]

These diverse spiritual and philosophical ideologies converge on a shared vision of harmony, humans flourishing, and responsibility towards the self and others, offering complementary views on dharma, virtue, and the pursuit of wisdom.

The late Buddhadasa, one of the most influential thinkers in contemporary Thailand, captured the essence of dharma as a holistic, interwoven concept. He summed it up by stating that the outcome of dharma is also part of dharma: 'Dhamma means (a) the state of nature as it is, (b) the laws of nature, (c) the duties that must be performed in accordance with the laws of nature, and (d) the results that are derived from the fulfillment of such duties.'[21]

Dharma, in this context, is not only a set of moral principals but also the natural order itself, and our duties are aligned with its unchanging laws. This idea echoes Mahavir Swami, the Jain Tirthankar, who stated: '*Vatthu Sahavo Dhammo*' (Dharma is nothing but the real nature of an object.) Just as the nature of fire is to burn and the nature of water is to produce a cooling effect, in the same manner, the soul's essential nature is to seek self-realization and spiritual elevation.[22]

The pursuit of inner truth is also reflected in the teachings of Guru Nanak, the founder of the Sikh tradition, who urged his followers: '*Taji sabh bharam bhajio paarbrahm. Kahu Nanak attal ih Dharma.*' (Renounce all your doubts and contemplate the Supreme Lord. Says Nanak, this is the eternal dharma.)[23]

Meanwhile, the African philosophy of *Ubuntu* resonates with this idea of interconnectedness: 'I am because you are.'[24] This sense of interdependence aligns with Confucius's teachings on the proper conduct of relationships, where he insisted that a harmonious world begins with a virtuous family, which begins with an individual cultivating their personal life. Confucius stated: 'To put the world in order, we must first put the nation in order; to put the nation in order, we must first put the family in order; to put the family in order, we must first cultivate our personal life; we must first set our hearts right.'[25] Although every social position carries within it a defined set of responsibilities or righteousness, Confucius insisted that the fulfillment of these duties should be inspired by human-heartedness, which he defined as 'loving others'.[26]

In a way, his values seem to complement both the Christian ideal of love and the Buddhist ideal of compassion. Since Confucius believed that humans were social animals, the proper conduct of relationships was crucial to him. It was only in relation to others that one could establish one's virtuous character. 'The man of human-heartedness is one who, desiring to sustain himself, sustains others, and desiring to develop himself, develops others; that may be called the way to practice human-heartedness.'[27]

In modern times, Stephen Covey, author of the international best-selling book *The Seven Habits of Highly Effective People*, describes dharma as: 'principles that govern human growth and happiness—natural law'.[28] His view ties into the ancient understanding of dharma as both a personal guide and a universal law in governing human well-being.

Finally, Taoism provides another complementary perspective, offering the concept of Tao as 'an emblem, meaning order, the whole, responsibility, efficiency'. Tao represents the total, responsible, efficient order of creation, the whole of what is multiplicity. The Taoist sage or grand prophet Lao-Tzu said: 'How deep and obscure! Yet its centre has essence. This essence is real, so, its center can be trusted.'[29] Tao and dharma, thus, point towards an eternal truth that binds all things together in a cohesive existence.

The Mahabharata says:

यतो धर्मस्ततो जयः

Yato Dharmastato jaya

(Victory is there where dharma is.)
[This shloka appears eleven times in the Mahabharata.][30]

We can interpret this in a contemporary context as: 'Dharma or actions aligned with truth and reality, brings success and victory.' Here, '*jaya*' refers to victory, glory, success, and so on.

The *Manu Smriti* declares:

धर्म एव हतो हन्ति धर्मो रक्षति रक्षितः
तस् - माद्धर्मो न हन्तव्यः मानो धर्मो हतोवधीत्

dharma eva hato hanti dharmo rakṣati rakṣitaḥ
tasmād dharmo na hantavyo mā no dharmo hato'vadhīt[31]

(Dharma only destroys [those] who destroy it. Dharma also protects those who protect it. Hence, dharma should not be destroyed. Know that if violated, dharma destroys us.)

If we focus on the phrase धर्मो रक्षति रक्षित (*Dharmo rakshati rakshitah*), meaning 'Dharma protects the protector of dharma', we can conclude: 'One who follows the path of dharma will always be sustained and safeguarded.'

Therefore, we can also say: 'Where there is dharma, or right action (action in tune with truth and universal ideals), there is victory.' When we put principles first in our lives, everything unfolds as it should, and there can be no failure.

Some contemporary expressions of dharma are as follows (from various anonymous sources):

- 'Dharma is very illusive. It is not easy to pinpoint or tackle.'
- 'Dharma seems to be an enigma, veiled in mystery and encased in puzzle.'
- 'Dharma is a tantalizer. It is a grand concept bristling with difficulties galore, both theoretical and practical. Everyone swears by dharma, but no two individuals agree on what constitutes dharma.'
- 'We can, however, unveil the mystery a little if we examine the meaning of dharma. The term is many-faceted in its implications. It stands for religion, customary observances of a community, law, usage, social welfare, ordinances, moral merit, virtue, righteousness, goodwill, justice, course of conduct, right, equity, piety, decorum, character, innate nature [svabhav], and a host of other allied connotations.'
- 'But this formidable list need not dismay us. It only implies that all these facets must be borne in mind when interpreting dharma. The word comes from the root 'dhr' 'to support': *dharanat dharmam ity ahuh*[32], it is the principle making for integrity and harmony in every context. Dharma is the rock on which all virtues are founded. It is the basis of all and the validation of all noble ideas. In other words, dharma is an evolutionary, holistic concept and not a fragmentary idea. Just as white light shines in different colours according to the medium it is passing through, dharma takes on diverse hues according to the individual or society through which

> it manifests itself. White light is single, but its constituent colours are multiple and distinct. Absolute dharma is a unity, but relative dharmas are multiform and different.'[33]

In the Mahabharata,[34] Yudhishthira asked Bhishma to explain the meaning of dharma. Bhishma replied:

तद्रिस्हो अयम् अनुप्रस्ह्नो यत्र धर्मह सुदुर्लबह
दुस्ह्कम्ह प्रलिसन्ख्यतुम् तत्केनत्र व्यस्वस्यथि
प्रभवर्थय भुतनम् धर्मप्रवछनम् क्रितम्
यस्यत् प्रभवसम्युक्तह स धर्म इति निस्छयह.

Tadrisho ayam anuprashno yatra dharmaha sudurlabaha
Dushkamha pralisankhyatum tatkenatra vysvasyathi
Prabhavarthaya bhutanam dharmapravachanam kritam
Yasyat prabhavasamyuktaha sa dharma iti nischayaha.

(It is most difficult to define dharma. Dharma has been explained to that which helps in the upliftment of living beings. Therefore, that which ensures the welfare of living beings is surely dharma. The learned rishis have declared that dharma is that which sustains.)

According to Swami Sastrananda:

> Among the great concepts and doctrines, the basic principles and directives of Hinduism, Dharma stands pre-eminent, with a vast deep and pervasive significance of its own. Having its rudimentary beginnings in the Vedas, it has, over the centuries grown like a mighty tree, with its numerous branches and secondary roots. In it there may be a lot of tangled growth and dead wood as well, yet it is majestic tree, living and life-giving, sheltering and sustaining numberless souls under its protection and shade. From simple beginnings, the term has now assumed various shades of meanings and significance, including righteous duty and code of conduct, virtues, justice, morality, and the moral principle or force integrating and sustaining man and the universe; the intrinsic,

inalienable nature and essence of a thing as also the attributes; and finally, religion, the deity of righteousness and God himself.[35]

[...]

When we study the Upanishads, we find that the vision of the [Rishis (sages)] was wholly integrated. They always saw clearly, as it were, a vast eye was spread out in the spiritual sky, the all-pervading Supreme Reality [Vishnu], and realized that all other entities and beings in the universe of experience are manifestations in different stages of that One Reality [*Sarvam khalu idam Brahma*], also called Brahman [The Infinite], Aksara [The Imperishable], and abide in it. From the subtlest to the grossest, and from the largest to the minutest, whether animate or inanimate, all entities are supported by and permeated with the Reality as the very essence of their being, as their very Self [Ātman].

This Reality, Brahman, hidden in the *Guha*, cave or *Hrdaya* [heart, i.e. the inmost recesses of consciousness] of all entities and beings as Ātman, like the tree in the seed, is spiritual, and its nature is Absolute Infinite Existence – Consciousness, Bliss [Sacchidananda]. The whole universe, with all its entities and beings, emerges from it, functions in it, and merges back into it, like waves into the ocean, and Brahman/Ātman envelopes them on all sides outwardly, as well as permeates them through and through inwardly. Brahman/Ātman controls and regulates them all from within [*antaryamin*] as the pervasive Great Law of their being [*rtam-brhat*]. None can dare transgress even a whit this Universal Great Law, including the Cosmic elements and divinities such as Agni [fire], Surya [Sun], Indra, Vayu, and even the frightful Death, all of whom meticulously perform their allotted functions. It is, as it were, a great Terror with raised powerful Sceptre like a thunderbolt [*Mahad-bhayam vajram udyatam*] diacritics, which none can resist. It is because of the rule [*prasasana*] of this Great law of Brahman, which is the Ultimate Imperishable Reality [*Aksara*], that the sun and the moon are held in their own courses, and everything in Nature obeys its own inner Law and the universe runs as well-regulated Cosmos.

And Dharma is this Cosmic Law which regulates inwardly the nature of entities and beings as their inherent property or characteristic, and outwardly the behavior and the functioning of individuals and groups in society and upholds the entire universe it's functioning.[36]

[...]

In olden days, Dharma meant much more than what we now understand from the term 'religion'. It stood for power to hold things together in perfect harmony.[37]

[...]

Dharma in its ultimate sense means the Supreme Spirit. '*Dharati lokan iti Dharmah*' diacritics, translation: Dharma is what sustains the worlds. Dharma and Brahman are the two topics that the Veda deals with '*Dharma-brahmani vedika vedye*: of these two, Brahaman is the end and Dharma the means'.[38]

[...]

The word Dharma connotes 'that on which everything rests'. This concept is unique to Indian culture, and being many faceted cannot be expressed by any other word in any other language. In fact, the ancient name for Hinduism is Sanatana Dharma (Perennial Philosophy enduring through time). Dharma is indeed the law of our being and therefore, it can be identified with God.[39]

Swami Vivekananda said:

Again and again, you hear this objection advanced: 'What good can religion [Dharma] do? Can it take away the poverty of the poor?' Supposing it cannot, would that prove the untruth of religion? Suppose a baby stands up among you, when you are trying to demonstrate an astronomical theorem, and says, 'Does it bring candy?' 'No, it does not,' you answer. Babies judge the whole universe from their own standpoint, that of producing gingerbread; and so do the babies of the world. We must not judge of higher things from a low standpoint ... Religion permeates the whole of man's life, not only the present but the past, present and future. Is it logical to measure its value by its action upon five minutes of human life?

Religion has made man what he is, and will make of this human animal a God. That is what religion can do. Take religion from

> human society and what will remain? Nothing but a forest of brutes.[40]
>
> [...]
>
> [Is] the manifestation of divinity already in man. It is being and becoming, not hearing and acknowledging.[41]

From another perspective, what virtues can be achieved through dharma? The *Manusmriti*[42] spells it out:

धृतिः क्षमा दमोऽस्तेयं शौचमिन्द्रियनिग्रहः ।
धीर्विद्या सत्यमक्रोधो दशकं धर्मलक्षणम् ॥

Dhritih kshama damosteyang shouca,indriyanigrahah
Dhirvidya satyamakrodho dashakam Dharmalaksananam.

(Fortitude, forbearance, self-restraint, non-stealing, purity, control of senses, discrimination [of good and bad], wisdom, truthfulness, and lack of anger are the ten characteristics of dharma.)

The Srimad Bhagavad Gita[43] says:

अहिंसा सत्यमक्रोधस्त्यागः शान्तिरपैशुनम्।
दया भूतेष्वलोलुप्त्वं मार्दवं ह्रीरचापलम्॥

Ahimsa satyamakrodhastyagah santiraoaisunam
daya bhutesvaloluptvam mardavam hriracapalam

(Non-violence, truthfulness, absence of anger, renunciation, peace, absence of malice, compassion towards living beings, lack of green, gentleness, modesty, and steadfastness are additional virtues of dharma.)

Finally, the *Brihadaranyaka Upanishad*[44] identifies dharma with truth and declares its supreme status:

स नैव व्यभवत्
तच्छ्रेयो रूपमत्यसृजत धर्मम्
तदेतत्क्षत्रस्य क्षत्रं यद् धर्मः

तस्माद्धर्मात् परं नास्त्य्
अथो अबलीयान् बलीयासमाशसते धर्मेण यथा राज्ञैवम्
धर्मेण यथा राज्ञा एवम्
यो वै स धर्मः सत्यं वै तत्
तस्मात्सत्यं वदन्तमाहुर्
धर्मं वदतीति धर्मं वा वदन्त सत्यं वदतीत्य्
एतद्ध्येवैतदुभयं भवति ॥ १४ ॥

sa naiva vyavabat
tacchreyo rupam atyasrjata dharmam
tad etat kshatrasya ksatram yad dharmah
tasmad dharmat param nasti
athoabaliyan baliyam sam asamsate dharmena
atha rajnaivam
yo vai sa dharmah
satyam vai tat
tasmat satyam vadantam ahur dharmam vadatiti
dharmam va vadantam
satyam vadati iti
etat dhyeavaitadubhayam bhavati

(There is nothing higher than dharma. Even a very weak man hopes to prevail over a very strong man through the strength of dharma, just as with the help of the king. So, what is called dharma is really truth. Therefore, people say that a man who declares the truth is declaring dharma, and one who declares dharma is speaking the truth. These two—dharma and truth — are one and the same.)

Hindu Dharma and Sanatana Dharma

Dharma etymologically means that which holds or sustains—sustenance. The questions that arise are: sustenance of what? What characteristics or qualities define an entity? What is the true nature of the self or a being? Survival must precede sustenance, followed by growth. Therefore, people must engage in activities, 'calls of duty', and abide by laws and rules for survival and sustenance. Thus, rules and laws are also part of dharma, as well as the duties and responsibilities that deliver justice to all. These principles apply to individuals, families, societies, and the environment.

For Hindus, everything is sacred. They view the world in this way: on one side is *adhyatma* (the inner nature and world), and on the other is *prakriti* (the outer, material world). Hindus were historically efficient in ensuring that while *moksha* is the final *purusarth* (the pursuits of life), dharma forms the foundation, with *artha* and *kama* as its supporting pillars. There is a material aspect, and a beyond-material aspect: *atmavidya* or *adhyatma* (the knowledge and science of self). Additionally, they have developed yogas as tools and methods to achieve the fulfillment of life's goals.

We tend to long for the boundless and infinite, and that is our true nature. We suffocate when this freedom of expansion is curtailed. Yet, we create artificial walls for our own protection, as well as for our experiences. Bhakti (devotion) is one subset of this, similar to expressions of devotion in other religions. To perform yoga, one must develop both the body and mind; hence, the popular practices of *hatha yoga* include *asana* and *pranayama*. As a byproduct of these practices, we remain healthy and lead fulfilling lives, while the higher goal is to experience oneness with the self and nature through *dhyana* and *samadhi*.

Moksha begins with freedom—freedom of choice and freedom of detachment. This freedom is no different from societal freedom or individual freedom within society. After experiencing these, emotional freedom (*bhakti*) and intellectual freedom (*jnana*) can be attained. This fundamental personal freedom is one end of the infinite spectrum known as *Moksha* or *Nirvana*.

Many people, especially Hindus, tend to refer to the 'Hindu religion' or 'Hinduism' as 'Hindu Dharma' or 'Sanatana Dharma'. First, 'Hindu Dharma' is a misnomer because dharma is universal. What people refer to as Hindu Dharma is the 'dharma-based system of living' developed by the Hindus. If this broader meaning is not forgotten, Hindu Dharma can be a useful compact term to describe the great Hindu Dharmic or dharma-based system. Many describe it as a 'way of life' and while this is true for all people and all religions, the term makes more sense when the idea of dharma is not confused with religion.

Now, regarding Sanatana Dharma. The standard translation of the word Sanatana is 'eternal'.[45] Some refer to it as '*philosophia perennis*'—the philosophy forever. Although universal in concept and beyond any sectarian identity, Sanatana Dharma first had to be identified as 'Hindu Dharma', as that is the term Hindus generally use for their dharmic system. Eventually, it came to be known as 'Hinduism' as the uninitiated struggled to understand it and sought to map it based on their understanding of the world beyond matter. However, once the concept is clear, there is no longer any need to use the term 'Hinduism'.

At least thirty ancient texts refer to the idea of 'Sanatana Dharma', including the Mahabharata (157 times) and the Ramayana (8 times). However, there is no single, clear definition to be found anywhere.

In the *Atharva Veda,* we find:

सनातन सनातनमेनमहुरुताद्या स्यात पुनण्रव्

Sanatan sanatanmenamhrutadhya punarnav

(Eternal, eternal, they call Him who is the origin, the one who is perpetually renewed.)

As mentioned earlier, the literal meaning of the term 'Sanatan' is eternal or 'always residing'—perpetual, permanent, everlasting, ancient. This means that which is Sanatan is continually renewed and thus remains new forever.

The complete verse from the *Atharvaveda*[46] reads:

सं॒नात॑नमे॑नमाहुरु॒ताद्य स्या॒त्पुन॑र्णवः।
अ॑होरा॒त्रे प्र जा॑येते अ॒न्यो अ॒न्यस्य॑ रू॒पयोः॑ ॥

sanātanam enam āhur utādyaḥ syāt punar navaḥ
aho rātre prajāyete anyo anyasya rūpayoḥ

(They call Him eternal, too; He may become new again today.
Day and night reappear fresh repeatedly,
one assuming the form of the other.)

If we take sustenance as the basic meaning of dharma, then the universe and its components must be sustained. The laws and actions, therefore, must be eternal. But how can they be eternal if they do not renew to adapt to new, ever-changing realities?

Practice of Dharma in Daily Life

It is enlightening to understand what the shastras and rishis say about dharma. So, what does it mean to follow dharma or be dharmic in our mundane, day-to-day living? First, what is the ideal human goal? A prosperous, peaceful, harmonious, evolutionary, and progressive society, where each individual can realize their full potential and be happy while achieving *adhyatmik* upliftment.

In defining dharma, the rishis noted two key aspects: for *abhyudaya* (material welfare and prosperity), we must follow *pravrttilaksana* (the nature of advancement in the world of action and achievement). For *nihsreyasa* (spiritual progress and achievement), we must follow *nivrttilaksana* (withdrawal from the material world and turning inward into the inner being). However, these two are not separate—they are two sides of the same coin. Without *adhyatma*, material prosperity can derail us, and without material fulfillment, *adhyatma* may become corrupt.

Individual Dharma

Be healthy—both mentally and physically. Be happy by performing our duties. The basic idea is to be honest and truthful—to oneself and others—be ethical, moral, and righteous, and follow natural and societal rules and laws. Finally, we perform our duties based on our roles in the family and society: parent, brother, sister, teacher, worker, leader, politician, businessman, scientist, artist, etc. If individuals follow the path of dharma, society, governance, the environment, and all sustaining goals will be cared for.

For *adhyatma*, one can start with essential duties and rituals for self-empowerment to perfect the body, mind, and actions—such as *puja*, *japa*, chanting, etc.—and use any or multiple branches of the science of yoga: Karma, Bhakti, Jnana, Hatha, and Mantra Yoga.

The above ideas, if realized, would sustain the earth, society, family, and individuals. This is the summary of dharma in practice.

CHAPTER 5

Samskriti and Culture

The primary goal of human life is survival for which food and shelter are essential. Once these basic needs are met, we strive for additional requirements such as comfort, wealth, health, and education. Julian Huxley, in his article, 'Evolution after Darwin', written for the centennial of Darwin's *The Origin of Species,* observed:

> Man's most comprehensive aim is seen not as a mere survival, not as numerical increase, not as increased complexity of organization or increased control over his environment, but as greater fulfillment—the fuller realization of more possibilities by the human species collectively and more of its component members individually. Once greater fulfillment is recognized as man's ultimate or dominant aim, we shall need a science of human possibilities to help guide the long course of psycho-social evolution that lies ahead.[1]

We act according to the needs of our lives, the availability of resources, and our individual nature. These actions may serve purely survival purposes, reflect highly creative pursuits, satisfy our senses or ego, or even help a person in need. Ultimately, all human efforts aim to achieve mastery over both our external and inner nature. Our thoughts prompt us to act. When we face a situation, knowingly or unknowingly, our thoughts drive us to respond. These thoughts are shaped by the prism of our worldview or philosophy of life. Some behaviours are instinctive or genetically preprogrammed, while others are learned neurologically and culturally from our environment.

As we grow and evolve, we gradually move beyond the ideologies of 'survival of the fittest' or 'might is right' and begin to consider others. This marks the first act of dharma—the initial step towards discovering the human spirit. One day, we may come to embrace the idea of '*Vasudhaiva Kutumbakam*'—the belief that the entire universe is a family. In doing so, we transcend physical and mental limitations and enter the realm of *adhyatma* (spirituality). Thus, we form a philosophy of life shaped by our understanding of how the world operates.

Although German philosopher Friedrich Hegel's influence in the West is visible via left-communist prism, while discussing culture, interestingly, he remarked, 'There was seen the strange spectacle of a cultured nation without metaphysics—like a temple richly ornamented in other respects but without a holy of holies.'[2] Like drops of water forming a wave, we contribute to the creation of ideals, profound thoughts, and behavioural patterns, all of which become elements of culture. Therefore, we need a way of living, which—essential for survival, growth, and sustenance—is culture itself. Living traditions that express the thinking, emotions, and way of life of a particular society are integral to its culture.

An individual's culture is a building block of the culture of a community, society, or nation, which collectively forms a civilization. As Samuel Huntington, Eaton professor of the science of government at Harvard University, noted:

> Civilization is the broadest cultural entity. Villages, regions, ethnic groups, nationalities, religious groups all have distinct cultures at different levels of cultural heterogeneity … Civilization is thus the highest cultural grouping of people, and the broadest level of cultural identity … that distinguishes humans from other species.[3]

The *UNESCO Chronicle* in May 1959 stated: 'Culture means the total accumulation of material objects, ideas, symbols, beliefs, sentiments, values, and social forms which are passed on from one generation to another in any given society.'[4] Culture can also be defined as the deepest insight into life and its highest aspirations, arising from the will to master both one's inner and external nature.

Sri Aurobindo described culture as the 'discovery of the freedom of spirit'. His perspective on culture and civilization is both profound and illuminating. He observed:

> True happiness in this world is the right terrestrial aim of man, and true happiness lies in the finding and maintenance of a natural harmony of spirit, mind, and body. Culture is to be valued to the extent to which it has discovered the right key of this harmony and organized its expressive motives and movements. And a civilization must be judged by the manner in which all its principles, ideas, forms, ways of living work to bring that harmony out, manage its rhythmic play, and secure its continuance or the development of its motives.[5]

The commentary on the Western concept of culture now brings us to the Sanskrit terms *samskara* and *samskriti*, which represent culture in its highest sense. The word *samskara* is derived from '*sam*' (harmonious, true to its dharma) and 'kara', or '*kri*'—to make or bring about. The meaning embedded in the name of our ancient language, Sanskrit, reflects this concept: it signifies that which has undergone *samskaran*—modification, purification, and the process of perfection.

Dharma refers to the innate potential and true nature of a thing, including the *adhyatmic* potential of human beings, which leads us beyond mundane material desires. *Samskriti*, as the refined condition of a substance, contrasts with *prakriti*, which refers to the raw or unrefined state. For example, *prakriti* can be likened to a crude gold alloy, while *samskriti* represents the process of refining it into a beautiful gold ornament. This, *samskriti* signifies 'the act of *samskara*'—the sum of all activities that bring life into alignment with its dharma. It implies purification and the transformation of something into a more developed refined state. *Samskriti* creates opportunities for growth, enabling the physical, mental, intellectual, and spiritual progress inherent in each individual.

However, the ultimate quest for human beings transcends these basic needs. It lies in the search for truth and the aspiration to uncover the reality of the universe. To fully realize our human potential, we must move beyond physical and mental limitations, striving for something infinite and eternal.

The Sanskrit word *adhyātma* (अध्यात्म) carries a profound meaning. Etymologically, it derives from *adhi* (above or transcendental) and *ātman* (self). Thus, *adhyātma* refers to the knowledge and practices that enable one to transcend the body, mind, and intellect, ultimately realizing the self, or atman. *Adhyatmikata*—for which there is no perfect English equivalent, though it is often rendered as spirituality—entails the discovery of the all-encompassing spirit of the world and the interconnectedness of all beings; it is, in essence, the science of the self.

Every act that strengthens us, deepens our wisdom, and opens us to the life of the spirit is part of *samskriti*. This concept of culture transcends the mere development of our creaturely potentials, focusing instead on the awakening of the divine soul or self within. This represents our higher dharma: the eternal truth about reality. Caring for others is central to understanding and experiencing this inner connections—hence the saying, 'Helping others is helping ourselves!' Dharma guides us to be mindful of these connections and act in alignment with them, making such actions an integral part of our *samskriti*.

Every action that aligns us with our dharma is a *samskritic* activity. The maxim *Dharma rakshati rakshitah* (Dharma protects the one who protects Dharma) underscores this relationship: *samskriti* serves as our protector, just as we uphold and protect it. Dharma and *samskriti* are, therefore, two sides of the same coin. A person's or society's culture can be judged by how balanced they are in thought, speech, and action—and by the synchronicity of these aspects. When there is imbalance or misalignment, it leads to '*vikriti*'—deviation, disharmony, or corruption from one's true divine nature. Such an entity requires *samskara*—a process of change, purification, and refinement.

The essence of a society's culture can often be discerned by observing its most respected individuals, who embody its highest standards of excellence.

As a final observation, our ways of communicating, our ethical principles, the methods we choose for entertainment, the food we consume, the books we read, and the television programmes we watch reveal our culture—and, simultaneously, shape it. When something impedes our growth, causes deviation from our true nature, or threatens to lead us to decline, we recognize that *vikriti* is present. In such cases, we must invoke *samskriti* to restore harmony and bring about positive transformation.

We solve one problem in life today, only to face another tomorrow. Why do these obstacles arise, and why do we struggle to move forward? It is because we have not cultivated our inner strength and motion properly. We fear change, lack a clear understanding of our path or dharma, have a weak life force, and have not yet developed a true sense of culture.

The culture of an individual should enable adaptation to the constant changes around us. It should protect their diversity and uniqueness while uniting them with the rest of humanity, fostering peaceful coexistence and keeping the banner of human progress aloft. Such a dharma is truly Santana—eternal and universal.

How Is a Culture Formed?

An apple falls, Newton observes it, and he discovers the hidden laws of nature. Scientists and engineers apply these laws to invent tools and machines that enhance human comfort. Inspired by his vision of individual freedom, Henry Ford fosters a culture of independence with the declaration, 'Every American must have a car.'

Similarly, Karl Marx, witnessing the suffering of the masses, formulates a worldview that becomes the foundation of a communist society and culture. The Buddha, seeing humanity's suffering, searches for a remedy, shares his insights, and inspires a new cultural framework. From these examples, we see that every powerful and enduring society is built on a vision, a worldview, or a philosophy of life. Families, communities, and nations create their own cultures, which eventually contribute to the shared global human culture.

A society or nation develops traditions, customs, social norms, values, and forms of creative expression we call the arts. All these elements collectively constitute a culture. Each individual, knowingly or unknowingly, participates in shaping personal, national, and global cultures. Thinkers and philosophers influence millions with their ideas, while traditions and customs are passed down to us by parents and neighbours, forming our heritage.

As children, our culture exists only in its most rudimentary form, inherited through past karma and genetics. Over time, we grow, cultivate values, and carve paths for our lives. This principle applies not just to individuals but to societies and nations as well.

According to Sri Aurobindo, the highest expression of human spirit or life consciousness appears as a worldview, often referred to as philosophy. This philosophy manifests in three significant aspects of life:

- Thoughts, ideals, an upwardly directed will, and the soul's aspirations shape spiritual traditions. These traditions are paths to realizing life's truth, often called 'religion'. Hindus, for example, have developed innumerable spiritual paths. As Sri Ramakrishna Paramhansa famously said, 'As many thoughts - so many paths.' Philosophy and spiritual realizations are ultimately translated into unique ways of living.
- Creative self-expression, intelligence, imagination, and appreciative aesthetics give rise to the arts, which serve as a medium for expressing our philosophy and ideals of life.

These arts include literature, music, visual arts, and more, reflecting the creative essence of a culture.

- The practical and outward manifestation of life consciousness takes shape in society and political systems. Social customs, traditions, festivals, civic and political structures, and laws are all built upon a society's ideals and values. These socio-political elements are integral to the fabric of culture.

Various Cultures of the World

In every society and culture, the basic needs of human beings remain the same. However, as the interests and tendencies of each culture differ, each places greater emphasis on specific aspects of human life. Swami Vivekananda, most likely, remarked that each culture has a fundamental idea to work out, a destiny to fulfil, a unique role to play in the world, and a contribution to make to the great human civilization. A culture can thrive only as long as it remains true to its foundational ideal. Until that ideal is lost or destroyed, a culture cannot perish—nothing can extinguish it. For Hindus, this ideal is dharma.

Cultures are often understood through the ways they express themselves. Their forms of expression are reflected in spiritual and social practices, arts and literature, sciences, customs, and sociopolitical systems. Broadly, cultures can be classified into the following types:

- Material or Physical Culture: A focused primary on material progress and existing at a sensory level is termed material or physical culture. Life's focus is on food, sleep, procreation, and fear of death.
- Mental or Intellectual Culture: A culture where the highest goal is intellectual or mental satisfaction is identified as a culture of the mind or intellect.
- Spiritual Culture: A culture dedicated to *adhyatmic* (spiritual) attainment is referred to as a spiritual culture.

While a particular culture may belong predominantly to one of these categories, it often contains elements of the other two.

However, the dominant characteristics of a culture are what determine its classification.

There are numerous cultures in the world among which the most distinct are Western, Hindu, Chinese, African, and Middle Eastern. This discussion will focus on Western and Hindu cultures.

Western culture is composed of several strands. The first originates from the political and social ideas of the ancient Greek city-states, particularly their emphasis on the values of truth, beauty, and a steadfast faith in reason and intelligence. The second strand is the dynamic Roman spirit, characterized by its formulation of administration systems, establishment of law, and a scientific mindset in pursuit of truth. The third strand consists of Christian principles, including the divinity of love and compassion, the brotherhood of humankind, and the Jewish values of righteousness and justice.

The Greek god of fire, Prometheus, was famous for achieving things, even defying the power of the king of gods, Zeus. The Promethean spirit of human excellence, often celebrated in Western traditions, is also intrinsic to Hindu culture, as exemplified in the Mahabharata. However, while Greece and Rome produced great philosophers like Socrates and Pythagoras, these societies ultimately rejected their teachings. Plato, despite his profound insights, was seen as otherworldly when he sought to guide his people towards the concept of 'Man, know thyself'. His social philosophy was absorbed, but his spiritual teachings remained misunderstood.

The absence of the *adhyatmic*—the inward spiritual dimension—has often led to a descent into materialism, a phenomenon evident in modern times. Religion, and the misunderstood notion of dharma, frequently devolves into empty forms, manifesting as ritualism, superficial displays of religiosity, and fervent exhortation to others to conform. In contrast, true *adhyatmikta* is a lived experience, not merely a proclamation. Closed and rigid systems are more likely to lead to the erosion or collapse of an *adhyatmic* system. This is particularly true for Dharmic or Hindu systems, which are inherently grounded in openness and flexibility.

This neglect, rooted in a movement away from introspection, hindered the further upward movement of the Western human spirit. It created a vacuum, and ultimately, Greek and Roman civilizations crumbled under their own weight. Early Christianity emerged as a spiritual alternative, but it soon imposed restrictions on freedom of expression. Christianity's emphasis on belief, its dogma of the 'only path', and its failure to satisfy the rational mind stifled aspirations for exploring the true inner universe. Early Christianity halted all experimentation in the realm of inner science or the science of life. It hindered the search for truth, both outwardly and inwardly.

It took many like Galileo to sacrifice their lives in pursuit of truth, and a long time passed before science regained the freedom it had lost. Once this freedom was restored after the Renaissance, Western society directed most of its energy towards searching for truth in the external world. As a result, the West became a field of action focused on the outer world, which became its specialization and led to the emergence of inventive geniuses. Currently, values of liberty, equity, democracy, and the rule of law flourished in the Western mind. The rejection of the theocratic states of medieval Europe and their oppression reinforced these values.

Although Judeo-Christian religious ideas and Greco-Roman inspirations for higher human achievements remain present in Western culture, it remains predominantly materialistic, with most people living on a sensate or intellectual plane. In contrast, Hindu culture has remained spiritual throughout the ages, despite occasional deviations due to foreign influence and a lack of inner strength, as seen today. Hindus have always perceived the divine presence in all things. By contrast, the Judeo-Christian tradition confines God to the church or temple. Western materialist society abandons the spirit altogether, cutting off human potential at the sensate level, which tends to focus solely on the outward. Hindus, however, would not 'kick' even a tree, for they believe the divine is present in all things, and such an act would shows disrespect according to their culture. Hindus would ask for forgiveness if they stepped on the Earth or plucked a leaf from a plant. In contrast, Western cultures have encouraged the exploitation of nature to such an extent that continued existence now seems uncertain.

At any moment, a 'survival of the fittest' mentality combined with inventive power may turn into the 'survival of none'. The vast stockpile of armaments held by various nations remind us of the comments made by Swami Vivekananda and Sri Aurobindo: We are still living in the barbaric phase of our so-called civilization and have yet to be 'civilized'. This is the outcome of material culture. British historian and philosopher Arnold Toynbee remarked, 'It is already becoming clear that a chapter which had a Western beginning will have to have an Indian ending if it is not to end in the self-destruction of the human race.'[6]

Greco-Roman culture focused on 'man in the society', or the external connections between human beings, while Hindu culture specialized in the 'human being in depth', or the inner connections of human beings. Dr S. Radhakrishnan, former President of India, beautifully illustrated this distinction when he said:

> The ideal man of India is not the magnanimous man of Greece or the valiant knight of medieval Europe, but the freeman of spirit, who has attained insight into the universal source [through] rigid discipline and [the] practice of disinterested virtues, who has freed himself from the prejudices of his time and place. It is India's pride that she has clung fast to this ideal and produced in every generation and in every part of the country, from the time of the Rishis of the Upanishads and Buddha to Ramakrishna and Gandhi, men who strove successfully to realize this ideal.[7]

Hindu Culture

What are the core principles of Hindu culture? Since the dharma of the self is sacred, divine, and illuminating, Hindus regard all of creation as divine. The divine's nature is described by the triad *Sat-Chit-Ananda*: *Sat* (the true or real), *Chit* (consciousness), and

Ananda (the bliss of love). This simple yet profound vision lays the foundation for a completely different cultural framework.

Truthfulness, respect, tolerance, acceptance, *ahimsa*, and honesty—these virtues were deeply cultivated in people's lives, resulting in the creation of a society with a high standard of culture.

As a result, this culture offers two great ideals to all of humanity:

अयं निजः परो वेति गणना लघुचेतसाम्।
उदारचरितानां तु वसुधैव कुटुम्बकम्॥

ayaṃ nijaḥ paro veti gaṇanā laghucetasām;
udāracaritānāṃ tu vasudhaiva kuṭumbakam.

('This person is mine, and that one is not,'
is the calculation of the narrow-minded. For those
of noble character, the entire world is one family.)
—*Maha Upanishad* (6.71–6.73)

Vasudhaiva Kutumbakam is the understanding that all of creation—humans, animals, plants, and nature—is interconnected and interdependent. We are one family.

And therefore, the all-inclusive and very common Hindu prayer is:

सर्वे भवन्तु सुखिनः सर्वे सन्तु निरामयाः ।
सर्वे भद्राणि पश्यन्तु मा कश्चिद्दुःखभाग्भवेत् ॥

sarvé bhavantu sukhinaḥ, sarvé santu nirāmayāḥ;
sarvé bhadrāṇi pashyantu, mā kashchid_duḥkha-bhāg-bhavét.

(Let everybody be healthy and happy, may all see what is
auspicious, and let there be no sorrow for anyone. The world is
one large family, which aligns with this thought.)

The source of this verse is not clearly known (it is not from the *Brihadaranyaka Upanishad*); however, two similar verses with very similar meanings can be found elsewhere:

सर्वेषां मङ्गलं भूयात् सर्वे सन्तु निरामयाः।
सर्वे भद्राणि पश्यन्तु मा कश्चिद्दुःखभाग् भवेत्।।

sarveṣāṁ maṅgalaṁ bhūyāt sarve santu nirāmayāḥ;
sarve bhadrāṇi paśyantu mā kaściddubkhabhāg bhavet.

(Let there be auspiciousness for all; let all be free from illness. Let all see what is auspicious, and let no one suffer from sorrow.)
—*Garuda Purana* 35.51

सर्वे भवन्तु सुखिनः सर्वे सन्तु निरामयाः।
सर्वे भद्राणि पश्यन्तु मा कश्चित्कष्टमाप्नुयात्।।

sarve bhavantu sukhinaḥ sarve santu nirāmayāḥ|
sarve bhadrāṇi paśyantu mā kaścitkaṣṭamāpnuyāt||

(Let all be happy, let all be free from illness. Let all see what is auspicious, and let no one encounter difficulty.)
—*Vājasaneya Samhitā*

'*Sarve*' or 'all' is the keynote of India; inclusiveness is its hallmark. Hindus do not seek to convert those who disagree with their point of view. Hindus do not kill others because of differing beliefs or viewpoints. Although local circumstances may cause a few exceptions, caste discrimination is a complete deviation from the foundation of dharma.

Hindu civilization uncovered the concept of dharma: the true nature of being and its paths, righteousness, and the laws of life and living. Everyone is duty-bound to unfold their potential to the fullest. The concept of Iswara and Brahman (the omnipresent, all-pervading supreme being) was the creation of the highest contemplating minds, a concept to which modern physics is approaching today. The law of karma is another profound discovery that binds us all together. Hindu sages proclaimed that 'we are the makers of our destiny', shaping who we want to be and what we can become. Every action yields a positive or negative result, affecting the individual, family, community, and society. Dharma is the central pivot of this civilization. Universality, humanism, and absolute freedom—or liberty—are the pillars of Hindu culture. As Swami Vivekananda said, 'Freedom is the first condition of growth.' Freedom from all limitations and attachments has manifested as the highest ideal in the concept of *mukti*. Hindus have excelled in the discoveries of the inner world, the science of spirit, and the science of consciousness: yoga.

These principles have given rise to many *adhyatmic* (spiritual) paths, panths, or sects, including Jainism, Shaivism, Shaktism, Vaishnavism, Buddhism, and Sikhism, along with newer groups like Swaminarayan in India. The term 'ism' was added by Western theologians much later, after the creation of these panths, to categorize them as 'religions' and separate them from Hindu Dharma. Hindus have produced vast literature and art across the world, with the concept of *adhyatma* as the central theme. Hindu sculptures, architecture, paintings, dance, and music are exceptional on a global scale, though much has been destroyed or stolen.

To fulfil the path of self-realization and self-actualization, Hindus have developed many systems tailored to people of various physical, mental, and spiritual capacities. The Karma, Bhakti, Jnana, Hatha, and Raja branches of yoga represent the highest achievements of this culture, all while acknowledging the aesthetic, intellectual, and material aspects.

Yet, it is a mistake to think that Hindus neglected material and mental needs. We must remember that Columbus was on his way to India, not searching for God, but for gold. The British did not go to India for its vast and diverse natural beauty, but to increase their material prosperity and feed their own poor. Hindus developed *shastras* and *vidyas*—branches of knowledge and technology—from Karma Yoga to kamasutra, natyashastra (the science of music and dance), shilpashastra (arts and architecture), rasayana (chemistry), ayurveda, astronomy, mathematics, and martial arts. In virtually every possible field, they left marks of excellence. Until today, a Hindu soldier's strength is described in Iran by the phrase 'the Hindu sword', symbolizing extreme harshness and fierceness. Indian ships were considered the best until the 18th century.

Hindus strove to perfect everything by associating sacredness with all aspects of life, following strict moral codes. A soldier would not attack an unarmed opponent. They would not exploit nature. Hindus were deeply aware of the importance of environmental harmony—not because of a biochemical concept of ecology, but due to a vision of the entire universe as a sacred living entity. This is called spiritualization: seeing the sacred everywhere. To call an animal, like a cow, 'mother' is an example of spiritualization, as is calling the sun the giver of all life, as in Suryadev or Lord Surya. To express one's identity with reference to the Supreme Being—'*Aum Tat Sat*' or '*Aham Brahmasmi*'—is nothing less than universal spiritual identity. Hindus, thousands of years ago, offered to the world what Julian Huxley once called 'the science of human possibilities'. It is true that Hindus have deviated from this path, mostly due to centuries of foreign control and oppression. However, the time has come for Hindus to return to their true heritage.

To clearly see the distinctive characteristics between cultures, we can examine the basic human act of relationship and communication—how people greet each other. Hindus' 'Namaste' is an expression of reverence from the entire body, mind, and spirit, acknowledging human divinity, whereas other cultures greet physically and intellectually. All societies grow according to *prakriti* or naturally. The distinction between Hindu culture and other societies can be explained this way: The Hindu culture of the Indian subcontinent was based on a vision, planning, and reorganization of the natural order of society, with *samskriti* as its foundation. For example, the main purpose of the varna system was for individuals and societies to evolve into a more perfect and harmonious states. The idea of dharma is to bind all into duties towards sustenance and sustainability. Most other civilizations grew according to *prakriti* without pre-planning or organization.

Now, the obvious question arises: Why are India and its people in such miserable conditions today? History can answer this question. Any entity can be destroyed if its inner strength weakens and external forces overpower it. Swami Vivekananda addressed this issue, saying:

> The social laws of India have always been subject to great periodic changes. At their inception, these laws were the embodiment of a gigantic plan, which was to unfold itself slowly through time. The great seers of ancient India saw so far ahead of their time that the world has to wait centuries yet to appreciate the full scope of this wonderful plan, that is the one and only cause of the degeneration of India. The degeneration of India came not because the laws and customs of the ancients were bad, but because they were not allowed to be carried to their legitimate conclusions.[8]

Indian Culture

Hindus have always welcomed people from abroad and were open to new ideas. Bharat provided shelter to persecuted people worldwide, including the Parsees, Jews, Tibetan Buddhists in the past, and Bangladeshis in more recent times. Yet, it is easier to say 'take the best of both worlds' than to do it. Culture is a living, organic ecosystem. One cannot simply impose an alien idea or practice on a culture; it must integrate into the system as if it were a natural part of our own body. Hindus did not merely adopt things from the outside but assimilated many ideas and adapted them to their own life and culture, which was already rich and diverse.

During the last thousand years of foreign invasion and occupation, Hindus have faced significant losses, most notably the erosion of their dynamism. During this period, society was compelled to focus on mere survival, which led to the ossification of social structures in an effort to protect itself. As a result, the ongoing process of reform and renewal (Sanatan), a hallmark of Hindu society, nearly ceased until the latter part of the 19th century.

Now, the time has come for Hindus to avoid imitating the West and instead examine their civilization through the wisdom of their own rishis. This perspective can help in removing unnecessary and damaging practices, both within India and globally.

Today, some may describe Indian culture as a composite one or even as a product of invaders' influence; this is, at best, misleading. The culture of Bharat remains firmly rooted in *adhyatmic* and yogic principles, as it has been throughout its history. Even non-Hindus in India exhibit these influences. Unfortunately, a small class of individuals who wield power and adhere to values alien to the nation attempt to foster a different kind of culture. Often, this is presented under the guise of being 'modern' or 'progressive'. However, this culture is neither a faithful replica of the West nor entirely disconnected from Hindu traditions. These individuals influence art, literature, music, and other forms of entertainment, including films. Many current forms of expression and entertainment, which are sometimes portrayed as art and culture in India, are far removed from Indian traditions.

India's willingness to accommodate contradictions often stems from a desire to avoid conflict. One such contentious issue is the contribution of Muslims to Indian culture. The fact remains that most Muslims in India are descendants of converted Hindus—whether due to poverty, neglect by Hindu society, or coercion—who continue to follow many Hindu practices, apart from religious rituals. However, the contributions of Islam to Indian culture are vastly outweighed by the destructive impact of Islamic invasions. This is evident in the thousands of Hindu, Buddhist, and Jain temples that were destroyed and often replaced by mosques, as well as in the burning of libraries and university towns like Taxila and Nalanda. During the Islamic period, there were sustained efforts to impose Persian, Turkic, and Arabic influences on the country. Like any other form of imperialism, Turko-Arab imperialism sought—and continues to seek—to control the lives of millions.

Islam served as a tool of pan-Arabic and pan-Turkic imperialism, which exacerbated local poverty. In India, this was compounded by the greed of Afghan and Turkic invaders, along with the Mongol zeal and cruelty exhibited by figures such as Ghori, Timur, and Babar. Many Muslims who remain fixated on the past glories of imperial influence—such as the Mughal or Pathan eras—continue to suffer from an identity crisis and a superiority complex. This has contributed to the erosion of indigenous culture and has alienated them from their country's natural and historic cultural ethos. Unsurprisingly, Pakistanis often perceived themselves as belonging to a different race or culture from Indians, aligning instead with Central Asia, Persia, or Arabia as the sources of their culture and history.

Max Muller offered a poignant commentary on the Islamic conquest of India, highlighting its profound impact on Indian society. He stated:

> The other epic poem too, the Mahabharata, is full of episodes showing a profound regard for truth [...] Were I to quote from all the law-books, and from still later works, everywhere you would hear the same key-note of truthfulness vibrating through them all [...] I say once more that I do not wish to represent the people of India as two hundred and fifty-three millions of angels, but I do wish it to be understood and to be accepted as a fact, that the damaging charge of untruthfulness brought against that people is utterly unfounded with regard to ancient times. It is not only not true, but the very opposite of the truth. As to modern times, and I date them from about 1000 after Christ [AD], I can only say that, after reading the accounts of the terrors and horrors of Mohammedan rule, my wonder is that so much of native virtue and truthfulness should have survived. You might as well expect a mouse to speak the truth before a cat, as a Hindu before a Mohammedan judge.
>
> When you read the atrocities committed by the Mohammedan conquerors of India from that time to the time when England stepped in and, whatever may be said by her envious critics, made, at all events, the broad principles of our common humanity

> respected once more in India, the wonder, to my mind, is how any nation could have survived such an Inferno without being turned into devils themselves.[9]

On the other hand, the concept of *Vasudhaiva Kutumbakam*—acknowledging everyone as part of one family—has resonated with many Muslims. Some Muslims recognize that they are part of the Indian cultural ethos, sometimes referred to as Hindutva, and are contributing positively to it. Certain Sufi saints, musicians, dancers, and singers exemplify this integration. However, it is worth noting that many Sufis during the Muslim period in India acted as agents of the ruling class and played a role in promoting Islamic aggression.

Despite the turbulent history marked by floods of hostility and battles, much of India remains the Bharat of Ram, Krishna, Sita, Draupadi, Shiva, and Parvati. Even Christians in Bharat have retained aspects of Hindu culture. Churches increasingly incorporate elements such as 'Aum' ('Om') and saffron, and some perform 'pooja' to Jesus. Similarly, many communists, while professing atheism, continue to engage in mantras and rituals, indicating the deep cultural roots that persist across ideologies. It seems that the current phase of confusion is temporary, and Bharat is slowly rediscovering her true dharma. A confused society, finding little of value to appreciate, tends to embrace anything that comes its way. It mimics others but struggles to assimilate these influences, as its mental faculties are not suited to certain types of external ideas. Consequently, the society suffers from cultural malnutrition. While the land has been freed from foreign rule, cultural alienation still persists among the elite—a trend initiated by India's first prime minister, Nehru. However, the responsibility for shaping the nation's destiny no longer lies solely with this alienated class. Today, many truly cultured individuals—those who possess *samskaras* and actively promote *samskriti*—are contributing to the national cultural awakening, helping Bharat reconnect with its rich heritage.

The Myth of a Common or Composite Culture in India

Many NeoCols would have us believe in the existence of a common or composite culture in India. Some modern Hindu *sadhus* often cite the phrase '*jato mat tato path*', a famous saying attributed to Sri Ramakrishna Paramhansa, to convey the idea that 'all religions are the same and valid'.

The story behind this saying is as follows: One day, Mahendranath Gupta, the biographer of Sri Ramakrishna and author of *Sri Sri Ramakrishna Kathamirta*, was engaged in a discussion with him. The subject was whether to follow Ishwara with a form (*sakar*) or without form (*nirakar*). Mahendranath preferred the latter. In response, Sri Ramakrishna explained, 'It is alright if one believes in one of them. Belief in the formless is well and good. But do not think this is the only truth; everything else is false. You should know that the path with form is also true, just as the formless is true.' It is within this context that Sri Ramakrishna is believed to have uttered the famous saying: '*jato mat tato path*'. The literal meaning of this Bengali phrase is, 'as many thoughts, as many ways (to achieve the goal)'. However, it was never intended to apply to 'religions' as a whole. Instead, it likely referred to the 'dharmic paths' and the *sadhana* (spiritual practices) within the *dharmic* traditions of the Hindus.

Another saying often quoted by champions of 'religious harmony' is '*Sarva dharma sama bhava*'. However, it is difficult to find an original reference for this phrase. Some attribute it to Sri Ramakrishna or Swami Vivekananda, while others suggest that Gautam Buddha uttered it along with '*ahimsa paramo dharma*' (non-violence is the highest dharma). Most likely, the phrase gained prominence through Gandhi, who used it to foster 'religious harmony' as part of his political activities.

Regardless of its origin, the saying was never intended to mean that 'all religions are equal or the same'. Religions or belief systems cannot support such sameness because each one claims exclusivity. For instance, many belief systems assert their prophet, scripture, or doctrine as the most authentic, true, or final—Islam being a prime example. Consequently, these religions inherently cannot 'agree to agree' on matters of belief and practice.

If the intended meaning is 'equal respect for all religions', it is still incorrect. The phrase implies respect from one 'religion' to another; however, 'Hinduism' is not a religion in the conventional sense. If the goal is to respect various traditions, including Abrahamic ones, we can strive for 'respect for all traditions'. However, it is unacceptable to condone any conflict with the law of the land or to permit practices that result in the loss of freedom or harm to another tradition due to inherent hatred and intolerance. A pertinent example is the idea and practice of iconoclasm, which involves desecrating or destroying *murtis* of *dharmic* traditions—a practice still occurring regularly in Afghanistan, Pakistan, India, Bangladesh, and many other places.

If we are speaking of dharma, then dharma must be what we strive for. In that context, we can assert that all dharmic paths (sustaining and harmonizing principles) are equally valid. However, it is important to recognize that not all paths lead to the same destination. Any sect asserting 'my way or the highway' holds a 'sectarian' view, which is inherently bound to conflict with others.

In the Mahabharata, we find a warning:

धर्मं यो बाधते धर्मो न स धर्मः कुधर्मकः|
अविरोधात्तु यो धर्मः स धर्मः सत्यविक्रमधर्मं ||

Dharmam yo badhate dharmo na sa dharmah kudharmkah;
avirodhattu yo dharmah, sa dharmah Satyavikrama.

(Any dharma that violates another's dharma is not true dharma. It is *kudharma* or bad dharma. The dharma that flourishes without harming the interests of others is indeed the true dharma, *aatyavikrama*.)[10]

According to the Merriam-Webster Dictionary, the word 'composite' means 'a thing made up of several parts or elements'.

When applied to culture, this suggests that these parts come from various religious and national traditions. However, dharmic traditions have very little in common with the Abrahamic ones. Regarding yoga, various 'religions' worldwide may share some rudimentary ideas and practices related to Bhakti yoga, but that is all. Even virtues like 'non-violence', 'love thy neighbour', etc., have been preached and practised by Hindus since time immemorial.

There is not much that Hindus needed in the past, nor need in the future, to learn from other religious traditions and nations such as Persia, Turkey, or Arabia. These nations benefitted the most from India prior to the era of Islamic invasions.

If 'composite culture' means an organic give-and-take, then what is there for Hindus to take? Others need to learn from Hindu ideals and traditions, not the other way around. The moment attempts are made to 'appease' opposing views of life and practices, confusion arises, damaging society's original fabric. The classic example is Gandhi. Many believe that he was the messiah of our time and sometimes compare him to Buddha. However, many may disagree if we study his beliefs and practice, as discussed below.

The False Narrative of Gandhi

Gandhi's perspective on religion was once of inclusivity, but his views have often been misinterpreted. He once said:

> I came to the conclusion long ago that all religions were true and that also that all had some error in them, and while I hold by my own religion, I should hold other religions as dear as Hinduism. So we can only pray, if we were Hindus, not that a Christian should become a Hindu; but our innermost prayer should be that a Hindu should become a better Hindu, a Muslim a better Muslim, and a Christian a better Christian.[11]

One example of Gandhi's efforts to blend religious traditions can be seen in his modification of sacred texts. A Vaishnava devotee

from the 17th century, Lakshmanacharya, collated the 108 names of Sri Rama in a text called *Shri Nama Ramayanam*. However, to bring Hindus closer to Muslims, Gandhi altered and tampered with this very sacred and beautiful song by inserting the names Allah, Rahim, and Karim into it.
Below are the original lyrics:

raghupati rāghava rājā rām
patita pāvana sītārām ||P||
sundara vigraha mēghashyām
gangā tuḷasi sẖālagrām |
bhadragirīshwara sītārām
bhaktajanapriya sītārām |
jānakiramaṇa sītārām
jayajaya rāghava sītārām ||1||

(O King Rama, you are the descendant of the Raghu clan and the uplifter of the fallen, worshipped with Sita. Your image is beautiful, and the colour [of your body] is dark blue, like a cloud. You are worshipped with Ganga water, tulsi plant, and shaligram [fossil rock]. You are the lord of Bhadrachalam Hill [Girisheswar], and together, you are called Sita Ram. You are a favourite of the devotees, O Sita Ram. Your consort is Sita. Victory to you, O descendent of the Raghu clan. Victory to Sita Ram.)

Here is Gandhi's altered version:

raghupati rāghava rājārāma,
patita pāvana sītārāma
sītārāma, sītārāma,
bhaja pyāre tu sītārāma
ishwara allaha tero nāma
saba ko sanmati de bhagavāna
rāma rahīma karīma samāna
hama saba hai unaki santāna
saba milā māṅge yaha varadāna
hamārā rahe mānava kā jñāna

(O Lord Rama, you are the descendant of the Raghu [clan] and the uplifter of the fallen. You and your beloved consort, Sita, are to be worshipped. All names of God refer to your name, including Ishwara and the Muslim Allah. O Lord, please grant wisdom to all, so that we may understand that Ram, Rahim, and Karim are all the same. We all are your children, and we all request this boon so that we may all possess the wisdom of humanism [manava jnana].)

Though Islam is against so-called idolatry, it also venerates the Kaaba. As we learn from the book *The Crash of a Civilization*, 360 different deities with murtis existed there. Mohammed banned and destroyed all but Allah. And this 'creator god' of Islam has ninety-nine names.[12]

Here are a few examples of these names, including Rahim and Karim, which Gandhi added in this prayer and their meanings:

- Raḥīm: The Most Merciful, Ever-Merciful, Merciful, Most Clement
- Karīm: The Noble, Bountiful, Generous, Precious, Honoured, Benefactor
- Raḥmān: The Beneficent, All-Compassionate, Most Gracious
- Mālik: The King, Lord, Sovereign, Dominion, Master, the One and Only
- Kabir: The Great, Ever-Great, Grand, Most Great, Greatly Abundant
- Shahīd: The Witness, Testifier, Ever-Witnessing
- Mujīb: The Responsive, Answerer, Supreme Answerer, Accepter of Invocation

Although these may appear to be great names, they are meant only for the followers of Islam. The Quran, which promotes various actions against 'kafirs' or infidels, raises the question: Why should the names of Allah be inserted into a sacred prayer of Hindus? Not only has Gandhi caused confusion among Hindus but he has also insulted Hindu tradition by doing so. This is a clear example of a failed attempt to coerce Hindus into accepting other ideas and ideals in the name of '*sarva dharma sama bhava*' and the creation of a 'composite culture'! However, he never attempted the reverse by inserting Hindu ideas or sacred names into Muslim prayer or prayer meetings exclusively for a Muslim audience.

This becomes even more evident when we examine his understanding and attitude towards Sri Ram. In fact, he does not seem to have prayed to the Sri Ram of Hindu tradition, even though he talked about a utopian kingdom, 'Ram Rajya'. On Ram Navami, 30 March 1928, he said the following in his speech at Sabarmati:

> The Rama of whom we sing is not the Rama of Valmiki, nor even the Rama of Tulsi—although his Ramayana is very dear to me and I consider it an incomparable work, I never seem to have enough of it once I start reading it. Today, however, we shall not think of Tulsidas's Rama or the Rama of Girdhar's Ramayana, much less Rama of Kalidasa or Bhavabhuti. There is great beauty in Bhavabhuti's *Uttararamacharita*. However, here is not the Rama whose name we may recite to cross to the other shore or whose name we may repeat in moments of despair. If someone is suffering unbearable pain I tell him to repeat Ramanama. If someone is unable to sleep I tell him too to repeat Ramanama. This Rama is not the son of Dasharatha or the husband of Sita. In fact he is not the embodied Rama. The Rama that dwells in our hearts cannot possibly have a physical form; the heart is no larger than a thumb and the Rama who dwells in some niche there could not have a body, nor could he have been born on the ninth day of the month of Chaitra in a certain year. He is birthless. He is the Creator, the Lord of the universe. Hence the Rama whom one wishes to remember, and whom one should remember, is the Rama of one's own imagination, not the Rama of someone else's imagination.[13]

On one hand, Gandhi acted as if he were a genuinely enlightened rishi, but his childish arguments reveal his limitations in understanding and appreciating Hindu pluralistic ideas. Was he truly a confused man? While Hindus regard Sri Ram as

'Purushottama', the highest-level human being, Gandhi played with the name of Ram, suggesting he was not the 'Perfect One'. Not only that, but perhaps Ram was just a petty murderer and a 'monster'! Consider the following:

> Many times we wonder how the Rama who slew Vali could be called the Perfect One. I too come across many such questions, and I am amused. What great achievement is there in having slain someone, by fair means or foul, or to have destroyed ten-headed Ravana, if ever there was one such. In this modern age, even if a Ravana is born, not with twenty but countless hands, a child standing behind a cannon can, by firing a single ball, send all his hands and heads flying. We should not regard such a being as Superhuman; we would look upon him as a big monster. I believe that we do not wish to acquire the strength of a super-monster. We would not attain peace by worshipping him. We should worship Him, the Inner Ruler, who dwells in the hearts of all, yet transcends all and is the Lord of all. It is He of whom we sing: Nirbalke bal Rama. The song also mentions Draupadi's despair. Now what had Draupadi had to do with an embodied Rama? Yet, the poet has sung that Rama saved Draupadi's honour. The Rama mentioned here is the One who is common to all and yet comprehended by none. It is this Rama whom we remember. Between this Rama, the Inner Ruler, and Krishna there is no difference.[14]

So, if Sri Ram was not the Ramayana-famous Hindu avatar to Gandhi, he invented a new version of Ram to fit his own Abrahamic mindset and agenda. This becomes clearer when we analyze how he altered the prayer.

In his mind, his idea of Ram had little to do with the Ram of the Ramayan. He removed the description of Sri Ram's physical body, '*sundara vigraha mēghashyām*', in order to establish his 'monotheistic' and 'formless' idea of God. Gandhi imposed this vision on the Hindu Ram by replacing it with '*ishwara allaha tero nāma*'. He also removed key elements of the Vaishnava puja tradition, such as the use of Ganga, tulsi, and shaligram. Who gave him the right to alter a Vaishnava song and turn it into an Abrahamic one? Was this an attempt to convert?

A true believer in the Abrahamic faith rarely appreciates original Indian icons like Ram, Krishna, Buddha, Mahavir, or, of course, any deity, Ishwara, or Bhagwan. The person who is called 'Mahatma' and 'father of the nation' may have done more harm by confusing Hindus than by bringing Hindus and Muslims together! It appears, from all his writings and activities, that like the missionaries, he failed to appreciate the term dharma and equated it with 'religion', thus making a mockery of Sanatana Hindu Dharma.

The often-quoted shloka used to support the idea of '*sarva dharma sama bhavo*' is '*ekam sat viprah vahudha vadanti*' (generally translated as 'truth is one, the learned express it in many ways'). However, it is frequently cited without considering its full context.

This verse, from the *Ṛigveda,* is often quoted only partially—the second part. The full verse reads as follows:

इन्द्रं मित्रं वरुणमग्निमाहुरथो दिव्यः स सुपर्णो गरुत्मान् ।
एकं सद्विप्रा बहुधा वदन्त्यग्निं यमं मातरिश्वानमाहुः ॥४६॥

Índraṃ mitráṃ váruṇam agním āhur
átho divyáḥ sá suparṇó garútmān;
Ékaṃ sád víprā bahudhā́ vadanty agníṃ
yamáṃ mātaríśvānam āhuḥ.

(They call Him Indra, Mitra, Varuṇa, Agni; indeed, He is the heavenly Garuḍa with beautiful wings. That which is One, the sages speak of as multifarious; they call Him Agni, Yama, Mātariśvan.)[15]

First, Abrahamic faiths would not agree with this verse. Second, this wisdom applies exclusively to Hindu Vedic context and not to Abrahamic traditions.

If a religion encourages its followers to seek the truth, foster natural spiritual aspirations, and allows critical thinking, it aligns with the elements of dharma. From a Western theological perspective, Indian *adhyatma* (spirituality) is entirely distinct from all Abrahamic traditions. None of the core values of the Vedas, Upanishads, or yoga find a place in these traditions, especially in Islam. Thus, for the Sanatanis there is not much to gain from these religions. Conversely, dharmic systems have much to offer humanity, irrespective of belief systems, race, nationality, or religion.

The practice of yoga, for example, benefits individuals when done correctly, without requiring belief. While Hatha yoga appeals to many, there are numerous other forms of yoga within the dharmic or yogic system of India. However, most Abrahamic authorities, including the Vatican, reject yoga. Acts of sustenance, order, justice, and righteousness—do these require belief, or are they intrinsic, natural human endeavours?

Hindus in India have historically been forced to 'live with' exclusivist traditions that came from outside. Unfortunately, there are religious leaders who insist that this accommodation is wrong. All the major Indian traditions—Hindu, Jain, Buddhist, and Sikh—share a common foundation rooted in dharma and yoga, concepts that are beyond the scope of the Abrahamic faiths.

Invaders destroyed thousands of Hindu temples, murtis, institutes of learning, and magnificent works of art and architecture. Why? Because of a belief in iconoclasm. They also slaughtered cows, which are sacred to most Hindus. How can there be a common or composite culture with those who view you as *kafir* or heathen or who humiliate you?

That said, all citizens of India can live with an attitude of coexistence. As long as no individual or group disrupts freedom, peace, harmony, or progress, everyone should be free to practise their beliefs in their own homes. However, we must reject the ideologies and figures of communism that promote the notion that all religions are equally false and lump Hindu Dharma into the same category to propagate their new 'religion'. Everyone has the right to pray and seek solace in a higher power, by whatever name they choose. Nobody has the right to impose their ideas, beliefs, or ideologies—whether religious or ideological (as in the case of communism)—on others. Attempts at religious conversions and the forcible imposition of ideologies on millions are crimes against humanity and civilizational offences that violate human rights.

The sooner we discard the illusion of '*sarva dharma sama bhava*', the better it will be for the world in general and Hindus in particular.

Role of the Hindus

Not too long ago, all of Asia was deeply influenced by Bharat's culture and philosophy—not through force, but by choice. Buddha and Ram continue to provide spiritual inspiration to many nations in Asia today, including China, Japan, Korea, Vietnam, Cambodia, Myanmar, Thailand, and Indonesia. Since Swami Vivekananda's arrival in America, Hindu Dharma has found a place in the hearts of many Americans, and numerous spiritual leaders have followed in his footsteps.

Marie Louise Burke observed: 'There are already many in the West who are in Vedanta philosophy. These "unsung devotees" find in Vivekananda's and Ramakrishna's teachings the ways of total sacrifice.'[16] Although Vivekananda's teachings are not central to mainstream Western thought and culture, the Christian Church in the West, both Protestant and Catholic, has taken a growing interest in Eastern ideas. Without always realizing the source, Americans are influenced by Vivekananda in their 'search for life within'.

That's not all—many other spiritual leaders, such as Paramhansa Yogananda, Srila Prabhupada, and others, have made significant contributions to shaping modern American minds. Their influence has also reinvigorated different cultures and brought about new waves of awakening in India. Millions of people around the world practise yoga in its various forms and benefit from ayurveda, India's ancient healing system. Both are grounded in *adhyatma*, or inner science.

What, then, should we do? What is our cultural debt to Bharat? What do we owe to the society we live in? Hindus living in predominantly non-Hindu lands must maintain their culture. However, it is equally important to allow them the freedom to develop new forms of expression for their Hindu values. This must be approached with great care.

One possible approach is to Hinduize selected native practices and festivals while reforming certain Hindu traditions. For example, in countries where the Thanksgiving festival is observed, Hindus can celebrate it as the harvest festival with Devi Lakshmi pooja. The priority should be to practise Hindu values and traditions at home and ensure that children receive *samskaras* (cultural and spiritual values). Have we truly learned what it means to be a 'Hindu Parent'? We must carefully reflect on what we practise and promote as our culture in our individual lives, homes, parties, communities, and organizations. It is our responsibility to uphold the essence of Hindu Dharma while ensuring its values resonate with future generations.

The Challenge Is Enormous

What, then, is the solution? Some suggest that science and spirituality must work in tandem. Even Einstein is often quoted as saying, 'Science without religion is lame, religion without science is blind.' Perhaps he too struggled to reconcile the unseen, infallible debate within the two realms. Let's consider the full context in which he made this statement:

> Now, even though the realms of religion and science in themselves are clearly marked off from each other, nevertheless, there exists between the two strong reciprocal relationships and dependencies. Though religion may be the one that determines the goal, it has, nevertheless, learned from science, in the broadest sense, what it means will contribute to the attainment of the goals it has set

> up. But science can only be created by those who are thoroughly imbued with the aspiration toward truth and understanding. This source of feeling, however, springs from the sphere of religion. To this there also belongs the faith in the possibility that the regulations valid for the world of existence are rational, that is, comprehensible to reason. I cannot conceive of a genuine scientist without that profound faith. The situation may be expressed by an image: science without religion is lame, religion without science is blind.[17]

This perspective provides a framework for understanding the interplay between science and spirituality, a relationship that continues to be debated today.

In this context, it is fitting to quote Sri Aurobindo, the modern Indian seer and philosopher, who offered a unique synthesis of these ideas:

> What Science could not provide India offers Brahman for the eternal goal, Yoga for the means of perfection, Dharma (*swabhavaniyatam karma*) for the rational yet binding law of conduct. Therefore, because it has something by which humanity can be satisfied and on which it can found itself, the victory of the Indian mind is assured.[18]

To many, the word 'spirituality' is more palatable than 'religion'. However, in practice, 'spirituality' often refers to the same age-old concepts of engaging in certain 'religious' activities. Some argue that the original meanings of the term 'religion'—such as respect for what is sacred, reverence for the gods, to reconnect, or return to the origin—are essentially the true essence of spirituality. Yet, it is evident that the contemporary use of both terms has drifted far from these possible original intents. For now, we can use the term spirituality in its broadest possible sense as a synonym for 'religion'.

Over the past century, a paradigm shift in thought has occurred. While scientific explorations delved into the realms of subatomic particles and the vast expanse beyond our solar system, thinkers like Thoreau and Emerson spearheaded the transcendental movement.

For the transcendentalists, ideal spirituality was not rooted in mental or intellectual exercises but in transcending these realms altogether. They believed true spiritual experience was achieved through the power of 'intuition', as opposed to the rigid theologies and prescribed religious practices of the world's various faiths.

These ideas were deeply influenced by the teachings of the Bhagavad Gita, India's most renowned philosophical text, as well as the writings and translations of the Upanishads by Raja Ram Mohan Roy. In 1893, Swami Vivekananda, the celebrated philosopher, monk, and reformer, coined the term 'science of spirituality'. At the World Parliament of Religions in Chicago, he presented Vedanta as an alternative worldview to the thinkers of the 19th century. His ideas resonated profoundly with the Western audience and left a lasting impression.

The transcendental and Vedantic movements liberated many from the intellectual confines of their time, becoming a cultural phenomenon in the US with an immediate and far-reaching impact. In 1976, the Smithsonian Institute recognized Swami Vivekananda in its list of the twenty-nine most influential people who ever visited America, noting that 'Vivekananda left an indelible mark on America's spiritual development'.[19] Yet the foundation for this wave of influence was laid earlier by Raja Ram Mohan Roy. As Sister Nivedita observed, 'He [Vivekananda] claimed himself to have taken up the task that the breadth and foresight of Ram Mohun Roy had mapped out.'[20]

On the one hand, those with a rational mindset appreciated the idea; some religious thinkers even took it seriously (Christian Science is a case in point). It has significantly enhanced the understanding of religions in general and Christianity in particular. However, the Church's missionary outlook felt threatened by this new influence of both material and 'spiritual' science, prompting many to incorporate greater rationality into their preaching.

Many thinkers' and scientists' understanding of religion or spirituality in the past was primarily shaped by the medieval form of Christianity. Consequently, they identified all other 'religions' of the world, including 'Hinduism', within the same framework. The study of Oriental ideas was also conducted through this narrow lens. Thanks to missionaries with vested interests, a distorted notion of our civilization was perpetuated.

Nevertheless, the original spirit of Indian thought did not escape the attention of thinkers like Emerson and Schopenhauer. Perhaps the real issue lies in the division of the world into religious and secular domains. Historically, religion has wrought havoc on civilization. Neither secular socialism nor capitalist leadership has offered much relief. Poverty, persecution, and exploitation remain widespread. Democracy and justice continue to be foreign concepts in large parts of the world.

'Survival of the fittest' has long been a mantra. The world urgently needs a mutual win-win approach, one not found in communism, capitalism, or any of the Abrahamic religions, which limit their ethical laws to their own followers. If you do not belong to one of these faiths, you are either expected to adopt their worldview or risk eternal condemnation.

In the West, religion can be broadly divided into three key aspects: the dogma or 'belief system', the ethical values it propagates, and the notion of divinity. The secular, material, and atheist perspectives often view divinity as a form of 'metaphysics'. Over time, the concept of 'divinity' has evolved from a matter of 'faith' into an unseen force associated with experiential and experimental inquiry—a 'science of spirituality'. The divide between the secular and the sacred has been profound.

The good news is that modern science, particularly quantum physics, has recognized consciousness as a significant factor, drawing some atheists closer to the idea of an all-pervading force. This force is often described using various names, such as Ishwar, Vishnu, or Substratum, reflecting diverse cultural interpretations.

Although 'interfaith' dialogues are plentiful, the idea of divinity and its applications remains so fragmented that reconciliation can seems unattainable. A cooperative system must be embraced for a true win-win scenario to emerge. Perhaps the starting point lies in addressing moral and ethical issues, where religion could play a constructive role.

Most religions begin their sermons with the message 'do good to others'. This fosters a degree of ethical awareness, either motivated by fear of punishment or the desire for rewards. Consequently, adherents tend to remain ethical to some extent. However, there is a fundamental problem: some religions do not extend this principle to those outside their creed. In some cases, outsiders are regarded as illegitimate and perceived as either targets for conversion or as enemies or infidels.

By contrast, today's secular ethical values, justice, and human rights are rooted in the so-called 'Golden Rule'.[21] It states: 'One should treat others as one would like others to treat oneself' and, in its negative or prohibitive form, known as the 'Silver Rule, 'One should not treat others in ways that one would not like to be treated'.[22]

However, this principle has its limitations. Prominent philosophers, including Kant, Nietzsche, and Bertrand Russell, have raised significant concerns about its application. Other universal codes of conduct for fostering a harmonious and productive world merit consideration. Non-violence and the pursuit of truth are two virtues frequently upheld in Indian ethical philosophy. Unfortunately, these too are insufficient. These values are often driven by religious doctrines or societal norms. Personal freedom, meanwhile, is typically safeguarded by 'the rule of law', whether secular or rooted in religious principles, such as Islamic Sharia.

In societies where corruption has become endemic, it is evident that conflicts will persist between survival needs, consumerist tendencies, the hunter-gatherer instincts of humanity, and the pleasure-seeking behaviours of individuals adhering to rules and codes. As meta-rule—a rule for creating rules—must be established to address this challenge, or the issue of applicability will remain unresolved.

What Is the Solution?

Some ethical codes require education, consistent practice, and the establishment of an environment and practical societal framework to support adherence.

Unfortunately, education systems across the globe have largely abandoned the responsibility of ethical orientation, leaving it instead to religious institutions. While the judicial system, courts, and law enforcement play a role by reducing violations through punishment and deterrence, these measures are largely reactive and insufficient as proactive solutions.

To truly uphold ethical values, individuals must cultivate self-discipline and foster an eagerness to engage with inspiring and uplifting ideas. As the English poet T.S. Elliot observed, this involves transcending 'the intellectual and emotional limitations of our time'.[23] Only then can creativity find true expression, and the full potential of individuals and societies be realized.

But even for that, one must have a sense of a more universal and interconnected existence and accept the fact that there is so much unknown in the universe, rather than being negative about it. One must be positive and say, 'Yes, there is something beyond our speech, mind, and even imagination, with or without form, in harmony with the order of the world and the rules of the universe, beyond human comprehension.' Call it Ishwara, Brahman, infinity, or any reasonable name.

If someone can say, 'Yes, I've experienced this infinity, I've realized that supreme connectedness, and I've felt like a part of the whole,' that is it! Now, one can affirm that there is something beyond the material, beyond our known rules. Once this wholesome vision of existence is developed, our attitude towards everything and our worldview will change. Our thoughts and actions will shift, and our collective attitudes and activities will define our culture. Many, especially in India, have experienced this wholeness and supreme consciousness; they are the rishis and sages.

Now, let us look at two basic human needs from a materialistic perspective: wealth and the physical/mental desires for survival, enjoyment, and happiness. However, this happiness can be thwarted by several factors, including consumerism and the violation of natural and social laws. Interpersonal conflict, disharmony with nature, and imbalance within one's own body, mind, and intellect can undermine our happiness.

Self-discipline and a lifestyle, at both the individual and societal levels, must be developed to realize our full potential. In the short term, this can help free people from bad habits and the limitations of body, mind, and time. In the long term, it can help us attain moksha, or salvation, which is freedom from the bindings of nature—both external and internal—leading to an actual state of freedom.

But all of this must be achieved by adhering to certain fundamental norms, laws, and orders. Some of the major concerns in today's world are climate change, global warming, the erosion of ethical and moral values in high places, corruption, terrorism, food shortages, and the health and water crisis. All of these contribute to a dangerous sustainability war. At the core of this is sustainability—physical, personal, emotional, intellectual, societal, and environmental.

This ties in with the idea that dharma embodies. What is dharma? At its core, it is a worldview and a 'sustainable way of life and living'—personal, social, national, and global. However, there are many ways to understand this multifaceted and complex term. Perhaps it is as potent and important, if not more so, than the broadest notion of Ishwara.

The Bharatiya ideas of *yama* and *niyama* provide a complete set of ethical values and rules (for example, *satya, ahimsa, saucha,* etc.); if followed, they would benefit any individual or society, irrespective of race, religion, or nationality. These also lead us to become more perfect, strong, and well-equipped, which brings us to yoga.

The first step in yoga is '*karmasu kaushalam*'—skill and excellence in work, as defined in the Gita (2.50). Then, gradually, one must extend the idea of yoga to different dimensions—body, mind, intellect, and finally, infinity, or the divine self and universe. The immediate gains are a healthy body and mind, realizing one's potential, and managing ethical values. In the long run, it will help reach out to the supreme divine. Here, nothing is secular; everything is sacred—something you don't want to destroy or lose but wish to use for self-evolution to the next level. Yoga is a vast science and technology of the self, the inner world, and consciousness. It has branched out in many directions of which today's popular yoga is only a minuscule facet.

Yoga-asana, dhyana, puja, aarti, mantra, and so on are a set of ways and tools to empower ourselves to be more peaceful, harmonious, efficient, and perfect. They help us live in accordance with the cosmic and divine order while invoking the powers or grace of the supreme divine. The divine is that which is sacred, 'ever-present', and enlightening. However, one must remember that ritualist practices are not the only ways, nor are they the sole benefits of the so-called rituals or spiritual acts. The study of these concepts is a vast subject that has been developed over millennia. Theologians may view these practices as a religion called Hinduism. However, much of this knowledge and practice has been misunderstood, lost, or corrupted, and some may require modifications.

It is important to note that yoga's current understanding is primarily related to 'hatha yoga', which represents specific physical postures for better control over the body and mind. Patanjali's *Yoga Sutras* mention the term 'asana' only twice among the 200-odd sutras. In contrast, apart from the four major branches of yoga commonly quoted—karma, bhakti, jnana, and raja—many more forms of yoga are found in the Gita itself and various other ancient Indian texts. Much of this knowledge is also lost.

Significantly, India's great personalities like Aryabhata, Varahamihir, Kanad, and Khana were both scientists and philosophers of various schools of thought, including yoga and Vedanta. In modern times, famous mathematicians and scientists such as Ramanujam, J.C. Bose, C.V. Raman, and Satyen Bose have all been followers of different forms and practices within India's age-old yoga traditions.

Bharat has always hesitated to promote a 'belief system'; instead, it has always had open scrutiny and debates among various thoughts and has never restricted another voice from being heard. There are terms such as 'panth', which denote a particular group or followers of a teacher. But India never called their paths universal; instead, Swami Vivekananda said that each person might have their own path to fulfillment, which is the *swadharma*. But even though that is not the same as religion, it is a great injustice to the term dharma to be represented by the word 'religion' and a civilizational loss if not understood and used correctly.

According to anthropologist and historian of religion Daniel Dubuisson, the concept of 'religion' as a discrete category is a Western construct, an invention of 19th-century scholars who created it as a field of scientific study. Prior to that time, there was little attempt to step outside religious experience and objectify it. In fact, the distinction between the 'secular' and the 'religious', as understood in the West, is meaningless in many non-Western cultures.[24]

Unfortunately, due to this categorization of ideas, Indian concepts such as dharma and karma are often treated in the same way as other 'religious' notions.

Many individuals and groups with specific agendas and vested interests have downplayed, subdued, and at times, attempted to extinguish India's open spirit. However, the good news is that many of the brightest minds of the past one and a half centuries, such as Emerson, Will Durant, and Toynbee, have understood, appreciated, expressed, and emphasized the adoption of the ideals of dharma and yoga-based Indian thoughts.

The stereotype surrounding Hindus and Indians are also rapidly disintegrating. They are no longer viewed simply as snake charmers or as Aryan nomads invading a land. Additionally, issues such as caste, sati, and poverty are no longer the defining images of India, as the world increasingly comes to terms with various ideologies and turns towards India. While the shift may not yet be visible in newspapers or on TV channels, Indian ways of thinking are gradually being embraced by many people, who adopt a lifestyle akin to that of Hindus through practice such as yoga and Ayurveda.

An unbiased, free mind should be able to appreciate this train of thought. Secular materialist minds often have negative experiences with religions—violence in the past, exploitation by religious authorities, persecution, and a lack of rational or scientific engagements with religious beliefs, often leading to conflicts. As a result, figures such as Hagel, Marx, and Lenin did not find much value in religion; to them, it became an 'opiate of the masses'. On the other hand, the Galileos of the world have been persecuted, and continue to be, even today in medieval societies dominated by conservative religious faiths.

However, in these debates, our experience of wholeness, divinity, and higher potential is suffering. The world must be rescued from this conflict if it is to progress. Of all the philosophies, systems, and ideas currently available, those propagated by Indian seers seem most apt for today's world. This is because they do not create a schism between the secular and the sacred, offer broader, universal ethical values, and provide a multitude of ways to experience the world and realize one's potential. They allowed freedom to the extreme, leading to moksha. The true evolution of the universe lies in the enlightenment of humanity at large. The expressions of the inner self, potential, creativity, and skills are nothing but dharma, guiding us towards realizing our full potential in a lifetime.

Yoga is the means, and moksha is the goal. Moksha, or liberation, does not have to be a distant, imaginary future. The small acts and expressions of freedom—from our daily greed, limited physical, mental, and intellectual abilities, emotional hijackings, and circumstantial challenges—are all small 'moksha steps' that contribute to the ultimate culmination.

Conclusion

Some thinkers argue that the next world war will be a war of cultures. People like Samuel Huntington believe that the clash of civilizations is inevitable. As Bertrand Russel stated, if cultures are 'billiard balls', they will inevitably collide with one other. Hindus, however, are an exception; they are flexible, absorbent, and open-minded people who have suffered greatly in this crucial matter, as they hold the powerful realization: '*Vasudhaiva kutumbakam*'. In this sense, Hindus hold the key to the peace and progress of the world of tomorrow. Hindus will contribute to minimizing conflicts and lighting the way for the world to recognize a single 'Global Human Culture', where unity in diversity is the central theme, and all cultures are seen as facets of a global and universal culture. However, for this to happen, Hindus must awaken from their slumbers and become true Hindus in practice.

CHAPTER 6

Divinity in Vedic and Hindu System

In ancient Indian philosophy, the pursuit of self-realization and understanding the nature of the Self has been central to spiritual teachings, as exemplified in the profound dialogue between Yajnavalkya and King Janaka. The Ramayana-famed Rajarshi Janaka, father of Sita Mata, was an ancient king of Videha, a region encompassing parts of Nepal and Mithila. He was called rajarshi (raja + rishi) because of his reputation as a great and benevolent ruler and as a highly *adhyatmic* person, possessing profound knowledge of the shastras and detachment from material wealth.

Yajnavalkya was a Hindu rishi (sage) whose teachings are recorded in the *Brihadaranyaka Upanishad.* On one occasion, he engaged in a profound dialogue with King Janaka about the knowledge of 'Self'. Janaka asked the rishi:

> 'O revered sage, what is the light that illumines a person, the light that awakens and impels him to perform all that he does?'
>
> Yajnavalkya gave a very straightforward answer by saying, 'The sun, O king, for it is the sun alone that is the source of all light and it is for this light that man sits, moves about, does all his work and returns.'
>
> 'That's right O venerable sage, but when the sun has set, what is it that helps man as light?'
>
> 'The moon; it is the moon that is the light of the man when the sun is not there,' was the reply of Yajnavalkya.

'All right, I agree, but when the sun is not there, the moon is also not there, then what is it that guides man as his light?' thus asked Janaka again.

Then Rishi Yajnavalkya replied, 'When the sun has set and the moon is not there, fire is our light, for by that we sit, work, go out and come back.'

'I am all in agreement with you,' said Janaka and continued asking 'but what then is the light when there is no sun, no moon and no fire?'

'Speech, indeed, is the light when all these are absent. Even though we cannot see our hand in the dark we can hear the voice and move towards the sound.'

Janaka was happy but had still one more question. He asked, 'O revered sage, when sun sets, moon is not there, fire is absent and there is no speech, then what is the light?'

'The Self, indeed, is our light O king, for by that we sit, move, work, go out and come back.'

Janaka was deeply touched by this but wanted to know from Yajnavalkya more about the Self that he referred to as the light of all lights. Yajnavalkya continued to impart the knowledge of the Self to King Janaka. He kept unraveling the mystery after mystery of the Self, and the whole teaching is given in the *Brihadaranyaka Upanishad* at length, but the essence of all that Yajnavalkya spoke to King Janaka about the Self is like this:

'The Self is the pure awareness that shines as the light within the heart, surrounded by the senses. It is this Self that is one with the Sole Reality, the Brahman. This Self is free from desire, from evil and from fear. The man who is union with the Self sees without seeing, smells without smelling, tastes without tasting, [speaks] without speaking, hears without hearing, touches without touching, thinks without thinking, knows without knowing, for there is nothing separate from him. This state of not having another is the state of unity, one without a second and that is the world of Brahman. This is the supreme goal of life, the supreme treasure, the supreme joy.'[1]

The aforementioned is an example of how the rishis of Bharat have attempted to define indescribable subject like atman. This chapter is a comparative study of how divinity is understood and conceptualized in different world traditions. We shall see that there is a conformity among various Bharatiya traditions regarding their ideas of divinity. In contrast, the Abrahamic and Western concepts of divinity are, at best, a subset—if not a minuscule aspect—of the Hindu idea of divinity.

When I use the English terms God, gods, or goddesses, what does that evoke for you? What image springs to mind, and what feelings are induced? Confusing, right? When it comes to divinity, Bharat has unique and original concepts. These include *devata, dev, devi, avatara, dhata, vidhata, ātman, paramātman, parameswar, Bhagwan, Brahman,* and *Ishwara.* There is no equivalent term for God or gods in Indian concepts, and the above terms are not easily translatable.

On the other hand, the term 'god' is not found in any original Abrahamic texts; it is a more modern introduction that came into existence long after the Hindu texts were formed. For example, the *shraddha* is generally translated as 'faith', but this is not an accurate translation. It is derived from *shrat* (श्रत्), which is akin to *sat* and *rta*, meaning 'truth' and *dha* (धा), a short form of *dharta* (धर्ता), meaning 'beholder of truth'.

Similarly, before progressing, we must clarify another Western/Abrahamic concept—theism and atheism. These two concepts are often superimposed on the Hindu notions of *astika* and *nastika.* The term theism was introduced in the mid-1600s by Ralph Cudworth, an English clergyman, and is derived from the Greek *theós* or *theoi,* meaning 'god(s)'.[2] Theism refers to a belief in the existence of supernatural divine beings and deities.[3] In contrast, atheism is derived from the Greek term *atheos*, which means 'without god(s)'. The Oxford Dictionary defines a deity as a god or goddess, meaning 'anything revered as divine'.[4]

These concepts introduce several terminologies used to classify various 'belief systems' according to the perspective of the so-called theologians regarding the idea of 'God'. Monotheism is defined as the 'belief in one deity or supreme being', as presented by the Abrahamic faiths.[5] Another term, polytheism, is introduced to denote religious faiths that believe in 'many gods' or deities. In that sense, the so-called 'Hinduism' is classified as a 'polytheist religion' according to theologians.

The term pantheism is defined as the belief that the entire creation is one with the supreme creator or being.[6] This includes all things in nature and celestial objects. Some suggest that Dutch philosopher Baruch Spinoza introduced this idea, but any Hindu can testify that the concept has deep Indian roots.[7] Eminent personalities such as Emily Dickinson, Nikola Tesla, Friedrich Nietzsche, Walt Whitman, Henry David Thoreau, Ralph Waldo Emerson, and Albert Einstein are believed to have been influenced by the idea of pantheism.[8]

German philologist and archaeologist Friedrich Gottlieb Welcker coined another term: henotheism, which refers to 'the worship of a single, supreme god that does not deny the existence or possible existence of other deities'.[9]

Finally, German Indologist Heinrich Zimmer, a scholar well-known like Max Muller, introduced yet another term, transtheism.[10] Transtheism is defined as being neither theistic nor atheistic, transcending these classifications. Zimmer used this term to describe 'Jainism', which does not deny the presence of devatas but asserts that one must go beyond them to achieve moksha. The term has also been applied to Buddhist thoughts by recent scholars such as Houlden.[11]

The word '*thi*' (as in *theos*) has a Sanskrit connotation, '*sthi*' or *sthito*, which means 'having a presence' or 'situated'. On the other hand, '*deo*' connects with *deva*, *dia*, or *theo*. Thus, historically, the concept of '*theo*' is not entirely removed from Hindu thought. However, the so-called 'theologists' created a convoluted usage of these terms to fit Western, colonial, Christian frameworks, attempting to describe others' practices related to divinity within their limited perspective.

But should Hindus give any importance to these terms? Clearly, it must be left to Hindus themselves to define and decide their practice and identity—not others.

As noted earlier, Western colonists and evangelists encountered various *darshanas* and practices in India, many of which they did not comprehend. Consequently, they imposed their own ideas on these traditions. Initially, they referred to the Hindu, Sikh, Jain, and Buddhist traditions as 'religion', as their only frame of reference was rooted in their experience and knowledge within Abrahamic and Western scholarship. Later, they added the suffix 'ism' to each tradition to fit them into narrow conceptual frames, dividing and separating them from the shared foundation of Indian traditions. Instead of highlighting the fundamental unity amongst these traditions, they emphasized the differences in thoughts and practices. This classification of Indian traditions as 'religion' and tagging them with 'ism' constitutes a gross insult and historical injustice. Most importantly, it dealt a significant blow to the idea of dharma, the cornerstone of all major traditions of Bharat.

Let us first examine their attempts to classify these traditions. Terms like theists, atheists, orthodox, and heterodox were superimposed on *astika* and *nastika*. They defined *nastika* simply as those who do not accept the absolute authority of the Vedas, and *astikas* are those who do. However, in reality, *asti* means 'is there'. What or who is there? *Ātman* or *paramātman*. Not the authority or knowledge of the Vedas. Was this a deliberate and clever attempt to disconnect Hindus from their foundational principles?

Now, let us take a quick look at the Jain and Buddha *darshanas* (*darshanas* are not the same as the Western concept of 'philosophy'; darshanas can be defined as a vision of reality through intuitive and meditative exploration) to examine whether their traditions evolved from the Vedas and Upanishads.

The Jain tradition does not believe in a special 'creator' divine being. Instead, it focuses on the saints called Jinas or Tirthankaras, whose teachings guide practitioners. Jains also have *kuladevatas* (family deities), and many worship key Hindu deities, such as Saraswati, Lakshmi, and Ganesha, along with the Vidya Devis or Shakti Devis, including Kali, Mahakali, and Gauri.

Jains revere the Ramayana and, by extension, Sri Ram. In Jain scriptures, he is described as one of sixty-three illustrious persons, known as śalākapuruṣa (शलाकपुरूष). These include nine sets of Balabhadra, Vasudeva, and Prati-Vasudeva.

According to Jain scholar and deputy chairman of the Institute of Jainology, Dr Harshad N. Sanghrajka, Sri Krishna, in Jain legends, was a cousin of Arishtanemi. 'Krishna as a Vasudeva (the 9th) is considered to be one of the [sixty-three] or *Triṣaṣṭiśalākāpuruṣa* born in each half-cycle,' he stated. He further asserted that Krishna is one of the nine 'Vasudevas' and suggested that Jains also accord him a status equal to that of a Tirthankara.[12]

Confusion and division arose not long ago when Buddha was deemed an 'atheist'. First of all, he was born a Hindu and practised an age-old yogic process to reach the dharmic height of 'Buddha'. Many of his sermons were based on the Upanishads. It is said that Bhagwan Buddha used to conclude his sermons with these words: *Charaiveti, Charaiveti.* This Sanskrit word *Charaiveti* (चरैवेति) is found in the *Aitareya Brahmana* and means 'go on' or 'move on'. This potent word, in true Upanishadic style, exhorts us to continue moving forward and to keep going.

The actual source of the phrase *Charaiveti, Charaiveti* lies in a hymn about the long, endless journey towards self-realization, which each of us must undertake. Each verse ends with the refrain: '*Charaiveti, Charaiveti*', meaning 'Oh traveller, march along, march along!' The original shloka is found in the *Aitareya Brahmana,* which is part of the 'Shakala Shakha' of the *Rigveda*[13]:

चरन्वै मधु विन्दति चरन्स्वादुमुदुम्बरम्सूर्यस्य पश्य श्रेमाणं यो न तन्द्र यते चरंश् चरैवेति चरैवेति ॥

Charanbai madhu vindati charantsvadu mudambaram.
Suryasya pasya sreemanam yo na tandrayate charan.
Yate charamsh Charaiveti, Charaiveti.

(The honeybee, through its motion, collects honey, and birds enjoy sweet fruits by constantly moving. The sun is revered because of its perpetual motion and shining presence. Thus, one should also remain in constant motion. Keep moving, keep moving on!)

The essence of this idea is beautifully expressed by Rabindranath in his poem 'Balaka':

হেথা নয়, হেথা নয়, আর কোন্‌খানে

Hetha noy, hetha noy, onno konokhane.

(Not here, not here, but somewhere else.)

A key Jain concept is *anekantavada,* which asserts that 'reality' cannot be defined in a single way; instead, a diversity of viewpoints exists. It strongly emphasizes the relativity of knowledge about reality and introduces *saptabhangi*, a seven-step theory or process that outlines seven possibilities:

- Maybe, it is.
- Maybe, it is not.
- Maybe, it is and is not.
- Maybe, it is inexpressible.
- Maybe, it is and is inexpressible.
- Maybe, it is not and is inexpressible.
- Maybe, it is and is not and is inexpressible.[14]

Moving from the Jain tradition to the Buddhist tradition, it is important to recognize the presence of several variations. Different sects may have significant differences, which can occasionally be contradictory. Buddha was born into a Hindu family and became the Buddha (the enlightened one) after practising existing teachings and techniques. He shared and preached his experiences and realizations, thus forming a new sect within the Indian traditions.

Could some of his teachings before enlightenment and during his search differ from his later teachings? It is possible. Over time, his followers and sponsors contributed further to his teachings, forming what later became a new dharmic tradition. This tradition was named 'Buddhism' by colonists, who categorized it as a separate 'religion'. However, Buddha himself did not create a new religion; his followers developed a new sect or tradition known as 'Bodhi Dharma'.

It is crucial to remember that various *darshanas*—such as Samkhya, Vaiseseka, and Vedanta—are ways of understanding reality. It is also said that Buddhadev studied under Samkhya gurus. Within mainstream Vedic traditions, there are Vaishnav, Shakta, and Shaiva streams, which share some similar views and practices, but also differ significantly.

When Western theologians arrived, they either failed to recognize the unity among these diverse *darshanas*, traditions, and practices or intentionally sought to separate them.

As we attempt to understand Buddha's life and teachings 2,500 years later, it is inevitable that many guesses and hypotheses will emerge. The term Hindu existed at the time; however, neither Hinduism nor Hindu Dharma as we know them today had appeared. Instead, there were many *darshanas*, including Samkhya, Mimansa, Charvaka, and Ajivika. Despite this diversity, there was one sure common thread running through dharma.

How was society then? How did Buddha grow up? What did he practise and preach at that time? Which aspects of 'Buddhism', as we know it today, were actually followed and taught by him? Logic suggests that since Buddha was part of the broader Hindu tradition, he utilized the tools and methods available to him and preached only what was appropriate for his time.

Buddha's main concern was the sorrow and pain inherent in life and how to transcend that predicament to a state he called 'Nirvana'. Is this state similar to the Vedantic concept of 'Moksha'? Is it a condition, a circumstance, or equivalent to the Upanishadic revelation—'knowing that, we don't need to know anything else', the Brahman?

Did Buddha worship deities such as Saraswati and Chandi? The answer seems affirmative. In Buddha's discourses, we find the invocation of various *devatas*, including the thirty-three *devas* mentioned in the Vedas. He also referred to the Vedas but only to three Vedas—the *Atharvaveda* appears to have been unknown, unused, or excluded.

The following is a Buddhist prayer that discusses divine beings just like the Vedas:

Transference of Merits to All Celestial Beings
May all beings inhabiting space and earth,
Devas and Nagas of mighty powers,
Having shared this merit,
Long protect the Dispensation!

May all beings inhabiting space and earth,
Devas and Nagas of mighty powers,
Having shared this merit,
Long protect the Teaching!

May all beings inhabiting space and earth,
Devas and Nagas of mighty powers,
Having shared this merit,
Long protect me and others!

May all Devas share this merit,
Which we have thus accumulated
For the acquisition of all kinds of happiness and prosperity!

May all Bhūtas share this merit,
Which we have thus accumulated
For the acquisition of all kinds of happiness and prosperity!

The following is an excerpt from the 'Mahā Jayamangala Gātha' (MJG), a revered Buddhist prayer to divine powers that is often recited for protection, blessings, and the well-being of individuals or communities:[15]

May all good fortune come my way.
May all the deities protect me.
By all the power of the Saṅgha,
May I always enjoy well-being. [MJG 15]

By the power of this protective recital,
May my misfortunes due to stars,
Demons, harmful spirits, and ominous planets
Be prevented and destroyed. [MJG 16]

May rain fall in due time.
May there be a rich harvest.
May the world be prosperous.
May the government be righteous. [MJG 17]

So, was Buddha a theist or an atheist? *Astika* or *nastika*? Was Buddha against the Vedas and Upanishads? Did he explicitly state that he did not believe in the authority of the Vedas? Should we accept this simply because some theologians define a *nastika* as one who does not believe in the authority, authenticity, or permanency of the Vedas?

We don't know—and may never know—whether Buddha regarded the Vedas as '*pramana*' (proof or authoritative knowledge) or denied them as such. He remained silent on many such questions, including the existence of Supreme Being.[16] This silence, however, was later interpreted by some of his followers as a denial of the validity of the Vedas as well as the existence of supreme Paramātman or Īshwara.

As noted earlier, various *devas* and *devis* (deities) and the planes of their existence are mentioned in Buddhist literature. Buddha may have advised his disciples to focus on their personal *sadhana* (spiritual practice) and to meditate on the virtues represented by the *devas* rather than on the deities themselves—even Mahabrahma. Interestingly, Mahabrahma and Brahma are still worshiped in Buddhist temples, particularly in Thailand, reflecting the syncretism and evolution of religious practices within the Buddhist tradition.

In *Mahanama Sutta* (MS 6), a key Buddhist text, we find the Buddha advising:[17]

> Furthermore, you should recollect the devas: 'There are the Devas of the Four Great Kings, the Devas of the Thirty-three, the Devas of the Hours, the Contented Devas, the devas who delight in creation, the devas who have power over the creations of others, the devas of Brahma's retinue, the devas beyond them. Whatever conviction they were endowed with that—when falling away from this life—they re-arose there, the same sort of conviction is present in me as well. Whatever virtue they were endowed with that—when falling away from this life—they re-arose there, the same sort of virtue is present in me as well. Whatever learning they were endowed with that—when falling away from this life—they re-arose there, the same sort of learning is present in me as well. Whatever generosity they were endowed with that—when falling away from this life—they re-arose there, the same sort of generosity is present in me as well. Whatever discernment they were endowed with that—when falling away from this life—they re-arose there, the same sort of discernment is present in me as well.'
>
> At any time when a disciple of the noble ones is recollecting the conviction, virtue, learning, generosity, and discernment found both in himself and the devas, his mind is not overcome with passion, not overcome with aversion, not overcome with delusion. His mind heads straight, based on the [qualities of the] devas. And when the mind is headed straight, the disciple of the noble ones gains a sense of the goal, gains a sense of the Dhamma, gains joy connected with the Dhamma. In one who is joyful, rapture arises. In one who is rapturous, the body grows calm. One whose body is calmed experiences ease. In one at ease, the mind becomes concentrated.
>
> Mahanama, you should develop this recollection of the devas while you are walking, while you are standing, while you are sitting, while you are lying down, while you are busy at work, while you are resting in your home crowded with children.[18]

Also, in *Paṭhamamahānāma Sutta* (AN 11.11) and the *Samgyutta Agama* (T. ii 237c9), the Buddha encourages disciples to emulate the qualities of the devas, including *saddha* (*shraddha* or faith), *sila* (ethics or moral conduct), *suta* (eagerness to learn), *cāga (tyaga* or renunciation*)*, and *pañña* (jnana, prajna, or wisdom).

The *Dhammapada*, a foundational Buddhist text, offers profound teachings that guide one towards ethical living, spiritual growth, and the transcendence of worldly attachments[19]:

- 'Just as a Brahman priest reveres his sacrificial fire, even so, should one devoutly revere the person from whom one has learned the Dharma taught by the Buddha.' (*Dhammapada* 392)
- 'Not by matted hair, nor by lineage, nor by birth does one become a Brahmin. But he in whom truth and righteousness exist—he is pure, he is a Brahmin.' (*Dhammapada* 393)
- 'What is the use of your matted hair, O witless man? What of your garment of antelope's hide? Within you is the tangle [of passion]; only outwardly do you cleanse yourself.' (*Dhammapada* 394)
- The person who wears a robe made of rags, who is lean, with veins showing all over the body, and who meditates alone in the forest—him do I call a Brahmin.' (*Dhammapada* 395)
- 'By telling the truth, by not growing angry, and by giving when asked, no matter how little you have: by these three things you enter the presence of devas.' (*Dhammapada* XVI 224)
- 'If knowledgeable people praise him, having observed him day after day to be blameless in conduct, intelligent, endowed with discernment and virtue: like an ingot of gold—who's fit to find fault with him? Even devas praise him. Even by Brahma he' s praised.' (*Dhammapada* XVI 229–30)

Was Buddha rejecting existing *darshanas* or was he redefining them? The latter seems more appropriate. Sanatana means that which is ever refined and ever renewed. One may refer to Buddha's idea of *pratītya-samutpāda* (the theory of dependent origination). According to this, dharma is about being and becoming, renewal and regeneration, all based on previous causation.

According to the legend, Buddha was asked, 'Does the Tathagata exist after death or not?' He remained silent. When asked about the idea of a Supreme Being, he again remained silent. This aligns with the silent admission of the Vedantic conclusion that Ishwara is *'abhang-manas-gochar'*, meaning Ishwara is beyond words, mind, and logic.

The core of Buddha's teaching can be summarized as *pratītya-samutpāda*, *anatman (*no-soul), and *nirvana* (the theory of dependent origination). *Anātman* is translated as 'no-soul', based on their definition of a soul. These three concepts have their roots in the Upanishads and Vedanta.

The Buddhist concept of consciousness is described as 'a flame on the candle of our body'. According to this idea, we leave the body at the moment of death, but this flame—particularly our 'flame of moral credit' or debit—transfers to a new body. In Buddhism, this 'karmic flame of consciousness' plays the same role as the idea of *ātman* or soul.

However, a key teaching of Buddha is the *anātman* theory, rooted in *pratītya-samutpāda*. According to this, there is no permanent agent called *ātman* because everything is relative. A relative entity cannot produce an unchanging, absolute entity like *ātman*. Everything in the mundane world is, therefore, without *ātman*.

The famous English Indologist and scholar of the Pāli language was Thomas William Rhys Davids (1843–1922). He played a major role in founding the British Academy and the London School for Oriental Studies. Though firmly pro-colonialist, he had a deep appreciation for Indian *darshanas*. The following is what he wrote about the Buddha:

> Gautama was born and brought up and lived and died a Hindu … There was not much in the metaphysics and principles of Gautama that cannot be found in one or other of the orthodox systems, and a great deal of his morality could be matched from earlier or later Hindu books. Such originality as Gautama possessed lay in the way in

> which he adopted, enlarged, ennobled, and systematized that which had already been well said by others; in the way in which he carried out to their logical conclusion principles of equity and justice already acknowledged by some of the most prominent Hindu thinkers. The difference between him and other teachers lay chiefly in his deep earnestness and in his broad public spirit of philanthropy.[20]

However, Davids acknowledged that the Buddha may have been opposed to the Vedas, largely because of the elements of ritual sacrifice present in them. Davids added, 'There are also opinions from some scholars and dialogues of Buddha that suggest that Buddha did support the "original, unaltered" form of Vedas and later, due to the way certain Brahmins interpreted sacrificial hymns, Buddha was compelled to reject their authority and sanctity.'[21]

Swami Vivekananda expressed the following about the Buddha:

> Buddha was one of the *sannyâsins* of Vedanta. He started a new sect, just as others are started even today. The ideas which now are called Buddhism were not his. They were much more ancient.
>
> Buddha was a reformer of Hinduism.
>
> Buddha was a great Vedantist [for Buddhism was really only an offshoot of Vedanta], and Shankara is often called a 'hidden Buddhist'. Buddha made the analysis, and Shankara made the synthesis out of it.
>
> He was a great man who gave the ideas power.[22]

Western neo-Indologists such as Diana Eck, Sheldon Pollock, Wendy Doniger, and others, who continue to create confusion about the understanding of India's heritage, *darshanas*, and *dharmic* traditions, are either not capable of understanding these subjects or are part of a deliberate effort to undermine Indian thought and to divide and separate.

The Bharatiya Idea and Meaning of Divinity

Before we proceed to demystify important Hindu concepts, let's first step back and understand the idea of the divine. The word divine is most likely derived from the Sanskrit word '*divya*', which means 'giver of light', or alternatively, knowledge, vision, and direction. In the Hindu system, the concept of *devata* is a derivative of the divine; *dai* and *div* mean 'to shine' or 'give light' and 'to show', respectively. Thus, *divya* (that which shines or gives light) and *daiva* (the cause of shining), which means 'to shine' or 'to show', refer to the ultimate cause or source. Each culture, in turn, has its own personified sacred objects, known as 'deities'.

Let us examine Persian and Avestan culture. Persian and Avestan history is like amber, preserving prehistoric life and elements in fossil form, capturing much of the civilizational knowledge found in language (ancient Persian and Avestan), architecture, and inscriptions.

Located about 60 km northeast of Shiraz, at the foot of Kuh-e Rahmat Mountain in the Fars province of Iran, lies the ancient, ruined city of Persepolis, also known as Takht-e Jamshid. It was the capital of the Achaemenid Empire and was later destroyed by Islamic invaders. While its pillars show similarities to those of Ashoka, three stone inscriptions (known as Achaemenid Royal Inscriptions) were found in Persepolis and the citadel of Pasargadae (Tachara Palace), which was built by Achaemenid Emperor Cyrus (559–530 BCE). The city was destroyed by Alexander around 330 BCE. The famous 'Daiva Inscription' called 'Xerexes', reveals ancient secrets from the time of Darius and Xerxes.[23]

The inscription is carved on four stone tablets found in a building located on the southeast corner of the Royal Complex.[24] It reads '*daivadānam viyakanam', meaning* 'I destroyed the house of devils' (*XPh* 37).

The term '*daiva*' appears frequently, and in the Avestan language, it evolved into *daēvāiš or Dēv-dād* (possibly Dev Dutta), meaning 'created or given by Deva'. This offers a glimpse of the Middle East, which was deeply influenced by Bharatiya ideas. The fact that the term 'divine' and 'divinity' are used in Europe and modern languages further demonstrates the influence of Vedic culture on the concept of 'higher beings' globally.

In the following section, we will look at more ancient and primary sources from Bharat and try to understand some of the most common words used for describing aspects of divinity.

Devata

The general meaning of the most frequently used Sanskrit term for divinity is *devata*: powers of *prakriti* (natural laws and existence) or the expressed forms of the Supreme Being, *Puruṣa*, or *Param Puruṣa*, nature itself.

According to the *Amarkosha*, the quality of a devata is *amar*—immortal, *nirjhar*—that which does not decay. Different forms of our consciousness are also immortal. *Devatas* never grow old. For example, Agni (fire) and Surya (sun).[25]

According to *Nirukta* of Yaskmuni, a *devata* has three aspects: *danad*—nourishment or giving powers, self-illumination powers, and energy-giving sources.[26] For example, physical nourishment is provided through offering to the *devas* in the form of *yajna*, while emotional nourishment occurs via *kala* (art and music), with offerings to Saraswati. The Mahabharata notes that a *devata* is 'the state or nature of a deity and light'.[27] A *devata* illuminates our emotions, intellect, and senses with knowledge.

In Bhagvada Gita, we have the following verse:[28]

देवान्भावयतानेन ते देवा भावयन्तु वः |
परस्परं भावयन्तः श्रेयः परमवाप्स्यथ ||

devān bhāvayatānena te devā bhāvayantu vaḥ
parasparaṁ bhāvayantaḥ śhreyaḥ param avāpsyatha

(By your sacrifices, the celestial *devas* will be pleased, and by cooperation between humans and the celestial *devas*, great prosperity will reign for all.)

The concept of 'thirty-three koti devata': The Vedas do not refer to thirty-three crore *devatas* but thirty-three types ('*koti*' in Sanskrit) of *devatas*. These are explained clearly in the *Shatpath Brahman* and many other scriptures. Among these are the eight Vasus, the eleven Rudras, the twelve Adityas, Indra, and Prajapati, as noted by Yajnavalkya in the *Brihadaranyaka Upanishad*.[29]

The following are some of the most prominent deities mentioned in the Vedas: Adityas, Agni, Apas, Aśvins, Brhaspati, Indra, Maruts, Mitra, Parjanya, Rudra, Savitr, Soma, Saraswati, Surya, Usha, Vāc, Varuna, Vishnu, Vishvakarman, and Yama.

Hindus have approached the universe, creation, and reality from many angles and perspectives and are not necessarily fixed in one way. They have debated and agreed to disagree across various streams of thought. There is no single way to see the world or express thoughts, nor is there any imposition on others: '*Ekam Sat Biprah Bahudha Vadanti*'—truth can be sought, realized, and expressed by many means and ways, as said by the wise. This philosophy applies only to those who support pluralistic ideas and thoughts, which exclude many of the world's religious and secular philosophies, as these tend to monopolize and impose.

Hindus have viewed the entire creation and existence within the spectrum of two endpoints: *Param* (the infinite) and *Shunya* (zero, the void, or nothingness). The infinite has been expressed in various ways, both with and without form. For example, infinite wealth and beauty are personified by Lakshmi, infinite knowledge by Saraswati, and infinite (shakti) power by Durga. These are deified attributes and forms of one Supreme or Infinite reality in different manifestations.

After *devata, deva*, and *devis*, the most commonly used term for divinity is *Bhagwan* or *Bhagavan* (details discussed later). *Bhagwan* has more earthly attributes. Then, there is the concept of Brahman, which denotes 'infinite greatness'. Finally, there is *Īśvara* or *Ishwara* (discussed in the following sections), which is formless in its original concept. However, it is also used to refer to Mahesvara, Bisveswara, Bateswara, and others as expressions of qualified divinity.

Moreover, there is the concept of *Brahman* (discussed later in this chapter). As previously noted, Hindu tradition does not have a direct equivalent to Western theological terms, such as 'God'. Therefore, whenever a Hindu uses the word 'God', they are deviating from their civilizational understanding of the universe, which is rooted in a universal and scientific view.

Brahmā (ब्रह्मा)

Brahmā is the *devata* (divine or ultimate cause), the source or creative force behind all creation, from which the entire universe is projected. He is the origin of all projections, the laws governing them, and the intelligence behind these projections, thus representing the essence of all creation. According to the Hindu Yuga concept, Brahmā is the first being to be created with each new *Maha Kalpa* (cosmic cycle).[30]

Brahmā creates everything within a particular cycle. A new Brahmā comes into existence at the beginning of every *Maha Kalpa* cycle. Brahmā is typically depicted with four faces or heads, known as *caturanana*. These four heads represent the four Vedas—*Rigveda*, *Samaveda*, *Yajurveda*, and *Atharvaveda*—the sources of all divine knowledge.

The name Brahmā is derived from the root *Bṛh* (बृह), which means 'to grow, increase, or expand', with the connotation of 'immense'. When combined with the suffix *manin*, it becomes Brahmān, signifying the primordial cosmic Creative Energy.[31]

Brahmā is one of the three cosmic aspects of creation, known as Trimurti (often erroneously compared to the Christian concept of Trinity):

- Creation and order: The *devata* is Brahma.
- Chaos, destruction, and renewal: The *devata* is Shiva.
- Balance or preservation: The *devata* is Vishnu.

A related term, *Brahmand,* refers to the 'egg' or seed of creation. Some would liken it to the state before the Big Bang. There are also several terms associated with Brahma, such as *Brahmacharya* and *Brahmavidya*.

Atmān and Paramātmān

Let us first explore how the West has viewed and described the esoteric concept of *ātman*. Generally, *ātman* and *paramātman* are translated into English as the 'individual soul' and the 'universal soul', respectively.

Thus, the common term used to denote ātman is 'soul'. However, it is important to clarify some Western and Abrahamic concepts related to this subject. Many cultures and traditions, often referred to as Paganism, existed before the rise of Abrahamic religions and were pushed to near extinction or fully destroyed after the emergence of Christianity and Islam.

The term Animism is used for those who believe that the entire creation has an unseen core or essence that enables the entity to sustain itself. The Latin term *animus* or *anima* means 'breath, spirit, and life'.[32]

However, modern religions no longer use the term *animus* to refer to the '*spirit*' in humans. Instead, they use the alternative term 'soul'. The Soul is defined as 'the immaterial aspect or essence of a human being'.[33]

The English word 'soul' has its root in Old English as *sāwol, sāwel,* which means 'life' or 'animate existence'. However, the Hindu concept of *ātman* cannot be adequately defined or described by any of these terms. *Ātman* has a much deeper and broader meaning.

Now, let us explore *atman*. In the Vedic tradition, *ātman* represents the 'conscious self'. It asserts that this is 'self-evident'. The earliest known use of the word atman is found in the *Rigveda*, appearing multiple times (I.115.1, VII.87.2, VII.101.6, VIII.3.24, IX.2.10, IX.6.8, and X.168.4). Here is one such revelation:[34]

यदिमा वाजयन्नहमोषधीर्हस्त आदधे ।
आत्मा यक्ष्मस्य नश्यति पुरा जीवगृभो यथा ॥

yad imā vājayann aham oṣadhīr hasta ādadhe |
ātmā yakṣmasya naśyati purā jīvagṛbho yathā ||

(As soon as I take these herbs in my hand, making [the sick man]
strong, the *ātman* of the malady perishes before [their application],
as [life is driven away from the presence] of the seizer of life.)

Ancient grammarian Yaska, commenting on this *Rigvedic* verse, suggests the following meanings of atman: 'the pervading principle', 'the entity in which other elements are united', and 'the ultimate sentient principle'.[35]

We have already discussed the idea of *'atamanam viddhi'* or 'know thyself' in earlier chapters, a central theme in the Upanishads, which essentially states that *ātman* is 'the ultimate essence of the universe', as well as 'the vital breath in human beings', representing the 'imperishable Divine within' that is neither born nor dies.

Now, let us examine how different Upanishads have described *ātman* in various contexts:

आत्मनि खल्वरे दृष्टे श्रुते मते विज्ञात इदं सर्वं विदितम् ॥[36]

ātmani khalv are vijñāte idam sarvam viditam

(Once the *ātman* is known, everything is known.)

All this (perceptible universe) is *ātman*:[37]

अथात आत्मादेश एवात्मैवाधस्तादात्मोपरिष्टादात्मा पश्चादात्मा पुरस्तादात्मा दक्षिणत
आत्मोत्तरत आत्मैवेदं सर्वमिति स वा एष एवं पश्यन्नेवं मन्वान एवं
विजानन्नात्मरतिरात्मक्रीड आत्ममिथुन आत्मानन्दः स स्वराड्भवति तस्य सर्वेषु लोकेषु
कामचारो भवति अथ येऽन्यथातो विदुरन्यराजानस्ते क्षय्यलोका भवन्ति तेषां सर्वेषु
लोकेष्वकामचारो भवति ॥

athāta ātmādeśa evātmaivādhastādātmopariṣṭādātmā paścādātmā
purastādātmā dakṣiṇata ātmottarata ātmaivedaṃ sarvamiti sa vā
eṣa evaṃ paśyannevaṃ manvāna evaṃ vijānannātmaratirātmakrīḍa

ātmamithuna ātmānandaḥ sa svarāḍbhavati tasya sarveṣu lokeṣu
kāmacāro bhavati atha ye'nyathāto viduranyarājānaste kṣayyalokā
bhavanti teṣāṃ sarveṣu lokeṣvakāmacāro bhavati ||

(The instruction on the *atman* is as follows: the *atman* is below; the *atman* is above; the *atman* is behind; the *atman* is in front; the *atman* is to the right; the *atman* is to the left. The *atman* is all this. He who sees in this way, thinks in this way, and knows in this way, has love for the *atman*, sports with the *atman*, enjoys the company of the *atman*, and finds joy in the *atman*, is supreme and can roam freely in all the worlds. But those who think otherwise are controlled of others. They cannot remain in the worlds they inhabit, nor can they move about in the worlds as they wish.)

Now, the term Brahman is introduced as synonymous with Brahma or *paramātman* (literally the absolute *ātman*). *'Ayam ātma brahma'* (This *ātman* is the Brahman):[38]

अयं धर्मः सर्वेषाम् भूतानाम् मधु
अस्य धर्मस्य सर्वाणि भूतानि मधु
यश्चायमस्मिन्धर्मे, तेजोमयोऽमृतमयः पुरुषः
यश्चायमध्यात्मं धार्मस्तेज्ōमयोऽमृतमयः पुरुषः
अयमेव स योऽयमात्मा, इदममृतम्, इदं ब्रह्म, इदं सर्वम् ॥

ayaṃ dharmaḥ sarveṣām bhūtānām madhu, asya
dharmasya sarvāṇi bhūtāni madhu; yaścāyamasmindharme,
tejomayo'mṛtamayaḥ puruṣaḥ, yaścāyamadhyātmaṃ
dhārmastejōmayo'mṛtamayaḥ puruṣaḥ, ayameva sa yo'yamātmā,
idamamṛtam, idaṃ brahma, idaṃ sarvam ||

(This righteousness [Dharma] is like honey to all beings, and all beings are like honey to this righteousness. [Similarly,] the shining, immortal being who is in this righteousness, and the shining, immortal being identified with righteousness in the body, are one and the same. These are but the Self. This Self-knowledge is the means of immortality; this underlying unity is Brahman; this knowledge of Brahman is the means of becoming all.)

Finally, the *Shvetashvatara Upanishad* reveals:[39]

स तन्मयो ह्यमृत ईशसंस्थो ज्ञः सर्वगो भुवनस्यास्य गोप्ता।
य ईशे अस्य जगतो नित्यमेव नान्यो हेतुर्विद्यत ईशनाय॥
यो ब्रह्माणं विदधाति पूर्वं यो वै वेदांश्च प्रहिणोति तस्मै।
तह देवंआत्मबुद्धिप्रकाशं मुमुक्षुर्वै शरणमहं प्रपद्ये॥

sa tanmayo hyamṛta īśasaṁstho jñaḥ sarvago bhuvanasyāsya goptā, ya īśe'sya jagato nityameva nānyo heturvidyata īśanāya. yo brahmāṇaṁ vidadhāti pūrvaṁ yo vai vedāṁśca prahiṇoti tasmai, taṁ ha devātmabudhdiprakāśaṁ mumukṣurvai śaraṇamahaṁ prapadye.

(He is the soul of the universe; He is immortal; His is the rulership; He is the all-knowing, the all-pervading, the protector of the universe, the Eternal Ruler. No one else is efficient to govern the world eternally. He who at the beginning of creation projected Brahma (that is, the universal consciousness), and who delivered the Vedas unto him—seeking liberation, I go for refuge unto that Effulgent One, whose light turns the understanding towards the *atman*.)

We have already explained the concepts of divinity and the creator god according to the Abrahamic religions. Here, let us explore their soul-like concept to differentiate between Vedic and Abrahamic ideas.

In Islam, *al-Ruh* primarily implies the 'breath of life' (*animus*), which is blown into a living being and departs from the physical body at the point of death. The Quran (32:9) states: 'Then He fashioned him [man] in due proportion and breathed into him His Ruh [soul created by Allah for that person], and He gave you hearing [ear], sight [eyes], and hearts.'

In the Hebrew Bible, the term '*nephesh*' refers to the essence responsible for feelings and sensations. Both humans and animals possess *nephesh*.

In Christian literature, a similar concept can be found. According to Matthew (10:28): 'And do not fear those who kill the body but cannot kill the soul. Rather, fear him who can destroy both soul and body in hell.' The first part of this verse seems to resonate with the Hindu idea of *ātman*, which 'cannot be killed, burnt, or destroyed'. This might reflect an influence or borrowing from Vedic literature. However, the second part reflects theological manipulation intended to instil the fear of 'God' and the consequences of the Day of Judgement.

Consider how an early Christian priest, John Damascene (7th century CE), described the soul:

> The soul, therefore, is a living essence, uncomplicated, incorporeal, invisible—in its proper nature—to the eyes of the body, immortal, reasoning and intelligent, formless, making use of an organic body and being the source of its powers of life, growth, sensation and generation, the intellect being its purest part though not in any way alien to it [as the eye is to the body, so the intellect is to the soul]. It has power over itself, its volition and energy, and is mutable, i.e., able to be changed, because it is created.[40]

Brahman ब्रह्मन्

Brahman is considered the 'highest universal principle' and the ultimate reality. It is the 'immaterial, efficient, formal, and final cause' of all that exists. Its nature is सच्चिदानन्द (*Saccidānanda)*—Sat-cit-ananda: all-pervasive, infinite, eternal truth, consciousness and bliss.

Let us briefly compare the terms *Brahman* and Ishwara. Swami Vivekananda provides clarity on this subject:[41]

> Who is Ishvara? *Janmâdyasya yatah*—'From whom is the birth, continuation, and dissolution of the universe,'—He is Ishvara—'the Eternal, the Pure, the Ever-Free, the Almighty, the All-Knowing, the All-Merciful, the Teacher of all teachers'; and above all, *Sa Ishvarah anirvachaniya-premasvarupah*—'He the Lord is, of His own nature, inexpressible Love.'

ॐ नमो भगवते वासुदेवाय
जन्माद्यस्य यतोऽन्वयादितरतश्चार्थेष्वभिज्ञः स्वराट्
तेने ब्रह्म हृदा य आदिकवये मुह्यन्ति यत्सूरयः ।

तेजोवारिमृदां यथा विनिमयो यत्र त्रिसर्गोऽमृषा
धाम्ना स्वेन सदा निरस्तकुहकं सत्यं परं धीमहि ॥[42]

oṁ namo bhagavate vāsudevāya
janmādy asya yato 'nvayād itarataś cārtheṣv abhijñaḥ svarāṭ
tene brahma hṛdā ya ādi-kavaye muhyanti yat sūrayaḥ
tejo-vāri-mṛdāṁ yathā vinimayo yatra tri-sargo 'mṛṣā
dhāmnā svena sadā nirasta-kuhakaṁ satyaṁ paraṁ dhīmahi

(I meditate upon Lord Sri Krishna because He is the Absolute Truth and the primeval cause of all causes—the creation, sustenance, and destruction of the manifested universes. He is directly and indirectly conscious of all manifestations, and He is independent, as there is no cause beyond Him. He alone first imparted Vedic knowledge into the heart of Brahmājī, the original living being. Even great sages and *devatas* are bewildered by Him, as one is misled by illusory representations—like water in fire or land seen on water. The material universes, temporarily manifested by the reactions of the three modes of nature, appear real only due to Him, though they are unreal. I meditate upon Lord Sri Krishna, eternally present in the transcendental abode, free from the illusory material world. I meditate upon Him, for He is the Absolute Truth.)

'From whom all things are born, by which all beings live, and unto whom they return—ask about it. That is *Brahman*.' *Brahman* alone existed in the beginning. From that One evolved everything. It projected a blessed form, the *Kshatra*. All these *devas* are Kshatras: Varuna, Soma, Rudra, Parjanya, Yama, Mrityu, Ishâna.

'*Ātman* alone existed in the beginning; nothing else vibrated. He thought of projecting the world and then created it.'

'Alone Nârâyana existed—neither Brahmâ, nor Ishana, nor Dyâvâ-Prithivi, nor the stars, nor water, nor fire, nor Soma, nor the sun. He did not take pleasure alone. After meditation, He created one daughter—the ten organs, and so on.'

In other descriptions, as the Srutis state, 'Who, living in the earth, is separate from the earth, who, living in the *Ātman*, is distinct from it,' thus emphasizing the Supreme One as the ruler of the universe.

However, in these accounts of the governance of the universe, there is no reference to the liberated soul having any role in ruling the universe. It is clear that such rulership is not ascribed to the liberated soul.

Eventually, *Brahman* is regarded as the 'cosmic creative principle'. According to various Hindu scriptures, *Brahman* is the 'projection of Brahma into creation'—the universe, the ultimate reality of all existence, and the totality of the cosmos, which is vast and expansive.

Sri Ramanuja, a proponent of the Vishishtadvaita school of Vedānta, provides a detailed explanation of Brahman in his commentary on the Brahma Sutras, the *Sri-Bhasya*: 'The word *Brahman* is derived from the root "*brh*" which denotes greatness or vastness, and is therefore applicable to all objects which have the quality of greatness, but more aptly to that object which by nature and qualities possesses this greatness to an infinite degree.'[43]

ब्रह्मैवेदममृतं पुरस्ताद्ब्रह्म पश्चाद्ब्रह्म दक्षिणतश्चोत्तरेण ।[44]
अधश्चोर्ध्वं च प्रसृतं ब्रह्मैवेदं विश्वमिदं वरिष्ठम् ॥

brahmaivedamamṛtaṃ purastādbrahma
paścādbrahma dakṣiṇataścottareṇa |
adhaścordhvaṃ ca prasṛtaṃ brahmaivedaṃ viśvamidaṃ variṣṭham ||

(All that is before is immortal *Brahman*. All that is behind is *Brahman*. Everything to the south, north, above, and below is Brahman, for the entirety of this universe is *Brahman*.)

सर्वं खल्विदं ब्रह्म तज्जलानिति शान्त उपासीत ।
अथ खलु क्रतुमयः पुरुषो यथाक्रतुरस्मिँल्लोके पुरुषो
भवति तथेतः प्रेत्य भवति स क्रतुं कुर्वीत ॥[45]

sarvaṃ khalvidaṃ brahma tajjalāniti śānta upāsīta |
atha khalu kratumayaḥ puruṣo yathākraturasmiṁlloke puruṣo
bhavati tathetaḥ pretya bhavati sa kratuṃ kurvīta ||

(All this is Brahman. Everything originates from Brahman, is sustained by Brahman, and returns to Brahman. Therefore, one should meditate upon Brahman with a tranquil mind. As a person thinks and wills in this life, so they become in the next. Thus, one should mediate with intent and focus.)

स य एषोऽणिमैतदात्म्यमिदं सर्वं तत्सत्यं स आत्मा तत्त्वमसि श्वेतकेतो इति भूय एव मा
भगवान्विज्ञापयत्विति तथा सोम्येति होवाच ॥[46]

sa ya eṣo'ṇimaitadātmyamidaṃ sarvaṃ tatsatyaṃ sa ātmā
tattvamasi śvetaketo iti bhūya eva mā bhagavānvijñāpayatviti
tathā somyeti hovāca ||

(That which is the subtlest of all is the Self of all this. It is Truth. It is the Self. 'That thou art, O Śvetaketu.' [Śvetaketu then asked,] 'Sir, please explain this to me again.' His father replied, 'Yes, Somya, I will explain it again.')

तं होवाच ।
यतो वा इमानि भूतानि जायन्ते ।
येन जातानि जीवन्ति ।
यत्प्रयन्त्यभिसंविशन्ति ।
तद्विजिज्ञासस्व ।
तद्ब्रह्मेति ॥[47]

taṃ hovāca |
yato vā imāni bhūtāni jāyante |
yena jātāni jīvanti |
yatprayantyabhisaṃviśanti |
tadvijijñāsasva |
tadbrahmeti ||

(To him, he verily said, 'From where are these beings born? By what means do they live after birth? Into what do they merge when they depart? Seek to know That, for That is Brahman.)

Now, we arrive at the final revelations and assertions:

प्रज्ञानम् ब्रह्म[48]
Prajnanam Brahma

(*Brahman* is the Ultimate Reality.)

एकमेवाद्वितीयं ब्रह्म[49]
Ekam Evadvitiyam Brahma

(*Brahman* is the only one without a second.)

Now, let us explore our true nature in relation to Brahman:

तत् त्वम् असि[50]

Tat Tvam Asi
(That thou art [That you are—you are *Brahman*].)

अयम् आत्मा ब्रह्म[51]
Ayam Atma Brahma
(This Self [Ātman] is *Brahman.*)

सो ऽहम्[52]
Soham
(I am He/That [Ātman].)

अहम् ब्रह्मास्मी
aham brahmāsmi
(I am *Brahman.*)

What is the importance of this knowledge to an average person? Are these merely poetic imaginations, or do they have practical value? This philosophy reveals that infinite possibilities lie within us. By practising yoga, one connects with the infinite, harmonizing life with creation and living more fully. Yoga is the process of connecting with infinity, but one must progress step by step:

- Achieve unity and harmony between body, mind, intellect, speech, and actions.
- Cultivate harmony with family, society, and the environment.
- Establish a connection with nature and Mother Earth.

Only then can one move beyond to infinite consciousness—*Brahman*.

However, if one repeats '*aham brahmāsmi*' continuously but still acts according to a sensate, selfish, egotistical mindset—lacking intelligence, kindness, and a sense of unity—the result would be nothing less than mockery and delusion.

ब्रह्म वा इदमग्र आसीत्, तदात्मानमेवावेत्, अहम् ब्रह्मास्मीति।
तस्मात्तत्सर्वमभवत्; तद्यो यो देवानाम् प्रत्यबुभ्यत स एव तदभवत्, तथार्षीणाम्, तथा
मनुष्याणाम्; तद्धैतत्पश्यन्नृषिर्वामदेवः प्रतिपेदे, अहम् मनुरभवं सूर्यश्चेति।
तदिदमप्येतर्हि य एवं वेद, अहम् ब्रह्मास्मीति, स इदं सर्वम् भवति, तस्य ह न देवाश्चनाभूत्या
ईशते, आत्मा ह्येषां स भवति; अथ योऽन्यां देवतामुपास्ते, अन्योऽसावन्योऽहमस्मीति, न स
वेद, यथा पशुरेवम् स देवानाम्।
यथा ह वै बहवः पशवो मनुष्यम् भुञ्ज्युः, एवमेकैकः पुरुषो देवान् भुनक्ति; एकस्मिन्नेव
पशावादीयमानेऽप्रियम् भवति, किंउ बहुषु? तस्मादेषाम् तन्न प्रियम् यदेतन्मनुष्याविद्युः॥

brahma vā idamagra āsīt, tadātmānamevāvet, aham brahmāsmīti |
tasmāttatsarvamabhavat; tadyo yo devānām pratyabubhyata
sa eva tadabhavat, tathārṣīṇām, tathā manuṣyāṇām;
taddhaitatpaśyannṛṣirvāmadevaḥ pratipede, aham manurabhavaṃ sūryaśceti |
tadidamapyetarhi ya evaṃ veda, aham brahmāsmīti, sa idaṃ
sarvam bhavati, tasya ha na devāścanābhūtyā īśate, ātmā hyeṣāṃ
sa bhavati; atha yo'nyāṃ devatāmupāste, anyo'sāvanyo'hamasmīti,
na sa veda, yathā paśurevam sa devānām |
yathā ha vai bahavaḥ paśavo manuṣyam bhuñjyuḥ, evamekaikaḥ
puruṣo devān bhunakti; ekasminneva paśāvādīyamāne'priyam

bhavati, kiṃu bahuṣu? tasmādeṣām tanna priyam
yadetanmanuṣyāvidyuḥ ||

(This [Self] was indeed Brahmān in the beginning. It knew only I—'I am *Brahmān*.' Therefore, it became All. Whoever among the *devas* came to know this became that Self; the same holds true for sages and others. The sage Vāmadeva, upon realizing this Self as That, knew, 'I was Manu.' To this day, whoever knows in the same way, 'I am Brahman', becomes the entire universe. Even the *devatas* cannot prevail over such a person, for they become the Self of the *devas*. Those who worship another, thinking, 'He is one, and I am another', do not understand. They are like animals to the *devas*. Just as many animals serve a man, so does each man serve the *devas*. Even if one animal is turned away, it causes distress; what then should happen if many animals are turned away? Therefore, men should not understand this as they do.)[53]

Modern Science and Brahmā-Vidya (Knowledge and Science of Brahmān)

First, let us share the thoughts of some great physical scientists of our time. One of the most outstanding scientists and geneticists, J.B.S. Haldane said, 'In the ultimate analysis, the universe cannot be nothing less than the progressive manifestation of God.'[54]

The great physicist, the father of quantum theory and quantum physics, Erwin Schrödinger, has said:

'The Bhagavad Gita ... is the most beautiful philosophical song existing in any known tongue. [...]
This life of yours which you are living is not merely a piece of this entire existence, but in a certain sense the whole; only this whole is not so constituted that it can be surveyed in one single glance. This, as we know, is what the Brahmins [wise men or priests in the Vedic tradition] express in that sacred, mystic formula which is yet really so simple and so clear; *tat tvam asi*, this is you. Or, again, in such words as 'I am in the east and the west, I am above and below, I am this entire world'.[55]

The multiplicity is only apparent. This is the doctrine of the Upanishads. And not of the Upanishads only. The mystical experience of the union with God regularly leads to this view, unless strong prejudices stand in the West.[56]
Hence this life of yours which you are living is not merely a piece of the entire existence, but is in a certain sense the whole; only this whole is not so constituted that it can be surveyed in one single glance. This, as we know, is what the Brahmins express in that sacred, mystic formula which is yet really so simple and so clear: Tat tvam asi, this is you. Or, again, in such words as 'I am in the east and in the west, I am below and above, I am this whole world'.[57]
It echoes:[58]

ब्रह्मैवेदममृतं पुरस्तात् ब्रह्म पश्चात् ब्रह्म उत्तरतो दक्षिणतश्चोत्तरेण ।
अधश्चोर्ध्वं च प्रसृतं ब्रह्मैवेदं विश्वमिदं वरिष्ठम् ॥

brahmaivedamamṛtaṁ purastād brahma paścād brahma dakśiṇataścottareṇa |
adhaścordhvaṁ ca prasṛtaṁ brahmaivedaṁ viśvamidaṁ variṣṭham ||

(All this is Brahman immortal, naught else; Brahman is in front of us, Brahman behind us, and to the south of us and to the north of us and below us and above us; it stretches everywhere. All this is Brahman alone, all this magnificent universe.)

Thus, you can throw yourself flat on the ground, stretched out upon Mother Earth, with the certain conviction that you are one with her and she with you. You are as firmly established, as invulnerable as she, indeed a thousand times firmer and more invulnerable. As surely she will engulf you tomorrow, so surely will she bring you forth anew to new striving and suffering. And not merely 'some day': now, today, every day she is bringing you forth, not once but thousands upon thousands of times, just as every day she engulfs you a thousand times over. For eternally and always there is only now, one and the same now; the present is the only thing that has no end.[59]
The earliest records, to my knowledge, date back some 2500 years or more... the recognition ĀTMAN = BRAHMAN (the personal

self equals the omnipresent, all-comprehending eternal self) was in Indian thought considered, far from being blasphemous, to represent the quintessence of deepest insight into the happenings of the world. The striving of all the scholars of Vedanta was after having learnt to pronounce with their lips, really assimilate in their minds this grandest of all thoughts [...] Again, the mystics of many centuries, independently yet in perfect harmony with each other (somewhat like the particles in an ideal gas), have described each of the unique experiences of his or her life in terms that can be condensed in the phrase: DEUS FACTUS SUM (I have become God).[60]

Physicist Robert Oppenheimer, reflecting on the profound intersection of science and spirituality, remarked:

> Access to the Vedas is the greatest privilege this century may claim over all previous centuries.
>
> The general notions about human understanding ... which are illustrated by discoveries in atomic physics are not in the nature of things wholly unfamiliar, wholly unheard of or new. Even in our own culture, they have a history, and Buddhist and Hindu thought a more considerable and central place. What we shall find [in modern physics] is an exemplification, an encouragement, and a refinement of old wisdom.
>
> The juxtaposition of Western civilization's most terrifying scientific achievement with the most dazzling description of the mystical experience given to us by the Bhagavad Gita, India's greatest literary monument.
>
> The Bhagavad Gita ... is the most beautiful philosophical song existing in any known tongue.[61]

Physicist Werner Heisenberg, reflecting on the intersection of science and Indian philosophy, stated:

> From the early great Upanishads, the recognition Ātman = Brahman (the personal self-equals the omnipresent, all-comprehending eternal self) was in Indian thought considered, far from being blasphemous, to represent, the quintessence of deepest insight

into the happenings of the world. The striving of all the scholars of Vedanta was, after having learned to pronounce with their lips, really to assimilate in their minds this grandest of all thoughts.

[From an essay on determinism and free will]

Most of my ideas & theories are heavily influenced by Vedanta.

There is no kind of framework within which we can find consciousness in the plural; this is simply something we construct because of the temporal plurality of individuals, but it is a false construction ... The only solution to this conflict insofar as any is available to us at all lies in the ancient wisdom of the Upanishad.[62]

In *Uncommon Wisdom: Conversations with Remarkable People*, Fritjof Capra writes about the conversation between Rabindranath Tagore and Werner Heisenberg: 'He began to see that the recognition of relativity, interconnectedness, and impermanence as fundamental aspects of physical reality, which had been so difficult for himself and his fellow physicists, was the very basis of Indian spiritual traditions.' Capra also recorded a conversation with Schrödinger in which he spoke about Heisenberg. He said:

I had several discussions with Heisenberg. I lived in England then [1972], and I visited him several times in Munich and showed him the whole manuscript chapter by chapter. He was very interested and very open, and he told me something that I think is not known publicly because he never published it. He said that he was well aware of these parallels. While he was working on quantum theory, he went to India to lecture and was a guest of Tagore. He talked a lot with Tagore about Indian philosophy. Heisenberg told me that these talks had helped him a lot with his work in physics because they showed him that all these new ideas in quantum physics were, in fact, not all that crazy. He realized there was, in fact, a whole culture that subscribed to very similar ideas. Heisenberg said that this was a great help for him. Niels Bohr had a similar experience when he went to China.[63]

He has also been quoted a couple of times saying, 'After the conversations about Indian philosophy, some of the ideas of quantum physics that had seemed so crazy suddenly made more sense.... Quantum theory will not look ridiculous to people who have read Vedanta.'[64]

Niels Bohr, a quantum physicist, stated, 'I go into the Upanishads to ask questions.'[65]

Nobel Laureate Physicist Prof. Brian David Josephson said, 'The Vedanta and the Sankhya hold the key to the laws of mind and thought process which are co-related to the Quantum Field, i.e., the operation and distribution of particles at atomic and molecular levels.'[66]

Max Planck, in a conversation with James Murphy, said, 'Science cannot solve the ultimate mystery of nature. And that is because, in the last analysis, we ourselves are part of nature and therefore part of the mystery that we are trying to solve.'[67]

And Sri Aurobindo said, 'What Science could not provide India offers B*rahmān* for the eternal goal, Yoga for the means of perfection, Dharma (*swabhavaniyatam karma*) for the rational yet binding law of conduct. Therefore, because it has something by which humanity can be satisfied and on which it can found itself, the victory of the Indian mind is assured.'[68]

Puruṣa (पुरुष) and Prakṛti (प्रकृति)

Our mortal identity as a living being is jīva (जीव). It is derived from the root *jīv*, which means 'to breathe' or 'to live'. *Jivan* is a word for 'life force' or life, and in that sense, what possesses this *jivan* is a *jīva*. The contrast between *jīvātman* and *paramātman* is that one exists in a 'living being', and the other is the 'Supreme Being'.

According to *Shiva Purana*:

अन्यतो भाव्यतेऽवश्यं मायया जन्म कथ्यते । जीर्यते जन्मकालाद्यत्तस्माज्जीव इति स्मृतः ।

anyato bhāvyate'vaśyaṃ māyayā janma kathyate |
jīryate janmakālādyattasmājjīva iti smṛtaḥ |

(Certainly, birth is induced by māyā as an extraneous source. The word jīva refers to that which undergoes decay from the time of birth.)

जन्यते तण्यते पाशैरजीवशब्दार्थ एव ही |
जनमपाशनिवृत्त्यर्थं जन्मलिंङ्गं प्रपूजयेत् ||

janyate tanyate pāśairjīvaśabdārtha eva hi |
janmapāśanivṛttyarthaṃ janmaliṃgaṃ prapūjayet ||

(This word *jīva* refers to that which is bound by the bonds of illusion. To end the bondage of birth, one must revere the symbols and signs of birth.)[69]

According to *Samkhya Darshana*, the manifest Ishwara is Brahman and has two aspects: *puruṣa* and *prakṛti*. The experience of the *jīva* is an interplay between the two. *Puruṣa* is conscious of the various combinations of our cognitive activities, while *prakṛti* is the manifestation. When the bondage of the *jiva* is overcome, that state is called *kaivalya* or moksha, which is also referred to as *jivanmukti* or liberated.[70]

The *Rigveda* states: 'पुरुष एवेदगं् सर्वं यद्भूतं यच्च भव्यम्' (Puruṣa is all that has been and all that is yet to be).[71] Metaphorically, *puruṣa* is the 'cosmic male' or 'father', and *prakṛti* is the 'cosmic nature' or 'mother'.

The *Shiva Purana* provides insights into the concepts of purusha and prakriti through the following verses:

व्यक्तांतरधिष्ठानं गर्भः पुरुष उच्यते |
सुव्यक्तांतरधिष्ठानं गर्भः प्रकृतिरुच्यते ||

vyaktāṃtaradhiṣṭhānaṃ garbhaḥ puruṣa ucyate |
suvyaktāṃtaradhiṣṭhānaṃ garbhaḥ prakṛtirucyate ||

(Puruṣa is the hidden, latent conception, while prakṛti is the manifest, inner conception.)

पुरुषत्वादिगर्भो हि गर्भवांजनको यतः |
पुरुषात्मप्रकृतो युक्तं प्रथमं जन्म कथ्यते ||

puruṣatvādigarbho hi garbhavāñjanako yataḥ |
puruṣātprakṛto yuktaṃ prathamaṃ janma kathyate ||

(Since it is the father who conceives first, the puruṣa holds the primordial conception. The unification of puruṣa and prakṛti is the first birth.)

प्रकृतेरव्यक्तता यातं द्वितीयं जन्म कथ्यते |
जन्म जन्मुर्मृत्युजन्म पुरुषात्प्रतिपद्यते ||

prakṛtervyaktatāṃ yātaṃ dvitīyaṃ janma kathyate |
janma jaṃturmṛtyujanma puruṣātpratipadyate ||
(Its manifestation in prakṛti is called the second birth. The creature, dead even as it is born, takes up its birth from the puruṣa.)[72]

The *Shiva Purana* defines *prakṛti* as another name for Shakti, the prime cause, created from the body of Ishwara:[73]

Īśvara, though alone, created the physical form of Śakti from his body. This Śakti did not affect his body in any way. This Śakti is known by various names: Pradhāna, Prakṛti, Māyā, Guṇavatī, Parā. She is the mother of Buddhi Tattva (the cosmic Intelligence), and Vikṛtivarjitā (without modification). That Śakti is Ambikā, Prakṛti, and the devis of all. She is the prime cause and the mother of the three deities.

Ishwara (ईश्वर)

Ishwara is, in a way, synonymous with *Brahman,* which refers to the Supreme Consciousness. The root of the word *Ishvara* comes from *īś-* or *Ish,* meaning 'capable of', 'able to', or simply 'potency' and 'owner, ruler, chief of'.[74] The second part, *vara*, means 'best, excellent, beautiful', 'choice, wish, blessing, boon, gift'.[75] Thus, *Ishvara* literally means 'Supreme and Infinite owner of all things', the universe's Supreme or infinite cause, source, and controlling entity. We do not find mention of *Ishvara* in the first two Vedas. However, the term is used in the *Yajurveda*, where the verb part *īś or Ishe* is employed.

The idea of Ishvara encompasses all that is ever denoted or connoted by the word 'real'. Ishvara is as real as anything else in the universe. After all, the term 'real' refers to precisely what Ishwara represents. Such is the philosophical conception of Ishvara.[76]

The First mantra of the *Yajurveda* reflects the invocation of divine energy and the importance of vitality and inspiration in life:

इषे त्वा ऊर्जे त्वा । वायव स्थ ।
देवो वः सविता प्रार्पयतु श्रेष्ठतमाय कर्मणऽ आ प्यायध्वम् अघ्न्या ऽइन्द्राय भागं प्रजावतीर्
अनमीवा ऽअयक्ष्मा मा व स्तेनऽ ईशत माघशमसो ध्रुवा ऽअस्मिन् गोपतौ स्यात बह्वीः ।
यजमानस्य पशून् पाहि ॥

Ishe tvorje tva vayava stha
devo vah savita prapayatu sresthatamaya karmana apyayadhva
maghnya indraya bhagam prajavati ranamiva ayakshma
va stena isata maghasamso dhruva asmin gopatau syata bhavir
yajmaanasya pasun pahi

(The creative potency is present in the higher levels of dynamic motion. What kind of inspiration does it provide? Inspiration for noble actions. Be vibrant like the wind, or as vital as air. Who grants this energy? The creator of the universe, who bestows energy, food, light, and life. Why does He gift these? To nourish the body, mind, and soul.)

The first verse of the *Isha Upanishad* says:

ईशा वास्यमिदं सर्वं यत्किञ्च जगत्यां जगत्।
तेन त्यक्तेन भुञ्जीथा मा गृधः कस्य स्विद्धनम् ॥

Isavasyam idam sarvam yat kim ca jagatyam jagatyam,
tena tyaktena bhunjitha, ma gridhah kasyasvid dhanam

(Whatever is in motion and subject to change in this ephemeral world is enveloped and permeated by *Īśa*. *Īśa* pervades the entire universe and creation.)

So, *Īśa* or Ishvara is omnipresent. Hence, Hindus perceive the same divine and sacred presence everywhere, including in all of nature—mountains, rivers, trees, animals, and even rocks. Mother, father, and guru are also revered as *devatas*.

The *Mandukya Upanishad* says:

ओमित्येतदक्षरमिदं सर्वं तस्योपव्याख्यानं भूतं भवद्भविष्यदिति सर्वमोङ्कार एव ।
यच्चान्यत्त्रिकालातीतं तदप्योङ्कार एव ॥

omityetadakṣaramidaṃ sarvaṃ tasyopavyākhyānaṃ bhūtaṃ bhavadbhaviṣyaditi sarvamoṅkāra eva | yaccānyattrikālātītaṃ tadapyoṅkāra eva || 1 ||

(*Aum*, the word, is all this. All that is past, present, and future is verily *Aum*. That which is beyond the triple conception of time is also truly *Aum*.)

सर्वं ह्येतद् ब्रह्मायमात्मा ब्रह्म सोऽयमात्मा चतुष्पात् ॥

sarvaṃ hyetad brahmāyamātmā brahma so 'yamātmā catuṣpāt || 2 ||

(All this is verily Brahman. This *atman* is Brahman. This *atman* has four *pādas* or quarters.)

जागरितस्थानो बहिष्प्रज्ञः सप्ताङ्ग एकोनविंशतिमुखः स्थूलभुग्वैश्वानरः प्रथमः पादः ॥

Jāgaritasthāno bahiṣprajñaḥ saptāṅga ekonaviṃśatimukhaḥ sthūlabhugvaiśvānaraḥ prathamaḥ pādaḥ || 3 ||

(The first *pāda* is *Vaiśvānara,* whose sphere [of activity] is the waking state, who is conscious of external objects, who has seven limbs and nineteen mouths, and whose experience consists of gross [material] objects.)

स्वप्नस्थानोऽन्तः प्रज्ञाः सप्ताङ्ग एकोनविंशतिमुखः प्रविविक्तभुक्तैजसो द्वितीयः पादः ॥

svapnasthāno'ntaḥ prajñāḥ saptāṅga ekonaviṃśatimukhaḥ
praviviktabhuktaijaso dvitīyaḥ pādaḥ || 4 ||

(The second *pāda* is the *Taijasa*, whose sphere [of activity] is the dream state, who is conscious of internal objects, has seven limbs and nineteen mouths, and experiences subtle objects.)

यत्र सुप्तो न कञ्चन कामं कामयते न कञ्चन स्वप्नं पश्यति तत्सुषुप्तम् ।
सुषुप्तस्थान एकीभूतः प्रज्ञानघन एवाऽऽनन्दमयो ह्यानन्दभुक् चेतोमुखः प्राज्ञस्तृतीयः पादः ॥

yatra supto na kañcana kāmaṃ kāmayate na kañcana svapnaṃ paśyati tatsuṣuptam | suṣuptasthāna ekībhūtaḥ prajñānaghana evā"nandamayo hyānandabhuk cetomukhaḥ prājñastṛtīyaḥ pādaḥ || 5 ||

(That is the state of deep sleep, wherein the sleeper does not desire any objects nor does he see any dream. The third *pāda* is the *Prājña,* whose sphere is deep sleep, in whom all [experiences] become unified or undifferentiated, who is verily a mass of consciousness entire, who is full of bliss and who experiences bliss, and who is the path leading to the knowledge [of the other two states].)

एष सर्वेश्वरः एष सर्वज्ञ एषोऽन्तर्याम्येष योनिः सर्वस्य प्रभवाप्ययौ हि भूतानाम् ॥
eṣa sarveśvaraḥ eṣa sarvajña eṣo'ntaryāmyeṣa yoniḥ sarvasya
prabhavāpyayau hi bhūtānām ||6 ||

(This is the Lord of all; this is the knower of all; this is the controller within; this is the source of all; and this is that from which all things originate and in which they finally disappear.)

In the Shakti/Tantra system, the female incarnation is *Isvari*. The term is used as part of many personified forms or manifested aspects of Ishvara, such as Maheshvara—the great Ishvara, Shiva, also called Mahadeva. Parameshvara or Parameswara refers to the supreme *Ishvara.* Other forms of Ishvara include *Jagadiswar,*

Jagdish, Jagadiswari, Jaganmata, Jagadhatri, Bhubaneswar, Ista devata, kuleswar, Nagar-iswar, among others.

The qualities of Ishvara are as follows. Generally, it is said that Ishvara is अवाङ्मनसगोचर (*Avāṅmanasagocara*), meaning beyond the power of thought and words—indescribable and inconceivable, beyond the reach of the senses.

The *Taittareya Upanishad* describes the nature of the ultimate reality, stating:[77]

यतो वाचो निवर्तन्ते। अप्राप्य मनसा सह।

yato vāco nivartante . aprāpya manasā saha

(Whence all speech, along with the mind, turns back,
not reaching It.)

The *Isha Upanishad* describes the nature of the Supreme Self as follows:[78]

तद् एजति तन् नैजति तद् दूरे तद् व् अन्तिके।
तद् अन्तर् अस्य सर्वस्य तद् उ सर्वस्यास्य बाह्यतः॥

tad ejati tan naijati tad dūre tad v antike |
tad antar asya sarvasya tad u sarvasyāsya bāhyataḥ

(It moves, and it moves not; it is far, and it is near. It is inside all
this; it is also outside all this.)

स पर्यगाच् छुक्रम् अकायम् अव्रणम् अस्नाविरं शुद्धम् अपापविद्धम्।
कविर् मनीषी परिभूः स्वयम्भूर् याथातथ्यतोऽर्थान् व्यदधाच् छाश्वतीभ्यः समाभ्यः॥

sa paryagāc chukram akāyam avraṇam asnāviraṃ śuddham
apāpaviddham |
kavir manīṣī paribhūḥ syayambhūr yāthātathyator'thān vyadadhāc
chāśvatībhyaḥ samābhyaḥ

(He [the Self] is all-pervading, bright, incorporeal, scatheless and veinless, pure, untouched by sin; a seer, all-knowing, superposed, and self-begotten. It is He who has duly allotted to the eternal creators their various duties.)

The *Yoga Sutras of Patanjali* mention Ishvara in several verses, with one of the most famous being '*Īśvara pranidhana*'. To Patanjali, Ishvara is पुरुषविशेष (*puruṣaviśeṣa)*—a special being.[79]

क्लेश कर्म विपाकाशयैरपरामृष्टः पुरुषविशेष ईश्वरः ॥

klesa karma vipaakaasayairaparaamrstah purusavisesa iisvarah

(This *purusa-viśeṣa* is the transformative catalyst or guide, aiding the yogin on the path to spiritual emancipation.)[80]

In the Mahayana Buddhist tradition, the word Ishvara appears in the compound '*Avalokiteśvara*' (lord who hears the cries of the world), referring to a bodhisattva who is often depicted as female and shares similarities with the Hindu devi Maheshvari. In Mahayana, Samantabhadra is a personification of the good, comparable to Ishvara.

Bhagavān (भगवान्)

The term most often used by Hindus to express divine infinity is Bhagwan or Bhagavān. While the term *Bhagha* is prominent in the Vedas, Bhagawan is not directly found there. According to some interpretations, '*bh*' stands for the 'cherisher and supporter' of the universe or creation in which all beings exist and which 'exist in all beings'. Meanwhile, 'ga' signifies the 'impeller or creator'.

The *Vishnu Purana* defines Bhagavān in terms that are very similar to the concept of *Ishvara*:[81]

उत्पत्तिं प्रलयं चैव भूतानामागतिं गतिम् |
वेत्तिं विद्यामविद्यां च स वाच्यो भगवानिति ||

utpattim pralayam caiva bhuutaanaamaagatim gatim |
vettim vidyaamavidyaam ca sa vaacyo bhagavaaniti ||

(He who understands the creation and dissolution, the appearance and disappearance of beings, the wisdom and ignorance, should be called Bhagavān.)

Let us now explore the ancient origins of the term 'Bhagavan', tracing its fragments from Persia to pre-history. Today's Baghdad seems to have some connection to this potent term, which appears in the form of 'baga' in Persia and Armenia.

An Achaemenid royal inscription from the period of Darius I (around 500 BCE) is found on a cliff at Mount Behistun in the Kermanshah province of modern Iran. This inscription, known as the Behistun Inscription, in called Bagastana in Old Persian, meaning 'the place of gods', signifying that Baghdad could be interpreted as 'created or given by the god[s]'. In Old Persian, the phrase '*haya maϑišta bagānām*' means 'who [is] the greatest among the gods', referring to Ahuramazdā. The term *baga* also means 'distributor'.[82]

In Old Persian, Baghdad means 'bestowed or given by God' (from Bagh or Bag = God and Dad = given).[83] Other cities in Iran today with names starting with 'Bag' include Bagram, Baghlan, and Bagshan.

In Sanskrit, the word *Bhagavān* is related to भग (*Bhagha*), which means beauty, fortune, blessing, divine radiance, excellence, majesty, splendour, power, and more. Some interpret *Bhagavān* as 'one who possesses [-*van*] the qualities of *Bhagha*', as mentioned earlier. Others connect it to the root भज् (*bhaj*), meaning 'to revere and adore', as seen in the term *bhajan*. In most Indian languages, the term *bhagya* refers to 'fortune' or 'destiny'.

The primary word for *bhagya* and *Bhagavān* is *Bhagha* (भग), which appears in the Vedas and is associated with the giver of fortune, wealth, and prosperity. *Bhagha* appears sixty times in the *Rigveda* and is invoked alongside deities such as Agni, Indra, Mitra, Varuna, the Ashvins, Pusan, Brahmanspati, Soma, and Rudra.

References to *Bhagavān* in Scriptures

One of the prominent mentions of Bhagavan is found in the *Rigveda* with the 'Bhagya Suktam' (*Rigveda* 7.41):

ॐ परातरग्निं परातरिन्द्रं हवामहे परातर्मित्रावरुणाप्रातरश्विना |
परातर्भगं पूषणं बरह्मणस पतिं परातः सोममुत रुद्रं हुवेम ||

Aum prātaraghniṃ prātarindraṃ havāmahe
prātarmitrāvaruṇāprātaraśvinā |
prātarbhaghaṃ pūṣaṇam brahmaṇas patiṃ prātaḥ somamuta
rudraṃ huvema ||

(At dawn, we invoke Agni, Indra, Mitra, Varuna and the Ashwins.
At dawn, we invoke Bhagha, Pushana, Brahmanaspathi, Soma,
and Rudra.)

परातर्जितं भगमुग्रं हुवेम वयं पुत्रमदितेयों विधर्ता |
आध्रश्चिद यं मन्यमानस्तुरश्चिद राजा चिद यं भगं भक्षीत्याह ||

prātarjitaṃ bhaghamughraṃ huvema
vayaṃ putramaditeryo vidhartā |
ādhraścid yaṃ manyamānasturaścid rājā
cid yaṃ bhaghaṃ bhakṣītyāha ||

(We will invoke the mighty, early-conquering Bhagha,
the son of Aditi, the great supporter.
Thinking of whom, the poor, the mighty,
and even the king himself say, 'Give me Bhagha'.)

भग परणेतर्भग सत्यराधो भगेमां धियमुदवा ददन नः |
भग पर णो जनय गोभिरश्वैर्भग पर नृभिर्न्र्वन्तः सयाम ||

bhagha praṇetarbhagha satyarādho
bhaghemāṃ dhiyamudavā dadan naḥ |
bhagha pra ṇo janaya ghobhiraśvairbhagha
pra nṛbhirnṛvantaḥ syāma ||

(Our guide, Bhagha, whose gifts are faithful,
favours this song and grants us wealth, O Bhagha.
Bhagha, augment our store of cattle and horses;
Bhagha, may we be rich in men and heroes.)

उतेदानीं भगवन्तः सयामोत परपित्व उत मध्ये अह्नाम |
उतोदिता मघवन सूर्यस्य वयं देवानां सुमतौ सयाम ||

utedānīṃ bhaghavantaḥ syāmota prapitva uta madhye ahnām |
utoditā maghavan sūryasya vayaṃ devānāṃ sumatau syāma ||

(May felicity be ours in the present,
when the day approaches, and at noontide.
And may we, O Bounteous One, still be happy in the deities' loving-kindness at sunset.)

भग एव भगवानस्तु देवास्तेन वयं भगवन्तः सयाम |
तं तवा भग सर्व इज्जोहवीति स नो भग पुरेता भवेह ||

bhagha eva bhaghavānastu devāstena vayaṃ bhaghavantaḥ syāma |
taṃ tvā bhagha sarva ijjohavīti sa no bhagha puraetā bhaveha ||

(May Bhagha truly be the bestower of bliss,
and through him, may the devatas bring us happiness.
As such, O Bhagha, all with might invoke thee;
be thou our Champion here, O Bhagha.)

समध्वरायोषसो नमन्त दधिक्रावेव शुचये पदाय |
अर्वाचीनं वसुविदं भगं नो रथमिवाश्वा वाजिन आ वहन्तु ||

samadhvarāyoṣaso namanta dadhikrāveva śucaye padāya |
arvācīnaṃ vasuvidaṃ bhaghaṃ no rathamivāśvā vājina ā vahantu ||

(To this, may all dawns incline, and come
to the pure place like Dadhikrāvan.
As strong steeds draw a chariot, may they
bring us Bhagha, who discovers the treasure.)[84]

The original concept of Bhagha has evolved into Bhagwan over time.

Qualities of Bhagavān in the Upanishads and Purana

In the Upanishads, the nature of Bhagavan is explored through profound questions and contemplations about the essence of knowledge and reality.

शौनको ह वै महाशालोऽङ्गिरसं विधिवदुपसन्नः पप्रच्छ ।
कस्मिन्नु भगवो विज्ञाते सर्वमिदं विज्ञातं भवतीति ॥[85]

śaunako ha vai mahāśālo'ṅgirasaṁ vidhivadupasannaḥ papraccha
|kasmin nu bhagavo vijñāte sarvamidaṁ vijñātaṁ bhavatīti ||

(Shaunaka asked if knowledge of the world's reality can be so complete that all the many things we see are understood. Can something so complete and excellent be found that, upon knowing it, one knows everything?)

द्वापरान्ते नारदो ब्रह्माणं जगाम कथं भगवन् गां पर्यटन् कलिं सन्तरेयमिति[86]

Dwaparante narado brhmanam jagam kathanm bhagvan gam paryatan kalim santareamiti

(At the start of the Dvapara Yuga, Narada went to Brahma and asked, 'O *Bhagavān*, how shall I, roaming over the earth, be able to overcome the effects of Kali Yuga?')

In the *Vishnu Purana*[87], we find a broad description of *Bhagavān,* with very specific opulence or qualities, and the meaning of Bhaga:

भगः अस्य अस्ति इति भगवान्

bhagaḥ asya asti iti bhagavān

(The one who has *bhaga* is called Bhagavan.)

ऐश्वर्यस्य समग्रस्य वीर्यस्य यशसः श्रियः।
ज्ञान-वैराग्ययोश्चैव षण्णां भग इतीरणा॥

aiśvaryasya samagrasya vīryasya yaśasaḥ śriyaḥ |
jñāna-vairāgyayoścaiva ṣaṇṇāṁ bhaga itīraṇā ||

(Absolute or Supreme prosperity, valour, success, wealth, divine knowledge, and dispassionate renunciation are the six Bhagas.)

One who is endowed with all the above attributes is called भगवान (Bhagwan).

The *Vishnu Purana*[88] summarizes the essence of Bhagavan as follows:

अशब्दगोचरस्यापि तस्य वै ब्रह्मणो द्विज ।
पूजायां भगवच्छब्दः क्रियते ह्युपचारतः ॥
शुद्धे महाविभूत्वाख्ये परे ब्रह्मणि शब्दिते ।
मैत्रेय भगवच्छब्दःसर्वकारणकारणे ॥
संभर्तेति तथा भर्ता भकारोर्थद्वयान्वितः ।
नेता गमयता स्रष्टा गकारार्थस्तथा मुने ॥

asabdagocarasyaapi tasya vai brahmano dvija |
puujaayaam bhagavacchabdah kriyate hyupacaaratah ||
suddhe mahaavibhuutvaakhye pare brahma.ni sabdite |
maitreya bhagavacchabdahsarvakaaranakaarane ||
sambharteti tathaa bhartaa bhakaarorthadvayaanvit.h |
netaa gamayataa srastaa gakaaraarthastathaa mune ||

(The word Bhagavat is a convenient term to be used in the adoration of that Supreme Being, to whom no term is applicable; therefore, Bhagavat expresses that supreme spirit, which is individual, almighty, and the cause of all causes. The letter 'Bh' implies the cherisher and supporter of the universe, while 'ga' is understood as the leader, impeller, or creator.)

The Gita is called Srimad 'Bhagavad' or 'Bhavavat' Gita, which means 'from the Bhagavan' or 'message from the Bhagavan'. This term is used extensively throughout the Gita. One of the most sacred mantras followed by devotees of Sri Krishna is the 'Dwadasakshari Mantra', or the 'twelve-syllable' mantra found in the *Shrimad Bhagavatam* and *Vishnu Purana*: ॐ नमो भगवते वासुदेवाय (*Om Namo Bhagavate Vāsudevāya),* which means, 'Om, I bow to Bhagavat Vāsudeva'.

When addressing divine figures, the term *Bhagavān* is used to show veneration. For example, Bhagwan Ram, Krishna, Shiva, Buddha, Mahavir, and other Tirthankaras are referred to in this way. Devi Durga is called Bhagawatī. In modern times, it has become common for many contemporary gurus to be addressed as Bhagwan as well. However, the *Vishnu Purana* clearly states that the term mahashabda (grand word) *Bhagavān* can only be used for the '*parabrahman*' and '*paramatma*', such as Vasudeva (Vishnu), and not for others:[89]

एवमेष महाशब्दो मैत्रेय भगवानिति।
परब्रह्मभूतस्य वासुदेवस्य नान्यगः ॥

evamesa mahaasabdo maitreya bhagavaaniti |
parabrahmabhuutasya vaasudevasya naanyagah

(The term *Bhagavān* is used exclusively for Parabrahman Vasudev.)

So, who exactly is Vasudev?

सर्वाणि तंत्र भुतानि वसन्ति परमात्मनि।[90]
भुतेषु च स सर्वात्मा वासुदेवः ततः स्मृतः।।

sarvaani tamtra bhutaani vasanti paramaatmani|
bhutesu ca sa sarvaatmaa vaasudevah tatah smrtah||

(All elements reside in *Paramatma,* and *Paramatma* resides in all elements. Therefore, *Paramatma* is also called *Vasudev.*)

Vidhātā (विधाता)

There are three terms used to express qualified divinity:

- Vidhātā: The exalted being in *Swarga Loka* (the heavenly realm), who is the leader of the Vidhātā Purush.
- Vidhih*:* The lord of the Vedas, the one who is in charge of *vidhi* (fate).
- Vidhān*:* The giver of law and *vidya* (knowledge).

Here are a few relevant verses from the *Rigveda* relating to Vidhātā:

ते नो॑ रु॒द्रः सर॑स्वती स॒जोषा॑ मी॒ळ्हुष्म॑न्तो॒ विष्णु॑र्मृळन्तु वा॒युः ।
ऋ॒भु॒क्षा वाजो॒ दैव्यो॑ विधा॒ता प॒र्जन्या॒वाता॑ पिप्यता॒मिषं॑ नः ॥[91]

te no rudraḥ sarasvatī sajoṣā mīl̲huṣmanto viṣṇur mṛl̲antu vāyuḥ |
ṛbhukṣā vājo daivyo vidhātā parjanyāvātā pipyatām iṣaṃ naḥ ||

(May Rudra and Saraswati, alike, well-asked, and Viṣhṇu and Vāyu, make us happy, sending rain; and Ribhukṣin, Vāja, the divine Vidhātā; and may Parjanya and Vāta grant us abundant food.)

उ॒भे द्यावा॑पृथि॒वी वि॑श्वमि॒न्वे अ॑र्य॒मा दे॒वो अदि॑तिर्विधा॒ता ।
भगो॒ नृशंस॑ उ॒र्व॑न्तरिक्षं॒ विश्वे॑ दे॒वाः पव॑मानं जुषन्त ॥[92]

ubhe dyāvāpṛthivī viśvaminve aryamā devo aditir vidhātā |
bhago nṛśaṃsa urv antarikṣaṃ viśve devāḥ pavamānaṃ juṣanta ||

(The all-pervading couples of heaven and earth, the divine Aryaman, Aditi, Vidhātā, and Bhagha deserve the praise of men; the spacious firmament and all the *devatas* honour the purified Soma.)

The *Manusmriti*[93] also mentions Brahman and Vidhātā:

विधाता शासिता वक्ता मैत्रो ब्राह्मण उच्यते ।
तस्मै नाकुशलं ब्रूयान्न शुष्कां गिरमीरयेत् ॥

vidhātā śāsitā vaktā maitro brāhmaṇa ucyate |
tasmai nākuśalaṃ brūyānna śuṣkāṃ giramīrayet ||

(The *Brāhmaṇa* is called Vidhātā—the ruler, the teacher, and the friend; therefore, one should not address unpleasant words to him nor use any harsh words.)

In Vaishnava literature, Vidhātā is equated with Brahma, carrying the meaning of 'organizer' or 'creator'.[94] In Theravada Buddhist literature, Vidhata appears as the name of a diety to whom sacrifices should be offered to obtain happiness.[95]

Avatāra (अवतार)

Avatāra is derived from *ava-tara*. The prefix *ava* denotes downward, and the root *tṛ* means 'to cross over', 'move', or 'land'. According to Monier Monier-Williams[96], avat*ā*ra means 'descent, alight, to make one's appearance'. Thus, it signifies 'descended', which can have multiple interpretations, such as a 'manifestation of a deity', 'bodily form on earth of a divine being', or the incarnation of a divine being.

While it is widely known that there are ten avatāras of Vishnu, referred to as the *Dasavatāras*, the *Bhagavata Purana* actually lists twenty-three avatāras of Vishnu. Additionally, the *Manava Purana* enumerates forty-two avatāras of Vishnu. However, that is not all; within Vedic and Puranic Hindu and Sikh traditions, there are avatāras or descents of Vishnu, Shiva, Parvati Devi, Lakshmi, and Ganesh.

The Guru Granth Sahib, the primary sacred scripture in Sikh tradition, mentions Puranic *devas* and *devis* such as Durga, Ram, Krishna, and Hari. The *Dasam Granth*, the second scripture, written by Guru Gobind Singh, mentions twenty-four avatars of Vishnu. It also refers to the avataras of Rudra (Shiva), including Dattatreya, Parshanath (a Jain Tirthankara), and the seven avatars of Brahma. The Guru Granth Sahib also mentions seven Brahma avatars: Valmiki, Kashyapa, Shukra, Baches, Vyasa, Khat, Kalidasa.[97]

According to the *Linga Purana*, *Kurma Purana*, and *Shiva Purana*, there are twenty-eight avatars of Shiva.[98] The *Linga Purana* lists the following: Shveta, Sutara, Madana, Suhotra, Kanchana, Lokakshi, Jagishavya, Dadhivahana, Rishabha, Muni, Ugra, Atri, Bali, Gautama, Vedashirsha, Gokarna, Guhavasi, Shikhandabhrit, Jatamali, Attahasa, Daruka, Langali, Mahakaya, Shuli, Mundishvara, Sahishnu, Somasharma, and Jagadguru.

The *Shiva Purana* mentions nineteen avatars of Shiva: Piplaad, Nandi, Veerbhadra, Sharabha, Ashwatthama, Bhairava, Durvasa Muni, Grihapati, Vrishava, Hanuman, Yatinath, Krishna Darshan, Vikshuvarya, Sureshwar, Krateshwar, Suntantakara, Brahmachari, Yaksheshwar, and Avadhut. Sheshanag is also considered by many to be a form of Shiva on earth.

Many forms of Parvati or Devi are also considered avatars, including Kali, Mahakali, Durga, Sati, Jagdhatri, Bhavani, and Maheshwari.

Four avatars of Ganesha are listed in the *Ganesha Purana*: Mohotkata, Mayureshwara, Gajanana, and Dhumraketu. The *Mudgala Purana* mentions eight avatars of Ganesha: Vakratunda, Ekadanta, Mahodara, Gajavaktra (or Gajānana), Lambodara, Vikata, Vighnaraja, and Dhumravarna.

Brāhmaṇa (ब्राह्मण) or Brāhmin

Today, a Brahmin is often seen as belonging to a so-called 'caste', although it originally referred to a *varna*. A professional priest is also referred to as a Brahmin. In its traditional sense, a Brahmin is a person belonging to a *varna* characterized by specific qualities (*gunas*), duties, and roles, such as acting as a purohit (priest). That is the ordinary understanding of term.

It is challenging to imagine or conceptualize either Brahma or Brahman. However, according to Hindu sages, there is a profound connection between all living beings and Brahma through creation and, consequently, the Brahman. A person who realizes this connection is considered a Brahmin, having lived as a *Brahmachari* in search of the Brahman.

Ultimate Brahmin-hood signifies a state or lifestyle where a person has realized or experienced the Supreme Brahman. Such a true Brāhmin sees Brahman in everything and everywhere, having attained liberation (moksha).

According to the *Śrīmad Bhāgavatam*:[99]

धृता तनूरुशती मे पुराणी
येनेह सत्त्वं परमं पवित्रम् ।
शमो दमः सत्यमनुग्रहश्च
तपस्तितिक्षानुभवश्च यत्र ॥

dhṛtā tanūr uśatī me purāṇī
yeneha sattvaṁ paramaṁ pavitram
śamo damaḥ satyam anugrahaś ca
tapas titikṣānubhavaś ca yatra

(In this world, the brāhmaṇas thoroughly study all the Vedas, and because they assimilate the Vedic conclusions, they are also to be considered the Vedas personified. The brāhmaṇas are situated in the supreme transcendental mode of nature, *sattva guṇa*. Because of this, they are fixed in mind control [*śama*], sense control [*dama*], and truthfulness [*satya*]. They describe the Vedas in their original sense, and out of mercy [*anugraha*], they preach the purpose of the Vedas to all conditioned souls. They practise penance [*tapasya*] and tolerance [*titikṣā*], and they realize the position of the living entity and the Supreme Lord [*anubhava*]).[100]

The Experience of Divinity

Most world religions teach that an intermediary or a 'middleman' or prophet is necessary to connect with the supreme form of divinity. However, Hindu and Vedic systems emphasize self-exploration and realization through personal practices known as '*sadhana*'. Various forms of yoga serve as techniques and pathways for this purpose, with Hatha Yoga, Mantra Yoga, and Tantra Yoga offering systematic processes to experience divinity both within and without.

During the Satya Yuga (Golden Era), people were naturally inclined towards these techniques and did not require imagery to aid their practices. As civilization transitioned into lower cycles, the need for visual representations arose, beginning with simple geometric forms such as circles, triangles, and rectangles. These evolved into intricate '*yantras*'. Most traditional temples worldwide, including the famous Ankor Wat Temple, are constructed based on a *yantra*.

With time, *mantras*—tools and techniques to empower the '*manah*' (mind) to connect with divinity—emerged. Later still, images and *murtis*, came into existence, serving as focal points for worship and mediation.

A key experience for all *sadhakas*—practitioners on the path to experiencing the whole, the divine, and the infinite—is found within one's own body, through the *Kundalini* and *Chakra* systems. Kriya Yoga and Tantra are powerful tools to awaken the divinity within, and the resulting practices and experiences are often referred to as 'mysticism' or 'occultism'. Similar experiences have been noted in world religions and by various 'saints' around the globe.

In the Hindu system, there are numerous paths to spiritual realization: Bhakti (surrender and devotion), Karma (selfless service to people and society), and Jnana (pursuit of knowledge through the search for truth in both the material and *adhyatmic* worlds), among others. These diverse approaches offer individuals the flexibility to choose a path that aligns with their dispositions and goals.

The Vedic vision of *Vasudhaiva Kutumbakam* reflects the culture and heritage of a land where divinity is perceived in rivers, mountains, trees, and animals. Even inanimate objects, such as stones, are believed to embody the same divine presences. This profound sense of interconnectedness forms the foundation of true spirituality and resonates with many traditions worldwide, including those of various Native American tribes.

Mysticism is the path of becoming one with the divine or the infinite and is, by definition, 'union with the Absolute, the Infinite, or God'.[101] It is suggested that Shamanism—found in Europe (for example, Celtic traditions) and Native or Pagan cultures—and certain Islamic sects, such as Sufism, represents paths of mysticism. Similarly, Kaabalah in Jewish tradition bears similarities to *Chakra sadhana*. Within the Hindu tradition, the practice of mysticism is particularly prevalent among certain sects and monks, especially those engaged in Shiva and Shakti sadhanas.

Divinity, however, can also be experienced through creative works such as paintings, poetry, and music. A profound example is the poetry and music of Poet Laureate Rabindranath Tagore and the *Baul* tradition of Bengal, which expresses spiritual themes in deeply resonant ways.

Those who dismiss spirituality or *adhyatmikata* without exploring or experimenting with it speak from a position of ignorance. Just as only someone who has studied and practised physics or biology is qualified to discuss these subjects meaningfully, the same applies to spirituality. One cannot credibly critique or deny its significance without first engaging with its practices and principles.

Conclusion

Once one has been exposed to the concept of divinity in the Hindu system, it is nothing short of overwhelming. This is a vast subject, developed over millennia by Hindu sages in their quest for truth and the ultimate meaning and essence of the world. It is akin to the Inuit tribe having more than 50 words related snow[102] or Bharat's tradition of recognizing 280 words for water,[103] each representing a specific quality. Similarly, Hindu sages have discovered, expressed, symbolized, and positioned the same divinity—infinite yet made finite—through myriad names and forms.

It should now be evident to the reader that the meaning of these concepts cannot be easily equated with the ideas of God, Allah, or Jehovah (Yəhōwā), which I discussed in detail in my previous book, *The Crash of a Civilization.* Hindus do not have many 'gods' or 'goddesses' in the conventional sense; instead, they have diverse ways of describing aspects of divinity through different names and forms. Each concept within the Hindu system is unique. Hindus would benefit greatly by familiarizing themselves with the deeper meanings of these concept and using them appropriately and contextually.

Furthermore, one must not forget the invaluable contributions of Hindu sages and scientists to various fields—contributions that form the pillars of modern civilization and continue to influence contemporary minds and sciences. These areas include mathematics and astronomy, cosmology, quantum mechanics, psychology and consciousness studies, co-evolution, environmental matters, nature-friendly architecture, yoga and ayurveda, and integrative health systems.

CHAPTER 7

The Hindu Dharmic System

Hinduism

As discussed in previous chapters, after encountering various practices in India related to divinity, Christian missionaries and theologians added an 'ism' to each distinct tradition, labelling them as a 'belief system in practice'. When preachers of the Abrahamic faiths arrived in India, they struggled to map or understand the complex and, to them, bewildering culture and practices of the Indians. As a result, they attempted to categorize them using their own framework. However, their tools were inadequate. Like the frog in the well, they could only compare the ocean to the well, and the best they could do was map the native systems according to their own worldviews, methods, and tools. Thus, the term 'Hinduism' came into existence.

To the Christian missionaries, Indian practices appeared to be strange forms of 'tribalism'. To them, the only true 'religion' was Christianity, and all others were false and would be labelled with the suffix 'ism', except for Islam. We have already discussed the history of Christian missionaries in India and how the terms 'Hinduism' and 'Hindu religion' were introduced in earlier chapters.

The term 'Hinduism' did not exist before the arrival of the British in India around the 1700s. At that point, the British grouped all native practices of the Hindus, Jains, Sikhs, and

Buddhists together. However, later, in their efforts to divide and rule, they created the caste system within the Hindu community. There is clear evidence now that the British superimposed their own social castes onto the Hindu *varnasharam* and jati system, categorizing people from thousands of jatis into four castes.[1] The jatis had lived independently for centuries, and caste was not a central concept in their daily lives; however, the British enforced it. They then separated the other major streams within the same Sanatana Dharma, forming Sikhism, Buddhism, and Jainism. As history has shown, whenever a society or race loses its means of protection against an external force, its ability to sustain its culture diminishes. Hindus survived because they had the valiant 'kshatriyas' to protect their land and society—today, this role is fulfilled by the police and military of the modern state.

India is an ancient society with deep and broad roots. Over centuries, it had strong and sustained interaction with much of the globe, through flourishing trade, the exchange of scholars and knowledge, and numerous internal military campaigns and invasions. A society with such varied interactions and exchanges over such a long period, one that has survived in its cultural, social, and intellectual states, could not have been anything but pluralistic. Thus, plurality is a natural, innate trait of the Indian mind; otherwise, it would not have survived for so long. The Christian missionaries and colonizers did not grasp this state of pluralism.

For a truly sustainable life on Earth, the messages of the great Indian thinkers and visionaries, and the lifestyle they recommended, are urgently needed for the world to reflect upon and help promote. A world that respects pluralism, teaches inclusiveness and tolerance, offers reverence for life and nature, and fosters a violence-free progressive mindset is very much possible if a critical mass, especially world leaders, acts upon these Hindu ideas.

Over thousands of years of experimentation in nearly all human domains, the Indian people created fields of knowledge. India's heritage has produced a great scientific and spiritual culture, unmatched artistic creations in sculptures, music, and dance, as well as grand social, political, economic, health, and educational systems from which the whole world has learned and benefitted. Did Einstein exaggerate when he said, 'We owe a lot to the Indians who taught us how to count, without which no scientific discoveries would have been possible?'[2]

Hindu history is rich with immense contributions in science, mathematics, grammar, and language, and has a glorious history of heroic valour against conquerors without attacking other nations. But the most significant contribution has been the knowledge of the 'self' or '*adhyatma*'. These contributions are treasured in Vedic and Vedantic as well as Jain, Buddhist, and Sikh literature.

Understanding Hindus and Hinduism

Shrouded in mystery and often misunderstood due to a lack of insight, exposure, and knowledge, 'Hinduism' is sometimes dismissed as a 'pack full of animistic/tribal rituals'.[3] Practices such as scarification, circumcision, penile subincision, and the knocking out of one or more incisors are some examples of rites of 'initiatory death' mentioned in connection with such interpretations in Eliade's works.[4]

Be that as it may, Hinduism—known by many names to its adherents, such as Hindu Dharma, Sanatana Dharma, Vedic Dharma, or simply dharma—represents the world's oldest continuous heritage and tradition. This chapter aims to introduce this great ancient tradition to those who lack sufficient knowledge and understanding of it.

Definition

Celebrated American historian Will Durant wrote in *Our Oriental Heritage*:

> India was the mother of our race and Sanskrit, the mother of Europe's languages. She was the mother of our philosophy, mother through the Arabs, of much of our mathematics, mother through

> Buddha, of the ideals embodied in Christianity, mother through village communities of self-government and democracy. Mother India is in many ways the mother of us all.[5]

'Hinduism' is often regarded as one of the oldest 'religions' in the world.[6] However, as already noted, the Hindu tradition does not fit the conventional definition of a religion, which typically includes a founder or prophet, a specific holy book, and a defined set of practices. Over its long history, innumerable personalities have enriched the Hindu tradition; some are known to us, while many others have been forgotten. However, several figures within this tradition enjoy prophetic stature and are referred to as *rishis*.

The Hindu tradition encompasses hundreds of sacred texts—addressing both spiritual and worldly topics—and its practices vary by region and family. Some define 'Hinduism' as a confederation of spiritual and cultural practices that are region-specific in India and across the globe. Adherents can choose from a wide range of practices within the vast Hindu system. In some families, each member may follow a distinct Hindu tradition, such as Shaivism, Vaishnavism, and others.

According to tradition, every Hindu's dharma or duty is to follow a sustainable lifestyle, which can, to some extent, be considered their personal 'religion' or *swadharma*. This acknowledges and follows the rules and order of both the cosmic and human realms. Hindus are encouraged to take the most appropriate actions in each context to create a sustainable life and world, thereby fostering progress and maintaining harmony and order not only for themselves but also for their family, society, nation, and all of creation. Dharma, or 'that which sustains', is a composite of order, duties, actions, and their attendant results. However, this worldview—and the way of life based on it—is often misinterpreted as 'religion'.

The Hindu tradition is not based on a 'belief system', which may sometimes resemble a 'fear system', where adherents are compelled to follow a 'religion' out of fear of 'sin-consciousness' and the threat of 'eternal damnation by burning in hell', or in pursuit of the reward of 'an everlasting heaven' following a judgement based on adherence to a specific path or prophet. Instead, the Hindu tradition is rooted in worldly experiences, logic, and a universal understanding of the nature of being. A striking contrast between India's traditions founded on dharma and the Abrahamic religions is the assertion that all beings are potentially divine, and divinity exists in all and sundry. Humans are seen as 'children of immortals', not as beings born into 'sin'.

Hindu tradition emphasizes personal actions and excellence in both spiritual and material domains. It is a tradition of deeds, not a creed. While a *guru* or teacher plays an important role, the responsibility for learning and practice rests on the individual, leading to spiritual attainment or the realization of one's full potential. A saviour, prophet, scripture, or even a religious place such as a temple becomes irrelevant to a *sadhak* or a 'practicing person [striving] to attain the *purusharthas* [pursuits of life]'.

The Hindu thought system is a conglomeration of hundreds of texts and spiritual authorities, and it does not require a central papal body. It is comparable to the academic tradition, which has produced a vast body of literature, is capable of self-correction, and continues to create new knowledge.

Tradition presents the truth and provides methods that, if followed, enable anyone to verify that truth. This is analogous to the empirical method, where replicating an experiment is necessary for acceptance within the scientific community. Hindus call this knowledge system *vidya* (a combination of knowledge and science).[7] Material knowledge is referred to as *Apar*a *Vidya*, while spiritual knowledge is called *Para Vidya*. For example, yoga practices for physical and mental health benefit millions, regardless of belief, faith, gender, or nationality. The Hindu system, rooted in and intertwined with the broader meaning of yoga, can be practised and experienced by anyone. Similarly, Ayurveda, the 'knowledge system of longevity', serves millions globally. It is based on yoga, herbal support, and natural remedial processes. *Jyotish* (Vedic or Hindu astrology), which significantly differs from its Western counterpart, also remains an integral part of Hindu life.

The Hindu system has no conflict with modern science, and many recent scientific discoveries align with concepts that were previously misunderstood. For instance, while glands in the human body were discovered in the 19th century, Hindus had long understood the existence and functions of endocrine and other glands.[8] Likewise, ancient Hindus accurately studied and predicted stellar bodies and planetary activities.[9] They were also major contributors to the number system and mathematics. Notably, physicists Carl Sagan observed that Hindu cosmology aligns with modern science thought.[10] Similarly, recent theories by Princeton Professor Paul Steinhardt echo ideas found in Hindu cosmology, particularly the *Vaisesika Sutras*.[11]

A unique aspect of the Hindu tradition is its emphasis on individual effort and experience, without creating a division between the spiritual and secular. Thus, it is not a religion in the conventional sense. Since Hindus view everyone as potentially divine (or possessing supreme consciousness), individuals can realize their full potential through *sadhana* (austere practice), leading to both material prosperity and spiritual attainment. A Hindu is empowered to discover the divine within by realizing 'I'm that' or by choosing a personal form of the divine (*Ishta Devata*) to invoke grace or surrender. The branch of knowledge that deals with divinity is known as *Adhyatma Vidya* or 'spiritual science'.

Identity and Demography

In ancient times, people living on the eastern side of the Indus River were called Hindus.[12] Today, anyone born into a Hindu family or adhering to its practices is referred to as a Hindu, regardless of their place of birth or nationality.

Population: Hindus constitute about 1.2 billion people, or 15 per cent[13] of the global population. However, from the perspective of Sanatana Dharma, the combined population—including Buddhists, Sikhs, and Jains—is significantly larger.

People of Indian origin, who are typically brown-skinned, reside across the globe. India itself has a population of about 1.3 billion, with 79 per cent identifying as Hindus. Other countries with significant Hindu populations include Nepal (23 million, or 81 per cent of the population), Bangladesh (15 million, or 10 per cent), Sri Lanka (2 million, or 10 per cent), and Pakistan (3 million, or 2 per cent). In the US, it is estimated that over 2 million people are of Indian origin, of whom 80 per cent or 1.6 million, are Hindus. Additionally, there are communities of Indian ancestry who were born or raised in countries such as the Caribbean and several African nations.[14]

It is essential to note that not all people of Indian origin are Hindu, and not all Hindus are of Indian origin or, for that matter, 'brown'. There are over 5 million practising Hindus worldwide who are Caucasian by birth. Yoga serves as a unifying thread across all Hindu traditions. Globally, over 100 million people—including 50 million American yoga practitioners—follow key elements of the Hindu tradition.

Languages: Sanskrit is one of the most ancient languages in the world and is considered the mother of most of the twenty-plus official languages of Bharat, as well as many European languages. It has greatly influenced Hindi, the national language of India, and Bengali, the national language of Bangladesh. Tamil, another ancient language of India, is widely spoken in Sri Lanka as well. In Nepal, a Hindu-majority nation, the primary language spoken is Nepalese.

Sects: Within Hindu tradition, there are four major sects based on spiritual practices. Shaiva are those who connect with Ishwara (the Supreme Bring) through the form of Shiva. Vaishnavas are those who revere Vishnu as their chosen form of divinity. Devotees who invoke the Supreme Being in the form of Shakti (the Divine Mother) are called Shaktas, while those who worship Lord Ganesha as their primary deity are known as Ganapatyas.

In modern times, these divisions are increasingly dissolving. It is common to find members of the same family observing and honouring multiple forms of divinity.

Fundamental Tenets

Worldview: Hindu Dharma is also known as Sanatana Dharma, meaning it is eternal, much like the laws of nature and spirit. The absolute foundation of the Hindu system is *Satya* (Truth). Truth is not only universal and accessible to all but it is also infinite, leading to an ongoing search for understanding in the eternal and universal aspects of life and creation.

A Hindu child is taught to respect and protect all aspects of creation, including nature, fostering an attitude of restraint in the use of natural resources. Great emphasis is placed on protecting the land, air, rivers, water, forests, mountains, and animals, advocating for a symbiotic relationship between humans and nature.

A Hindu child learns the simple equation that to be happy, those around them must also be happy. Some of the key concepts have already been discussed in detail; here are some glimpses:

- एकं सद्विप्रा बहुधा वदन्त (*Ekam Sat Viprah Bahudha Vadanti*):[15] The truth or reality can be discovered and realized in many ways, and the learned find multiple ways to perceive and express it. This means that truth is one but can be realized in diverse ways. It encourages acceptance of pluralism in thought and practice, as opposed to exclusive viewpoints where a single thought or idea is imposed on all. The Hindu view of the Omnipresent, Omniscient, and Omnipotent Supreme Being is one, experienced differently by individuals, rather than imposing a specific, exclusive identity of the same.
- वसुधैव कुटुम्बकम् (*Vasudhaiva Kutumbakam*):[16] The entire creation is one family. All beings—humans, animals, plants, and nature—are interconnected and interdependent.
- सर्वे भवन्तु सुखिनः सर्वे सन्तु निरामयाः । सर्वे भद्राणि पश्यन्तु मा कश्चिद्दुःखभाग्भवेत् ॥

(*Sarve bhavantu sukhinah sarve santu niramayah sarve bhadrani pashyantu ma kasthit dukhavag bhhavet*):[17] A key prayer recited by Hindus is, 'Let everybody be healthy and happy, and let there be no sorrow to anyone.'

- जननी जन्मभूमिश्च स्वर्गादपि गरीयसी (*Janani Janmabhumischa swargadapi gariyasi*):[18] Hindus, regardless of their place of birth, give the highest respect to their mother and motherland (*matribhumi*). Their primary duties lie towards their country.

Purusartha or Goals of Life

Every human being must have pursuits in life. Beyond mere survival, realizing one's full potential and achieving prosperity from a material perspective are essential. On the other hand, spiritual or *adhyatmik* aspirations set the highest goal—to return to the source, or to *Devattwa* or *Ishwaratta* (the English equivalent being Godhead), the supreme consciousness, through karma (action) and *sadhana* (disciplined effort that leads to transformation and the evolution of higher consciousness). This is often referred to by terms such as Moksha, Nirvana, Liberation, or Mukti, while similar, are not identical.

Hindus are expected to pursue *artha* and *kama* through *dharmic* means, leading to mukti or liberation. There are three key pursuits of life, known as *purusartha*[19], namely: *artha* (material resources), *kama* (fulfillment of life's desires and goals), and *moksha* (liberation), based on one's dharma in general and *swadharma* in particular.

Darshanas or Philosophical Schools of Thoughts

The term *darshanas*[20], loosely translated as 'philosophy', means the 'vision of truth'. The *darshanas* in India are divided into six *āstika* schools, which accept the final authority of the Vedas, and three *nāstika* schools, which do not follow or recognize the supreme revelations and authority of the Vedas.

The *āstika darshanas* are:

- *Samkhya*: A strongly dualist theoretical exposition of mind and matter that denies the existence of a particular creator or Ishwara.
- *Yoga:* A school emphasizing knowledge and self-discovery through meditation, closely based on *Samkhya.*
- *Nyaya*: The school of logic.
- *Vaisheshika*: An empirical school of atomism.
- *Mimamsa*: An anti-ascetic and anti-mysticism school of orthopraxy.
- *Vedanta*: The logical conclusion to Vedic ritualism, focusing on mysticism. Vedanta is the most dominant of all the current Hindu traditions.

Traditions that follow the *nāstika darshanas* include Buddhism, Jainism, and *Cārvāka*, an agnostic materialist worldview that waned into oblivion in the 15th century, with its primary texts also being lost at that time.

Key Concepts

Dharma: We have already discussed dharma in earlier chapters. To summarize, we can say it represents the cosmic order, the rule of law, the code of conduct, and duties based on one's role in society. The literal meaning is 'that which sustains'.

A Hindu is not afraid of the changes necessary in response to the needs of time, while keeping in view the eternal and universal aspects of life and creation. In fact, a common Indian term for 'world' is *samsara*, which denotes its ever-changing and transient nature. Another term is *jagat*, which signifies that the world is ever moving and expanding.

Karma: Karma refers to mental or physical activities and duties in general, but more accurately, it signifies appropriate actions guided by dharma to achieve the pursuits of life. Ultimately, karma is a means to realize a person's full potential and attain the final goal—*mokhsa.*

Divinity: The word divinity has roots in the Sanskrit terms deva, divya, and daiva, all of which relate to the sacredness of all creation, signifying the presence of the Supreme Being, Ishwara, in everything. Another name for the Supreme Being is Brahman, which is distinct from the class of Brahmin. Additionally, Brahma is not the same as Brahman—Brahma is part of the Trinity and represents the creator aspect of Brahman or Ishwara.

The one and only Ishwara is represented in the Hindu Trinity, which includes the three main cosmic aspects of the Supreme Being: creation, preservation, and destruction, thus enabling renewal. These are viewed as the male aspects of Ishwara, and each is inseparably dependent on the female aspect, Shakti. The female counterparts of Shiva, Brahma, and Vishnu are Durga (or Shakti), Saraswati, and Lakhsmi, respectively. Saraswati is the bestower of knowledge, arts, and music; Lakshmi represents wealth and beauty; and Durga embodies Shakti or protective force in many forms, including that of a mother.

All six key forms of divinity have hundreds of different names based on specific qualities and forms, as the pluralistic system allows. For example, Vishnu is called by various names such as Narayan (protector of the masses), Venkateshwara, Balaji, and Hari (the remover of sorrow), while Shiva is also known as Mahadeva (the great divine), Yogeshwara (lord of yoga), Nataraja (lord of the cosmic dance), among others. There are many other forms and names of divinity in Hindu tradition. Some of the most common are the elephant-headed Ganesha or Ganapati (remover of obstacles) and Subramanya or Karthikeya or Murugan. The monkey-faced Sri Hanuman or Bajrangbali, a devotee of Sri Ram, is also a prevalent divine form.

The relationship between the adherent and Ishwara varies extensively depending on the darshana followed. For instance, one may deny a physical form of divinity, have a personal relationship (such as with a mother, father, or friend), or completely surrender to their *Ishta* (the favoured form) of Ishwara or deity.

Yoga: Although yoga in the West is understood as a popular health management tool or set of practices, it literally means 'union', from which comes the term yoke. Originally, it referred to the union between the soul[21] of an individual and the Supreme, or the connectivity of the individual's existence with the cosmic. This idea is unique to the Hindu tradition, which is sometimes overlooked by other *dharmic* traditions, such as Buddhism. In a spiritual sense, yoga advocates ways to reach *Devattwa*, and for this, one needs to be healthy and stable to carry out the activities.

Practically, yoga aims to attain excellence in both the material and spiritual worlds. One key definition of yoga is '*Yogah karmasu kaushalam*' or 'excellence in action is yoga'. Hence, yoga's current usage as a health tool represents only a small aspect of the tradition, which is deeply rooted in Hindu heritage and tradition. The popular Hatha yoga was introduced to the West only a century and a half ago, and it has since taken many names and forms as it has been commercialized in a big way.

There are many different types of yoga found in various Hindu texts, including eighteen described in the Bhagavad Gita. However, four stand out in modern days: Hatha or Raj Yoga (the commonly known one), Karma Yoga (realization through righteous actions), Bhakti Yoga (realization through *Shraddha,* faith, and reverence), and Jnana Yoga (realization through acquiring higher knowledge by seeking truth). Many recommend following a path that combines one or more of these yogic disciplines.

Punarjanma (reincarnation or rebirth): Each being is born with the goal of returning to the supreme consciousness or *Devattwa*. If this is not attained in one life, one takes many births until the goal of moksha or nirvana is achieved. The special birth of supreme divine beings in human form is called an *avatar*.

Caturashrma: In traditional Indian philosophy, the concept of Caturashrma outlines the four key stages of a person's life: *Brahmacharya* is a path of self-control, restraint, and integration, known as *Sanyam.* This stage is about 'living in the company of the creative and formative divine form called Brahma' and training the basic instincts to harness higher powers within. It is a process of preparing the ground for self-actualization and represents the student's life. *Grihastha*, or family life, focuses on enjoying the world within a family structure. *Vanaprastha,* or the retired life, is dedicated to serving society. *Sannyas*—the 'saging in aging' stage—is spent in the company of or contemplating the divine or higher consciousness.

The first stage prepares an individual to deal with the world, the second allows for enjoyment of the world within a family framework, the third expands responsibilities beyond the family into society, and the final stage is devoted to higher consciousness and preparing for the next life or attaining moksha.

It is remarkable that based on these four stages of life, each of which typically lasts for twenty-five years, India's life expectancy would logically exceed seventy-five years, as suggested by the fourth stage. It is also important to note that the marriageable age was higher because one had to complete the first stage of life before entering into marriage.

Social classes: *Varnasharam* was originally a social division based on one's aptitude and professional excellence[22] (a modern Western example would be 'blue-collar' and 'white-collar' professions). Those devoted to knowledge or spiritual attainment were called the Brahmins. Those who served the people and the country by providing protection, justice, and law and order, including kings and soldiers, were classified under the Kshatriya *varna*. Those engaged in business and trade were called the Vaishya, and those who did not fit into any of these categories were called the Shudras.

Originally, these professional groups were also referred to as '*jati*', a term that was later misunderstood as 'caste'. The system did not depend on birth, but over time, due to a lack of social reforms and foreign rule, it became a 'by birth only' system, leading to significant social unrest and discrimination. Fortunately, these class distinctions are gradually withering away. Further details on this topic will be discussed later.

Holy person: A holy person can be a purohit (someone who conducts ritual acts for the benevolence of the '*pur*' or town), a priest, or a *pujari* who performs puja or worship activities aimed at spiritual attainment and divine grace. A person who has renounced the material world in pursuit of spiritual growth is called by many names, including *sant,* the etymological origin of the word 'saint'. In Hindu tradition, a person can progress from the first stage of life to the fourth stage and become a *sannyasi* or *sadhu* (ascetic). A *guru* is a spiritually (and sometimes materially) experienced person who 'removes darkness or ignorance', prepares a *shishya* (student) to acquire knowledge, and teaches both spiritual and material subjects.

Sacred texts: The most sacred scriptures are the Vedas, which are considered 'divine knowledge' and are revelations to innumerable, mostly unknown *rishi*s (sages) of yore. The four Vedas are the *Rigveda*, *Samaveda*, *Yajurveda*, and *Atharvaveda.* There are also the Upanishads and Puranas. The most famous scripture, considered the essence of all scriptures, is the Bhagavad Gita, a part of the world's grandest epic, the Mahabharata. The Mahabharata serves as a commentary on an ancient period in history. The Ramayana is another famous Hindu text, even older than the Mahabharata, and speaks of a time further in the past. It should be noted that all knowledge—and, for that matter, all texts on both spiritual and material subjects—are sacred.

Vegetarianism: It is unclear when Hindus were first advised against eating meat. Hindu tradition strongly recommends the use of nature in a sustainable, '*dharmic*' way. Killing animals contributes to a sense of violence, and today, it is well-known that meat consumption poses many health challenges.[23] However, many Hindus do eat meat, fish, and eggs. In Hindu tradition, milk and milk products such as butter and yogurt are considered vegetarian. Since cows represent Mother Nature and are revered and protected by Hindus at all costs, even those who may not be vegetarian would not touch beef or beef products.

Today, people around the world are promoting the ethical treatment of all animals. While animals used in circuses are banned, the ethical procuring of milk that does not harm the cows or their calves—especially the male calf—is emphasized. This contrasts with practices in the dairy and meat industries, where cows are often confined to small spaces, force-fed, injected with steroids, milk-producing hormones, etc., and the male calf is usually killed at birth as it is considered a by-product in veal production. In many cases, calves are also deprived of their rightful share of their mother's milk. This is *adharma*. This, coupled with health concerns, gave rise to the practice of veganism, where no dairy products are included in a meal.

Ethics and Morality

While Hindus explore and experience the ultimate and infinite in relation to ethics and morality, these principles are well-defined and universal in nature, applying to any person or society at any time. They are based on the concept of dharma, which also stands for order or norm. There are established norms by which one wishes others to view or treat him/her. The 'Golden Rule'—'Treat others as you would like to be treated'—forms the basis of modern-day human rights tenets and finds its origin in many elaborate terms in Hindu concepts such as *yama* (not to be confused with Yamaraja, the king of death) and *niyama*. In many ways, these concepts address and resolve criticisms of the Golden Rule made by many modern thinkers.

Based on the *yamas*[24] (observances and recommended practices related to interactions with the world and society) and the *niyama* (personal observances) that sustain an individual, a home, a family, a society, a country, and, ultimately, the entire creation, one must follow fundamental principles. Without these, sustenance and progress will be disturbed, peace will be absent, and the overall harmony and evolution of civilization will be hindered.

Originally, there were ten yamas and niyamas, which were later simplified to five each in the *Patanjali Yoga Sutras*. Yama prepares the individual to be the best citizen through specific interpersonal behavioural practices. Here are the five yamas:

- *Ahimsa:* The attitude of reducing violence in any form—towards oneself, others, and Mother Nature.
- *Satya:* The firm commitment to truth and the path of truth.
- *Asteya:* Not stealing, which means not possessing or taking things without true ownership.

  Brahmacharya: Limit sensual pleasures and indulgences to allow the various faculties and senses to mature and function effectively over a long period. According to Pramhansa Yogananda[25]: 'The art of taming one's natural tendencies is not in the application of futile brute force, but in gradual psychological steps.' This is Brahmacharya.
- *Aparigraha:* Not possessive or greedy, which involves letting go of unnecessary attachments and cultivating contentment with what is needed.

According to the Bhagavad Gita:[26]

सर्वाणीन्द्रियकर्माणि प्राणकर्माणि चापरे ।
आत्मसंयमयोगाग्नौ जुह्वति ज्ञानदीपिते ।।

sarvāṇīndriya-karmāṇi prāṇa-karmāṇi chāpare
ātma-sanyama-yogāgnau juhvati jñāna-dīpite

(Some, inspired by knowledge, offer the functions of all their senses and life energy in the fire of the controlled mind, which is illuminated by knowledge.)

Niyamas prepare the individual to grow within, with a commitment to evolve, develop self-discipline, and realize their full potential through personal behaviour:

- *Saucha*: Mental and physical cleanliness and following order in one's personal life, home, and the world.

- *Santosha*: Contentment with whatever one received after making all efforts.
- *Tapas:* Austerity, discipline, and hard work.
- *Swadhy*aya: Self-study, regularly observing one's actions and behaviour, and evolving higher thinking through contemplation and reading inspiring, uplifting material, including scriptures.
- *Ishwar Pranidhana*: Realizing one's physical limits and striving to work beyond them to reach the highest potential, evolving from a mere animal to a human, and eventually to divinity (*Devattwa*). This requires the grace of the divine, and surrendering to adoption of this path and process is essential for the progress of civilization.

The Bhagavad Gita takes one much deeper and presents twenty essential values of true knowledge and dharma. Many management gurus are incorporating the knowledge of the Bhagavad Gita into their programmes.

Amid the over-emphasis on non-violence, one often forgets that the Hindu ideal was to ensure the protection of life, rights, and the delivery of justice. There would, at times, be occasions to fight. The Kshatriyas (the protectors) in society were assigned this duty. Hence, during the early invasions of India (including those by Alexander), the Hindus fought back valiantly, with female soldiers among them, as they had some of the best warriors in the world. Because of their courageous resistance, much of India remains predominantly Hindu, continuing to follow dharmic traditions.

Adhyatmic Symbolism

Murthy, murti, or moorthy: A murti is a physical representation of divinity, often mistakenly referred to as an 'idol' (a term traditionally used to mean a 'false god'). It is revered and worshipped as a deity, representing a specific aspect of *Devattwa*. Murtis can be crafted from metal, clay, stone, or other materials. These sacred forms, also known as *pratima* and *vigraha*, hold profound significance for Hindu devotees.

Tika/tilak: During spiritual practices or prayers, Hindus apply special substances to their foreheads and between their eyebrows. According to Hindu tradition and yoga, this area is considered the seat of the third eye, symbolizing higher knowledge and illumination. Both men and women use materials such as sandalwood paste, vermillion, turmeric paste, and similar substances, which vary in shape and size depending on the occasion and specific tradition. Married women also apply vermillion to their foreheads and the parting of their hair.

Clothes: Traditional Hindu attire is simple and typically consists of one-piece clothing: dhoti for men and saree for women. Other garments such as salwar and kurta are also considered traditional attire. However, many Hindus now wear Western clothing as well.

Mala: Rosaries or beads (mala) are worn by many Hindus around their necks, arms, wrists, and sometimes their waists. Some also wear chains with pendants featuring Om or other sacred symbols. Male Brahmins wear a 'sacred thread', a tradition that dates back to the Vedic era when all men and women across varnas and jatis wore this thread after undergoing a ceremony (*upanayan*) to mark their entry into student life.

Greetings: Namaste is the folded-hand gesture commonly used for greetings in India and by Hindus worldwide. It signifies, 'I observe and bow down to the divinity in you.' This is the most widely used form of greetings in Indian traditions. In southern India, *Vannakam* is another common term for greeting. Hindus also greet by invoking divine names, such as Jai Sri Krishna, Jai Sri Ram, Ram Ram, or Jai Siya Ram.

Head coverings: While some Hindu traditions encourage men to cover their heads with a turban or a cap and women to use a scarf or the pallu of a saree, especially during sacred occasions, this practice is no longer essential in modern times. In contrast, Sikhs are required to grow their hair and beard and wear a turban as part of their tradition.

Swastika: The word *swasti* in Sanskrit means 'may it be well with you', 'farewell', 'hail', 'adieu', or 'peacefulness'. The swastika symbol is used to promote peace and harmony. However, it acquired negative connotations due to its misuse by the Nazis, who adopted an inverted version of the Hindu swastika as the hooked cross.[27] Despite this, Hindus continue to use the swastika, which can be seen decorating many Hindu homes worldwide.

Avatar: An avatar is the incarnation of *Devattwa* (divine essence). The term literally means 'that force which descends'. According to the Bhagavad Gita, divine beings, particularly Vishnu—the protector of creation—manifest in human form whenever chaos and adharma (lawlessness) prevail in society. The most revered *avatars* are Sri Ram and Sri Krishna. Buddha is also considered the tenth *avatar* of Vishnu.

Practice

Samskaras: Hindus are traditionally expected to follow sixteen key sacred ceremonies or sacraments, known as *samskaras*[28] (originally there were forty), marking different phases of life from birth to death. Below are the most significant ones in order:

- The very first *samskara* is *garbhadhan*, the ceremony of conception or impregnation of the mother.
- The fifth *samskara* is *namakarana,* the naming ceremony conducted after the birth of the child.
- The seventh is *annaprasana*, when the child is fed their first cereal, usually around six months of age.
- The eleventh is *samvartana,* or the ceremony marking graduation from formal education.
- The twelfth is *vivah,* the sacred ritual of marriage.
- The sixteenth is *antyesthi,* the funeral rites and post-funeral rituals.

Pooja or puja: The terms puja or pooja are often translated into English as 'worship', but this translation does not fully convey their essence. *Puja* encompasses a set of rituals and processes involving adoration, oblation, offerings, the utterance of sacred words and verses, devotional songs, music, and meditation. These acts are performed to invoke the divine presence and seek blessings. Puja is typically carried out in front of a *murti* or *murtis,* which are physical representations of one or more aspects of divinity or deities known as *devata* or *devis.*

Teertha or pilgrimage: To Hindus, every part of creation is sacred. They hold profound reverence not only for human rights but also for animals, plants, and even inanimate aspects of creation, such as the earth, water, rivers, and mountains. However, certain places are of particular importance due to their association with divine grace, often empowered through the penance of sages. Hindus visit these sacred sites in large numbers, as the atmosphere is believed to preserve divine grace and impart it to devotees when they engage in proper spiritual practices.

India is home to many such *teerthas* (pilgrimage sites) that date back thousands of years. Some of the most revered sites include Kashi and Varanasi (Benares), Tirupati, Kamakshya, Prayag, Haridwar, Mathura and Vrindavan, Ayodhya, Amarnath, Puri, and Vaishno Devi. The land of Hindu Dharma, Bharat, is referred to as the 'Holy Land' and is honoured as the divine mother, 'Bharat Mata' (Mother India).

Many pilgrimage sites are centred around temples (*mandirs*), which are found not only in India but also in countries where Hindus reside. For instance, there are over 1,000 Hindu temples in the US.[29]

Vivah or marriage: *Vivah* or *vivaha* is one of the twelve *samskaras* performed when a Hindu completes their studies and enters family life through marriage. It is considered a union of two *ātmans* (individual souls). Both spouses take several vows to ensure a long-lasting and happy life together.

The traditional form of marriage is arranged marriage, where both families are involved in assessing compatibility and the relationship potential. However, other forms of marriage also exist in Hindu tradition. One such form is *gandharva vivah* or love marriage.

Seva or service: 'Service to man is service to God' is a well-known quote attributed to many Indian personalities, including Gandhi. It originates from the concept of *tyaga*—the act of selfless 'giving' for the benefit of all. According to Hindu scriptures, *tyaga* is the path to attaining *moksha* (liberation).

Seva refers to service performed without any expectation of reward, forming the foundation of Hindu life. The *Isha Upanishad*[30] emphasizes this idea with the verse:

तेनं त्युक्तेनं भुञ्जीथा:

tena tyaktena bhunjitha

(Let it go and rejoice—perform *tyaga*.)

***Rṇa* or debts/obligations:** Hindus recognize several duties or obligations called *rnas*, which help preserve and continue the traditions of the *rishis* through specific practices. The *Rigveda* refers to the *ṛṇatraya*—the three debts under which every human being is born. These are further elaborated in Vedic texts such as the *Taittiriya Samhitā*[31] and are collectively known as *trayo rnas* (three obligations). The term *ṛṇa* is sometimes translated as debt. The three main *rnas* are: *rsi-ṛṇa* (obligations to seers and teachers), *deva-rna* (obligations to divine manifestations of power), and *pitri-rna* (obligations to ancestors and parents). The *Satapatha Brahmana*[32] introduces an additional rna: *nri-rna* (compassion and duties towards fellow human beings and society at large).

Specific activities, ceremonies, and *yagnas* are performed to fulfil these obligations. Hindus honour divine forces, rishis, and ancestors to ensure their memory and influence continue. This includes respecting and supporting teachers to foster education and caring for family and kin as a tribute to ancestors.

Death: Hindus view death positively. Hindu tradition extends the concept of karma to the cosmic level, rejecting the notion that life ends after death or continues eternally in places like heaven or hell. Instead, the goal of life is to return to *Devattwa.* If one's life does not allow for the attainment, the process begins again in the next birth, continuing from where it was left off. Preserving the body may hinder this process, which is why Hindus cremate their dead, also conserving the earth's land resources.

As mentioned earlier, Hindus cremate their dead, this practice is based on two fundamental principles. First, once the body no longer contains life, it is believed to have fulfilled its purpose in this life and must return to the source—the five essential elements: earth, air, water, energy and space (or ether). Second, since life undergoes transformation and evolution through many births, the destruction of the body is seen as part of the rebirth process. After death, family members follow several ritual practices.

Personal behavioural observances: Shoes are considered unclean, and the feet—especially when used or shown—are viewed as symbols of disrespect. Hindus do not wear shoes in sacred places (leather shoes hold additional significance, as they are made from dead animal, such as cows). Many Hindus also refrain from bringing shoes into the central part of their homes. Striking someone with shoes is considered the worst insult, as is stepping on someone or something. Hindus avoid stepping on sacred objects, including people (who are seen as abodes of *devatas*), money, and books. If this happens by accident, they seek for forgiveness and show respect by offering a '*pranam*' (salutation). Things considered unclean, such as dead bodies, spit, faeces, and urine, are avoided during all sacred practices and rituals.

What Does It Mean to Be a Hindu?

A person who identifies as a Hindu accepts, follows, and practices the core values of Hindu Dharma is a Hindu. These values include the fundamental *darshanas,* key concepts such as dharma, karma, yoga, and divinity, adherence to ethics and morality, and other practices, as outlined in earlier sections.

To be successful in life, to be happy, and to realize one's full potential are essential goals for any human being. Hinduism offers a structure that allows individuals to choose their own path in the pursuit of life's goals (*purusarthas*). Along this path, one must be fit physically, mentally, intellectually, and spiritually, and aligned with the entire creation. This process is called yoga.

Ultimately, Hindu life is about leading a non-dogmatic, rational, yet emotionally satisfying existence. A duty-bound life provides structure, reducing doubt and stress, while encouraging respect and actions to safeguard the living space and all life forms from harm. It also emphasizes the importance of upholding dharma, including fighting against adharma and those who threaten the welfare of society. As the saying goes, '*Dharmo rakshati rakshitah*'[33] (Dharma, when upheld, protects the adherent).

Thus, to be a Hindu is to follow the principles necessary for a peaceful, harmonious, sustainable, and progressive world, all based on dharma.

Other Bharatiya Traditions

The foundation of all Hindu traditions and sects is rooted in the concepts of dharma, karma, and yoga. Dharma represents both the goal and path, while yoga is the means to achieve it. Even the ancient tradition of Zoroastrianism is based on ideas similar to those of dharma ('*Daena*' -> '*Din*') and shares a connection with the Vedic tradition.

Jain: Jainism, one of the oldest traditions in India and a strong proponent of the principle of non-violence, has a lineage of enlightened gurus known as Tirthankaras, literally 'ford-makers'.

While the practices, observances, and activities in Jainism differ significantly from mainstream Hindu traditions, Jains connect with the idea of Sanatan Dharma, particularly through their primary emphasis on *yama* and *niyama*. Around 4.2 million people follow the Jain tradition in India, and 6 million worldwide.[34]

Buddha: Although much of Buddha's experience has been assimilated by mainstream Hinduism, his teachings, which began around 550 BCE and were carried forward by his disciples after his death, formed a new tradition. In many ways, the teachings and practices of Buddhism align with the Sanatana Dharma traditions. There are several common deities that later emerged in the Mahayana branch of Buddhism, such as Saraswati and Shakti, who are also revered in mainstream Hinduism. Buddhists have placed significant emphasis on yoga, particularly in the forms of tantra and meditation. Estimates suggest there are between 350 and 500 million Buddhists worldwide[35], with 3 per cent (35 million) in India, 15 million in Sri Lanka, and over 250 million across various other Asian countries. The actual number of practising Buddhists in China is debated, with estimates ranging from 33 per cent to 80 per cent, as China was once predominantly a Buddhist country. In North America, nearly 7 million people follow the Buddhist tradition.

Sikh: Guru Nanak (1469 CE–1539 CE) founded the Sikh tradition, which emerged from the Hindu tradition. Many of the practices are similar to mainstream Hindu Bhakti Yoga. In the 16th century, when most dynasties had already been established, the Mughal Empire sought to displace them, leading to the rise of Islamic aggression. The last of the Gurus, Guru Gobind Singh (1666–1708) established the Khalsa, a community where the firstborn son of a Hindu family became a Sikh to protect Sikhism from the Mughals, particularly Emperor Aurangzeb. Sikhs were required to adopt a special dress code, which included wearing a beard and keeping a comb. The Sikh tradition is rooted in the foundation of Sanatana Dharma. Today, there are over 25 million Sikhs worldwide[36], with approximately 20 million living in India, and about 700,000 in the US, Canada, and the UK.

Common Misperceptions about Hindus and India

Though Hindu tradition is rich in honouring life, its long history has seen many inevitable turns and societal experiences that have unfortunately led to contradictory ideas and practices marring Hindu societies over the years. Power struggles among elites have resulted in exploitation in all societies, and Hindus are no exception. The hallmark of Hindu tradition is its ability to adapt and sustain itself through constant reforms. Historically, deviations, foreign invasions, and colonial rules contributed to the consolidation or emergence of certain social evils, such as caste discrimination, which can be traced back at least as far as the *Manusmriti*.

Caste: Social classification originally did not pertain to a group of people across generations but was instead based on an individual's traits and profession. This system was known as *varna* and *jati*. The term caste is not synonymous with *varna* and was used erroneously. The classifications can be simplified as thinkers (Brahmin), protectors (Kshatriya), traders (Vaishya), and service providers (Shudra). Exploitation by corrupt powers and a lack of reforms, coupled with consolidation by vested interests, led to caste or class discrimination. During periods of invasion, society entered a survival mode and became stagnant. Evidence suggests that during British rule, the concept of caste was manipulated for the rulers' benefit[37], transforming it into a major social evil. The word *dalit* means a persecuted person. *Asprishyata* (untouchability) was another issue, but these practices have no sanction in the main scriptures.[38] Such discriminations go against the founding principles of Hindu Dharma, as reflected in the Hindu worldview. Discrimination based on caste or creed is now illegal in India and punishable by law.

Dowry and child marriage: In ancient texts, the age of marriage is well-defined for both males and females, typically between

21 and 25. The first of the four stages of life, *Brahmacharya* or studentship, lasted until around the age of twenty-five[39], after which men and women entered the next stage, *Garhasthya* or family life. Over time, various factors influenced the age of marriage for women, which gradually decreased. However, many believe that child marriage and dowry practices emerged primarily during the Muslim invasions. Members of the Muslim ruling class were known to kidnap or forcibly marry young Hindu women. To counter this, many parents began marrying their daughters at a young age to protect them. This also gave rise to late-night weddings, held in secrecy, in many parts of India.[40]

Sati: Sati is the rare and uncommon practice of self-immolation by a widow on her deceased husband's funeral pyre. Evidence of this act in ancient times is scarce, and it was neither sanctioned nor prescribed by any scriptures or law books of India.[41] It may have started as a voluntary act but later became seen as a 'respectable practice' or even a '*de riguer*' custom in certain sections of Hindu society during the British period.[42] A mass instance of Sati occurred during the Muslim invasion of western India, where Hindu women, fearing capture after a military defeat, chose to jump into the fire. This tragic event is known as *Jauhar* (1303 CE, 1535–65 CE).[43] The practice is now banned by law, and in recent decades, only a few such cases have been reported.

Poverty: Hindu tradition suggests that poverty is not a desirable living condition. India was one of the wealthiest nations until the 17th century, when Christopher Columbus sought its riches. The Muslim invasions, followed by British colonialism, devastated India's economy, transforming it into one of the poorest countries. Many believe that the vast wealth stolen from India by European powers significantly contributed to the Industrial Revolution.

The *Atharvaveda* states: 'One may amass wealth with hundreds of hands, but one should also distribute it with thousands of hands. If someone keeps all that he accumulates for himself and does not give it to others, the hoarded wealth will eventually prove to be the cause of ruin.'[44]

Poverty is abhorred by the scriptures, which identify eight *durbhagyas* or misfortunes, one of which is *daridrata* or poverty. *Yaachana*, meaning begging or living in a state of dependence, and *runam*, being in debt, are also identified as *durbhagyas*. Ancient texts suggest that *durbhagyas* arise from bad karma, and thus, every Hindu is encouraged to engage in good karma to avoid misfortunes such as *daridrata*.

Cow worship: 'Worship' is not an appropriate term to describe the Hindu practice of respecting and invoking divinity. Thus, the phrase 'cow worship' is a misnomer. Hindus regard the cow as the most revered animal, although they advocate for the respect and protection of all living beings. This reverence stems from historical and practical reasons.

First, killing animals contradicts the principle of avoiding unnecessary destruction of life, which aligns with protecting the environment, economy, and overall well-being. Cows provide essential resources such as nutrition, fuel, and manure for farming. Furthermore, the cow symbolizes motherhood and the safeguarding of civilization, serving as a representative of nurturing and protection in the animal kingdom.

Hindu traditions also feature divine forms with animal attributes, such as Ganesha with an elephant's face and Sri Hanuman with a monkey's. Many animals, including cows, bulls, snakes, lions, tigers, eagles, peacocks, mice, swans, and owls, are associated with various deities as *vahanas* (vehicles). While each *vahana* has a profound symbolic meaning, these associations reflect a deep reverence for the animal kingdom.

Conclusion

For a truly sustainable life and a liveable earth, the messages of great Indian thinkers and visionaries, along with the lifestyle they advocated, are urgently needed for the world to reflect upon and promote. A world that embraces pluralism, fosters inclusiveness and tolerance, reveres life and nature, and cultivates a violence-free and progressive mindset is achievable if a critical mass—particularly world leaders—acts upon these Hindu principles.

The words of Arnold Toynbee, the renowned thinker and historian, remain strikingly relevant: 'Today we are still living in a transitional chapter of the world's history, but it is already becoming clear that a chapter which had a Western beginning will have to have an Indian ending if it is not to end in the self-destruction of the race.'[45]

How Some World Thought Leaders Viewed the Hindu System

Henry David Thoreau, American poet and philosopher:

> 'In the morning I bathe my intellect in the stupendous and cosmogonal philosophy of the Bhagvat Geeta, since whose composition years of the gods have elapsed, and in comparison with which our modern world and its literature seem puny and trivial.'[46]
>
> 'What extracts from the Vedas I have read fall on me like the light of a higher and purer luminary, which describes a loftier course through a purer stratum. It rises on me like the full moon after the stars have come out, wading through some far stratum in the sky.'[47]

Arthur Schopenhauer, German philosopher and writer:

> 'There is no religion or philosophy so sublime and elevating as Vedanta.'[48]

Ralph Waldo Emerson, American poet, essayist, and philosopher:

> 'I owed a magnificent day to the Bhagavad-Gita. It was as if an empire spoke to us, nothing small or unworthy, but large, serene, consistent, the voice of an old intelligence which in another age and climate had pondered and thus disposed of the same questions which exercise us.'[49]

Mark Twain, American writer, humourist, and essayist:

'Land of religions, cradle of human race, birthplace of human speech, grandmother of legend, great grandmother of tradition. The land that all men desire to see and having seen once even by a glimpse, would not give that glimpse for the shows of the rest of the globe combined.'[50]

Julius Robert Oppenheimer, American theoretical physicist:

'The general notions about human understanding ... which are illustrated by discoveries in atomic physics are not in the nature of things wholly unfamiliar, wholly unheard of, or new. Even in our own culture, they have a history, and in Buddhist and Hindu thought a more considerable and central place. What we shall find [in modern physics] is an exemplification, an encouragement, and a refinement of old wisdom.'[51]

'Access to the Vedas is the greatest privilege this century may claim over all previous centuries.'[52]

Werner Karl Heisenberg, German theoretical physicist:

'The startling parallelism between today's physics and the world-vision of eastern mysticism remarks, the increasing contribution of eastern scientists from India, China and Japan, among others, reinforces this conjunction. Physical science has now become planetary and draws into its fold an increasing number of non-westerners who find in its new vision of the universe many elements that are quick to note, one cannot always distinguish between statements made by eastern metaphysics based on mystical insight, and the pronouncements of modern physics based on observations, experiments and mathematical calculations.'[53]

Albert Einstein, German-born American theoretical physicist:

'When I read the Bhagavad-Gita and reflect about how God created this universe everything else seems so superfluous.'[54]

Prof. Brian David Josephson, physicist and a Nobel laureate:

'The Vedanta and the Sankhya hold the key to the laws of mind and thought process which are co-related to the Quantum Field, i.e., the operation and distribution of particles at atomic and molecular levels.'[55]

Harvey Cox, Harvard Divinity School:

'I agree that the quest for Truth is the quest for God. This is the core teaching of all religions. The Scientist's motivation is to seek the very kind of truth that Krishna speaks about in the Bhagavad Gita. I also agree that the word Religion is an invention of modern western thought.'[56]

Sir V.S. Naipaul, author and Nobel laureate:

'The key Hindu concept of dharma—the right way, the sanctioned way, which all men must follow, according to their natures—is an elastic concept. At its noblest it combines self-fulfillment and truth to the self with the ideas of action as duty, action as its own spiritual reward, man as a holy vessel.'[57]

Prof. A.H.L. Heeren, German historian:

'The historians who have inquired into the religion and learning of the East have almost always been obliged to revert to India for information in their researches. That distant country, however, as at no former period attracted the attention of Europeans in these particular years so much as the present day. From the time that it became subject to the English, it has excited their regard, not more by its productions than by its arts and literature. And the learned of Great Britain now flatter themselves, that they had at length discovered the sources from which, not only the rest of Asia, but the whole Western World derived their knowledge and their religion.'[58]

CHAPTER 8

Bengal's Contribution to Modern Patriotism and Nationalism

Bengal in Modern Indian History

Bengal has a long tradition of Jain, Buddhist, and Vedic Hindu practices. During the 4th–3rd centuries BCE, Bengal was entirely under the influence of the Jain tradition. Jainism remained prevalent throughout Bengal until the 11th century. While the Buddhist influence had been present since the time of the Mauryan Empire, including Ashoka's reign from the end of the 2nd century BCE, it became more prominent around 750 CE with the advent of the Pala Dynasty. By the 9th century, Buddhist influence had waned, and the Vedic Hindu tradition was reestablished. However, due to the long-standing influence of Jain and Buddhist traditions, the Brahmin and Kshatriya classes suffered, and a weakened social order prevailed by the time the Muslims arrived in Bengal.

In the 14th and 15th centuries, when Turko-Afghan Islamic forces were attacking much of India, Bengal remained distant from the central action around Delhi. The Sufis played a central role in the Islamic conversion in eastern India. Forcible conversion was initially practised, but it is widely accepted that 'the single most important factor that contributed to the large-scale conversion to Islam in Bengal was the influence of the Sufis.'[1] Sufi religious preachers, sometimes referred to as 'saints', were also known as

Pir, Darvish, and other titles. These religious mendicants, who arrived in Bengal from West and Central Asia by the 15th century, established their ummahs and dargahs around the graves of revered individuals across Bengal. These establishments became centres for preaching, conversion, and the initiation of followers.

The second wave of proselytism was carried out by Turkish mercenaries and Middle Eastern traders who arrived with the Muslim forces in eastern India at the beginning of the 13th century and began settling in Bengal. While forcible conversion was the initial approach, later, lower-caste Hindus were attracted to Islam. The Buddhist groups, weakened by a lack of political power and support, were particularly vulnerable. Their 'non-violent' nature, with no means to resist the armed Muslims, led to their easy defeat or conversion.

During this time, the Hindu upper caste, especially the Brahmins, held significant influence, not only because of their caste status but also due to their involvement with the Mughals. Their local representatives granted them many privileges, and they became landlords. Not many from this group were forcibly converted, but some accepted conversion for special privileges and wealth. Many Hindus, particularly the poor and illiterate peasants, were deceived into accepting the Sufis as gurus and converted. These Sufis played a crucial role in establishing Muslim rule in Bengal. Makhdum Shah and Jalal Shah were two prominent figures in this process. Khan Jahan Ali was another key figure in South Bengal during the 15th century.

Hazrat Khan Jahan Ali, a Muslim strongman and preacher from Jessore, Bengal, was highly influential. One local Brahmin leader, Gobindalal Roy, who knew Jahan Ali, was tricked into converting to Islam. Gobindalal took the name Mohammad Tahir Pir Ali and became very wealthy. Although his relatives did not convert, they were ostracized by the orthodox Hindu Brahmins and were thereafter derogatorily called the 'Pirali Brahmins'.[2]

Jagannath Bandyopadhyay, belonging to the Rarhiya Brahmin class of the Kushari (Sandilya gotra) division, was the zamindar (landlord) of Pithabhog in Jessore district, Bengal, and married a daughter of a 'Priali' Brahmin named Sukhdev. Jagannath's grandson Panchanan later moved to the western part of Bengal, to a settlement on the bank of the Ganga called Govindapur, one of the three settlements that would form modern-day Kolkata. Due to their high priestly status, the locals referred to them as 'Thakurs' (Godmen). The English associates of the East India Company, unable to pronounce 'Thakur', called them 'Tagore' (as in Rabindranath Thakur/Tagore).[3]

Throughout history, there are certain *yuga sandhi* or transitional periods in the history of nations that lead them in a new direction. The 1700s marked such a period for Bengal as it witnessed several significant events. The first major historical event was the Battle of Plassey (Palashi) on 23 June 1757, followed by the arrival of the British East India Company (EIC). The EIC had attacked and captured Calcutta on 2 January 1757.

In the following century, three major personalities were born in the eastern part of India, each responsible for the country's spiritual, social, and political reawakening. Raja Ram Mohan Roy, born in 1772, played a pivotal role in reforming Hindu society, creating political awareness among Hindus, and redefining Hindu thoughts and practices regarding divinity. Just three years after his death in 1833, Ramakrishna Paramhansa was born in 1836. His disciple, Swami Vivekananda, who invigorated the nation, was born in 1863. This hundred-year period marked a turning point for India's return to its original heritage and tradition. The movements that followed gave rise to many of India's great leaders.

Raja Ram Mohan Roy (1772–1833)

Raja, or Rajarshi, Ram Mohan Roy was a 'Yuga Purush' or 'Renaissance Man' during a transitional period in Indian history when the influence of the Mughals ended and Western colonial and imperial forces arrived in India.

Apart from the Thakurs or Tagores, another prominent family in Bengal was that of the so-called 'Pirali Brahmin' family of Ram Mohan Roy. Members of the Roy family served in the Mughal administration for three generations. Krishan Chander Banerjee, Roy's great-grandfather, was in the service of Murshid Quli Khan, the *subedar* (governor) of Bengal. For his excellent service as a revenue officer, he was honoured with the title '*Raya Rayan*' (in Sanskrit, *Raya* means Raja, *Rayan* means Rajan or king). Over time, *Raya Rayan* became Roy or Ray. His grandfather, Braja Binod Roy, a devout Vaishnava, served under the Bengal nawabs, Murshid Quli Khan, and his successor Ali Vardi Khan. Ram Mohan's father, Rama Kanta, also served in the nawab's administration and procured a zamindari (landlordship) after the EIC defeated the nawab in the Battle of Plassey in 1757. Roy worked for several EIC officers while maintaining connections with the Mughal legacy. Roy's paternal great-grandfather, Krishan Chander Banerjee (or Bandyopadhyay), is believed to be a descendant of Narottama Dasa Thakura (also known as Shri Thakura Mahasaya), a follower of Sri Chaitanya Mahaprabhu.[4]

Who was Raja Ram Mohan Roy? This is what Rabindranath Tagore said about him: 'Our futility will be in the measure of the greatness of Ram Mohan Roy.'[5] He is often referred to as the 'Renaissance man of modern India'. Yet, some people who have never even read his original writings continue to criticize him, accusing him of being anti-Hindu, anti-Sanskrit, a British agent, pro-Christian, and a supporter of conversion, among other things. To truly understand him, one must study his life and work from original sources. Many people who have not done the basic research on Roy spread biased opinions based on secondary and tertiary sources.[6]

If we look back at Roy's roots, we can gain insight into his influences. As the son of a Mughal official, he was sent to a madrasa in Patna at the age of nine to learn Arabic and Persian, the court language of the time. This education was necessary for him to secure a good job. Some suggest[7] that his ideas of 'monotheism' and resentment against 'idolatry' were developed by the influence of the Quran. While it is possible that a nine-year-old might have been influenced, it is unlikely that what is often attributed to him is entirely accurate—he never became an 'iconoclast'.

He was equally proficient in Sanskrit and travelled to Varanasi at the age of eleven, where he studied the scriptures in their original form and later translated many of them. He spent ten years in Varanasi. Additionally, he spent several years in Tibet, learning about the Buddhist tradition.

His real education in the *shastras* took place at home, under the tutelage of Nandakumar Vidyalankara, also known as Hariharanandanath Tirthaswami Kulabadhuta, a Sakta *vamacara tantrika sannyasi* (*abhadoot*). Roy developed the idea of one Brahman manifesting in many forms, most likely from his practice of tantra, initiated by his friend and guru, Hariharananda Bharati. One of his early works was the translation of the *Mahanirvana Tantra* and *Kularnava Tantra*. He was born near a Shaktipeeth—Ratnavali (dedicated to Adi Shakti in the form of Kumari) and near Tarakeswar, which is famous for its Shiva temple. Although he may have expressed criticism of murti puja, he himself studied tantra under the guidance of his guru and undoubtedly visited these temples.

After moving to Calcutta (now Kolkata), Roy studied many scriptures, including the *Brahmasutrabhasya* and the *bhasyas* of Sankaracharya on the *Talavakara*, *Isha Upanishad*, *Katha Upanishad*, *Mandukya Upanishad*, and *Mundaka Upanishad*. He studied these texts at the *'tol'* (Sanskrit school) of the eminent Vedanta scholar and Supreme Court pandit Mrtyunjaya Vidyalaya Sivaprasad Sharma. Later, Ramacandra Vidyabagis, the brother of Hariharananda, became Roy's guru. Ramacandra was a student of Vidyavacaspati Goswami Bhattacharya of Santipur, one of the few *mathas* (hermitage schools) in 18th-century Bengal. Therefore, it is clear that Roy was a product of the traditional *matha* system in Bengal.

Not content with just Sanskrit and English, Roy also learned Hebrew and Latin to read biblical texts in their original form. This allowed him to challenge the Christian missionaries on their activities in India and confront the discrimination and malpractices of the EIC. Roy also addressed the siphoning of Indian wealth to Britain, which deprived Indians of their resources. His battles with Christian missionaries and the EIC disprove the notion that he had any allegiance to either the Christians or the British administration.

In the 19th-century, the Mughal king in Delhi, Akbar Shah II (1760–1837), was merely a figurehead and had to live under the control of the EIC. Initially, the EIC recognized the Mughals and, to appease them and enhance their power structure, had the Mughal king's name minted on coins alongside the royal logo. Akbar II was secular and nominated his son, Mirza Jahangir, as his heir apparent. However, a conflict arose between Mirza and the British resident, Archibald Seton, resulting in Mirza being imprisoned. Akbar II desperately requested Roy to go to London to persuade the British to undo this injustice and increase his pension.

Akbar Shah re-honoured Roy with the title of Raja, which his family had already held (Raya, Roy), and sponsored his trip to England in 1829. This provided Roy with a great opportunity to travel to England to pursue some of his own goals. He had heard that the British might overturn the bill banning Sati and wanted to ensure that this did not happen. Roy also sought to confront, debate, and defeat the Christian evangelists by bringing the battle between India and missionaries to their own territory. He dreamed of proving that Hindu Dharma was the 'mother of religions', a vision that Vivekananda realized at the Parliament of Religions in Chicago in 1893, sixty-four years later.

When Roy arrived in Liverpool, England, in 1830, he was greeted with great fanfare and honoured by aristocrats, reformers, and scholars. His name quickly spread to America. In 1833, after three years of eventful activities, success, and achievements, Roy became physically exhausted and unwell. While in Bristol, he contracted meningitis and soon passed away. During that time, there was little provision for cremation in England, so, he was buried by his hosts in Arno's Vale Cemetery near Bristol. Minister Lant Carpenter delivered a funeral sermon to a crowd of a thousand people at Lewin's Mead Chapel.

Contrary to the false propaganda that he adopted Christianity, Roy had taken a Brahmin cook on his trip to England, wore the sacred thread, and uttered the sacred 'Aum' sound during his final moments.[8] Many Hindus are unaware that there is a tradition of '*samadhi*' for saintly individuals, a special burial rather than cremation. There are many examples of this, such as the Sankaracharyas and the founder of the International Society for Krishna Consciousness (ISKCON), Srila Prabhupada, who were buried in the Hindu tradition.

It seems that Roy's final wish was to go to England to challenge Christianity and promote Vedanta. Although he did not live long enough to fully realize this mission, it was later accomplished when Swami Vivekananda followed in his footsteps, beginning in 1893.

According to his biographer, Robertson:

> Any kernel of similarity between Judeo-Christian and Advaita theology is not an example of a shared common core, but something that was originally, and more perfectly, prefigured in the Vedas and Upanishads. Roy's view was that it was this Upanishadic Advaita theology, predating Islam and Christianity by a millennium, was the highest form of religion.[9]

A grave injustice has been done to Roy by not giving him sufficient presence in history books. The people of India have forgotten him and exiled him, while his mortal remains rest in Bristol, England. As a humble attempt to rectify the lack of knowledge about Roy, we shall examine his life and works in the following pages. We begin by reflecting on Raja Ram Mohan Roy, his contributions, and his influence on other great Indian leaders.

In an address entitled 'Inaugurator of the Modern Age' in India, Rabindranath Tagore said:

> He was born at a time when our country having lost its link with the inmost truths of its being, struggled under a crushing load of unreason, in abject slavery to circumstance. In social usage, in politics, in the realm of religion and art, we had entered the zone of uncreative habit, of decadent tradition and ceased to exercise our humanity. In this dark gloom of India's degeneration [Ram Mohan] rose up, a luminous star in the firmament of India's history, with prophetic purity of vision and unconquerable heroism of soul.[10]

Sri Aurobindo declared: 'Raja [Ram Mohan] Roy was a great man in the first rank of active genius and set flowing a stream of tendencies which have transformed our national life.'[11] Gopal Krishna Gokhale referred to him as the 'Father of Modern India'.[12] Swami Vivekananda said:

> The great Hindu reformer, Raja Ram Mohan Roy, was a wonderful example of this unselfish work. He devoted his whole life to helping India. It was he who stopped the burning of widows. It is usually believed that this reform was due entirely to the English; but it was Raja Ram Mohan Roy who started the agitation against the custom and succeeded in obtaining the support of the Government in suppressing it. Until he began the movement, the English had done nothing. He also founded the important religious society called the Brahmo-Samaj, and subscribed a hundred thousand dollars to found a university. He then stepped out and told them to go ahead without him. He cared nothing for fame or for results to himself.[13]

According to Sister Nivedita, 'He [Vivekananda] claimed himself to have taken up the task that the breadth and foresight of Ram Mohun Roy had mapped out.'[14]

Netaji Subhas Chandra Bose, in turn, said:

> Ram Mohan urged a return to the original principles of Vedantism and for a total rejection of all the religions and social impurities

> that had crept into Hinduism in later times. He also advocated an all-around regeneration of the social and national life and the acceptance of all that is useful and beneficial in the modern life of Europe. Raja Ram Mohan Roy, therefore, stands out against the dawn of the new awakening in India as the prophet of the new age ... Raja Ram Mohan Roy has come to be called the Maker of Modern India.[15]

Chittaranjan Das said:

> There is no doubt that he was the first who held before us the ideal of freedom. He was the first to sound the note of freedom in every department of life and in every different culture that has met today in India. It may be that we have to modify that, it may be we have to analyse that more carefully and more in detail for the purpose of scientific study but it is enough for our purpose to say that he inaugurated many reforms – you might call that reforming activity. He inaugurated the reforms which again, in turn, gave rise to reaction which, again, gave rise to further reforms which made the nation turn on itself, till at last, it began to be self-conscious.[16]

Yes, indeed, he is the Father of the Indian Renaissance, the Father of Modern India, the initiator of the Hindu awakening that gave rise to the Hindutva movement, and the maker of modern India. While he was given the title Raja, the more befitting title, after understanding all his contributions, is *Rajarshi* (Raja and Rishi in one).

Sophia Dobson Collet, a biographer of Roy, noted:

> Rammohun Roy taught the people to realise that everything that had come down from the past was not ideal and that a living society stood in constant need of readjustment to varying circumstances. Thus a new era of conscious, active reform was inaugurated in the Hindu society of which Raja Rammohun was the leader and pioneer.[17]

Collet also observed that Roy 'presents a most instructive and inspiring study for the new India, of which he is the type and pioneer'.[18] She added, 'He embodies the new spirit, its freedom, its large human sympathy, its pure and sifted ethics, along with its reverent but not uncritical regard for the past and prudent disinclination towards revolt.'[19]

Finally, she concluded:

> There is here in germ the national aspiration which is now breaking forth into cries for representation of India in the Imperial Parliament, 'Home Rule for India' and even 'India for the Indians.' The prospect of an educated India ... seems to have never been long absent from Rammohun's mind, and he did, however vaguely, claim in advance for his countrymen the political rights which progress in civilisation inevitably involves. Here again, Ram Mohan stands forth as the tribune and prophet of New India.[20]

According to Professor Lynn Zastoupil, '[Ram Mohan] has often bestowed with the title of the Father of modern India ... While impact of [Ram Mohan's] ideas and activities on Indian society is generally accepted to have been extensive, [Ram Mohan] also exerted considerable influence in Victorian British society.'

The author locates Ram Mohan within a nexus of British (and to a lesser extent, North American) social, political, and religious reformers—including Unitarians, radicals, early feminists, and advocates of liberty of the press and free trade—and 'analyzes the ways in which [Ram Mohan's] passions intersected with the projects of reformers and humanitarians in Britain'.[21]

Zastoupil further noted:

> His celebrity should thus be read as evidence of Victorian society in the making: Britons thronged to see Rammohun because in him they could see reflected what the dismantling of the established order held in store for themselves. This, and Roy's dialogue and correspondence with the Unitarians in the 1820s, suggests that, whilst he was partly influenced by Western ideas, he also had a profound influence on the thinking of Westerners.[22]

When Henry Ware asked Roy in a letter in 1824 about the possibility of converting Hindus to Christianity, he responded, 'No human possibility exists of converting the Hindoo to any sect of Christianity.' Raja Ram Mohan Roy spoke more directly about the success of the Unitarian missionaries, responding firmly in the negative. Examples of these can be found in his letters.[23]

An example like this shows us the problems Roy had with Christianity. He had started to translate some Christian texts into Bengali and Hindi but stopped midway as he rejected the Christian doctrine of the Trinity. Instead, he wrote the 'Precepts of Jesus'. The same was the case with his biography of Muhammad. It is apparent that, after much research, Roy felt that these works would expose Christianity and Islam in a very negative light or that he found so much incompatible with his Vedantic vision that he could not continue. The 'Precepts of Jesus' was essentially an exercise in analyzing Jesus and Christianity through Hindu lenses.

The fundamental Christian belief in the Trinity of the Father, Son, and the Holy Ghost was 'completely discarded as baseless and destroyed the key pillars of Christianity'.[24]

After Roy published the booklet 'Precepts of Jesus' for the Baptists, it was reviewed in a Christian missionary publication, *Friends of India*, which expressed the fear that 'Precepts of Jesus' might 'greatly injure the cause of truth' (that is, Christian doctrines).[25] He then openly invited the Baptists for a public debate. Roy presented Jesus in the booklet as a great human but not as the Messiah or the Son of God. He suggested that Jesus would be remembered primarily for his nature, not his message. He 'did not grant Jesus any authority except the power of his message'.[26]

Raja Ram Mohan Roy's Key Contributions

He conceived and propagated the Brahmo Sabha, later known as the Brahmo Samaj, alongside Dwarakanath Thakur. This platform became a major institution for India's spiritual, social, and political transformation.

Reform of Hindu Spiritual and Religious Practices

Roy had to grapple with the concepts of 'religion' and 'theology' in order to articulate his tradition not only to the Christians but also to his fellow countrymen. During his time, he had to adopt the same terminologies used by the English people, as this was the language of communication. Although Roy is often credited with coining the term 'Hinduism', it was actually introduced by the evangelists decades earlier. Roy merely used their terms to facilitate communication.

Hindu society, at the time, was heavily immersed in rituals and lacked a deep understanding of the original texts, such as the Vedas and Upanishads, which were accessible only to a select few. This gap in knowledge is what triggered Roy's struggle with orthodoxy. His main intention was to guide people away from ritualistic, sometimes convoluted practices, and encourage them to focus on original sources, such as the Vedas, to bring back the authentic Bharatiya *adhyatmic* traditions. Roy worked towards educating the general public by translating these texts from the original Sanskrit. He also read translations of Greek philosophers.

He strongly believed that religious reform was essential for both social reform and political modernization. In 1815, in Rangpur, he conceived the idea of setting up as reformist religious association, the Atmiya Sabha. This vision culminated in the establishment of the Brahmo Sabha in 1828, which later became the Brahmo Samaj, a platform for religious, social, and political transformation.

On one hand, Roy focused on the internal reform of Hindu society, seeking to restore the true essence of Sanatan Dharma through the study of the Vedas and the Upanishads. On the other hand, he had to fight against Christian missionaries in order to halt conversions. Rabindranath Tagore remarked, '[Ram Mohan] brought back the life into Hindu Dharma ... A Christian revolution was inevitable if [Ram Mohan] did not crush it. For that, Indians are indebted to him forever.'[27] Tagore also said,

'Roy saved Hindu Dharma; he also revived and reinstated the Vedic Sanatan Dharma.'[28]

In his introduction to the *Isha Upanishad*, Roy wrote: 'From considerations like these, it has been that I (although born a Brahmin and instructed in my youth in all the principles of that sect), being thoroughly convinced of the lamentable errors of my countrymen, have been stimulated to employ every means in my power to improve their minds and lead them to the knowledge of a purer system of morality.'

> It was a matter of time that [Ram Mohan] passionately pleaded and worked for social change; yet he was not a revolutionary. He had, in fact, the shrewdness to understand that Indian society of his time simply did not admit of revolutionary transformation, but it did have the flexibility for slow adjustment. And thus, his effort at making reforms – social, religious and economic – from within. It was in this context that [Ram Mohan] challenged the prevailing priestly class which invented and perpetuated certain corrupt dogmas and doctrines and derived benefits from them … to the utmost of their, power, by keeping the knowledge of their scriptures concealed from the rest of, the people.[29]

Girijashankar Raychaudhuri stated that Ram Mohan, for the first time in this era, revived the immense wealth of the Vedas and the Upanishads, which had been forgotten for a long time.[30]

Preventing Mass Conversion to Christianity

As India was beginning to recover from centuries of Islamist occupation, Roy developed critical views on Islam and Muhammed, despite having attended a madrasa during his early childhood. His sarcastic remarks about Muhammad provoked the ire of local Mullahs, prompting him to move to Calcutta.

In Calcutta, where he worked under the EIC, Roy engaged with Englishmen and encountered several Christian missionaries. He realized that unless the missionaries were challenged, they would continue their unchecked efforts at mass conversion. To confront them, he studied Biblical literature in its original Hebrew and Latin, and soon began publicly debating with the evangelists. Meanwhile, he strategically built a relationship with the Unitarians, who were less orthodox than the Baptists. Roy's goal was to reform Christianity through connections with the Unitarians. It may not be an exaggeration to say that Roy was one of the first to challenge Christianity in both India and England.

It is remarkable to recall his work during those days when he was boldly challenging the missionaries, at a time when political power lay with the all-powerful nation of Britain and the EIC. As a genius endowed with both intellectual and *adhyatmic* power, he relied on logic and facts, presenting only the truth.

While Roy worked closely with the Unitarians, he distanced himself from them towards the end, as he had already achieved success in his mission. It is now clear that his aim was to diminish the zeal of the missionary zealots and see them fade away. By subtly creating a rift among Christian groups, he ultimately benefitted Hindu society, as the Unitarian Society never maintained much popularity and shut down in the early months of 1828.[31]

Gradually, all Christian missionaries, except a few Unitarians, began leaving Calcutta. In the two centuries since Roy's time, many more missionaries have come to India, but the Christian population in Bengal remains minuscule, and Hindus owe this to Rajarshi.

Education

According to Raja Ram Mohan Roy, 'For by a reference to history, it may be proved that the World was indebted to our ancestors for the first dawn of knowledge which sprang up in the East, and thanks to the Goddess of Wisdom, we still have a philosophical and copious language of our own, which distinguishes us from other nations.'[32]

Raja Ram Mohan Roy's vision for India's education was rooted in realism. He founded Hindu College (1817) and Vedanta

College (1825), where both the ancient knowledge of the Vedas and modern developments could be imparted. He envisioned promoting subjects like mathematics, geography, and Latin, which were necessary to help Indians keep pace with the rest of the world.

He opposed Sanskrit as the medium of education since it was no longer a spoken language. He was also against the establishment of the Sanskrit College, which was promoted by the British. Had he supported the Sanskrit College, proposed and managed by the British, it would have led to indirect control over Brahmin Pandits by 'buying' them, much like the Islamic rulers did. This would have enabled the British to control society through the institution.

While some critics still blame Roy for Sanskrit not becoming the national language, he genuinely promoted it through the establishment of Hindu College and Vedanta College. He revitalized Hindu Sanatan Dharma and Sanskrit education in his Vedanta school. Rajnarayan Basu (1826–99), also a Brahmo, was a prominent writer and leader of the Renaissance movement in Bengal. Along with Nabagopal Mitra, he started the Hindu Mela. He studied at the Vedanta and Hindu Colleges, both founded and supported by Ram Mohan. He was the maternal grandfather of Sri Aurobindo.

Unfortunately, figures like Macaulay took advantage of the English medium for education, conspiring to build a Western colonial system designed to create 'clerks' for their use. Even then, geniuses like Vivekananda, Aurobindo, and Netaji made use of the same system to learn about world affairs and developed their own inspiring ideas and methods to cultivate patriotism among the masses.

Society and Women

Raja Ram Mohan Roy's social reforms included the abolition of sati, child marriage, polygamy, and *purdah* (female seclusion). The practice of seclusion or physical segregation of women, introduced by Islam in India, required women to cover their bodies (concealing their skin, form, and appearance). This practice was later imposed on Hindu women, particularly those from the 'upper-classes'. Roy also campaigned for women's education, the right to inherit property, inter-caste marriage, and the right of widows to remarry. Many of these pioneering efforts were later advanced by Vidyasagar. Roy also fought against caste discrimination and untouchability.

Authorities and legal experts in England consulted him on the Bengal Sati Regulation case. In 1832, he attended the three-day hearing before the Privy Council, which upheld Bentinck's law banning sati. After the victory, Roy rejoiced, saying, 'As we [Indians] can no longer be guilty of female murder, we now deserve every improvement, temporal and spiritual.'

Legal and Governance Reform

Roy's biographer wrote:

> [Ram Mohan] Roy's presence in this country made the English people aware, as they had never seen before, of the dignity, the culture and the piety of the race they had conquered in the East. India became incarnate in him, and dwelt among us, and we beheld her glory. In the court of the King, in the halls of the legislature, in the select coteries of fashion, in the society of philosophers and men of letters, in Anglican church and non-conformist meeting-house, in the privacy of many a home, and before the wondering crowds of Lancashire operatives, [Ram Mohan] Roy stood forth the visible and personal embodiment of our eastern empire. ...Wherever he went, there went a stately refutation of the Anglo-Indian insolence which saw in an Indian fellow subject only a 'black man' or a 'nigger', as he had interpreted England to India, so now he interpreted India to England.[33]
>
> Indeed, the thoroughness and vigor of the Raja's political efforts were astonishing. Even at an early age he carried his political agitations to the very center of the seat of authority. His visit to England, fraught as it was with the manifold consequences, had a far-reaching effect on the politics of India.

> One of the main objectives which he had in view in going to England was to lay before the British public the cause of India, and in this mission, he was remarkably successful.[34]

As a statesman, Roy navigated the British legal system with exceptional professionalism. His well-researched arguments, delivered with remarkable precision, left a significant impact wherever he presented them. During his visit to London, he advocated for several judicial reforms and was largely successful. Below are a few examples of his advocacy work:

- Substitution of English for Persian as the official language of the courts of law.
- Appointment of native assessors in civil courts and the introduction of jury trials.
- Separation of the offices of judge and revenue commissioner, as well as those of judge and magistrate.
- Codification of criminal and civil law in India.
- Significant employment of Indians in the civil service.
- Consultation of public opinion before enacting legislation.

Roy convinced the Parliament to allow imported salt to compete with the salt monopoly in India. He also demanded the abolition of taxes on tax-free lands and worked to reduce export duties on Indian goods, advocating for the abolition of the EIC's trading rights. While India continues to carry the legacy of British administrative services, nearly 200 years ago, he called for the Indianization of these service posts and the separation of the executive from the judiciary. Finally, he demanded equality between Indians and Europeans in various services.

Although he himself was a zamindar (landlord), he championed the cause of agricultural peasants against the zamindars. He demonstrated that, although the zamindars had greatly benefitted from the Permanent Settlement of 1793, the condition of the actual cultivators and farmers remained as miserable as ever, with zamindars at liberty to constantly increase rents. 'Such is the melancholy condition of agricultural labourers,' he wrote, 'that it always gives me the greatest pain to allude to it.' What remedy did he propose? First, the prohibition of any further rent increases, and second, a reduction in the revenue demanded from zamindars by British authorities to ensure a corresponding reduction in rents.

Collet concluded:

> Thus [Ram Mohan] was the champion of the people at large and not of the class to which he himself belonged. Many of the reforms he advocated have already been carried out, and the political leaders of the present day are still working out the programme he laid down. Babu Surendra Nath Banerjee thus acknowledges in the address already referred to the political foresight of the Raja: 'It is remarkable how he anticipated us in some of the great political problems of today.'[35]

Later, we will explore how he sowed the seeds for freedom, nationalism, and politics.

Globalizing Hindu Thoughts

Roy was the first Indian to propagate the knowledge of the Vedas and Vedantic ideas outside India, spreading these teachings across Europe and America. The American Transcendental movement found its origin in Roy's works. Through his connections with the Unitarians in Calcutta, his writings reached a wide audience in both Britain and America. In a letter written in 1821, the renowned American Unitarian Ralph Waldo Emerson remarked:

> We have in Calcutta, a very learned native, a Hindoo of very large fortune, and a Brahmin ... and is now what we should call Free-thinker ... He is one of the first scholars in India, Europeans not excepted, quite a critic of the dead European languages, and is altogether one of the first men of the age. The Brahmin's name is [Ram Mohan] Roy.[36]

Roy had studied and grappled with the exotic facts about India, which had been appearing with increasing frequency in

New England (northeast America) journals and travel accounts since the turn of the century.[37]

The *Christian Register* and other periodicals in England frequently discussed Roy. The *Christian Observer* of London wrote about him as early as 1816. In Boston, Ram Mohan was introduced to the locals. The *Christian Disciple* and *Christian Examiner* in 1824 referred to him as a 'remarkable Hindoo Reformer'. The *North American Review* published an article titled 'Theology of the Hindoos, as taught by Ram Mohun Roy', citing several long passages from Roy's translations of the *Kena Upanishad* and *Isha Upanishad*.[38]

Hodder writes:

> According to Kenneth Walter Cameron, Emerson borrowed ideas from these Upanishad's to write his poem for his Harvard College graduation, 'Indian Superstition'. Cameron also noted: '[In] the publicity about [Ram Mohan] Roy who was for the young Emerson and his contemporaries a living representative of all those virtues of idealism and high mindedness which Emerson found refracted here and there throughout India's sacred books'.[39]

According to Zastoupil, the Unitarians had a broad political and social impact in 19th-century Britain, as they actively participated in civic life and social reform, while also circulating their own and Roy's ideas widely.[40] He had a significant influence on the British Unitarians.

His father, William Emerson, was the editor of the *Monthly Anthology* and *Boston Review*, which printed items on India as early as 1803.[41]

Emerson was impressed and influenced after reading Roy's translations, particularly the *Isha Upanishad* (1820) and Thoreau's translation of the *Principal Vedas* (1850). Emerson was assigned the topic 'Indian Superstition' as his thesis for graduation at Harvard College in 1821. He read Roy's translation of the Hindu scriptures and, together with Henry David Thoreau, the American naturalist, essayist, poet, and philosopher, promoted Transcendentalism in New England (America), which profoundly influenced the American spiritual reawakening.[42] This later made it somewhat easier for Swami Vivekananda to spread when he visited America half a century later in 1893.

The translations of the *Harivansh*, *Laws of Manu*, the Bhagavad Gita, and the *Samkhya Karikas* deeply influenced Thoreau.[43] After 1850, however, references to Oriental religions in his journals became less frequent. One notable episode in this regard during the following decade was the arrival in Concord of a truckload containing forty-four Oriental books from Thoreau's English friend, Thomas Cholmondeley. This event held greater significance for the broader transmission of Oriental ideas than for their formative impact on Emerson and Thoreau themselves. Nonetheless, Thoreau described it as a 'princely gift', thanked Cholmondeley profusely, and even built a special case from driftwood to house the collection.[44]

Henry David Thoreau was dissatisfied with the spirituality he found in Christianity. In a letter to his friend H.G.O. Blake in 1849, he wrote: 'Depend upon it, that rude and careless as I am, I would fain practice the yoga faithfully. To some extent, and at rare intervals, even I am a yogin.'[45]

India was regarded as the 'cradle of the human race', a sentiment famously expressed by Mark Twain. However, we find a similar view in Thoreau's writings decades before Twain. Thoreau believed: 'Farthest India is nearer to me than Concord or Lexington.'[46] He also wrote: 'Was not Asia mapped in my brain before it was any Geography? In my brain is the [Sanskrit], which contains the history of primitive times. The Vedas and their Angas are not so ancient as my serenest contemplations.'[47]

'Though neither Emerson nor Thoreau made any significant reference to Roy in his writings, it is well known that they were familiar with his work. Emerson read Roy's translation of [Isha Upanishad] in 1820 and Thoreau's translation of the Principal Vedas in 1850. The correspondence between Roy and British

Unitarians was published in Boston in 1824 by Henry Ware, a prominent American Unitarian.'

Emerson and Thoreau influenced Walt Whitman, the American poet, essayist, and journalist, who, in turn, inspired Edward Carpenter, an English socialist, poet, and philosopher.[48] Emerson also influenced two prominent philosophers: Friedrich Nietzsche (German) and William James (American).

Thoreau's writings went on to influence many public figures, including US President John F. Kennedy, American civil rights activist Martin Luther King Jr, US Supreme Court Justice William O. Douglas, and the Russian author Leo Tolstoy. American economist Murray Rothbard noted that 'all spoke of being strongly affected by Thoreau's work, particularly Civil Disobedience'.[49]

Thoreau also inspired numerous artists, authors, and other prominent figures, including Marcel Proust (French Novelist), William Butler Yeats (Irish Poet), and Ernest Hemingway (American novelist),[50] as well as Frank Lloyd Wright (American designer), John Muir (American naturalist),[51] and even George Bernard Shaw.[52]

Dr John Thornton Kirkland, then president of Harvard University, exchanged correspondence and held meetings with Ram Mohan Roy. In London in 1831, a special meeting of the Unitarian Association was held in Roy's honour, where Kirkland was present. On this occasion, he said, 'It is well known that the Rajah is an object of lively interest in America, and he is expected there with the greatest anxiety.'[53]

Similarly, Swami Vivekananda influenced many eminent figures in both Europe and America, ensuring that the globalization of Indian ideas and thought—initiated by Raja Ram Mohan Roy—would continue for centuries to come.

It is said that Roy 'was the toast of London, Philadelphia, and Boston'. He was an international celebrity and a world-class statesman, known to President Thomas Jefferson's inner circle, President John Quincy Adams, Ralph Waldo Emerson, Arthur

Schopenhauer, Jeremy Bentham, and the movers and shakers of Parliament.[54]

His portrait was painted in London by renowned artists such as Samuel De Wilde[55] and two of America's greatest painters: Gilbert Stuart Newton of Boston and Rembrandt Peale of Baltimore. Even Napoleon Bonaparte's court painter created a portrait of him.[56]

Although Emerson never met the Raja, he paid tribute to him with these words: 'It is a faithful saying, worthy of all acceptation, that a reasoning man, conscious of his powers and duties, annihilates all distinction of circumstances.'[57]

Raja Ram Mohan Roy can undoubtedly be called the Father of Modern India's Renaissance and the greatest reformer of the 19th century, as he inaugurated 'the age of enlightenment and liberal reformist modernization in India'. At the same time, he remains one of India's most important global leaders and icons.

Brahmo Samaj

Founded on 20 August 1828 by Raja Ram Mohan Roy and Dwarakanath Tagore, the Brahmo Sabha began in Calcutta and became the first and most influential religio-social-political reform movement in 19th-century India, playing a pivotal role in the making of modern India.[58] This movement, also known as the Bengal Renaissance, pioneered religious, social, educational, and political reforms.

In 1861, Brahmo Sabha members in Lahore, led by Pandit Nobin Chandra Roy, along with several Bengalis from the Lahore Bar Association, renamed the organization Brahmo Samaj and formally inaugurated it.[59] Soon after, branches were established in various parts of India, including Punjab, Quetta, Rawalpindi, Amritsar, and Calcutta. As a young man, Swami Vivekananda actively participated in Brahmo Samaj activities.[60]

The Brahmo Samaj began criticizing the British Crown for its unjust practices, and the Brahmo movement gradually transformed into Hindutva (Hindu-ness) and nationalism (Indian-ness).

Subsequently, the Tagore family initiated a powerful Swadeshi movement called the Hindu Mela. In April 1867, the Hindu Mela was established on Chaitra Sankranti, the last day of the Bengali calendar.

The event featured an exhibition showcasing indigenous artwork, handicrafts, cottage industries, and more. Within the formal structure of a committee, Gajendranath Tagore (great-grandson of Dwarakanath and nephew of Rabindranath) became the first secretary, while Nabagopal Mitra, the organizer of the mela, served as assistant secretary. Among the eminent figures involved in Calcutta were Raja Kamal Krishna Bahadur, Girish Chandra Ghosh, Ramanath Tagore, Peary Charan Sarkar, Kristodas Pal, Rajnaryan Basu, and Dwijendranath Tagore.

By 1875, the Hindu Mela had gained significant popularity. That year, it was presided over by Rajnarayan Basu, one of the most revered personalities of the time and the maternal grandfather of Sri Aurobindo. He used the Hindu Mela as a platform to spread nationalist sentiments among Indians. At the age of fourteen, Rabindranath Tagore wrote and recited his first known poem, '*Hindu Melar Upahar*' (Hindu Mela's Gift) in which he expressed a desire for the rule of King Sri Ram and King Yudhisthira. In the poem, he honoured the sacrifices of Raja Prithviraj Chauhan, Rani Durgavati, and other women warriors, while voicing his anguish and pain at living under foreign rule.

In 1872, a new vision of Hindu nationalism was introduced in Calcutta by Adi Brahmo Samaj President Rajnarayan Basu through his lecture, 'The Superiority of Hinduism'.[61]

In 1874, members of the Brahmo Samaj formed the Samadarshi Party. On 26 July 1876, politically minded members founded the Indian Association to promote the nationalist ideology of Surendranath Banerjee. This initiative was led by Surendranath and Anandamohan Bose,[62] with Rajnarayan Basu also playing a significant role. Using this platform, Surendranath Banerjee organized two sessions of the Indian National Conference in 1883 and 1885. A decade later, this movement paved the way for the formation of the Indian National Congress (INC).

Although Surendranath Banerjee was a founding member of the INC, disagreements led him to break away and establish the Indian National Liberation Federation in 1919. Prominent leaders of this organization included Tej Bahadur Sapru, V.S. Srinivasa Sastri, and M.R. Jayakar.

Ram Mohan's farsighted vision thus sowed the seeds of a national political organization. Surendranath Banerjee later wrote: 'Let it be remembered that [Ram Mohan] was not only the founder of the Brahmo Samaj and the pioneer of all social reform in Bengal, but he was also the father of constitutional agitation in India.'[63]

Bipin Chandra Pal once said of Raja Ram Mohan Roy: 'Raja was the first to deliver the message of political freedom to India. He so keenly felt the loss of this freedom by his people that even as a boy, yet within his teens, he left his country and travelled to Tibet, because he found it difficult to tolerate the domination of his country by another nation.'[64]

In addition to the Nobel Laureate Rabindranath Tagore, nationalist leaders such as Surendranath Banerjee and Bipin Chandra Pal were prominent members of the Brahmo Samaj.

Nascent Hindu National Identity

Raja Ram Mohan Roy was also an eminent and independent journalist who believed in using the news media for mass communication. He ventured into the field of education, addressing a wide range of issues affecting the Indian masses, and aimed to form public opinion on matters impacting daily life in British India.

Following in his footsteps, Nabagopal Mitra, one of the founding fathers of nationalism in India, became the editor of the *National Paper*, which was started by Devendra Nath Thakur. This marked the first time in India's long history that ideas were examined through the lens of Indian thought. As a result, Mitra envisioned reviving the ancient Hindu identity and ideals, inspiring many educated youths to rally behind him in a fight against the 'cultural colonialism' of the British by revitalizing the best aspects of ancient Hindu civilization.

This movement was fully supported by members of the Tagore family, both morally and financially. Nabagopal Mitra founded the Hindu Mela (which was inaugurated by Rajnarayan Basu), the pioneering institution behind the genesis of Hindu nationalism. In addition to the *National Press*, he also started the National Society, National School, National Theatre, National Store, National Gymnasium, and even the National Circus, earning him the nickname 'National Mitra'.[65]

Rishi Bankim Chandra Chattopadhyay (1838–94)

The land of India has been called by various names throughout history and in various texts, including Bharatavarsha,[66] Aryavart,[67] and Brahmavarta.[68] The latter two names referred to specific regions. Earlier still, the landmass was known as Nabhivarsa and Jambudwipa. In most cases, India has been adorned with titles such as Punyabhumi (sacred land) or, at times, Devabhumi (land of the divine). The modern concept of this sacredness of the land, often framed as a motherland, was reinforced by great personalities like Rana Pratap and Shivaji. This patriotism also embodied a deep-rooted cultural identity and pride.

With the decline of Mughal power and the rise of English rule, a new concept of love for the land and its culture began to take shape towards the end of the 17th century. This gave birth to the hope for the revival of India's ancient heritage. The nation began to be envisioned as a mother, and the idea of Hindutva took root with Bankim Chandra Chattopadhyay, who composed India's national song, 'Vande Mataram', and the mantra for the revolutionaries of the Indian independence movement in 1882, in his famous novel *Anandamath*.

The story is as follows: on his deathbed, as one of his daughters attended to him, Bankim Chandra Chattopadhyay had a conversation about the poem 'Vande Mataram'. The editor of a magazine had been constantly pestering him for an overdue article, yet he had been unable to start it. One night, however, he sat down to write, and what flowed from his pen was the beautiful poem 'Vande Mataram'. Bankim told his daughter that he did not truly write it—that Devi Durga had written it through his pen. He also mentioned that the poem and the mantra 'Vande Mataram' would become powerful long after his death in 1894. In reality, the mantra proved to be highly influential for leaders in the independence movement, including the revolutionaries.

Bankim was honoured with the title of a 'rishi', as he was believed to possess the ability to see the future. He was able to foresee the decline of the Muslim rulers and the impact of British rule on Indian society. He envisioned the nation as a mother, much like the famous sentiment expressed in the Ramayana. Bankim sought to use the metaphor of Devi Durga to describe the motherland in the form of Bharat Mata.

Later, Rabindranath Tagore's brother, Abanindranath Tagore (1871–1951), painted the first image of Bharat Mata[69] and Sri Aurobindo elevated this idea, inspiring the revolutionaries in their fight for independence.

Shri Chandranath Bose (1844–1910)

Chandranath Bose was the head of Bangiya Sahitya Parishad, a literary society in Bengal that introduced the ideas of Hindutva to the common people.

Although he is largely forgotten today, Bose was a deputy magistrate in Dacca, holding degrees in history and law. He was regarded as 'the doyen of economic nationalism in Bengal'. In 1892, he introduced the concept of Hindutva as taking pride in being a Hindu through a book titled *Hindutva*[70], written in Bengali. For inspiration, he credited Bankim Chandra Chattopadhyay and Bhudev Mukhopadhyay, a Bengali nationalist writer and contemporary of Bankim.

In his book, Bose discussed how Hindus were weak and explored the causes behind this weakness. He emphasized the importance of cultivating specific qualities in every Hindu to embody true Hindutva. He argued that false pride should be replaced by strength, with the goal of achieving excellence in all areas of life. Bose suggested the following principles for Hindus to adopt: *soham* (I am that—I am Brahma), *loy* (aligning all activities with a grand plan—ultimate Brahminhood), *Nishkam Dharma* (selfless duty), *dhruva* (tenacious determination), endurance and perseverance, and attention to detail while keeping the final goal in mind. While the book is primarily written with a spiritual bent, it also reflects certain orthodox views on contemporary social norms in Hindu life.

Many dispute the idea that Hindutva and Hinduism are the same. They are not. 'Hinduism' was imposed as a set of 'religious' practices, but there is substantial literature that states one does not have to be 'religious' to be a Hindu. Even Swami Vivekananda said he would be 'an atheist if he does not believe in himself'. He also believed that the term 'Hindu' should evoke a 'galvanic shock'. This was also Chandranath Bose's assertion: 'to talk about Brahma in you and experience it'.

Swami Vivekananda (1863–1902)

Then came Swami Vivekananda, a spiritual master and a revolutionary sannyasi. His arrival in India was a great blessing for its land, heritage, and people. He stands out as the turning point for India after 1,000 years of subjugation. In 1897, he gave a clarion call to set aside all other deities and, for the next fifty years, worship only one living devi—Bharat Mata. India gained independence from the British exactly fifty years after his proclamation. The great leader of India, Netaji Subhash Chandra Bose, called him 'the maker of modern India'. In a 1963 speech, Dr S. Radhakrishan described Swamiji as the 'embodiment of the spirit of this country'.[71]

This is how Swami Vivekananda awakened the Hindus to their identity and self-respect:

> Mark me, then and then alone you are a Hindu when the very name sends through you a galvanic shock of strength. Then and then alone you are a Hindu when every man who bears the name, from any country, speaking our language or any other language, becomes at once the nearest and the dearest to you. Then and then alone you are a Hindu when the distress of anyone bearing that name comes to your heart and makes you feel as if your own son were in distress. Then and then alone you are a Hindu when you will be ready to bear everything for them [...]
>
> You may see thousands of defects in your countrymen, but mark their Hindu blood. They are the first Gods you will have to worship even if they do everything to hurt you, even if every one of them send out a curse to you, you send out to them words of love. If they drive you out, retire to die in silence like that mighty lion, Govind Singh. Such a man is worthy of the name of Hindu; such an ideal ought to be before us always. All our hatchets let us bury; send out this grand current of love all round.[72]

Swami Vivekananda then laid the foundation for the feeling of being a Hindu, which in essence is Hindutva:

> We Hindu must believe that we are the teachers of the world ... We are Hindus. I do not use the word Hindu in any bad sense at all, nor do I agree with those that think there is any bad meaning in it. In old times, it simply meant people who lived on the other side of the Indus; today a good many among those who hate us may have put a bad interpretation upon it, but names are nothing. Upon us depends whether the name Hindu will stand for everything that is glorious, everything that is spiritual, or whether it will remain a name of opprobrium, one designating the downtrodden, the worthless, the heathen. If at present the word Hindu means anything bad, never mind; by our action let us be ready to show that this is the highest word that any language can invent.
>
> [...]

> It has been one of the principles of my life not to be ashamed of my own ancestors. I am one of the proudest men ever born, but let me tell you frankly, it is not for myself, but on account of my ancestry. The more I have studied the past, the more I have looked back, more and more has this pride come to me, and it has given me the strength and courage of conviction, raised me up from the dust of the earth, and set me working out that great plan laid out by those great ancestors of ours. Children of those ancient Aryans, through the grace of the Lord may you have the same pride, may that faith in your ancestors come into your blood, may it become a part and parcel of your lives, may it work towards the salvation of the world![73]

It should be noted that Swami Vivekananda was one of the first leaders to vehemently reject the Aryan Invasion Theory. He then prescribed how the 'Hindu nation' should be 'regenerated':

> There are among us at the present-day certain reformers who want to reform our religion or rather turn it topsy-turvy with a view to the regeneration of the Hindu nation. There are, no doubt, some thoughtful people among them, but there are also many who follow others blindly and act most foolishly, not knowing what they are about. This class of reformers are very enthusiastic in introducing foreign ideas into our religion. [...]
>
> There is another class of men among us who are intent upon giving some slippery scientific explanations for any and every Hindu custom, rite, etc., and who are always talking of electricity, magnetism, air vibration, and all that sort of thing. Who knows but they will perhaps someday define God Himself as nothing but a mass of electric vibrations! However, Mother bless them all![74]

In a letter to Alasinga, he wrote, 'The Hindu must not give up his religion, but must keep religion within its proper limits and give freedom to society to grow.'[75]

The celebrated poet laureate Rabindranath Tagore is fondly called 'Gurudev' or 'Teacher par excellence'. He is sometimes portrayed as the epitome of 'secularism' and as someone who was against all forms of nationalism, mostly by communists. Many of these people failed to understand him, and some even accused him of supporting British colonialism, claiming that the Indian national anthem, 'Jana Gana Mana', was written in praise of George V, the British king-emperor, during his visit to India.[76] More on this controversy later.

Tagore is also presented as a universalist and an internationalist, opposed to any form of nationalism, by those who fail to grasp his true philosophy.[77] When the occasion arose, he saluted not only the '*desher maati*', the soil of the land, but also expressed profound love for his province, Bengal, through 'Amar Sonar Bangla', which is now the national anthem of Bangladesh.

During his early years, he also held the view that Hindu nationalism might have divided Hindus and Muslims, particularly in their involvement in the freedom movement. He even said: 'As our nationalists put on Hindu overtones, the Muslims also start feeling they should assert their separate Muslim identity. The Muslims now want to be equal with the Hindus in all respects. We should whole heartedly support this effort of the Muslims.'[78] However, his view changed after analyzing the Islamist global agenda in the Khilafat Movement, where many Islamist leaders pledged allegiance to the Turkish Caliph rather than to a free, democratic India.

> A very important factor which is making it almost impossible for Hindu-Muslim unity to become an accomplished fact is that the Muslims cannot confine their patriotism to any one country. I had frankly asked the Muslims whether in the event of any Mohammedan power invading India, they [the Muslims] would stand side by side with their Hindu neighbours to defend their common land. I was not satisfied with the reply I have obtained from them … Even such a man as Mr. Mohammed Ali has declared that under no circumstances it is permissible for any Mohammedan, whatever be his country, to stand against any Mohammedan.[79]

But in fact, Tagore was a very practical and visionary man, and his observations on true religious communalism were expressed very bluntly: 'There are two religions in earth, which have distinct enmity against all other religions. These two are Christianity and Islam. They are not just satisfied with observing their own religions, but are determined to destroy all other religions. That's why the only way to make peace with them is to embrace their religions.'[80] He further added: 'When two-three different religions claim that only their own religions are true and all other religions are false, their religions are only ways to Heaven, conflicts cannot be avoided. Thus, fundamentalism tries to abolish all other religions. This is called Bolshevism in religion. Only the path shown by the Hinduism can relieve the world from this meanness.'[81]

Therefore, it is clear that he eventually accepted that the universal Hindu ideals, whose fountainhead is the Vedas and which form the essence of Hindutva, were an essential part of India's rejuvenation. Hence, his Viswa Bharati University was based on the ancient traditions, values, and practices of the Vedas. He observed the lack of pride and unity among the Hindus and regretfully wrote:

> Whenever a Muslim called upon the Muslim society, he never faced any resistance - he called in the name of one God 'Allah-ho-Akbar'. On the other hand, when we (Hindus) call we will call, 'come on, Hindus', who will respond? We, the Hindus, are divided in numerous small communities, many barriers-provincialism-who will respond overcoming all these obstacles? 'We suffered from many dangers, but we could never be united. When Mohammed Ghouri brought the first blow from outside, the Hindus could not be united, even in those days of imminent danger. When the Muslims started to demolish the temples one after another, and to break the idols of Gods and Goddesses, the Hindus fought and died in small units, but they could not be united. It has been provided that we were killed in different ages due to out discord. Weakness harbors sin. So, if the Muslims beat us and we, the Hindus, tolerate this without resistance-then, we will know that it is made possible only by our weakness.

> For the sake of ourselves and our neighbour Muslims also, we have to discard our weakness. We can appeal to our neighbour Muslims, "Please don't be cruel to us. No religion can be based on genocide" – but this kind of appeal is nothing, but the weeping of the weak person. When the low pressure is created in the air, storm comes spontaneously; nobody can stop it for sake for religion. Similarly, if weakness is cherished and be allowed to exist, torture comes automatically – nobody can stop it. Possibly, the Hindus and the Muslims can make a fake friendship to each other for a while, but that cannot last forever. As long as you don't purify the soil, which grows only thorny shrubs you can not expect any fruit.'[82]

Although Muslim and British historians led us to believe that the Hindus were not united and easily lost to the invading forces, the real story in not as simple. Earlier in this book, we have seen that for over 300 years, the Hindus valiantly kept the invaders at bay. It took them a long time to conquer Sindh, and then they gradually entered the mainland. Rabindranath did not have access to the details we have today. In any case, Hindu unity has always been a problem, and more so today. Hindus identify themselves through provincial identity, caste or jati identity, and sectarian religious identities, but not necessarily as Hindus. The modern Hindutva movement seeks to unite all Hindus, though they are more diverse than any society or nation in the world. This is what the NeoCols are worried about, and they engage in constant propaganda to prevent this unity. It is the most significant hurdle to their mission of converting India into either a communist or an Islamic state, or breaking it into pieces.

In an earlier section, Rabindranath simply reminded the Hindus to shake off weakness, unite, and fight for justice for all. His appeal is clear, and his warning to the Hindus is equally direct:

> The terrible situation of the country makes my mind restless and I cannot keep silent. Meaningless ritual keep the Hindus divided in hundred sects. So we are suffering from series of defeats. We are tired and worn-out by the fortunes by the internal external enemies. The

> Muslims are united in religion and rituals. The Bengali Muslims the South Indian Muslims and even the Muslims outside India-all are united. They always stand untied in face of danger. The broken and divided Hindus will not be able to combat them. Days are coming when the Hindus will be again humiliated by the Muslims. 'You are a mother of children, one day you will die, passing the future of Hindus society on the weak shoulders of your children, but think about their future.'[83]

And he provided a clear indication of the solution:

> That kingdom of idiocy – the fatal lack of commonsense – was continuously invaded by the Pathans, sometimes by the [Mughals] and sometimes by the British. From outside we can only see the torture done by them, but they are only the tools of torture, not really the cause. The real reason of the torture is our lack of common sense and our idiocy, which is responsible for our sufferings. So we have to fight this idiocy that divided the Hindus and imposed slavery on us ... If we only think about the torture we will not find any solution. But if we can get rid of our idiocy, the tyrants will surrender to us.[84]

Rabindranath was also a follower of Rishi Bankim Chandra Chattopadhyay, much like the founder of the Rashtriya Swayamsevak Sangh (RSS), Dr Keshav Baliram Hedgewar, who dreamed of India as an undivided Hindu empire. Tagore wrote his famous poem eulogizing Chhatrapati Shivaji, whose mission was to defeat the invading Islamic forces ruling the country from Delhi.

As part of the effort towards the national awakening of Hindus, Balgangadhar Tilak, the great freedom leader, initiated the Ganesh Utsav and Shivaji Utsav in 1894 to inspire collective consciousness. Many freedom fighters drew inspiration from these events, particularly from the ideals of Shivaji. Rabindranath Tagore contributed to this movement by penning his famous poem 'Shivaji Utsav' in Bangla. Below is a translation of a few of its most relevant stanzas:

A few distant centuries ago, on a nondescript day
I can barely imagine
Upon what craggy hilltop, within a dense sunless forest
O sovereign Shivaji
Lightning-like, across your forehead, there flashed
The thought from above—
'With a singular religious thread [ekdharmapashe], this torn-up, fragmented
Bharata, I shall bind in One.'
[...]
Then came the day when from the plains of Maratha
The flaming tongues of your thunderbolt
Carved out in every corner of the sky the message of a new age:
The *mahamantra* of unification.
Upon the crown of the *Mughals* that tempestuous morn
The message arrived, writ upon a scroll—
And yet, that thunderous proclamation of Maratha
Bengal heard not, hence knew not its intent.
[...]
Where were you then, O contemplative One, Hero of Maratha
Where was your valiant name!
Your saffron insignia, scattered in the dust, crushed
Into nothingness by decree of fate.
The mocking annals of the invaders brand you as bandit
As they break into raucous laughter—
All your noble efforts nothing more than a robber's failed work
What all have since known.
[...]
O Royal Savant, those soaring, unifying thoughts of yours
In the store-house of Fate are preserved
Forever, could the hands of Time, ever purloin
The minutest speck of it?
That sacrifice of yours at the shrine of your Motherland
That resolute *sadhana* for the Truth
Who would have known—these became from thence
Till the end of time, Bharata's inheritance!

[…]
Nay—the Truth never dies beneath the oblivion
Of a hundred centuries—
Apathy kills it not, it stirs not nor weakens by insult
It takes a hundred knocks but stands tall.
The One considered long since vanquished and silenced
Beyond the field of action
That Truth is today arrived, clad as a venerable guest
At Bharata's door.

Yet today, its potent mantra, its generous eyes
Gaze upon the future
With rapt attention—what glorious vision it sees
Who is to tell?
O ethereal sage, you are arrived today
Manifest in your meditative image
Yet brought with you your legendary power
To fulfill your mission.

You have not today your ensigns, warriors or steeds
Nor your fierce weapons—
The skies are not rendered insane today
By booming chants of Hara! Hara! Hara!

[…]

No one had imagined in these three centuries
Nor dreamt in their sleep—
That your hallowed name one day, without battle
Would unite Bengal and Maratha.
The power of your penance, long curtailed in oblivion
Abruptly, today
Like an everlasting message, would instill a fresh new life
Upon a fresh new dawn!

[…]

With your head held high, seated upon the throne
Of Death—the royal diadem
Upon your temple, never shall its divine radiance
Be concealed, ever.
You are revealed, revealed today to us, O Royal One
You are indeed the Maharaja.
Four score million children of Mother Bengal
Shall bow to you with their royal tribute.[85]

The National Anthem—'Jana Gana Mana' Controversy

Some people believe that 'Jana Gana Mana' was written in praise of King George V. However, anyone even fleetingly familiar with Rabindranath Tagore's work would find it inconceivable that this great genius of India—who consistently refined and continues to refine the consciousness of India and others around the world—could have written a song in praise of the British emperor of India.

Despite belonging to perhaps the most 'elite' family of Bengal and his time, Rabindranath Tagore used every moment of his long, creative life to understand, empathize with, and defend India's history, culture, and people. He was deeply proud of his heritage—and with good reason. Tagore harboured profound disdain and contempt for colonial rule and its rulers. The famous French scholar Romain Rolland, who was also a great admirer of Ramakrishna and Vivekananda, described Tagore as 'a moral guide of the independent spirits of Europe and India'.

Tagore actively participated in the Swadeshi freedom movement. He wrote many patriotic songs that inspired freedom fighters during his time and later. His songs also played a role in the 1971 Bangladesh Liberation War. For instance, his '*O amar desher maati, tomar pore thekai matha*' ('O the soil of my country, on you, I rest my head') served as an anthem of inspiration during that struggle.

In 1915, Rabindranath was knighted by King George V. He accepted the knighthood to demonstrate that he was not a 'nigger'—a term the British often used to demean Indians—but an equal to any British citizen. However, in 1919, following the Jallianwala Bagh massacre in Amritsar, where British troops killed over 400 unarmed Indian demonstrators, Tagore renounced his knighthood in protest.

Rabindranath Tagore also played a pivotal role in promoting Hindu philosophy in Bengal, arguably more than most religious leaders in recent times. He brought complex Vedic and Upanishadic concepts into the language of the common man through the medium of popular culture. His songs, music, dramas, and dances continue to resonate and remain ever-popular even today.

He composed the music for 'Vande Mataram' himself and sang it in 1896 at the Calcutta Congress Session. He remarked: 'Vande Mataram! These magic words will open the door of his iron safe, break through the walls of his strong room, and confound the hearts of those who are disloyal to its call to say Vande Mataram.'[86] His poem 'Shivaji Utsav' (1904), as quoted earlier, can be considered one of the most eloquent pro-Hindu compositions in contemporary Indian literature.

He introduced 'Rakshabandhan' and 'Shivaji Utsav' (following Tilak's example) in Bengal to foster patriotism and unity. At his university, Shantiniketan, students were required to formally initiate into Brahmacharya through a structured process. Lastly, one must recognize the profound depth of his personality and the significance of his contributions, which deserve far more respect and seriousness that is often accorded. After all, this is the man who composed:

Where the mind is without fear and the head is held high,
Where knowledge is free,
Where the world has not broken up into fragments by narrow dogmatic walls,
Where the clear stream of reason has not lost its way
into the dreary desert sand of dead habit,
Where the mind is led forward by thee
Into ever widening thought and action—
Into that heaven of freedom, my Father, let my country awake!

Now, let us delve into the history of the controversy surrounding the national anthem. A book addressing this issue, titled *Our National Anthem*, was published in 1972 by Prabodh Chandra Sen, the then vice-chancellor of Vishwabharati/Shantiniketan. The book presents some simple yet significant facts about the song:

- In December 1911, Tagore was requested to write a poem in praise of the king to welcome him during the Congress session in Kolkata.
- He was upset and unhappy with this request. After a long night's struggle, he composed 'Jana Gana Mana'.
- He sang the song at the Congress session.
- At the end of that session, a Hindi song written by Rambhuj Chaudhary was sung, but some newspapers mistakenly referred to it as being written by Tagore.
- Pro-British Aglo-Indian newspapers reported: 'Tagore sang a song in Hindi in praise of the King'—a distortion no different from today's media often praising those in power by misrepresenting facts.
- Netaji Subhas Chandra Bose later adopted 'Jana Gana Mana' as the national anthem for the Indian National Army (INA). In 1950, this song was officially adopted as India's national anthem, while 'Vande Mataram' became the national song.
- In 1937, responding to a friend's query about the origins of 'Jana Gana Mana', Tagore explained that a loyalist friend had requested him to write a song in praise of the king. Tagore had felt angered by his friend's presumption about his loyalty. It his highly likely that this anger inspired him to compose 'Jana Gana Mana'.
- On one occasion, during a visit to India, the renowned Irish poet W.B. Yeats recounted a conversation with Tagore. The account, later printed in the *Indian Express* newspaper, included the following version: 'He [Tagore] got up very early in the morning and wrote a very beautiful poem .... When he came down, he said to one of us, "Here is a poem which I have written. It is addressed to God, but give it to Congress people. It will please them."'[87]

A slightly different version is also found:

> The National Congress people asked Tagore for a poem of welcome. He tried to write it but could not. He got up very early in the morning and wrote a very beautiful poem, not one of his best, but still beautiful. When he came down, he said to one of us, 'Here is a poem which I have written. It is addressed to God, but give it to Congress people. It will please them.' All Tagore's own followers knew it meant God, but others did not.[88]

Rabindranath himself said that he felt greatly pained by the unjustness of the charge. In a letter to Pulin Behari Sen, Tagore later wrote:

> A certain high official in His Majesty's service, who was also my friend, had requested that I write a song of felicitation towards the Emperor. The request simply amazed me. It caused a great stir in my heart. In response to that great mental turmoil, I pronounced the victory in Jana Gana Mana of that Bhagya Vidhata [God of Destiny] of India who has from age after age held steadfast the reins of India's chariot through rise and fall, through the straight path and the curved. That Lord of Destiny, that Reader of the Collective Mind of India, that Perennial Guide, the great Charioteer of man's destiny in age after age could never be George V, George VI, or any other George. Even my official friend understood this about the song. After all, even if his admiration for the crown was excessive, he was not lacking in simple common sense.
>
> I should only insult myself if I cared to answer those who consider me capable of such unbound stupidity as to sing in praise of George the Fourth or George the Fifth as the Eternal Charioteer leading the pilgrims on their journey through countless ages of timeless history of mankind.[89]

Everyone should read all five verses of the song with a proper translation to truly appreciate the genius of Rabindranath. Here is a general analysis of the song, including linguistic and cultural references, along with questions to ponder.

Consider these keywords from Indian culture that appear in this song—who do we normally associate these with?

- *Vidhata*: Bestower of the results of karma
- *Ashish*: *Aashirwaad* (blessings)—who does an Indian seek *aashirwaad* from?
- *Shubha*: Auspicious
- *Mangala*: All-purpose welfare—who gives *mangala*, George V or God?
- *Hey*: Thou
- *Vani*: Oracle/Message
- *Chirasarathi*: Eternal charioteer—Krishna?
- *Sankatadukatrata*: *Sankatmochan-kari*—Durga?

The key adjectives used (almost one unique adjective in each verse) carry profound meanings:

- *Jana gana mangala daayak* (verse 1): Dispenser of all-purpose welfare
- *Jana gana okiya vidhaayak* (verse 2): Bestower of unity and harmony among the people
- *Jana gana patha parichaayak* (verse 3): The giver/shower of proper direction to the people
- *Sankat dukhatrata* (verse 3): The rescuer from dangers and grievances
- *Jana gana dukha trayaka* (verse 4): The remover of all sorrows of the people
- *Rajeshwar* (verse 5): Lord of lords/kings

Finally, for the consolation of those who wish to review whether 'Jana Gana Mana' should remain the national song, Rabindranath himself provided some insights:

> In the course of our history, India had once deeply realised her geographical entity; she established in her mind an image of her own physical self by meditating on her rivers and hills... In my song of the victory of Bharat-vidhaata composed a few years ago, I have

> put together a number of Indian provinces; Vindhya-Himachala and Yamuna-Ganga have also been mentioned.
>
> I feel, however, that a song should be written in which all the provinces, rivers and hills of India are strung together in order to impress upon the minds of our people an idea of geography of our country. We are nowadays profuse in the use of the term National Consciousness, but what kind of national consciousness can there be, devoid of actual geographical and ethnological realisations?[90]

In the 1930s, a Congress sub-committee shortlisted several 'national' songs that could be sung alongside or instead of 'Vande Mataram'. Rabindranath suggested that only the first two stanzas of 'Vande Mataram' should be sung.

In the late 1940s, further debates arose over 'Vande Mataram', as its invocation of the nation as goddess was considered controversial. This conflicted with Islamic theology, which forbids the worship of any deity other than Allah. Netaji Subhas Chandra Bose adopted 'Jana Gana Mana' as the national anthem.

In 1950, 'Jana Gana Mana' was officially chosen as the national anthem, prevailing over both 'Vande Mataram' and Iqbal's 'Sare Jahan Se Accha'. However, 'Vande Mataram' was given 'equal status'. One of the reasons for its selection was that 'Vande Mataram' could not be played effectively by a band as a signature of the country. Additionally, 'Jana Gana Mana' enjoyed a favourable international reputation. It had been well-received at the United Nations in New York, where it was first played as an orchestral arrangement in 1947. Many regarded it as superior to most national anthems worldwide. Within India, the overwhelming majority of provinces supported its nomination.

Swami Pranavananda (1896–1941)

The founder of the Bharat Sevashram Sangha, Swami Pranavananda, was a great spiritual leader and reformer in undivided Bengal. He was a staunch proponent of Hindu unity, strengthening Hindus and Hindu society by adhering to their *shastras* and practising *sadhana*. He was also an advocate for the idea of a 'Hindu Raṣhṭra'.

Below are some of the most relevant excerpts from *Shri Shri Pranavananda Upadesh*, which clearly articulates his Hindutva mission:

- This country has maintained close contact with God throughout its life and intends to do so in future. This country is not that country which has accepted materialism as the sum mum bonum of life. This country implies more importance to morality, religion and spiritualism. [I]
- We must banish indolence, drowsiness and indifference and cultivate vigorous capacity for hard work so that it can inspire us to high endeavour, infuse power and awaken us again. [II]
- To resuscitate this decaying nation and to install new energy in its heart, we should spread wide the indomitable influence of the spirit of unity of the Sangha throughout the whole country and awaken its moral and religious sense of opening up the fountain of power within, through selfless service. [III]
- You shall have to follow the footsteps of the Arya Rishis [saints] by cultivating the ancient ideals to lead this degraded country and degenerated nation to the path of spiritualism and religion. Build up the vast Sangha-spirit [the spirit of unification] by uniting and integrating the small units. Grid up your lions to invigorate this weak and enfeebled nation. [IV]
- To replace the religious atmosphere at present prevailing in India, millions of selfless workers are needed immediately. It is the influence of these selfless persons that will change the attitude of the people of the whole country and then in that changed atmosphere and attitude a new nation will build up. [VI]
- To rescue the inert nation from the deep embrace of somnolence, shake off the chain of slumber and wake up to a life of action and appear before the country. Drown your errors and illusions in the abyss of oblivion, awaken your own self-memories in your heart and go ahead with the task of revitalizing the weak and inactive nation ... Thus equipped with purified

and emancipated attitude, uphold the depressed, protect the distressed, shelter the shelter less, bring peace and pleasure to the afflicted and step heroically into the field of courage fortified with unlimited courage, vigour and energy for work. Work for the welfare of the country, the nation and the society. [VII]

- We must exert all our energy for the upliftment of this degraded nation. We should have to give protection to and embrace the neglected castes and tribes. If you can infuse the elevating influence of spiritualism in the hearts of the backward castes and tribes with your untiring efforts, the greatest good of the country shall have been surely achieved. You have now taken vow of championing the cause of the backward untouchables under the leadership of an exalted personality of the Divine Dispensation. Such exalted privilege and good luck can only stem from a life replete with virtuous deeds. So, attend to your respective tasks with utmost vigour and enthusiasm. [VIII]
- You are the sons of Immortal Spirit. There is endless strength and vigour within you and you need not be perturbed under any circumstances. You are sacred and pure by yourselves. You should have no fear. Who can destroy you? Have patience and be composed and self-confident. The power within will manifest itself spontaneously. [XII]
- The Hindus have all-education and erudition, knowledge and intelligence, wealth and prosperity and ability as well. But they are divested of harmony, unity and integrity. For lack of concord, integrity and reconciliation, they are scattered and so they face failure in every sphere. They are torn asunder in different ways for this internal quarrel, racial problems, religious differences and factional strife. So, the first and foremost thing we need is their reconcilement, re-formation and rapprochement.
- The Hindus are untouchable to the Hindus! What a despicable idea! What an inhuman system! Untouchability is a grave sin! It is, as if, an incurable social disease! As soon as this grave sin is swept away, the Hindu-society will become strong and well-off. No Sastras, no reasons and no cultural heritage support this grave sin of untouchability.[91]

The account unfolds as follows: Swami Pranavananda, a great spiritual master, grew increasingly concerned about the future of Bengal during the last three years of his life. He approached numerous leaders, businessmen, intellectuals, and newspaper editors, warning them: 'You may not see it, but I see that Bengal and the Bengalis are on the path of total ruin and a calamity in the offing. A time will come when Bengalis shall run like mad in the street. There won't be a place to stay; they'll die like fleas in the street. Stand behind me, so I can try to save them.'[92]

Despite his appeals, no one paid heed to him. As he sought a leader who would unite and safeguard the Hindus of Bengal, Swamiji identified Syama Prasad Mookerjee (1901–53) as the ideal candidate for this responsibility. He requested a meeting with Syama Prasad Mookerjee, but circumstances repeatedly delayed it.

Syama Prasad Mookerjee was a lawyer and academician, the son of the renowned Ashutosh Mookerjee, famously known as the 'Tiger of Bengal'. Ashutosh Mookerjee, a celebrated educationist, lawyer, and mathematician, became the second vice-chancellor of the University of Calcutta. Following in his father's footsteps, Syama Prasad Mookerjee achieved great academic and administrative milestones. In 1934, at just thirty-three years old, he became the youngest vice-chancellor of the University of Calcutta,[93] serving until 1938.

In August 1940, a grand Hindu conference was planned on the occasion of Janmashtami. Justice Manmatha Mukherjee of the Calcutta High Court was to inaugurate the event, and Syama Prasad Mookerjee was the presiding guest. When Syama Prasad arrived, Swamiji offered him his own garland and declared, 'I've found the right person to stand tall for the Bengali Hindus.' He then blessed Syama Prasad Mookerjee.

In October 1940, Swamiji was in Kashi during Durga Puja. One day, he said, 'Bring Syama Prasad here.' His disciples, surprised at how he knew of Syama Prasad's presence in Kashi, made inquiries and confirmed that Syama Prasad was indeed there with his family, staying at Banaras Hindu University. Syama Prasad agreed to visit Swamiji, saying, 'I'll come to offer my puja to Durga on the day of Maha-Ashtami and will seek blessings from Swamiji.'

On Maha-Asthami, Syama Prasad, accompanied by his family, visited the ashram, offered puja, and had an intimate and long conversation with Swamiji. It is believed that Swamiji transferred his spiritual power to Syama Prasad Mookerjee during this meeting.

Swamiji entrusted Syama Prasad Mookerjee with the mission of propagating the idea of a united India, including Kashmir and West Bengal. It was through his efforts that West Bengal remained a part of India. His close associate and freedom fighter, Nalinaksha Sanyal, played a crucial role by persuading members of the Bengal Assembly to vote against a separate 'United Bengal', thereby ensuring that West Bengal stayed within India.

In 1951, Syama Prasad Mookerjee founded the Bharatiya Jana Sangh (BJS, Indian People's Organization), which later became the precursor to today's Bhartiya Janata Party (BJP, meaning the Indian people's party). In 1977, the BJS merged with several other parties to form the BJP.

Syama Prasad Mookerjee worked tirelessly to integrate Kashmir into India. He famously stated, 'A single country can't have two constitutions, two prime ministers, and two national emblems', referencing the unique provisions granted to Jammu and Kashmir under Article 370. His vision was ultimately realized in 2019 when Article 370 was abolished by the Modi Government.

While in Kashmir to create political pressure for integration, Syama Prasad Mookerjee was arrested and died in custody under mysterious circumstances. Many believe he was murdered, with allegations of an Abdullah–Nehru conspiracy surrounding his death.[94]

The land through which the sacred Ganga culminates her journey from the Himalayas to Gangasagar, as King Bhagirath invited and led her, has made it fertile for vegetation and the birth of great personalities whose contributions in the past few centuries significantly impacted the whole country. The spiritual renaissance from Sri Chaitanya to Sri Ramkrishna to Sri Aurobindo and the sociopolitical and scientific revolutions by innumerable great personalities of Bengal have been significant in the modern history of Bharat. Great personalities such as Bankim Chandra, Ram Mohan Roy, and Rabindranath reintroduced the age-old knowledge of the Vedas and the Upanishads to the masses. Many of them also have helped shape a renewed ideal of love for the motherland and a new national identity. Unfortunately, Gopal Krishan Gokhale's famous assertion, 'what Bengal thinks today, India thinks tomorrow', is no longer valid. Bengal needs another revolution to rise again.

CHAPTER 9

Hindutva

The legend in the Ramayana tells us: The fierce battle is over. The dead bodies and vultures have vanished. There is no sound of war drums or the rumbling of fiery weapons. No wails of women mourning the loss of their children or husbands. Peace has finally dawned in Lanka.

Sri Ram and Sita sit together after their long separation following Ravana's abduction of her. Sri Ram and his soldiers have defeated Ravana's forces and slain him. The war did not occur solely because Ram sought to kill Ravana; it was fought to rescue his beloved wife, Sita.

The couple had been in *vanavaas*—exile in the forest—for fourteen long years. Poverty and suffering must have weighed heavily on Lakshmana. Meanwhile, Lanka, the golden city, was a land of immense wealth and material abundance. Awestruck by its prosperity, Lakshmana requests Sri Ram: 'Brother, let us stay here in this land of wealth and rule the country that we have earned.'

Hearing this, Sri Ram utters:

अपि स्वर्णमयी लङ्का न मे लक्ष्मण रोचते |
जननी जन्मभूमिश्च स्वर्गादपि गरीयसी ||

Api swarnamayi lanka na me Lakshman rochate,
janani janmabhoomishch swargaadapi gasriyasi

(Lakshmana, even this golden Lanka does not appeal to me.
Mother and motherland are superior even to heaven.)[1]

This passage illustrates the profound and ancient love for the motherland among Bharatiyas.

There exists another version of this shloka. When Sri Ram arrived at the ashram of Rishi Bharadwaja, he inquired about his brother Bharata, his mothers, and the state of Ayodhya. The sage informed him of everything and recited:

मित्राणि धन धान्यानि प्रजानां सम्मतानिव |
जननी जन्म भूमिश्च स्वर्गादपि गरीयसी ||

mitraani dhana dhaanyaani prajaanaam sammataaniva |
jananii janma bhuumisca svargaadapi gariiyasii | |

(Friends, riches, and food grains are highly
valued in this world. Yet, mother and motherland
are far superior to even heaven.)[2]

One of these shlokas may be a later addition and not part of the original Valmiki Ramayana. It doesn't necessarily follow the flow of earlier shlokas either. Nevertheless, it is a Sanskrit verse of great meaning. The above shlokas give us an essence of patriotism.

*****

What is Hindutva? Simply speaking, Hindutva is Hinduness: feeling like a Hindu, acting as a Hindu, and taking pride as a Hindu. To an Indian, just as '*aham Brahasmi*' or '*so-aham*', Hindutva means '*aham Hindu asmi*' (I am a Hindu). It's as simple as that—the feeling, the identity, the *asmita*, and the pride, all together. It is akin to the Indianness of an Indian.

Most people in Bharat identify their country as 'Bharat', not 'India'. The term 'Bharat-ness' or *Bharatiyata* is not commonly used in their vocabulary either. Hence, most people identify themselves as Hindus and take pride in their heritage. This is an inner sense and 'who I am', found in a name and in the term Hindutva or Hinduness.

Many in India and around the world call this country 'Hindustan'—the land of the Hindus. India's official salutation is also 'Jai Hind' (Victory to Hind or Hindustan, Salute to Hindustan, that is, India). Unless one rejects their heritage for personal reasons, this is simply an expression of how an Indian citizen feels about being an Indian—about their Indianness and their identity as a Hindu, expressed as Hindutva. Hindutva does not mean opposition to others; it is simply a self-identity.

The Oxford English Dictionary describes Hindutva as: 'Originally: the state or quality of being Hindu; "Hinduness".' In later use, a further definition was added: 'An ideology seeking to establish the hegemony of Hindus and the Hindu way of life; Hindu nationalism.'[3] According to Merriam-Webster's Encyclopedia of World Religions, Hindutva is a concept of 'Indian cultural, national, and religious identity'. The term conflates a geographically based religious, cultural, and national identity: 'A true Indian is one who partakes of this Hindu-ness.' It goes further, stating that 'even those who are not religiously Hindu but whose religions originated in India—Jains, Buddhists, Sikhs, and others—share in this historical, cultural, and national essence. Those whose religions were imported to India, meaning the country's Muslim and Christian communities primarily, may fall within the boundaries of Hindutva only if they subsume themselves into the majority culture.'[4]

As we can see, the term is used to represent the tradition, heritage, and culture of this ancient land. Some have noted a similarity between the relationship of Hindutva to India and that of Zionism to Israel.

We must not forget that India's Hindu system has been pluralistic from the beginning of its history. It allows all ideas and thoughts to flourish. Having said that, one must recognize that there cannot be a single monolithic definition of Hindu Dharma and, for that matter, Hindutva. People should not be forced to fit into one idea or 'package', unlike most other cultures based on a singular thought in the world.

Love for the '(mother)land' and a sense of Hindu/Bharatiya identity are present among the inhabitants of Bharat. Before the foreign invasions, 'Hindu identity' may have been dormant, but cultural and spiritual unity was organically present throughout the subcontinent. The Hindu identity is not very explicit in the *shastras* and other historical literature. Yet, numerous saints were born during the invasions and foreign occupations to safeguard the land, heritage, and society. All Bharatiya spiritual traditions were given an umbrella identity as Hindu by Raja Ram Mohan Roy, which has been discussed in the previous chapter.

Saints of India during the Islamic Occupation

Before the Islamic invasions and occupations of Indian territories, there were two types of institutions, sometimes independent and sometimes combined: centres for learning in the form of universities and *mandir*-based learning centres. The former would have provided more formal training in material subjects, while the *mandirs* would focus more on society, culture, and *adhyatma* (spirituality). Thus, *jnana* (the search for truth) and karma (experiments with natural sciences, laws, and associated technological development) were found more in universities such as Nalanda. The *mandir*-centric institutes had a greater emphasis on cultural and social reforms, ensuring the continuity of the 'Sanatana' tradition.

After repeated invasions and continuous foreign occupation, these learning centres were largely damaged and destroyed, including numerous libraries. In this dire situation, the only way to preserve the heritage was through the path of Bhakti and a deep dive into inner *adhyatma,* especially where external support, such as a *mandir*, was missing. During this period of extreme hardship and crisis, numerous great saints emerged. The following section lists the most notable saints, although many others also came forward as saviours of the people and society. The actual birthdates and birthplaces of some of these saints remain a subject of debate.

Sri Ramanuja (1060–1118, born at Sriperumbudur, Tamil Nadu) was the proponent of *vishishtadvaita* (qualified non-dualism) *darshana.* His philosophy complemented the Dvaita Vedanta of Madhvāchārya and Advaita Vedanta of Ādi Shankaracharya, giving rise to the three most influential Vedantic *darshanas* of the second millennium.

Nimbarkacharya (born between the 7th and 11th century at Nimbapuri, Karnataka) was the chief proponent of the Dvaitadvaita Vedanta *darshana.*

Namadeva (1270–1350, born at Narsi, Hingoli, Maharasthra) was a great poet and saint, devoted to Lord Vitthal (Krishna).

Madhavacharya (1238–1317, born in Pajaka near Udupi, Karnataka) was the proponent of Dvaita Vedanta. His philosophy was called *Tattvavāda,* meaning 'arguments from a realist viewpoint'.

Jnandeva Sant Dnyaneshwar (1275–96, born at Apegaon near Paithan in Maharashtra) was also known as Jnaneshwar. He was a great Marathi saint, poet, philosopher, and yogi of the Nath Vaishnava tradition.

Lalleshwari (1320–92, born in Kashmir) also known as Lal Ded, was a saint of the Kashmir Shaiva order. She created a style of mystic poetry called *vatsun* or *vakhs,* meaning 'speech'. Her poems represent some of the earliest known works of Kashmiri literature.

Vallabhacharya (1479–1531, born at Champaranya, Chhattisgarh) was a Vaishnava devotional poet-saint. He founded the Krishna-centred Pushti Margiya Vaishnava tradition and propagated the Shuddha Advaita Vedanta *darshana.*

Shankar Dev (1449–1568, born at Alipukhuri near Bordwa, Assam) was a great saint-scholar, poet, playwright, dancer, actor, musician, artist, and social-religious reformer who popularized Vaishnava bhakti in Assam.

Sant Surdas (1479–1584, born at village Ranukta or Renuka in Uttar Pradesh) was a blind Vaishnava poet and singer, famous for his works written in praise of Sri Krishna.

Ramananda (born in the 15th century at Prayag) was the guru of disciples such as Kabir, Ravidas, and Narahari. He has been described as 'the bridge between the Bhakti movement of the South and the North'.

Mirabai: (1498–1546, born at Kidki in the Pali district of Rajasthan) was born into a Rajput royal family. She was a celebrated Vaishnava mystic poet and a devoted follower of Sri Krishna.

Tulsidas (1532–1623, born at Sookar, Uttar Pradesh) was also known as Goswami Tulsidas. He was a Ramanandi Vaishnava Hindu saint and poet, and a great devotee of Sri Rama. Tulsidas wrote several popular works in Sanskrit and Awadhi, including the epic *Ramcharitmanas*, a retelling of the Sanskrit Ramayana based on Rama's life in the vernacular Awadhi.

Narsi Mehta (born in the 15th century in Talaja, Gujarat) was a great saint-poet who popularized the Vaishnava tradition in Gujarat. He made significant contributions to Gujarati literature.

Kabir (born in the 15th century near Varanasi) was a disciple of Ramananda, a mystic poet and saint whose writings influenced the Bhakti movement. His verses also found their place in the Guru Granth Sahib.

Guru Nanak (1469-1539, born in Nankana Sahib, currently in Pakistan) was born into a traditional Hindu family and was the founder and first guru of the Sikh Panth. He believed in social harmony and introduced meditation in the name of Ishwara in many forms, including Ram and Hari. Later, various gurus contributed significantly to spirituality and social reforms, culminating in the foundation of the Khalsa by Guru Gobind Singh to protect society from Muslim domination.

Sant Eknath (1533–99, born at Paithan, Maharashtra) was a philosopher, saint, and poet. He was a devotee of Krishna and a significant figure of the Warkari tradition.

Sant Tukaram (born in the 17th century) was a Marathi poet, saint, and a great devotee of Shri Vitthal (Krishna). He is best known for his devotional poetry, called a*bhanga* and *kirtans*.

All these great saints shared various forms of Bhakti and other *darshanas* and practices, which led to tremendous sociocultural reforms and contributed significantly to literature, music, and the arts. Some were more directly engaged in dealing with Islamic onslaughts. Bharat owes much to the Sikh gurus, especially Guru Gobind Singh. We also know about Samarth Ramdas, the spiritual guru of Shivaji Maharaj, who awakened the Kshatriya spirit among the masses.

Great Personalities Who Shaped Hindu Identity

In the following section, we will examine a list of 'great personalities' who have shaped the Hindu identity.

Samarth Ramdas (1608–81, born in Jamb Village, Maharasthra), also known as Sant Ramdas or Ramdas Swami, was a Marathi saint, poet, writer, spiritual master, and the guru of Chhatrapati Shivaji. Samarth Ramdas taught Advaita Vedanta and yoga; he was a devoted *bhakta* of Ram and Hanuman and promoted Kshatriya dharma, inspiring Shivaji in his battles. The idea and identity of being a Hindu were perhaps instilled in Shivaji by him.

Sri Chaitanya Mahaprabhu (1486–1534, born in Nabadwip, West Bengal) was a prominent reformer who played a key role in the development of the ideas of Hindutva. An early reflection of the idea of Hindutva can be found in his reform efforts. When thousands of so-called low-caste Hindus were preyed upon for conversion by the Islamists, partly due to injustices shown to them by 'upper-caste' people and the pressure of Islamic conversion campaigns, Sri Chaitanya introduced the *maha-mantra* of 'Hare Krishna', to be chanted by anybody and everybody, thus removing caste barriers in divinity-related activities. This helped restore the feeling of being Hindu. Most people have forgotten the ancient adage '*sangha shakti kalou yuge*' (in Kali Yuga, the true power lies in the unity [of Hindus]), which was the theme and motto of Sri Chaitanya. There is a very commonly used verse about how one can be empowered in every yuga. Though the source for this verse is hard to find, the verse is as follows:

त्रेतायां मंत्रशक्तिश्च, ज्ञानशक्तिः कृते युगे।
द्वापरे युद्धशक्तिश्च, संघशक्तिः कलौ युगे॥

Tretayam mantrashaktischa gyanshaktih krite yuge
Deapare yudhashaktischa sangha shakti kalou yuge.

(In Treta Yuga, shakti is achieved via mantra, jnana in Satya Yuga, battle power in Dwapar, and organizational unity in Kali Yuga.)

Sri Chaitanya flooded the entire eastern areas of India with a new understanding of Hindu Dharma, awakening the ideals of dharma.

Chhatrapati Shivaji (1630–80, born in Shivneri, near Junnar, Maharasthra) introduced the idea of Hindu identity, unity, and the expression of Hindutva in the form of a nation of awakened Hindus. He is believed to have used the phrase *Hindavi Swarajya* (Hindu self-ruled kingdom) in a letter to Dadaji Naras Prabhu Deshpande of Rohidkhore on 17 April 1645. The letter stated: 'Shri Rohireshvar, the divine master of your valley, has given us success, and He will satisfy all our desires by enabling us to establish *Hindavi Swarajya*.'[5]

According to Pagadi, *Hindavi* had the sense of 'the sons of the soil' within this context.[6] Author G.S. Banhatti attributed this statement to Swami Vivekananda:

> Shivaji is one of the greatest national saviours who emancipated our society and our Hindu dharma when they were faced with the threat of total destruction. He was a peerless hero, a pious and God-fearing king and verily a manifestation of all the virtues of a

> born leader of men described in our ancient scriptures. He also embodied the deathless spirit of our land and stood as the light of hope for our future.[7]

On another occasion, it is recorded that Swami Vivekananda had much to say about Shivaji, the 'Hindu king' who brought much Hindu pride—in other words, the feeling of Hinduness and Hindu identity:

> [Shivaji,] the greatest king that India had produced within the last three hundred years; one who was the very incarnation of Siva, about whom prophecies were given out long before he was born; and his advent was eagerly expected by all the great souls and saints of [Maharashtra] as the deliverer of the Hindus from the hands of the Mlechchas and one who succeeded in the establishment of the Dharma which had been trampled under foot by the depredations of the devastating hordes of the [Mughals].[8]

He continued in the same conversation:

> Is there a greater hero, a greater saint, a greater bhakta and a greater king than Sivaji? Sivaji was the very embodiment of a born ruler of men as typified in your great Epics. He was the type of the real son of India representing the true consciousness of the nation. It was he who showed what the future of India is going to be sooner or later, a group of independent units under one umbrella as it were, i.e., under one supreme imperial suzerainty.[9]

Shivaji's contemporary was the great poet Kavi Bhushan (1613–1715), who served in the courts of Bundeli King Chhatrasal. He met Shivaji in Agra for the first time and attended Chhatrapati Shivaji's court. Bhushan presented many of his poems at the grand coronation of Shivaji Maharaj. He said, 'Had there not been Shivaji, Kashi would have lost its culture, Mathura would have been turned into a mosque and all would have been circumcised.'[10]

The importance of Hindu emperor Shivaji becomes clearer when we read Rabindranath's famous poem in tribute to Shivaji.

The momentum to throw off the yoke of British colonial rule was also driven by Hindu social movements, prominent among which was the Arya Samaj. A brief overview follows:

Arya Samaj

Swami Dayanand Saraswati was once invited as the chief guest at the annual festival of the Adi Brahmo Samaj. Basu's famous speech and writing were titled 'Hindu Dharmer Shreshthata'. Basu gave a copy of this to Swami Dayanand Saraswati and met him several times. He also met Devendranath Thakur. These interactions significantly impacted his thoughts and work, prompting him to start a similar organization.[11]

Saraswati founded the Arya Samaj in Bombay on 10 April 1875, but the organization gained momentum three years later in Punjab after the establishment of the Lahore Arya Samaj. The Arya Samaj remained at the forefront of political agitation against British colonial rule, with Lala Lajpat Rai, a prominent member, being an important leader of the revolutionary section of the INC. After Swami Dayananda gave the clarion call for Swaraj as 'India for Indians' in 1876, Bal Gangadhar Tilak took up the idea and famously declared, 'Swaraj or freedom is my birthright.'

Similar to the Brahmo Samaj, the Arya Samaj influenced a host of great freedom fighters and leaders. Here is a short list: Bal Gangadhar Tilak, Ram Prasad Bismil, Bhikaji Rustom Cama, Pandit Lekh Ram, Swami Shraddhanand, Shyamji Krishna Varma, Kishan Singh, Bhagat Singh, Bhai Parmanand, Lala Hardayal, Madan Lal Dhingra, Mahadev Govind Ranade, Ashfaq Ullah Khan, Mahatma Hansraj, Lala Lajpat Rai, Bipin Chandra Pal, Yogmaya Neupane, and Vinayak Damodar Savarkar.

Veer Vinayak Damodar Savarkar (1883 –1966, born in Bhagur, Maharasthra) was disillusioned with the leadership of the Congress Party and saw through the design of the Muslim leaders and their collaboration with the British to create Muslim rule in a potentially independent India. Recognizing that Muslims were not aligned with the broader independence movements but rather with a pan-Islamic rule under the Caliph, he introduced 'Hindutva' to inspire pride and assertion among Hindus, emphasizing their long history and rich heritage.

He sought to motivate assertive Hindus and popularized this ideology in his book *Essentials of Hindutva* (1921–22). It is possible that he was influenced by the writings of Bankim Chandra Chattopadhyay and Chandranath Basu's concept of 'Hindutva', since he was closely connected with the revolutionaries of Bengal. Savarkar was one of the few 'secular' Hindu leaders who sought to revive civilizational glory. His 'secularism' was not about observing or performing religious rituals, but about a broader vision of national identity. His *Six Glorious Epochs of Indian History* was perhaps the first-ever written history of the Hindus/Indians since the time of the invasion, a period when much of Indian history had been written by the conquerors.

As a revolutionary, Veer Savarkar inspired numerous freedom fighters both in India and abroad, putting his life at risk many times. Like Netaji, Savarkar posed a significant challenge to Britain. He was arrested in 1910 while in London[12] and was subsequently put on a ship called 'Moriya' and extradited to Mumbai. However, Savarkar had studied international law and devised a plan to escape from the ship and seek asylum in France.

On 8 July 1910, when the ship was anchored at the port of Marseilles, he went to the toilet and covered the glass on the door with his clothes. He then jumped through the toilet window, plunged into the ocean, and swam swiftly towards the French port. Despite British soldiers following him in a boat, they were unable to catch him. Savarkar then surrendered to the French police and sought asylum. However, the French authorities arrested him, as entering French territory without permission was also illegal. British officers bribed the French officials and secured Savarkar's custody. He was sent to the Andaman Jail for trial and sentenced to fifty years of rigorous imprisonment.[13]

To Savarkar, as was the case with his predecessors, 'Hindu' was an inclusive term for everything that was Indian. To him, a Hindu was 'first and foremost someone who lives in the area beyond the Indus River, between the Himalayas and the Indian Ocean'. He based his ideology on three pillars: *rashtra* (nation), *jati* (race), and *sanskriti* (a common cultural heritage). His secularism also indicates that Hindutva was not a 'religious' term to him. As he explained in his book, the close association of the terms Hindu and Sindhu is a clear indication that he was more concerned with geography, history, and culture, as Prof. Arvind Sharma states: 'religion did not figure in his ensemble'.[14]

Today, leftists criticize this ideology and compare Hindu pride with Hitler's Nazi pride. First, all nations take pride in their history and heritage. Second, when the majority does not get their fair share, they are often expected to act against their adversaries. Finally, any conquered nation would rewrite its history once the conquest is over. There can be no comparison between Hitler's ideology and Savarkar's. Hitler misappropriated and misconstrued two Indian ideas. First, to motivate thousands to create a 'nation of pure race', that is, the Aryan (misunderstood) race, and then caused the Holocaust of the Jews, leading to the death of millions. Second, he also misused the Swastika, a symbol revered in India and many other ancient cultures. Hitler turned the symbol, which is sacred in every Hindu household as a symbol of '*swasti*' (peace), into a tool of hate, giving it a bad name.[15]

Now, the NeoCols found it inconvenient to accuse Savarkar of being a so-called fascist—perhaps because he also used the word 'Arya' in his ideas. However, in the Indian context, the word Arya does not denote a race. Its mention can be traced back to the oldest of the Vedas, the *Rigveda*:[16]

इन्द्रं वर्धन्तो अप्तुरः कृण्वन्तो विश्वमार्यम् ।
अपघ्नन्तो अराव्णः ॥

Om Indram vardhanto apturah krinvanto vishwamaryam,
Apaghnanto aravnah.

(Let us uplift Indra [symbolizing the soul] through good deeds,
removing attitudes of misery and evil.
Let us make the whole world noble.)

Here, the word 'Arya' does not refer to any particular race, caste, or creed. Instead, it means a virtuous and cultured person. Ascribed to the *Vasistha Smriti* by some, the following verse further explains:[17]

कर्तव्यमाचरन् कर्म, अकर्तव्यमनाचरन्।
विष्ठति प्रकृताचार: यः स आर्यः स्मृतः॥

Kartavyamacharn Karma, Akratvyamanacharan
Vishthti Prakritachare yeh sa Arya smriteh

(He is an Arya who performs his duties diligently, avoids what should not be done, holds traditions in high regard, and upholds them. By his or her nature, an Arya is a caring person.)

Despite his limited access to information while in jail, Savarkar himself expressed doubts about the Aryan Invasion Theory. He wrote:

> So far we have not pinned our faith to any theory about the original home of the Aryans. But if the most widely accepted theory of their entrance into India be relied on, then a natural curiosity arises as to the origin of the names by which they called the new scenes of their adopted home. Did they coin all those names from their own tongue? Could they have done so? Is it not generally true that when we meet a new scene or enter a new country, we call them by the very names—may be in a slightly changed form so as to suit our vocal ability or taste—by which they are known to the native people there? Of course, at times we love to call new scenes by names redolent with the memory of the clear old ones—especially when new colonies are being established in a virgin and but thinly populated continent. But this explanation could only be satisfactory when it is proved that the name given to the new place already existed in the old country and even then it could not be

> denied that the other process of calling new scenes by the names which they already bear is more universally followed.[18]

As noted earlier, the term Hinduism does not align with the definition of religion as understood by theologians. Savarkar himself had reservations about using the term, which he considered narrow and sectarian, shaped by external portrayals. He observed: 'It is imperative to point out that we are by no means attempting a definition or even a description of the more limited, less satisfactory, and essentially sectarian term Hinduism.'[19]

Savarkar clearly differentiated between Hindutva and Hinduism and preferred the usage of Hindutva over Hinduism. To him, Hindutva represented broader concept encompassing the pantheon of philosophical ideas, practices, and the uniquely inclusive culture and value system of the Hindus. He explained:

> Hindutva is not identical with what is vaguely indicated by the term Hinduism. By an 'ism' it is generally meant a theory or a code more or less based on spiritual or religious dogma or creed. Had not linguistic usage stood in our way then 'Hinduness' would have certainly been a better word than Hinduism as a near parallel to Hindutva. Hindutva embraces all the departments of thought and activity of the whole Being of our Hindu race.[20]

Returning to the story of Savarkar's life: though he was handed over to the British police and denied asylum, the case became an international issue, highlighting violations of human rights. It even reached the Hague, and as a result of the controversy, the French President was compelled to resign.

Nevertheless, Savarkar had already been given the maximum sentence of fifty years. He endured horrific tortures in prison. He was regularly flogged, chained, and kept in solitary confinement. He was forced to perform gruelling labour, including serving as a human yoke to pull the oil mill. He had no access to toilets or sanitation and was often given rotten, worm-infested food to eat. His crime? 'Crimes against the government.' This torment continued for years, with no hope of relief in sight.

Many freedom fighters subjected to these unbearable tortures went insane, and some even committed suicide. Savarkar himself contemplated suicide numerous times, but his unwavering character and commitment to India's cause prevented him from giving in.

The story does not end there. His elder brother, Ganesh (known as Babarao), was also sentenced to the same prison for twenty-five years.[21] He faced similar brute torture. Upon discovering that his brother was in the same jail, Babarao managed, after great effort, to send a note to Savarkar. He wrote, 'I had hopes that you would work for our motherland and taste success. This hope had made my own transportation bearable. I thought that you would carry on the work for which I had to sacrifice myself.' He wondered what had caused his brother to endure the same hellish imprisonment. In response, Savarkar wrote:

> Baba, success and failure are but coincidences. It is not our fault if we failed in our first battle. In fact, we are fortunate to have stood our ground in the face of failure. It is a matter of pride for us that we are bravely enduring those sufferings, which we exhorted others to undergo. It is now our life mission to languish in this prison and if need be, accept the abuses of those for whom we suffer. Remaining free and achieving fame whilst fighting is no doubt considered glorious. But it is equally glorious to die unknown and suffer abuse. Not just fighting and becoming famous but dying unknown and unsung is also essential for final victory. As far as the loss to our cause is concerned, I can only say that our absence shall not bring our War of Independence to a halt. This army of countless warriors, whose charioteers are the proud Sri Krishna and Sri Ram, shall not halt in our absence![22]

It is perhaps a human tendency to place leaders on a very high pedestal. However, the truth remains that no human being is perfect in their ideas or thoughts—errors are a part of human nature. Knowledge evolves, and we progress from lower to higher understanding. Especially concerning our past, absolute certainty about historical facts is elusive unless based on direct experience.

That said, the NeoCols often undermine India's great thinkers by pointing out factual inaccuracies in their interpretations of history. A classic example is the Aryan Invasion Theory. Today, we can unequivocally demonstrate that there was no 'Aryan invasion' of India. However, leaders like Tilak and Savarkar, relying on the information available to them from contemporary historians, formed their views to the best of their ability.

Having said that, Savarkar's tone and language in his book *Hindutva* approach the Aryan Invasion Theory with caution, yet the NeoCols celebrate his supposed support for it. As noted earlier, he wrote his book *Essentials of Hindutva* in 1921–22 while imprisoned in the Cellular Jail in the Andamans, with limited access to historical source material. The Aryan Invasion Theory was prevalent at the time. However, he was cautious and wrote:

> Although it would be hazardous at the present state of oriental research to state definitely the period when the foremost band of the intrepid Aryans made it their home and lighted their first sacrificial fire on the banks of the Sindhu, the Indus, yet certain it is that long before the ancient Egyptians, and Babylonians had built their magnificent civilization, the holy waters of the Indus were daily witnessing the lucid and curling columns of the scented sacrificial smokes and the valleys resounding with the chants of Vedic hymns—the spiritual fervour that animated their souls.[23]

The NeoCol propaganda has become even more insidious, aiming to diminish the contributions of prominent figures to tarnish their public image. Two notable cases are J.C. Bose and Savarkar. There has been a persistent effort to portray them as 'mediocre' personalities with minimal achievements. Their fault? They celebrated India's glorious past.

Savarkar's *The Indian War of Independence* (1909), written during the later part of his life, and *Six Glorious Epochs of Indian History* (published posthumously in 1971) exposed the inaccuracies of colonial historians. At a time when there was neither the internet nor even telephone, this genius, working from London, meticulously compiled information for his books.

The language skills of Nehru and his creation of *Discovery of India* were a significant attempt, but in terms of content, it was far inferior to the *Six Glorious Epochs of Indian History* or even *Essentials of Hindutva*. He urged his contemporaries:

> O Hindus, consolidate and strengthen Hindu nationality; not to give wanton offense to any of our non-Hindu compatriots, in fact to anyone in the world but in just and urgent defense of our race and land; to render it impossible for others to betray her or to subject her to an unprovoked attack by any of those 'Pan-isms' that are struggling forth from continent to continent. As long as other communities in India or the world are not respectively planning India first or humanity first, but all are busy organizing offensive and defensive alliances and combinations on an entirely narrow racial or religious or national basis, so long, at least, so long O Hindus, strengthen if you can those subtle bonds that like nerve threads bind you in one organic social being. Those of you who, in a fit suicidal, try to cut off the most vital of those ties and dare to disown the name Hindu will find to their cost that in doing so, they have cut themselves off from the very source of our racial life and strength.
>
> Equally certain it is that whenever the Hindus come to hold such a position whence, they could dictate terms to the whole world—those terms cannot be very different from the terms which Gita dictates or the Buddha lays down.[24]

Bengal: Birthplace of Nationalism and Hindutva

As explained in the previous chapter, both the Hindutva movement and Indian nationalism took root in Bengal. It all began with Raja Ram Mohan Roy. Savarkar was in touch with Bengal's revolutionaries and must have been influenced by the ideals and ideas of Bankim, Chandranath, and Vivekananda.

The founder of RSS (national volunteer organization, 1925), Keshav Baliram Hedgewar (1889–1940), came to Calcutta to study medicine and was in contact with revolutionaries, especially Sister Nivedita (a direct disciple of Vivekananda who had connections with the Irish Republican Army [IRA]) and Sri Aurobindo. The idea of forming RSS came to him during his time in Bengal, and the seeds of his nationalism and Hindutva were sown early on. Bankimchandra profoundly influenced him, and while studying at Neel City High School in Nagpur, he was expelled for chanting 'Vande Mataram'[25], which had been made unlawful by the British government at that time. Is it possible that he was also inspired by the novel *Anandamath* to start RSS? According to scholar and writer Uday Mahurkar, Hedgewar may also have been influenced by Swami Pranavananda, the founder of Bharat Sevashram Sangha.

The second chief (*sarsanghchalak*) of the RSS, Madhav Sadashiv Golwalkar (1906–73), became a monk under the discipleship of Swami Akhandananda (a brother monk of Swami Vivekananda) at the Sargachi Ramakrishna Mission Ashram, an organization founded by Vivekananda.

The first president of the BJS, which later became the BJP, was inspired and initiated by Swami Pranavananda. Prime Minister Narendra Modi was also associated with the Ramakrishna Mission, where he attempted to become a monk but did not succeed. He later became a *pracharak* (full-time worker) of the RSS.

An interesting point to note here is that today's Congress Party is not the original INC. Prime Minister Indira Gandhi was expelled from the INC for violating party discipline in November 1969. She then split the party into Congress (O), with many senior leaders like K. Kamraj and Morarji Desai remaining in it, and the new party of Indira was called Congress (I). Congress(I) is today's Congress Party. Congress (O) merged into the Janata

Party in 1977.[26] It is a major blunder to call this party the 'Old Mighty Congress Party'—in reality, it is a party of the Gandhi clan today!

Legal Aspects of Hindutva

The Right to Freedom of Religion is stated in Article 25(2)(b) of the Constitution, which falls under the category of 'Right'. This article includes the following definition: 'Hindus shall be construed as including a reference to persons professing the Sikh, Jain, or Buddhist religion.' Savarkar's idea was very similar—he believed that Hindutva encompassed all Indian traditions, that is, Hindu, Buddhist, Jain, and Sikh. He confined 'Hindu nationality' to 'Indian religions' (traditions), as they all shared a common origin in India, built on shared values where ideas such as dharma, karma, yoga, etc., form the foundation of each. However, there is no clear definition of Hinduism. Now, let us examine what the Indian legal system has to say about 'Hinduism'.

Article 25 in the Constitution of India, 1949

Freedom of conscience and free profession, practice, and propagation of religion

(1) Subject to public order, morality and health and to the other provisions of this Part, all persons are equally entitled to freedom of conscience and the right freely to profess, practise and propagate religion.

(2) Nothing in this article shall affect the operation of any existing law or prevent the State from making any law —

(a) regulating or restricting any economic, financial, political or other secular activity which [may be] associated with religious practice;

(b) providing for social welfare and reform or the throwing open of Hindu religious institutions of a public character to all classes and sections of Hindus.

Explanation I.— The wearing and carrying of kirpans shall be deemed to be included in the profession of the Sikh religion.

> Explanation II.— In sub-clause (b) of clause (2), the reference to Hindus shall be construed as including a reference to persons professing the Sikh, Jaina or Buddhist religion, and the reference to Hindu religious institutions shall be construed accordingly.[27]

In 1966, a five-judge constitutional bench consisting of Chief Justice P.B. Gajendragadkar, K.N. Wanchoo, M. Hidayatullah, V. Ramaswami, and P. Satyanarayanaraju, in the 'Sastri Yagnapurushadji' case (1966 SCR [3] 242), attempted to define Hinduism. Justice Gajendragadkar, in his verdict, noted:

> The historical and etymological genesis of the word 'Hindu' has given rise to a controversy amongst Indologists; but the view generally accepted by scholars appears to be that the word 'Hindu' is derived from the river Sindhu, otherwise known as Indus, which flows from Punjab. 'When we think of the Hindu religion, we find it difficult, if not impossible, to define the Hindu religion or even adequately describe it. Unlike other religions in the world, the Hindu religion does not claim anyone prophet, it does not claim any one prophet, it does not worship any one god, it does not subscribe to any one dogma, it does not believe in any one philosophic concept, it does not follow any one set of religious rites or performances, in fact, it does not appear to satisfy the narrow traditional features of any religion or creed. It may broadly be described as a way of life and nothing more.'[28]

In a way, they followed in the footsteps of the second President of India, Dr Sarvepalli Radhakrishnan, who was also a Hindu scholar. The Supreme Court adopted his view that Hinduism is complex and that 'the theist and atheist, the sceptic and agnostic, may all be Hindus if they accept the Hindu system of culture and life'.

In 1990, a series of decisions were taken by the Supreme Court to define Hindutva, known as the 'Hindutva Judgments'. The then president of the Supreme Court Bar Association, Ram Jethmalani, interpreted in 1995 that 'Ordinarily, Hindutva is understood as a way of life or a state of mind and is not to be equated with or understood as religious Hindu'.[29]

He also suggested that the Supreme Court had provided clarity on the 'true meaning' of the term, stating that 'Hindutva is not hostile to any organized religion, nor does it proclaim the superiority of any religion over another'. At the same time, there are some opposing views, though they are minuscule.

Over the past 600 years, many great personalities have given an identity to the cause of Hinduness or Hindutva, not necessarily using the term but through their actions. Attempts have been made to distinguish between Hindutva and 'Hinduism'. As we have already discussed, the term 'Hinduism' is not appropriate for the Hindu dharmic system, so there is no meaningful comparison. The same applies to the term 'Hindu religion'—it does not fit the definition of a religion. What about the Hindutva ideas of Chandranath Basu and Savarkar? If we deeply contemplate it, they did not present different ideas; essentially, they are the same. Perhaps each has its own dimension—one is more *adhyatmic* and social, while the other is more sociopolitical. Both are essential elements of Bharatiya heritage, but they are not separate or different concepts. The question is, do the proponents of Hindutva today fully understand it?

CHAPTER 10

Nationalism: Meaning and Scope of Freedom

Bharat is undergoing a period of transformation. Indians are re-evaluating their unique knowledge system and critically examining what has been imposed upon them by external forces—first during the medieval Islamic invasions, then by Western colonists, and more recently by Marxists. The process of decolonization and de-Marxization of Indian thoughts has made notable progress in recent times, though much work remains.

Liberty and Nationalism: The Bharatiya Way

Bharatiya *sabhyata* (Indian civilization) expresses its essence through unique and broad concepts such as dharma, Ishwara, rashtra, *varna,* yoga, *darshana, atman*, and many more. These ideas have often been expressed through non-Indian terminologies, which offer limited and often derogatory interpretations—such as religion, God, nation, caste, philosophy, relaxing exercise, soul, etc. This has resulted in considerable harm, not only by distorting India's own understanding of its ideas and hindering its socio-economic and cultural progress but also by misrepresenting the scope and potential of individuals and civilizations at large. Institutions like Jawaharlal Nehru University have played a role in perpetuating this process because of significant presence of certain communist streams and leaders.

Despite enduring numerous assaults over millennia, Bharat has maintained a continuous tradition of knowledge and wisdom, much of which remains available for the world to 'rediscover'. Freedom (particularly freedom of expression) and nationalism are the central themes of today's discourse—age-old topics that deal with our true nature as individuals and our relationship to the world around us.

The debate surrounding fundamental ideas of life can be invigorating. These ideas encompass notions such as the preference for various forms of government, the roles of citizens and the state, the constitution, race, caste, gender, and more. A debate is valuable if it brings enlightenment. It should not deepen divisions but rather contribute to progress and peace.

Let us first examine how the West, often regarded as the torchbearer of modern democracy, expresses the concept of freedom in a secular context. British scholar Isaiah Berlin proposed two types of freedom: negative and positive.[1] Negative freedom refers to the space within which an individual can act as they wish, free from interference. Positive freedom, on the other hand, involves adherence to laws that we prescribe to ourselves, ensuring that no one can enslave themselves.

English philosopher Maurice W. Cranston[2] accepted Berlin's ideas and refined the concept of positive freedom into two forms: individualist 'rational freedom' (as proposed by Kant), which finds freedom in self-discipline, and 'compulsory rational freedom' (as proposed by Hegel), which sees freedom as arising from discipline alone, thus becoming a social ethic or obligation.

In turn, American philosopher Mortimer J. Adler discussed two types of freedom: 'circumstantial' and 'acquired' freedom.[3] Circumstantial freedom refers to unimpeded actions that allow the individual to pursue their own good as they see fit, thereby fulfilling their desires. This type of freedom depends on the circumstances that affect an individual's ability to carry out their wishes. Acquired freedom, on the other hand, involves doing what one ought to do. It depends on the state of mind or character that enables an individual to act according to the moral law or an ideal that is in keeping with human nature.

What is the difference? 'The acquired freedom of being able to will as one ought, and the circumstantial freedom of being able to do as one pleases.'[4] The idea of 'acquired freedom' aligns with the thoughts of Plato, the Stoics, Kant, and Hegel.

Most of the world discusses 'rights'—human rights, women's rights, black rights, minority rights, and so on. These discussions arise because these rights are not properly granted; their freedom is restricted. Bharat, however, is unique in that it places primary emphasis on 'duty' (*kartavya* and dharma as duty) rather than 'rights'. Bharat believed that all entities in a society performed their 'dharma' (dharma, meaning duties and not 'religion') according to their position and role, and in doing so, all rights would be taken care of.

Bharat has long since lost much of this righteous norm, which is why corruption, discrimination, and nepotism are so prevalent today. However, Bharat can return to its natural order. By doing so, it can not only transform its own state and destiny but also have a profound impact on global civilization.

With this contextual framework, let us examine the Indian concepts of 'freedom'. In recent times, four Indian thinkers and leaders have significantly contributed to this area of thought: Swami Vivekananda, Rabindranath Tagore, Sri Aurobindo, and Mahatma Gandhi. Their perspectives give little credence to socialistic ideas (Sri Aurobindo, in particular, severely criticized socialism and communism, highlighting their internal contradictions and limitations). These luminaries also evaluated Western secular thoughts and connected them with the higher and broader ideas of liberty rooted in Bharat. The following quote by Swami Vivekananda illustrates the profound characteristics of Indian thought of freedom:

> There is one wonderful phenomenon, connected with our lives, without which 'who will be able to live, who will be able to enjoy life a moment?' – the idea of freedom. This is the idea that guides

each footstep of ours, makes our movements possible, determines our relations to each other – nay, is the very warp and woof in the fabric of human life.[5]

For Bharat, freedom is sacred and inherently spiritual. But what kind of freedom was Swami Vivekananda referring to? He articulated:

Liberty of thought and action is the only condition of life, of growth and well-being. Where it does not exist, the man, the race, the nation must go down. Caste or no caste, creed or no creed, any man, or class, or caste, or nation, or institution which bars the power of free thought and action of an individual – even so long as that power does not injure others – is devilish and must go down.[6]

Sri Aurobindo analyzed the dual aspects of freedom: outer and inner. He observed:

Nature does not manufacture, does not impose a pattern or a rule from outside; she impels life to grow from within and to assert its own natural law and development modified only by its commerce with its environment. All liberty, individual, national, religious, social, ethical, takes its ground upon this fundamental principle of our existence. By liberty we mean the freedom to obey the law of our being, to grow to our natural self-fulfilment, to find out naturally and freely our harmony with our environment … If a real, a spiritual and psychological unity were effectuated, liberty would have no perils and disadvantages; for free individuals enamoured of unity would be compelled by themselves, by their own need, to accommodate perfectly their own growth with the growth of their fellows and would not feel themselves complete except in the free growth of others. Because of our present imperfection and the ignorance of our mind and will, law and regimentation have to be called in to restrain and to compel from outside.[7]

He cautioned against the overreach of human-made rules and laws:

Carried too far, an imposed order discourages the principle of natural growth which is the true method of life and may even slay

> the capacity for real growth. ... And all repressive or preventive law is only a makeshift, a substitute for the true law which must develop from within and be not a check on liberty, but its outward image and visible expression. Human society progresses really and vitally in proportion as law becomes the child of freedom; it will reach its perfection when, man having learned to know and become spiritually one with his fellow-man, the spontaneous law of his society exists only as the outward mould of his self-governed inner liberty.[8]

He further elaborated:

> [The] more the outer law is replaced by an inner law, the nearer man will draw to his true and natural perfection ... This further evolution demands the growth of a higher form of freedom ... The solution lies in ... a spiritual, an inner freedom that can alone create a perfect human order.[9]

Finally, he concluded, 'Therefore the truest order is that which is founded on the greatest possible liberty; for liberty is at once the condition of vigorous variation and the condition of self-finding.'[10]

Rabindranath Tagore expressed similar thought in the following manner:

> Neither the colourless vagueness of cosmopolitanism, nor the fierce self-idolatry of nation-worship, is the goal of human history. And India has been trying to accomplish her task through social regulation of differences, on the one hand, and the spiritual recognition of unity on the other ... from the early time of the Upanishads up to the present moment, a series of great spiritual teachers, whose one object has been to set at naught all differences of man by the overflow of our consciousness of God. In fact, our history has not been of the rise and fall of kingdoms, of fights for political supremacy. In our country records of these days have been despised and forgotten, for they in no way represent the true history of our people. Our history is that of our social life and attainment of spiritual ideals.[11]

From the Indian perspective, the highest form of freedom is 'spiritual freedom' or *adhyatmic* freedom. While Berlin's concept of 'positive freedom' and Cranston's notion of 'rational freedom' echo certain aspects of Indian ideas, many Western thinkers, such as John Laird and H.J. Mueller, criticized and dismissed Indian philosophies as meaningless and irrelevant. The rejection stems from their materialistic worldviews and differing understandings of human nature, which are often disconnected from the idea of an Absolute and its significance in the political and spiritual realms.

According to Berlin, 'Negative Freedom wants to curb authority as such. Positive Freedom wants it placed in their own hands.'[12] Bharat, however, does not view negative and positive freedom as two distinct or irreconcilable concepts. Instead, they are seen as two ends of the same spectrum. Indians perceive freedom from all forms of bondage—physical and mental, material and psychological, political and social—as one end, and freedom to realize one's harmony with all of existence and beings, culminating in self-realization in the material world, as the other end.

Swami Vivekananda provides a profound illustration of this thought by interconnecting the concepts of God, nature, the individual self, and freedom:

> The God of heaven, becomes the God in nature, and the God in nature becomes the God who is nature, and the God who is nature becomes the God within this temple of the body, and the God dwelling in the temple of the body at last becomes the temple itself, becomes the soul and man—and there it reaches the last words it can teach. He whom the sages have been seeking in all these places is in their own hearts; the voice that you heard was right, says the Vedanta, but the direction you gave the voice was wrong. That ideal of freedom that you perceived was correct but you projected it outside yourself, and that was your mistake. Bringing it nearer and nearer until you find that it was all the time within you, it was the Self of your own self.[13]

He also addressed the material dimension of human nature:

> What, again, is the meaning of liberty? Liberty does not certainly mean the absence of obstacles in the path of misappropriation of wealth etc., by you and me, but it is our natural right to be allowed to use our own body, intelligence or wealth according to our will, without doing any harm to others; and all the members of a society ought to have the same opportunity for obtaining wealth, education or knowledge ... One should raise the self by the self... Let each work out one's own salvation. Freedom in all matters, i.e., advance towards Mukti, is the worthiest gain of man. To advance one's self towards freedom, physical, mental and spiritual, and help others to do so, is the supreme prize of man. Those social rules which stand in the way of the unfoldment of this freedom are injurious, and steps should be taken to destroy them speedily. Those institutions should be encouraged by which man advance in the path of freedom.[14]

This inner freedom begins by loosening the grip of pre-programmed instincts and emotions, progressing towards rationality, and ultimately reaching the *adhyatmic* level. The first step towards ultimate freedom—the attainment of moksha—is freeing oneself from greed, anger, jealousy, and deep attachments to material pleasures. Only then do the virtues and interpersonal principles of *ahimsha (*non-injury*), satya (*commitment to truth-seeking and living*), asteya (*not taking possession of things without proper ownership or consent*), brahmacharya (*managing sensual pleasures and instincts*)*, and *aparigraha* (avoiding unchecked accumulation of wealth and limiting greed*)* acquire real meaning for both social and individual existence.

The power to transcend lower impulses and instincts lies within us. The Indian yoga system serves as a pathway for individuals and societies to evolve towards higher levels of conscious living. Modern evolutionary and developmental psychologists such as Clare Graves, Don Beck, Robert Kegan, Kurt Fischer, and Jenny Wade pointed towards a sociocultural evolution of humans and societies—an evolution that aligns closely with the wisdom offered by Indian seers long ago.

This profound understanding of freedom is echoed in the words of American economist Samuel Bowles, 'The cause of Freedom is the cause of God!'[15]

Role of Freedom, Adhyatma, and Dharma

To Dwight D. Eisenhower, the power of freedom is inherent and vital: 'Freedom has its life in the hearts, the actions, the spirit of men and so it must be daily earned and refreshed—else like a flower cut from its life-giving roots, it will wither and die.'[16]

The debate surrounding the concept of nationalism in India has several limitations, making it essential to clearly understand the terms patriotism, nationalism, nation, state, and country. These terms are often interpreted and expressed differently by different individuals.

Life is a series of changes requiring decisions (or indecisions) and actions (or inactions), all shaped by our worldview. Human decisions are driven by various faculties: instincts (reactions stemming from genetic programming), emotions (responses generated by the neural networks of the brain), and logic (based on the processing of available facts). However, facts are often incomplete, and instincts and emotions frequently dominate. Occasionally, a rare 'other voice' emerges—what we call 'intuition'.

Intuition, which has become a subject of significant modern study, has long been central to spiritual traditions. It is viewed as a power of consciousness closest to the original source of all knowledge—*jnana* or *gyana*. Yoga serves as the methodology and path to attaining this true knowledge.

What is 'spirituality'? Spirituality is the closest English equivalent to the Bharatiya concept of *adhyatma*. It is defined as the 'science of self'—a means to understand one's inner core in relation to the rest of creation, with or without the presence of a 'creator' being. Importantly, this concept transcends the boundaries of religion.

Swami Vivekananda remarked, 'Religion [dharma] is the manifestation of divinity already in man. It is being and becoming, not hearing and acknowledging.'[17] In my view, spirituality is the ability to recognize the position of the self while simultaneously connecting with the world as both a part of and an extension of oneself. This understanding is central to yoga, which transcends concerns with 'religion'.

Adhyatma is experienced and expressed through dharma—the sustaining principles and actions that govern harmonious relationships between the self and creation. These relationships extend symbiotically to encompass family, society, country, land, rivers, air, plants, and animals. Thus, *adhyatma* is neither a religion nor a belief system; it is the lived experience of yoga or union in everyday life. This is a concept that an atheist, a secularist, and a religious person alike can appreciate and agree upon.

J. Allen Boone, a lesser-known author and expert in non-verbal communication, particularly with animals, beautifully articulated this sense of universal connectedness: 'We are members of a vast cosmic orchestra in which each living instrument is essential to the complementary and harmonious playing of the whole.'[18]

In addition to spiritual frameworks, a social and legal force emerges from the collective decision-making of society and the judiciary. This force plays an integral role in daily life, blending utility, ethics, and intuitive formulations to create and maintain a harmonious social order.

Let us revisit dharma once more:

धारणात् धर्म इत्याहुः धर्मों धारयति प्रजाः।
यः स्यात् धारणसंयुक्तः स धर्म इति निश्चयः।।

Dharanat dharmam ityahu dharmo dharayate praajah
Yah svadharansamyuktah sa Dharma iti nischayah.
—'Karnaparva' (69.59), Mahabharata

(The word dharma is derived from *dharana* [sustenance]. Dharma sustains society, and that which has the capacity to sustain is indeed dharma.)

In Shankaracharya's introduction to the *Commentary on the Gita*, he defines the twofold dharma, which has roots in Rishi Kanada, the founder of the Vaiseshika *darshana*, as follows:

द्विविधःहिवेदोक्तःधर्मः, प्रवृत्ति–लक्ष्मनःनिवृत्ति–लक्ष्मनःच
तत्रएकःजगतःस्थिति–कारणंप्राणिनांसाक्षाद्अभ्युदय–निःश्रेयस–हेतुः

dvividho hi vedokto dharmah; pravítti-laksano nivritti-laksanah ca tatraekah jagatah sthiti-karanam praninam sakshat-abhyudaya-nihshreyas-hetuh

(The dharma taught in the Vedas is of twofold nature, characterized by *pravritti* [outward action] and *nivritti* [inward contemplation, or the power and tendency to detach]. It is meant for the stability of the world and ensures *abhyudaya* [material prosperity and socioeconomic welfare], as well as *nihshreyasa* [spiritual freedom and attainments] for all beings.)

Modern society is on the verge of finding a solution to the conflicts between material and moral wars. Bharat responded to this dilemma long ago, stating that we need both action and meditative contemplation to create a sustainable, dharma-based world.

According to the Confucian concept of *jen*, human-heartedness and righteousness form the foundation of individual and social responsibilities, where the proper conduct of relationships is paramount. Self-development and sustenance rooted in this inner morality, in turn, help develop and sustain others. *Jen* is a fundamental virtue that refers to the principle of common humanity. This is strikingly similar to the concept of dharma.

According to Taoism, dharma is described as 'an emblem, meaning order, the whole, responsibility, efficiency', and 'it is the

Responsible Efficient, Total Order, creation as a whole, the whole of what is, multiplicity'.[19]

Management guru Stephen R. Covey (author of *The 7 Habits of Highly Effective People*) has categorically referred to these as: 'principles that govern human growth and happiness – natural laws'. He also stated, 'Every human has four endowments- self-awareness, conscience, independent will and creative imagination. These give us the ultimate human freedom ... The power to choose, to respond, to change.'[20] This is the power of *nivritti*—the power of deeper contemplation and harmony.

It is surprising to see many atheists and communists (anti-spiritualists) in India today quoting Rabindranath's views on nationalism. The same communists once called him 'a poet of the bourgeois'. They seek shelter in what they do not have faith in: spirituality. Rabindranath always believed in humanism, which is rooted in India's age-old vision of '*vasudhaiva kutumbakam*' (the entire creation is one large family), '*sarve bhavantu sukihna, sarve santu niramayah*' (let everyone be happy and healthy), and other similar sage concepts. He perhaps saw the impatience and tendency to copy the West and feared that Indian leaders would adopt alien ideas imported from the West for their national life, such as 'religion' or 'nationalism'. India, however, has dharma and *desh-bhakti* (reverence for the land), which are broader and distinct from the Western political framework. He was deeply disturbed about the future and mission of India: 'Light to the world.' To steer the thoughts of his countrymen in the right direction, he prayed:

Where the mind is without fear and the head is held high
Where knowledge is free
Where the world has not been broken up into fragments
By narrow domestic walls
Where words come out from the depth of truth
Where tireless striving stretches its arms towards perfection
Where the clear stream of reason has not lost its way
Into the dreary desert sand of dead habit

Where the mind is led forward by thee
Into ever-widening thought and action
Into that heaven of freedom, my Father, let my country awake.[21]

This ideal of freedom in Bharat is based on the ultimate concept of freedom—*mukti* or *moksha*. But alas! The tragedy in Bharat today is that many supporters of religious and ideological terrorism and separatism are trying to find shelter in Rabindranath, like 'devils quoting the scriptures'!

What is the love of a son for his mother like? Why do we form attachments to things, living and non-living? Biology provides a helpful explanation. We create neural circuits in our brain in the form of 'memories', and our nervous system also forms 'pleasure' and 'pain' centres. These centres can be activated when certain internal or external stimuli trigger specific memories. Each time we recall pleasant memories, the pleasure centres are activated, possibly releasing 'feel-good' chemicals like dopamine. The reverse is also true. Since childhood, we have built these neural circuits, continuously pruning them while retaining the baseline. Our DNA, hormones, and neurons control our thoughts and actions, which we may refer to as 'instincts'.

Beyond instincts, we are thinking and utilitarian beings, which leads us to develop emotions and attachments. Nature has done this to prioritize survival, creating space for higher forms of living. Through this process, we grow in empathy and compassion. That is where purely animalistic material living ends. Gradually, emotions, intellect, logic, and ultimately, intuitive powers intertwine with the human spirit of interconnectedness, reaching the doorsteps of spirituality, or *adhyatma*.

In India, deep impressions of the external and inner world are referred to as *samskaras.* Positive *samsakaras* lead us towards progressive actions, while negative ones push us towards destructive behaviours. Thus, our animal instincts, combined with negative *samaskars,* can make one's thoughts and actions demonic—such as those of suicide bombers, destroyers of harmony, or individuals who relentlessly seek the accumulation of power and wealth.

Let's extrapolate instinct, emotions, compassion, and love for our parents, family, and clan to our birthplace. We share a similar bond, faith, love, attraction, affinity, and even weakness with our birthplace, which reflects the true nature of the world. This is why love for our country or motherland feels so natural.

As Bernard Shaw noted: 'Patriotism: Your conviction that this country is superior to all other countries because you were born in it.'[22]

However, the Marxists attempted to defy both biology and the human spirit of compassion. For them, the family is a 'structural conflict' in the pursuit of a 'classless' society. The family, as the basic unit of societal living, was something Marxists could never fully accept: 'Abolition of the family! [...] The bourgeois family will disappear, in the course [of history] as its supplement [private property] disappears, and both will vanish with the destruction of capital.'[23]

Moreover, Indian communists never truly sought a united Bharat. Therefore, when they speak of nationalism, it is, at best, a travesty.

Love for a country is somewhat akin to the love and affinity we feel for a parent, family, or clan. Our being is shaped by the impulses from which we create our identity. You may call it kinship, but it also forms the foundation for love of one's country. Filial love is similar to the love we feel for the nation into which we are born. Simply put, this love for your country is patriotism. Bharat has embraced this love for its motherland since the early days of its history, as reflected in the Ramayana and encapsulated in the great motto: 'Mother and motherland are greater than heaven.'

At first, love for one's mother and motherland is emotional. But it evolves as every inhabitant of the land takes on duties and obligations towards the land that provides them with sustenance. This is both a moral and social responsibility, with legal duties involved as well—everything is part of what Bharat calls 'dharma'. This includes acts and responsibilities to uphold, protect, and serve the land. From the rulers' point of view, this is *Raj Dharma;* for the citizens of the country, it is *Praja Dharma.*

What Are Nationalism and Patriotism?

Generally, people use 'patriotism' and 'nationalism' interchangeably, but there is often no clear agreement on their definitions.

According to the Oxford Dictionary, nationalism is defined as:

- A feeling of loving your country very much and being very proud of it; a feeling that your country is better than any other
- The desire by a group of people who share the same ethnic group, culture, language, etc., to form an independent country

Merriam-Webster, on the other hand, defines nationalism as:

- An ideology that elevates one nation or nationality above all others and that placed primary emphasis on promotion of its culture and interests as opposed to those of other nations, nationalities, or supranational groups
- A nationalist movement or government

In contrast, Merriam-Webster defines patriotism simply as the 'love for or devotion to one's country'.

Many thinkers around the world have abhorred the ideas of nationalism and patriotism. The most substantial criticism came from the Russian author and religious thinker Leo Tolstoy, who said: 'The feeling of patriotism – It is an immoral feeling because, instead of confessing himself a son of God ... or even a free man guided by his own reason, each man under the influence of patriotism confesses himself the son of his fatherland and the slave of his government, and commits actions contrary to his reason and conscience.'[24] Tolstoy also influenced Rabindranath Tagore.

Indian-born British author George Orwell claimed that 'nationalism is the worst enemy of peace'. From our experience over the past two centuries, we can say that there is often a degree of a 'superiority' complex in those who declare themselves nationalists. Hitler's assertion of a superior German race serves as an example of extreme nationalism. Nationalism can also be construed as racism. British nationalism, for example, resulted in the subjugation and persecution of millions across Asia and Africa.

So, what is the difference between the two? The famous American journalist Sydney J. Harris simplified it as follows: 'The difference between patriotism and nationalism is that the patriot is proud of his country for what it does, and the nationalist is proud of his country no matter what it does; the first attitude creates a feeling of responsibility, but the second a feeling of blind arrogance that leads to war.'[25]

Therefore, it appears that the critical issue with these two concepts lies in the assertion of superiority—whether culture, moral, or economic—or through military power. The fine line is between 'pride' and 'superiority'. Anyone using the words nationalism or patriotism without considering this connotation of aggression might simply define them as 'love, loyalty, and duties for a nation or country'.

People have also confused these terms with love for a particular government or political party. Scottish poet Thomas Campbell said, 'The patriot's blood is the seed of Freedom's tree.'[26] Mark Twain warned, 'Patriotism is supporting your country all the time, and your government when it deserves it.'[27]

Irish historian and politician James Bryce offered a balanced view: 'Our country is not the only thing to which we owe our allegiance. It is also owed to justice and to humanity. Patriotism consists not in waving the flag, but in striving that our country shall be righteous as well as strong.'[28] This assertion echoes the Indian concept of Raj Dharma and Rashtra Dharma, the sacred duties of the ruler and the nation to their subjects.

When it comes to Bharat, it has never invaded any nation to impose its superiority. Instead, it has welcomed people from all over the world. In the field of learning, institutions like Taxila, Nalanda, and many others opened their doors to people from across the globe. In terms of embracing people with different worldviews, including Muslims and Christians, Bharat voluntarily welcomed them and provided space for them to establish their bases (this was before the invasions and proselytization campaigns of missionaries began). Thus, Bharat has become—and remains—the ideal pluralistic, open society, home to all the major religious groups, seculars, and atheists, who have coexisted for centuries. When it comes to providing shelter to the persecuted, Bharat has an exemplary record. From the Zoroastrians to the Jews, to the Tibetans, and even to people from Bangladesh, Bharat has never turned away those seeking refuge. Why is this so?

Because inherently, the Indian ethos is pluralistic and motherly, it is not about world domination or conquering others. This pluralism gave birth to great kings like Chandragupta, Samudragupta, Harshavardhan, Shivaji, and monumental spiritual leaders like Mahavir, Buddha, Nanak, Chaitanya, Sri Ramakrishna, and many others. This civilization declared:[29]

आनोभद्राःकरतवोकष्यन्तुविश्वतो.अदब्धासोअपरीतासउद्भिदः |
देवानोयथासदमिदवर्धेअसन्नप्रायुवोरक्षितारोदिवे–दिवे ||

ā no bhadrāḥ kratavo kṣyantu viśvato adabdhāso aparītāsa udbhidaḥ
devā no yathā sadamid vṛdhe asanaprāyuvo rakṣitāro dive-dive

(May auspicious knowledge come to us from all sides, which harm no one, is unimpeded, and victorious over the forces of division. May the *devatas* always be with us for our growth, never moving away from us, but guarding us day by day.)

Bankim Chandra's 'Vande Mataram' and the idea of the 'mother' are not expressions of superiority. They are an offering to what Sri Aurobindo referred to as the 'collective consciousness of people', a sentiment that Rabindranath Tagore saluted in '*Jana gana mana adhinayaka*'.

American writer George W. Curtis echoed this sentiment of Sri Aurobindo, stating that a country is not merely a piece of land: 'A man's country is not a certain area of land, of mountains, rivers, and woods, but it is a principle; and patriotism is loyalty to that principle.'[30]

India's concept of a nation-state, or Rashtra, is not purely political. It is akin to federalism, with a most benevolent ruler or ruling system. The concept of Rashtra carried a deep and profound meaning; it is not just land, a country, or a nation but also encompasses the ethos, principles, obligations, duties, and the collective will of the people.

According to Aurobindo: 'Nationalism [Rashṭra-bhakti] is simply the passionate aspiration for the realization of that Divine Unity in the nation, a unity in which all the component individuals, however various and apparently unequal their functions as political, social or economic factors, are yet really and fundamentally one and equal.'[31]

Finally, Netaji Subhas Chandra Bose takes this idea of nationalism to a new dimension: 'Nationalism is inspired by the highest ideals of the human race: satyam [truth], shivam [highest ideal of Devattwa], sundaram [beauty and creativity]. Nationalism in India has … roused the creative faculties which for centuries had been lying dormant in our people.'[32] This thought—the concept of a Rashtra—is unique to Bharat.

In Sanskrit, love and devotion for the nation is called देशभक्ति (*deshbhakti*). There is also a Sanskrit term for the people's relationship to their country: देशआत्माबोध् (*deshatmabodh*); here, *desh* stands for country, and *atma* is used as in *atmiya,* meaning one who is connected to the *atman*, commonly a relative. So, *Bharatiya deshatmabodh* refers to the relationship of the individual to the *atman* of the nation.

There is a Vedic concept called ऋत (*ṛta*)—the 'natural order', the 'universal order', truth, and rule. Alongside this is the concept of dharma—the reciprocal sustaining principles and acts, both in the material and spiritual sense. The Vedic idea of Rashtra has direct links to *ṛta* and dharma. The *Rigveda* (9.7.1) declares:

असृग्रमिन्दवः पथा धर्मन्नृतस्य सुश्रियः ।
विदाना अस्य योजनम् ॥

asṛgram indavaḥ pathā dharmann ṛtasya suśriyaḥ |
vidānā asya yojanam ||

(With the support of and along *ṛta*, the principle of truth and order, flow soma essences [of life]; dharma stands parallel to the path, [which includes the principles, path, and acts for reciprocal sustainability and, ultimately, for 'being and becoming' what we are destined to be].)

Rashtra provides the framework for each citizen to follow dharma, thereby achieving progress and harmony with the rulers' firm commitment to dharma. Bharatiya society must evolve to the next level by paving the way for true patriots and leaders, discarding current-day political norms such as number games, caste division, and offering freebies to stay in power. Instead, we need an ambulance of leaders dedicated to serving the people sincerely. The 'business' and 'profession' of politics must shift, where politicians no longer run for election solely for money and power but for the true purpose of governance.

Hence, the *Rigveda*[33] offers this prayer:

ॐसंगच्छध्वं संवदध्वं
सं वो मनांसि जानताम्
देवा भागं यथा पूर्वे
सञ्जानानाउपासते||

saṃgacchadhwaṃ saṃvadadhwaṃ
saṃ vo manāṃsi jānatām
devā bhāgaṃ yathā pūrve
sañjānānā upāsate ||

(May you move in harmony, speak in one voice, and let your minds be in agreement, just as the ancient *devatas* shared their portion of the sacrifice.)

The key to Bharatiya thought is diversity and harmony, not homogeneity and uniformity. Incidentally, some scholars have suggested that the '*Sanjanana*' mentioned in the last *shloka* refers to Devi Saraswati, the goddess associated with wisdom and knowledge, and the goddess of *ganatantra* (democracy).

We can also meditate upon another *sukta* from the *Rigveda:*[34]

समानी व आकूतिः समाना हृदयानि वः |
समानमस्तु वो मनो यथा वः सुसहासति ॥

samānī va ākūtiḥ samānā hṛdayāni vaḥ |
samānam astu vo mano yathā vaḥ susahāsati ||

(Let your intentions and inner self [*hṛdayāni*] be one—mutually equal [*samānā*] and in harmony. Let our minds and intellects reside in harmony [*susahāsati*] within us. Let your hearts be alike.)

Society can progress in harmony once responsible citizens and those in power adhere to the mandate outlined above; challenges should be analyzed and resolved amicably together.

Interestingly, people today often gather more under a political party banner than the national flag. There are over 2,500 political parties in India. Most of these parties claim to serve the nation (with the exception of partisan ones like the communists and the Muslim League), but in reality, they divide society and its people. The lack of collective effort, as suggested in the Vedic mantra *saṃgacchadhwaṃ* described earlier, must be addressed by removing divisiveness in the name of politics, religion, or caste.

Social and judicial laws largely pertain to the masses. While living within an Indian Rashtra system, we have discussed moral duties. People should observe and fulfill a few ऋण (ṛṇa), which can be loosely translated as debts, obligations, or commitments.

The *Rigveda*[35] refers to the *ṛṇatraya,* the three obligations under which every human being is born. These obligations are elaborated in Vedic literature, such as the *Taittiriya Samhitā*[36], and are associated with certain offering or *yajna* (rituals), often referred to as the *'pancha maha yajnas':*

- *Pitri-rna (Pitri Yajna)*: Duties to ancestors (including female ones) to ensure that the institution of parenthood is respected, protected, and strengthened. Activities include the highest respect for parents and ancestors, *shradda* (rituals for the departed), and *tarpana* (obsequies ceremonies).
- *Deva-rna:* Duties to all natural and divine forces, which involve observing, understanding, and utilizing divine powers through the performance of yajnas or Vedic sacrifices.
- *Rishi-rna (Brahma Yajna):* Duties to the seers and teachers to ensure that the institution of learning is respected, protected, and propagated. Activities include *svādhyāya* (self-study or study of scriptures) and *tapas* (austerity and penance).

Is it possible that the original concepts of Rashtra were inspired by terms like *ra-tra* or *rna-tra,* or *ṛṇatrayaṃ,* where all citizens were obliged to fulfill these *rnas*?

The *Satapatha Brahmana*[37] notes two additional *rnas*:

- *Nri-rna (Manushya Yajna*): This refers to compassion and duties towards fellow human beings. Activities include *athithi satkara* (honouring guests), serving guests at home, feeding unannounced guests, helping relatives and neighbours, and serving the poor.
- *Bhuta-rna* (*Bhuta Yajna*): This involves compassion, protection, and preservation of nature, including plants and animals.

The Practical Implications of Patriotism and Free Speech

Now, let us return to our primary duties towards our land and her people, according to the standards of a modern democratic system. Mark Twain sums up these duties nicely:

> My kind of loyalty was to one's country, not to its institutions or officeholders. The country is the real thing, the substantial thing, the eternal thing; it is the thing to watch over, and care for, and be loyal to; institutions are extraneous, they are its mere clothing, and clothing can wear out, become ragged, cease to be comfortable, cease to protect the body from winter, disease, and death.[38]

Thomas Paine spoke about the nature of such a nation: 'Those who expect to reap the blessings of freedom, must, like men, undergo the fatigue of supporting it.'[39]

However, Indian communists neither believe in a nation nor a state. They advocate for a utopian 'world communism—a worldwide stateless communist society, similar to an Islamic world or Islamic Khilafat, or *Dar-ul-Islam*'. We also know quite a bit about those who have little to no respect for the Indian flag; after all, one of the favourite role models of the NeoCols, Arundhati Roy, said: 'Flags are bits of colored cloth used first to shrink-wrap people's brains and then as ceremonial shrouds to bury the dead.'[40] Unfortunately, many in Bharat also share this view.

We must understand the broader concepts of Rashtra, dharma, *rna*, and others to rescue the nation from the crisis it has faced. These concepts are immensely valuable for the foundation of an advanced human civilization. On a more specific note, I support the views of American politician Adlai E. Stevenson II: 'Patriotism is not short, frenzied outbursts of emotion, but the tranquil and steady dedication of a lifetime.'[41]

We must remind rational people who value democracy of the warning given by Theodore Roosevelt:

> Patriotism means to stand by the country. It does not mean to stand by the president, or any other public official save exactly to the degree in which he himself stands by the country. It is patriotic to support him insofar as he efficiently serves the country. It is unpatriotic not to oppose him to the exact extent that by inefficiency or otherwise he fails in his duty to stand by the country.[42]

Is Bharat free from British colonial thoughts, rules, and laws? Does the Indian Constitution truly allow freedom to the people, or is it merely an instrument to perpetuate foreign ideologies through the hands of Indians themselves? In the wisdom of Rabindranath Tagore: 'Political freedom does not give us freedom when our mind is not free. An automobile does not create freedom of movement, because it is a mere machine. When I myself am free I can use the automobile for the purpose of my freedom.'[43]

Is freedom, like the world's largest constitution, in consonance with the ethos and aspirations of the people of Bharat? Does it grant true freedom to all? It may be time to ask these questions, including revisions, clarifications, and perhaps the elimination of many outdated rules, such as the 150-year-old British Sedition Law of 1860 (Indian Penal Code Chapter VI, Sections 121–30, Offences against the State).

According to Kautilya:

> [The State] must be based on sound economic foundations, so that it enables men to realize the aims of his life, to lessen as much as possible, the struggle of existence at home, to lessen the dependence of the community on the outside world, to be in a position to help other sections of humanity in distress, and thereby to ensure an existence conducive to the happiness of men in this life and paving the way to a brighter beyond.[44]

For Kautilya, the state is not merely a materialistic concept, but a spiritual one. And 'spiritual' does not mean 'religious'—it refers to an inner connection between one's self and the rest of creation, including the social and political spheres.

Sri Aurobindo has provided us with a roadmap for a higher social structure and political framework, where societies and political systems evolve from the current models into a society 'in which respect for individual liberty and free growth of the personal being to his perfection is harmonized with respect for the needs, and efficiency, solidarity, natural growth and organic perfection of the corporate being'.[45]

He envisioned that nation-states would evolve into a true 'world union' of states, allowing for maximum diversity among all inhabitants—individuals, ethnic groups, races, and creeds—to realize their highest potential. These are the long-term goals of our civilizations.

Similarly, according to Rabindranath Tagore:

> [Man] will have to exert all his power of love and clarity of vision to make another great moral adjustment which will comprehend the whole world of men and not merely the fractional groups of nationality. The call has come to every individual in the present age to prepare himself and his surroundings for this dawn of a new era when man shall discover his soul in the spiritual unity of all human beings.[46]

This has been the message of Bharat all along. Bharat does not believe in the aforementioned 'negative freedom'. It believes in absolute freedom—moksha—for all of humanity. However, for one to attain this, one must first have material prosperity, security, and equal opportunities, which can only be created by a nation-state, or more precisely, by the Rashtra.

Thus, before one aspires to serve the universe as a global citizen, one must begin at home—serving the family, the state, and the country first. Charity begins at home. While loving and serving all of humanity can be a noble slogan and ideal, it becomes a hypocritical expression if we fail to serve those closest to us. Unfortunately, Bharat is still the hub of romantic and utopian ideologues who dream of a 'classless' world!

Therefore, for now, as far as the boundaries and walls around the country are concerned, while the ultimate goal may be a borderless world, the current jihadist and neo-colonial expansionism necessitates strong borders—especially when forces of domination and destruction, whether in the name of jihad or trade, are continuously attempting to cross them to cause harm. Those who cannot agree are free to voluntarily travel to the other side of the border.

A final reminder to some of the misguided youth of Bharat—as Andre Gide, the French Nobel Laureate, said, 'To know how to free oneself is nothing; the arduous thing is to know what to do with one's freedom.'[47]

Free speech is truly free only if it does not undermine the privileges provided by freedom itself. If free speech has the imminent potential to harm people or national interests—such as security, unity, and social harmony—then it comes at a cost! If one cannot respect a nation's flag, national song/anthem, constitution, law, and judicial system, one is free to leave and live in another fantasy dreamland. Such individuals lack a sense of gratitude, reciprocity, or commitment to the land's progress and its people. In that case, they belong to a culture of ingratitude and are nothing but parasites in society.

Today, Bharat needs millions of dedicated *deshbhaktas*—patriotic citizens and leaders committed to the *rnas*—to change the course and cleanse the curse of the crash that befell her.

CHAPTER 11

Misperceptions about the Hindu Dharmic System

If you are a victim of caste-related discrimination, you should be empowered to resist it through the legal system, and you must work to change your destiny. After all, affirmative action for historically 'backward' classes has been in effect for over a century; it's time to catch up. The British began offering quotas for certain neglected communities as early as 1882.

Manuvad and Casteism

If you are an apologetic Hindu and believe that Hinduism would be great if not for casteism and 'Brahmanism', there is hope. And if you are a Hindu who is seriously interested in understanding the history and finding remedies for the wrongs committed against the 'lower castes', please read on.

How many Hindu households have a copy of the Ramayana, the Mahabharata, or the Bhagavad Gita? I am sure the number would be quite high. But how many households have a copy of the *Manusmriti*? I would say it's close to zero. How many Hindu priests own a copy, or how many of them teach the *Manusmriti* to their congregations? It would still be near zero.

So why is there so much noise against a book ascribed to Manu—one that Hindus themselves have almost forgotten? The answer lies with the Marxist 'historians' and groups shedding crocodile tears to advance their divisive agendas.[1] The so-called 'Dalit' advocates needed to find a target, a scapegoat, and a source to vilify the entire Hindu society to establish their hegemony. Then came their eureka moment: the *Manusmriti*.

These NeoCols, who long dominated the field of historiography, used this text to peddle their narratives. Until recently, only a handful of academics and scholars dared to challenge their pet theories and expose their fraudulent historical accounts.

Ah, the *Manusmriti*—the supposed fountainhead of all caste discrimination and the oppression of women! But have you read it? Perhaps not. I have. And what does it really say? According to their claims, it states that 'low castes and women do not have any rights and their lives are made difficult by the upper castes'. But does it, really? Let us examine a few *sutras* from the *Manusmriti,* widely available in the market, primarily translated by British 'scholars' and later by Marxist 'academics'. In reality, the original manuscript is lost, because of which we do not have any manuscript to verify the validity of currently available translations!

The NeoCols made us believe that the *Manusmriti* caused all the issues in Indian society through a few negative *shlokas* about lower castes and women. However, they conveniently ignore other *shlokas* that express the opposite, praising women. For example:[2]

पितृभिर्भ्रातृभिश्चैताः पतिभिर्देवरैस्तथा ।
पूज्या भूषयितव्याश्च बहुकल्याणमीप्सुभिः ॥

pitṛbhirbhrātṛbhiścaitāḥ patibhirdevaraistathā |
pūjyā bhūṣayitavyāśca bahukalyāṇamīpsubhiḥ ||

(Women must be honoured and adorned by their fathers, brothers, husbands, and brothers-in-law, who desire their own welfare.)

यत्र नार्यस्तु पूज्यन्ते रमन्ते तत्र देवताः ।
यत्रैतास्तु न पूज्यन्ते सर्वास्तत्राफलाः क्रियाः॥[3]

yatra nāryastu pūjyante ramante tatra devatāḥ |
yatraitāstu na pūjyante sarvāstatrāphalāḥ kriyāḥ ||

(Where women are honoured, the gods are pleased, but no sacred rite yields rewards where they are not honoured.)

शोचन्ति जामयो यत्र विनश्यत्याशु तत् कुलम् ।[4]
न शोचन्ति तु यत्रैता वर्धते तद् हि सर्वदा ॥

śocanti jāmayo yatra vinaśyatyāśu tat kulam |
na śocanti tu yatraitā vardhate tad hi sarvadā ||

(Where female relations live in grief, the family soon wholly perishes, but that family where they are not unhappy ever prospers.)

जामयो यानि गेहानि शपन्त्यप्रतिपूजिताः ।[5]
तानि कृत्याहतानीव विनश्यन्ति समन्ततः ॥

jāmayo yāni gehāni śapantyapratipūjitāḥ |
tāni kṛtyāhatānīva vinaśyanti samantataḥ ||

(Not being duly honoured, the houses on which female relations pronounce a curse perish completely, as if destroyed by magic.)

The tactics of the NeoCols were clear: omission and commission, selective use of sources, and the whitewashing or sanitization of any dark spots on Islamic rulers and Islamist organizations.

The real issue, however, lies with the Hindus themselves. Their understanding, practice, and education about the Hindu dharmic system were poorly demonstrated during the post-independence era. A generation of Hindus, mostly educated in the British-introduced system, has grown increasingly distant from their roots—a situation further exacerbated by the NeoCols.

To address this, let us trace back the original source of *varna*, which was later interchangeably used as 'caste'. This misrepresentation has done a grave injustice to the rishis. The earliest reference to the origin of the four *varnas* or groups is found in the famous *Rigveda*: 'The Brahmana was His Mouth; the Kshatriya His Arms became. His Thighs the Vaisya was; of His Feet, the Sudra was born.'[6]

The Bhagavad Gita states: 'I created the fourfold order according to the divisions of quality *(guna)* and work *(karma)*; though I am its creator, know Me to be incapable of action or change.'[7]

Many social and political movements have abolished much of the caste system, often with the stated aim of 'liberating' or protecting the life, liberty, and livelihood of the so-called lower castes, the Dalits, and the untouchables. The term 'Manuvad' is frequently invoked in this context. The *Manusmriti* is often cited for its discriminatory and derogatory prescriptions against Shudras and women and is blamed for institutionalizing the birth-based caste system, supposedly the root cause of discrimination against the so-called lower castes.

However, which texts are the most popular and deeply intertwined with people's lives in terms of practice? These are the Ramayana, the Mahabharata, and the Bhagavad Gita (which is part of the Mahabharata). And what about the *Manusmriti*? As mentioned earlier, the *Manusmriti* is barely known by even a minuscule proportion of Hindus, let alone followed by the general Hindu population worldwide.

Moreover, the *Manusmriti* contains many contradictory verses, providing clear evidence of alterations, insertions, and interpolations. A careful reading of the available Sanskrit text reveals verses that differ in language, context, and flow, indicating that many of these were later additions. Even Dr B.R. Ambedkar, a champion of the neglected and backward classes, acknowledged the existence of fraudulent insertions into various scriptures, including the *Manusmriti*.[8]

According to J. Sinha, 'less than half, or only 1,214 of the 2,685 verses in *Manu Smriti*, may be authentic'.[9]

Yet, Ambedkar himself, along with latter-day leaders and followers of the 'Dalit' movements, made the *Manusmriti* and an imaginary 'Manuvad' (Manu-ism) the source of all societal evils.

They credited it as a conspiracy against the lower castes and formulated it as the bedrock of anti-Brahmanism.[10]

Some believe that since Brahmins were highly revered and held significant authority over other groups of people, they became the first to be empowered during the Muslim and British periods of rule. In turn, they were used as tools to control other groups, facilitate religious conversion, and enforce the rulers' divide-and-rule policies. During the Muslim period, this process was made easier by the creation of adverse rules for the lower classes, which led to their marginalization. Many were abandoned by the mainstream, leaving them vulnerable to absorption by Muslim preachers and clerics.

Additionally, there is evidence suggesting that the British, especially figures such as William Hunter and Thomas B. Macaulay, undertook deliberate projects aimed at altering ancient Indian texts for their own missions in India.

Sections of the *Manusmriti* that appear unfavourable to Shudras are often misunderstood, particularly when individual *shlokas* are read in isolation rather than as part of a broader context. While some verses seem to debar Shudras from learning Vedic knowledge, these interpretations often overlook the scripture's overall treatment of all four *varnas,* not solely the Shudras. For example:[11]

> As the son of a Shudra may attain the rank of a Brahmin if he were to possess his qualifications, character and accomplishments, and as the son of a Brahmin may become a Shudra, if he sinks to his level in his character, inclinations and manners, even so must it be with him who springs from a Kshatriya; even so with him who is born of a Vaishya. In other words, a person should be ranked with the Class whose qualifications, accomplishments, and character he possesses.
>
> [...]
>
> In [a case of] theft the guilt of a Shudra shall be eightfold, that of a Vaisya sixteen-fold, that of a Kshatriya two-and-thirty fold That of a Brahmana sixty-fourfold, or quite a hundredfold, or [even] twice four-and-sixtyfold; [each of them] knowing the nature of the offence.[12]

This example clearly shows no inherent bias towards the Brahmins. What about the fifth category—*Antyaja*/Untouchable/Dalit?

The so-called *harijans*, untouchables, *antyajas*, and Dalits also fall into certain *jatis*. Over time, the Shudra *varna* has been inaccurately conflated with these 'lower castes', or Dalits, and the scheduled castes (SC) and scheduled tribes (ST).

It is true that discrimination based on an individual's 'caste', especially by the so-called 'upper caste' against the 'lower-caste', has existed and continues in some places. However, today, the so-called 'caste-discrimination' has evolved into a 'class struggle' between the so-called SC and other backward classes (OBC) groups and others, largely a construct of the British era and now perpetuated by the NeoCols.

In reality, this has been reframed into a conflict of 'Dalits' versus the rest of society, classic Marxist strategy. In the current scenario, reverse discrimination is also evident due to the reservation system. The quota system has created challenges for the so-called upper-class groups, particularly in areas such as college admissions and government job placements.

Additionally, Christian missionaries worldwide have aligned themselves with this narrative, framing caste discrimination as a 'human rights violation' to facilitate their conversion agendas more effectively.

However, this portrayal overlooks that fact that the most common Hindu prayers focus on the well-being of all. Millions of Hindus chant the following prayers daily:

ॐ सर्वे भवन्तु सुखिनः सर्वे सन्तु निरामयाः ।[13]
सर्वे भद्राणि पश्यन्तु मा कश्चिद्दुःखभाग्भवेत् ।
ॐ शान्तिः शान्तिः शान्तिः ॥

Aum Sarve sukhina santu sarve santu niramayaha, s
arve bhadrani pashyantu ma kashshit dukhavag bhavet,
Aum Shantih Shantih Shantih

(May all be happy, may all be healthy, may all be blessed, may no one experience sorrow. Peace, peace, peace [be unto us].)

सर्वमंगलमांगल्ये शिवे सर्वार्थसाधिके ।[14]
शरण्ये त्र्यम्बके गौरी नारायणि नमोऽस्तु ते ।

Sarva managa mangalyam shive sarvarthsadhike
sharenyatrambake gauri narayani namostute |

(O Devi Durga, who bestows all-round welfare and goodness. O Shiva's consort, fulfiller of all desires, O refuge of all, O three-eyed Gauri, O Narayani, we bow to you.)

It is indeed puzzling that a Hindu who chants such inclusive and benevolent shlokas could engage in discrimination or persecution in the name of *jati* or caste. Any practice of discrimination and persecution in the name of jati, caste or gender violates the spirit of Dharma..

So, when did the *jati* or *varna* discrimination start? The Chinese traveller Hueng Tsang (630 CE) wrote extensively about Indian society.[15] However, his writings make no mention of social discrimination. While there were undoubtedly diverse social classes, there appears to have been a symbiotic coexistence.

Alberuni, who accompanied the invader Mahmud Ghaznavi, wrote about Indian society around 1030 CE. He mentioned the four *varnas,* as well as another group, the *antyaja* (such as leather merchants and *chandals*), who lived outside the mainstream. He observed, 'Much, however, as these classes differ from each other, they live together in the same towns and villages, mixed together in the same houses and lodgings.'[16] This observation suggests that a rigid and discriminatory system may have initially emerged as a response to the Islamic invasions, intended to protect each group. Later, it was further entrenched by the divisive policies of the British.

The *jati* system became more rigid due to foreign domination[17] and colonial rule, which lasted for centuries. There is clear evidence of various *jatis* fighting against the invaders, with many being forced to abandon the mainstream and live on the social fringes. At times, they lived in forests and, in the long run, became part of the 'lower' *jatis* due to a lack of interaction with the mainstream.

Scholar Ram Swarup has written, 'With the advent of Islam ... the [jati] system also acquired undesirable traits like untouchability ... during the Muslim period, many Rajputs were degraded, and they became scheduled castes and scheduled tribes. Many of them still retain the Rajput gotra.'[18]

Even during the 16th and 17th centuries, European travellers mentioned the caste system in passing, though without much emphasis.

The modern-day study of the Indian social system gained prominence with the 1891 Census, which introduced the 'Index of Castes'. The colonial Portuguese introduced the word 'caste' from their own 'casta', meaning lineage, breed, or race, to describe the Indian social system. Later, the British superimposed this term on the Indian *jati* system and further imposed the concepts of *varna* upon it.[19]

Only recently, alongside the theory of Aryan racism and invasions, people have started questioning the caste system's validity as an Indian apartheid system. Scholars such as Nicolas Dirks (Columbia University) have argued that the caste system contradicts Indian tradition. He squarely blamed the British for it, describing it as 'the product of a historical encounter between India and British colonial rule'.[20]

It also turns out that the scholars who wrote the dictionaries and textbooks conflated the Indian concepts of *jati*, *kula*, and *varna* with the Portuguese term 'casta'.[21] On one hand, they were influenced by their own European 'caste system'.[22] On the other hand, they failed to understand Indian society due to their ignorance. Still, Indians fell into the same trap: the British-educated Indians accepted what their white masters said and failed to study it independently.

The understanding of caste also took a wrong direction due to certain preconceived notions, particularly the belief that the Brahmins were the cause of all social evils in India. In his 1993 book *Interpretation of Caste,* Declan Quigley wrote:

> Unable to visualize a general structure of caste which would displace Dumont's theory;[23] they hang on to it unremittingly even though

> their own evidence shows again and again that this theory simply does not explain what is known about India ... The entrenched idea that 'Brahmans are the highest caste' has done most to hinder an alternative formulation of how caste systems work.[24]

Today, we are gradually learning about the superimposition of the Portuguese *casta* on Hindu *varna*. For over 100 years, scholars, writers, and sociologists parroted the British version of the caste story, which depicted India as a casteist society before the world, while they were part of creating a divisive 'caste system'.

Why did the British rulers do this? The simple answer is 'Divide and Rule'!

A renowned thinker and scholar, Dharampal took it upon himself to study India's past. While going through British archives, he uncovered many of India's hidden stories, leading to a shocking rediscovery of Bharat that challenged numerous myths about India's culture, tradition, and history. He wrote several books based on his discoveries, including *The Beautiful Tree: Indigenous Indian Education in the Eighteenth Century* (1983), *Indian Science and Technology in the Eighteenth Century* (1971), and *Civil Disobedience and Indian Tradition* (1971). While British rule fostered the belief among the educated Indian class that there was little to be proud of in India's past, Dharampal highlighted that India's own science and technology, education, and industries existed long before the British arrived and ultimately destroyed them.

Dharampal wrote in his book *Rediscovering India: Collection of Essays and Speeches, 1956–1998*:

> For the British, as perhaps for some others before them, caste has been a great obstacle, in fact, an unmitigated evil not because the British believed in casteless-ness or subscribed to non-hierarchical system but because it stood in the way of their breaking Indian society, hindered the process of atomization, and made the task of conquest and governance more difficult.[25]

By caste, Dharampal meant *jati*.

Scholar Koenraad Elst goes into more depth, writing:

> Christian and Muslim missionaries found it very difficult to lure Hindus away from their communities. Sometimes castes [*jatis*] were collectively converted to Islam, and Pope Gregory XV (1621–23) decreed that the missionaries could tolerate caste distinction among Christian converts. Still, by and large, caste remained a significant hurdle to the destruction of Hinduism through conversion. That is why the missionaries started attacking the institution of caste and, in particular, the Brahmin caste. This propaganda has blossomed into a full-fledged anti-Brahminism, the Indian equivalent of anti-Semitism ... This decentralized structure of civil society and of the Hindu religious commonwealth has been crucial to the survival of Hinduism under Muslim rule. Whereas Buddhism was swept away as soon as its monasteries were destroyed, Hinduism retreated into its caste structure and weathered the storm.[26]

Koenraad further explained:

> Abbe Dubois [1816], a French missionary, was one of the most influential European travelers. Dubois had difficulty in converting Hindus to Christianity. He attributed this difficulty to the Hindu 'caste prejudices'. Hindus are addicted to their superstitions and prejudices born of caste affiliation. Nobody can change them. Christian missionaries, in general, were frustrated in getting Hindus to convert to Christianity. All the abuse was heaped on the institution of caste and on crafty Brahmins who kept the masses duped.

Indian Thinkers on Jati

Yet, the concept of *jati* was progressive and scientific. It embodied the Indian idea of 'unity in diversity', promoting multiplicity. This was true multiculturalism, where each tradition could thrive without becoming a 'melting pot'. The idea of pluralism gave each *jati* a distinct place and role in society, enabling their contributions to be maximized.

Swami Vivekananda said:

> Though our castes [*jati*] and our institutions are apparently linked with our religion, they are not so. These institutions have been necessary to protect us as a nation, and when this necessity for self-preservation will no more exist, they will die a natural death. In religion, there is no caste. A man from the highest caste and a man from the lowest may become a monk in India and the two castes become equal. The [currently degenerated] caste system is opposed to the religion of Vedanta.[27]

Jati Advantages: A Shield against Invaders

Let us pause to analyze a darker part of Indian history. In doing so, we will see how the Indian social system helped protect the country from sinking into the dark medieval ages, dominated by religious fanatics. The following are a few observations on how the so-called caste system (or *jati*) played a role in safeguarding India from total sociopolitical and cultural annihilation by foreign forces by creating strong group resistance to fight and creating barriers against mass conversion.

Swami Vivekananda noted, 'Caste [*jati* system] is an imperfect institution, no doubt. But if it had not been for caste, you would have had no Sanskrit books to study. This caste made walls, around which all sorts of invasions rolled and surged but found it impossible to breakthrough.'[28]

Scholar Ram Swarup wrote: 'With the advent of Islam, the Hindu society came under great pressure; it faced the problem of survival. When the political power failed, castes took over; they became defense shields and provided resistance passive and active.'[29]

According to scholar K.S. Lal:

> So well coalesced was the Hindu social structure that it not only saved India from the fate of countries like Iran, Iraq, Syria, and Egypt when they confronted the Islamic onslaught, but did not rest content till it had supplanted the Muslim political power in the land even though it took a thousand years to do so. Hindus had

> suffered only a military defeat against Muslim invaders. It was not a collapse of the Hindu social system.[30]

To put this information into proper perspective, we can consider what French sociologist Emile Durkheim observed:

> A nation can be maintained only if between the state and the individual there is interposed a whole series of secondary groups near enough to the individuals to attract them strongly in their sphere of action and drag them, in this way, into the general torrent of social life ... Occupational groups are suited to fill this role, and that is their identity... community orientation creates trust among the members of the society.[31]

There exists intrinsic trust among jati or clan and tribe members which protects members from foreign interventions. Trust also help support each other including financial support. American political scientist and economist Francis Fukuyama noted that trust has an economic value. He said:

> [The] ability to associate depends, in turn, on the degree to which communities share norms and values and can subordinate individual interests to those of large groups. Out of such shared values comes trust and trust as we will see has a large and measurable economic Value and trust results in social capital.[32]

Former director of the Tamil Nadu Institute of Urban Studies, P. Kanagasabapathi, defined social capital in the following way:

> From time immemorial groups of people have created strong communities based on commonly observed rules and mutual self-help. These social links discourage deviant behavior through ostracism and other social penalties, create a climate of trust in which agreements are honored and grievances redressed and facilitates collective action against threats from outsiders and risks from natural disasters. This is the social capital. Unlike financial or human capital, it cannot be owned by individuals only by social groups. Being less

> tangible than financial or human capital, it is difficult to measure and so has been ignored in the past. Yet it is an invaluable asset.[33]

Jati has clearly provided this social capital to India to date. Should *jatis* still exist? Who are you to judge my clan or *gotra*? It should be left to the people, as long as it does not harm anyone.

Varnashrama: The Original Idea

Swami Vivekananda once said:

> What [*varna*] really is, not one in a million understands.
>
> [...]
>
> And that is the line of work that is found in all our books, in spite of what you may hear from some people whose knowledge of their own Scriptures and whose capacity to understand the mighty plans of the ancients are only zero.
>
> [...]
>
> We believe in Indian caste [*varna*] as one of the greatest social institutions that the Lord gave to man. We also believe that through the unavoidable defects, foreign persecutions, and above all, the monumental ignorance and pride of many Brahmanas who do not deserve the name, have thwarted in many ways, the legitimate fructification of this glorious Indian institution, it has already worked wonders for the land of Bharata and it destined to lead Indian humanity to its goal.[34]

The great saint and reformer, Swami Dayananda Saraswati, was highly critical of the caste system. However, he opined that it is important to recognize that *varna* is not based on birth or heredity but on the nature and merits of the individual. He said, 'The Class and Order of an individual should be determined by his merits alone.'[35]

Dr B.R. Ambedkar said, '[Vedic] varna and caste are two very different concepts. Varna is based on the principle of each according to his worth, while caste is based on the principle of each according to his birth. The two are as distinct as chalk from cheese.'[36]

Gandhi expressed:

> I believe that if Hindu society has been able to stand, it is because it is founded on the caste system ... A community which can create the caste system must be said to possess unique power of organization ...
>
> I believe that caste has saved Hinduism from disintegration. But like every other institution, it has suffered from excrescences. I consider the four divisions alone to be fundamental, natural, and essential.[37]

India's great modern sage, Sri Aurobindo, similarly said, 'Caste [*varna*] therefore was not only an institution which ought to be immune from the cheap second-hand denunciations so long in fashion, but a supreme necessity without which Hindu civilization could not have developed its distinctive character or worked out its unique mission.'[38]

What is the *varna* system, then? What is its true meaning and relevance to us today? To understand the *varna* system, we must first explore the concept of *gunas*. *Gunas* are said to be the guiding principle of one's nature, temperament, and behaviour in life, influencing actions from moment to moment.

- Tamas: Inward, instinctive—under nature's control, veiling; it represents the principle or state of darkness, ignorance, and dullness
- Rajas: Outward—fighting to conquer nature, expressing, creating, protecting
- Sattva: Inward, intuitive—above nature, illuminating, guiding, uniting

The Self can express and illuminate when the laws and secrets of nature are understood and applied to elevate our life, both externally and internally. The state of complete freedom from nature is *moksha*. There are four fundamental needs of society:

- Knowledge: Inquisitiveness
- Protection: Protection and preservation
- Living Resources: Acquiring, collecting, sharing, exchanging, and interchanging

- Service: Serve, serve, serve

While all three *gunas* interplay in our lives constantly, at any given moment or stage of our life, one remains dominant.

We can now view tamas as nature's veiling and raw power. Those incapable of removing the veil and overcoming the raw power are indeed Shudras. A Shudra is like a newborn child, lacking experience and knowledge of the world's operation, ignorant or incapable of finding the path to higher knowledge for self-evolution. The state of tamas can happen to anyone at any moment regardless of the dominant guna or state one belongs to. That means a 'Brahmin' can also have a tamas moment, and a tamasic person can get out of it through effort.

It is said that every human being is born as a Shudra and, through their own effort, can earn a position in one of the other *varnas*, such as Vaishya, Kshatriya, and Brahmin. The *Skand Puran* says:[39]

जन्मना जायते शूद्रः संस्कारात् द्विज उच्यते
शापानुग्रहसामर्थ्यं तथा क्रोधः प्रसन्नता ||

janmanā jāyate śūdraḥ saṃskārāddvija ucyate |
śāpānugrahasāmarthyaṃ tathā krodhaḥ prasannatā

(Everyone is born at the stage of a Shudra [ignorant of the path to spiritual knowledge] until, through samskara [purification, enrichment, and education], they become *dvija* [the second born]. The ability to curse and bless, to control anger and delight, and to be foremost in all three worlds, are qualities found only in the Brahmana [one who seeks the path to higher knowledge].)

One cannot become a Brahmin by birth. Dwija means 'born again', but this second birth is not physical; rather, it signifies a transformation in one's attitude and aptitude.

The Bhagavad Gita says:[40]

चातुर्वर्ण्यं मया सृष्टं गुणकर्मविभागशः।
तस्य कर्तारमपि मां विद्ध्यकर्तारमव्ययम्।।

catur-varnyam maya srstam
guna-karma-vibhagasah
tasya kartaram api mam
viddhy akartaram avyayam

(According to the three modes of *guna* [inner qualities and nature] and karma [the work ascribed to them or chosen by them], the four divisions of human society were created by Me. And, although I am the creator of this system, you should know that I am yet the non-doer [uninvolved], being unchangeable.)

However, Hindu sages did not view the *varnas* as hierarchical but rather as key pillars of society, representing a 'spectrum' of potentials and possibilities. According to *Varnadharma,* the other three *varnas* (beyond Shudra) are explained based on their potentialities and temperaments.

Through acquisitive power, using *rajas*, Vaishyas, who are also influenced by *tamas*, attempt to overcome it by accumulating, gathering, and distributing the essentials of life.

Those who can use *rajas* to shake off this veil and express and assert themselves through valour are the Kshatriyas, who hold *kshatra* (umbrella)—protecting and safeguarding.

Those who transcend this and use the illuminating power of *sattva* can truly escape the veil and cycles of nature (*maya*), attaining true freedom in *moksha;* they are indeed the Brahmins.

The Grand Plan!

Swami Vivekananda noted:

> The social laws of India have always been subject to great periodic changes. At their inception, these laws were the embodiment of a gigantic plan, which was to unfold slowly through time. The great seers of ancient India saw so far ahead of their time that the world must wait centuries yet to appreciate the full scope of this wonderful plan, which is the one and only cause of India's degeneration. The degeneration of India came not because the laws and customs of the

ancients were bad, but because they were not allowed to be carried to their legitimate conclusions.[41]

What was that 'gigantic plan', and what would possibly be the 'legitimate conclusions'?

Vivekananda explained:

> What is the plan? The ideal at the one end is the Brahmana, and the ideal at the other end is the chandala, and the whole work is to raise them, and slowly you will find more and more privileges granted to them. It is the duty of the Brahmana, therefore, to work for the salvation of the rest of mankind, in India. If he does that and so long as he does that, he is a Brahmana.[42]

What the Swami meant by salvation was the process of evolving to higher states. Of course, this 'Brahmana' refers to the individual who has reached the highest peak of inner human development in the evolutionary process, while the 'Chandala' is the one who has not evolved as much. This is not determined by birth or classified arbitrarily.

Vivekananda said: 'In the land of Bharata [India], every social rule is for the protection of the weak. Such is our ideal of varna, as meant for raising all humanity slowly and gently towards the realization of the great ideal of spiritual man, who is non-resisting, calm, steady, worshipful, pure, and meditative. In that ideal there is God.'[43]

The *varna* system is an organic and ecological model of human society, functioning like the human body. This idea is very important for the ecological age and holds universal value. Human society should function as an integral whole, much like the human body. The different *varnas* do not have separate identities but can only function in mutual harmony for the good of the whole. Once we realize this, we will begin to work for the overall good of society as our own greatest good. The true message of the *varna* system is human unity and the growth of individuals and societies, not warring castes and classes, which would be like the limbs and organs of the body fighting with one another. However, this requires openness to understand it without biases and to honour wisdom and spiritual values.

In the words of Sri Aurobindo:

> We must realize that the ancient Aryan Rishis meant by the Chaturvarnya, not a mere social division, but a recognition of God manifesting Himself in fundamental Swabhava [individual nature], which our bodily distinctions, our social orders are merely an attempt to organise in the symbols of human life, often a confused attempt, often a mere parody and distortion of the divine thing they try to express. Every man has in himself all the four Dharmas, but one predominates, in one he is born and that strikes the note of his character and determines the type and cast of all his actions; the rest subordinated to the dominant type and helps to give it its complement. No Brahmana is a complete Brahmana unless he has the Kshatratejas in him, the Vaishyashakti and the Shudrashakti, but all these have to serve in him the fullness of his Brahmanyam. God manifests Himself as the four Prajapatis or Manus, catvāro manavah of the Gita, and each man is born in the amśa of one of the four; the first characterised by wisdom and largeness, the second by heroism and force, the third by dexterity and enjoyment, the fourth by work and service.
>
> The perfected man develops in himself all four capacities and contains at once the god of wisdom and largeness, the god of heroism and force, the god of skill and enjoyment, the god of work and service. Only one stands dominant and leads and uses the others.[44]

The Importance of Rediscovering the Varnashrama Dharma System

Only in recent times has there been an effort to understand the 'conscious evolution' of individuals and societies. Now that we are aware of and conscious about evolution, a concept that can be termed 'evolutionary consciousness', we can work towards fulfilling the dream of a truly sustainable future. This can be achieved by developing the idea that humans can guide and manage the process of evolution, particularly in mental states.

Modern developmental psychology studies the growth and development of the mind—essentially, interior development. Some notable scholars in this field include Clare Graves, Abraham Maslow, Deirdre Kramer, Cheryl Armon, Jan Sinnot, Kurt Fischer, Jenny Wade, and Robert Kegan. Philosopher Ken Wilber has made efforts to identify classes based on aptitude and characteristics. More thought leaders are expected to explore the area of 'conscious evolution', creating models to accelerate the upward movement of individuals and societies. This can be accomplished by leveraging the interplay of the three *gunas,* which influence individuals and societies from *tamas* to *sattva.*

For civilization to survive and progress, we must consider the individual and the 'herd instinct' as primitive, focusing entirely on the 'group imperative'—the ideals of *sarve bhavantu sukhina* and *vadudhaiva kutumbakam.*

American philosopher Ken Wilber developed an evolutionary mapping system for individuals and societies through a 'spiral mapping' approach in his 'Integral Theory'.[45] Wilber introduced a four-quadrant grid model that attempted to integrate individual's psychological and spiritual development, collective shifts in consciousness, and levels or holons in neurological functioning and societal organization. By doing so, he has attempted to integrate Indian thought into a model more aligned with Western methodologies. The original idea of Integral Humanism, proposed by Sri Aurobindo, has been reinterpreted and redrawn by Wilbur. Jean Gebser and Georg Feuerstein were among the first to explore this concept. While many of Wilbur's ideas were appreciated, secular academia did not offer much commentary on them. Maslow and other well-known researchers acknowledged the idea of evolution within human classes and societies. Wilbur also attempted to create imagery to explain why certain human beings and societies behave the way they do. His classification bears a resemblance to the Indian *varnashrama* system.

Sri Aurobindo broadly defined various states of human consciousness, based on Indian philosophies such as the physical, vital, mind, and super mind. Wilbur developed a model with states defined by different colours: archaic, magic, mythic-rational, rational, and integral. This model aims to define, identify, quantify, and predict the progress of conscious human evolution.

Therefore, rather than dismissing the *varna* system, the time has come for modern thinkers to recognize its profound implications for the planned and projected conscious evolution of humankind, as Rishi Aurobindo foresaw:

Our early approaches to the Infinite
Are sunrise splendours on a marvellous verge
While lingers yet unseen the glorious sun.
What now we see is a shadow of what must come.[46]

Social scientists need to engage in classifying people and societies, formulating ways to identify, quantify, and accelerate the process of the 'conscious' evolution of humans and societies. This is the only way forward for our civilization to address the beastly behaviours driven by greed, revenge, and violence. Yoga, a system that has existed for millennia, has been instrumental in aiding this evolutionary process.

Today, we also have a window of opportunity to confront potential challenges arising from artificial intelligence. Many people concerned about the proliferation of artificial intelligence in our lives can better cope with scientific developments by raising the inner consciousness level, which ultimately can help prevent the universe from falling into the sphere of demonic forces. Our inner power of yoga can help us rise above these challenges and create new opportunities for the upward movement of individual and societal evolutionary trajectories.

CHAPTER 12

Dharma Is the Future

We are all familiar with the idea of a Global Village as we are now interconnected via technology. Borders are gradually vanishing, and the concept of 'One World' is no longer merely an expression. Any small event occurring in a remote part of the earth is instantly shared with the rest of the world, thanks to global connectivity.

The World Today

Climate change and global warming do not discriminate based on national boundaries. In the post-COVID-19 era, we have grown accustomed to 'online' activities—connecting, talking, and even seeing one another from the farthest corners of the globe. However, the same advanced connectivity enabled by rapid transport technologies has also contributed to the swift spread of diseases like COVID-19.

As each day passes, we increasingly rely on technology, not only for our daily needs—including the 'Internet of Things' (IoT)—but also for groundbreaking research in previously unimaginable fields. Yet, a pressing concern looms: Are we in control of technology, or are we on the brink of witnessing technology take full control of our lives? Will robots, artificial intelligence (AI), machine learning (ML), and similar advancements erode our thinking abilities and identities? Are we approaching the era of technological 'singularity',[1] where machines might surpass all human intelligence, as Kurzweil predicted?[2] Could human society, along with its ethical systems, eventually be governed by non-human, non-living entities?

There is much to come, and we must all take the time to reflect on our worldview, lifestyle, and daily activities, including our responsibility towards morality and sustenance. For now, let us consider where we stand today as a civilization. To better understand the reality, let's imagine our Global Village as a community of 100 people. Here's how the world would look:

- Four children die before reaching the age of five.[3]
- Thirty-three people lack access to safe drinking water.[4]
- Twenty people (equivalent to about 1.6 billion in actual numbers) live without adequate housing, and two people (around 150 million) are homeless.[5]
- Fourteen people are unable to read or write.[6]
- Seven people hold a college degree.[7]
- Nine people regularly face starvation.[8]
- Twenty-five people do not have basic sanitation.[9]
- And yet, one person owns half the wealth of the village.[10]

According to a UN report, a child under fifteen dies every five seconds around the world.[11] On top of the devastating impact of COVID-19, the global economy remains grim. The pandemic-induced 'lockdowns' forced millions of factories to shut down, halted manufacturing, and disrupted distribution system.

Most significantly, this pandemic has had an enormous impact on the global food system. The report estimates that between 83 and 132 million people may go hungry due to the economic turmoil we are experiencing worldwide.

Now imagine what could happen if we faced another pandemic-like situation caused by new germs, so-called superbugs,[12] or even the outbreak of another world war!

From the perspective of women's safety, the situation is equally grim. Even in a 'developed' country like the US, an American is sexually assaulted every 92 seconds. On average, 3,21,500 individuals aged twelve or older become victims of rape or sexual assault in the US each year.[13]

The leading causes of death from diseases today are no longer primarily due to invisible organisms like viruses and bacteria, thanks to the advancements in modern medicine and healthcare systems. It seems the days of 'communicable diseases' (apart from the looming threat of potentially catastrophic 'superbugs') are numbered. However, ironically, it is our so-called 'development' and modern lifestyle that are now largely responsible for our deaths. These are known as non-communicable or lifestyle diseases.

The following chart highlights some of these lifestyle diseases:

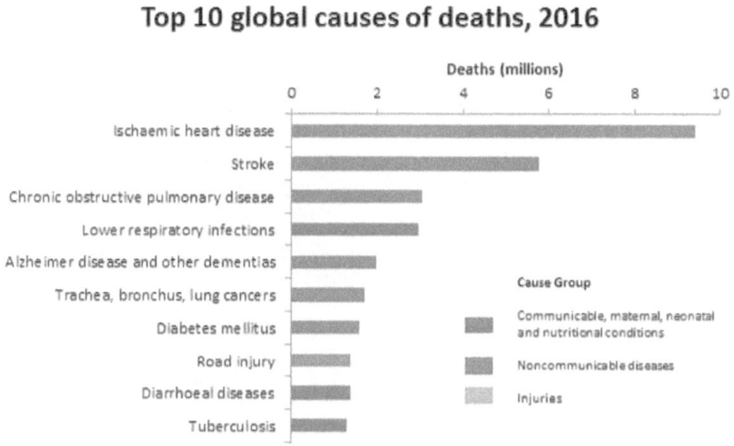

Source: Global Health Estimates 2016: Deaths by Cause Age, Sex, by Country and by Region, 2000-2016. Geneva, World Health Organization; 2018

Now, let's examine the major causes of death from injuries in our 'developed' world. Nearly one-third of the 5.8 million global deaths from injuries are caused by violence, suicide, homicide, and war, while nearly one-quarter are the result of road traffic crashes. Other leading causes of death from injuries include falls, drowning, burns, and poisoning.

In total, injuries account for about 10 per cent of global deaths, which is 32 per cent higher than the combined fatalities from tuberculosis (TB), HIV/AIDS, and malaria.[14] Additionally, 4.4 million people—approximately 8 per cent of all deaths worldwide—die from violence and injuries annually.[15] Here is a breakdown of these deaths:

- Road traffic: 23 per cent
- Homicide: 11 per cent
- Suicide: 15 per cent
- War: 3 per cent

A study examining the causes of death in 2004, along with projections for 2030, presents a grim picture.[16] It increasingly highlights that more than half of the top ten reasons of death are linked to our lifestyle and human behaviour:

Total 2004	
1	Ischaemic heart disease
2	Cerebrovascular disease
3	Lower respiratory infections
4	Chronic obstructive pulmonary disease
5	Diarrhoeal diseases
6	HIV/AIDS
7	Tuberculosis
8	Trachea, bronchus, lung cancers
9	Road traffic crashes
10	Prematurity and low birth weight
11	Neonatal infections and other
12	Diabetes mellitus
13	Malaria
14	Hypertensive heart disease
15	Birth asphyxia and birth trauma
16	Suicide
17	Stomach cancer
18	Cirrhosis of the liver
19	Nephritis and nephrosis
20	Colon and rectum cancers
22	Homicide

Total 2030	
1	Ischaemic heart disease
2	Cerebrovascular disease
3	Chronic obstructive pulmonary disease
4	Lower respiratory infections
5	Road traffic crashes
6	Trachea, bronchus, lung cancers
7	Diabetes mellitus
8	Hypertensive heart disease
9	Stomach cancer
	HIV/AIDS
	Nephritis and nephrosis
	Suicide
	Liver cancer
	Colon and rectum cancer
	Oesophagus cancer
	Homicide
	Alzheimer and other dementias
	Cirrhosis of the liver
	Breast cancer
	Tuberculosis

Over the past decade, terrorists have killed an average of 21,000 people worldwide each year.[17] As technology advances, it seems our happiness index is being adversely affected—why else would the suicide rate be rising so rapidly?

Is this the progress we have achieved in the age of space exploration, genetics, AI, and ML? While we have made remarkable advancements in recent decades, we still have a long way to go in achieving equal opportunities, equitable minimum living standards, and enabling everyone to realize their full potential as human beings.

Not long ago, Paul Ehrlich, Bing professor of Stanford University, warned us in his books *One with Nineveh* and *The Population Bomb* about the explosion of the human population and its subsequent impact on food, health, and resources.[18] He predicted that the rising population would soon lead to a global catastrophe. Today, we find ourselves on the brink of an environmental disaster far worse than the collapses of the Harappan, Egyptian, Mesopotamian, or even Greek civilization. While their downfalls were regional, ours is shaping up to be global.

How do we propose to address such a looming crisis? Who is influencing the world and shaping our lives today?

Consider Samuel Huntington of Harvard University, whose thesis, *The Clash of Civilizations* (1993),[19] has profoundly impacted the thought processes of many world leaders. Huntington argued that the next 'Great War' would be fought between cultures, with the superior culture ultimately prevailing. Does this seem reminiscent of neo-Darwinism—natural selection and the survival of the fittest?

Political fortune-tellers like Francis Fukuyama of George Mason University argued in his book *The End of History and the Last Man,* 'We have all the best things already happened. Liberal Democracy, Equal Rights, Capitalism. Nothing more human beings can think of to make things any better. This is it!'[20]

Ray Kurzweil of MIT, regarded as one of the leading inventors of our time, discusses in *The Age of Spiritual Machines*, the emergence of real cyborgs and polyborgs. Similarly, Gregory Stock, director of the UCLA School of Medicine's Program of Medicine, predicts in *Redesigning Humans: Our Inevitable Genetic Future* that humanity will assimilate with super-intelligent machines to bypass biological evolution. This fusion, according to Stock, will supercharge not only our minds but also our bodies, which will be remade and redesigned in virtually any form we find compelling and useful.

And yet, here we are, grappling with poverty, illiteracy, disease, climate change, conflicting ideologies, and terrorism. That is our reality. Instead of addressing these global challenges, humanity remains entangled in religious conversions, genocide, and ideological wars.

Hindu seers, with their profound foresight, envisioned the future of humanity and established societies in Bharat and across the world based on that vision. Although invasions and colonial rules caused significant damage to the Indian system and diminished people's understanding of its significance, some dogmas and unscientific practices emerged during this prolonged period of decline. Yet, what remains of Bharat today continues to carry hope for humanity.

What Is Our Fate?

Is it sealed within the double helix of our DNA? Will political ideologies and systems, built on limited and fragmented views of reality, continue to dictate our lives? Will intellectuals, scholars, scientist-turned-philosophers, or politician-turned-leaders determine our destiny? Or will the corporate world reduce us to mere statistics, ignoring our capacity to think, cooperate, and love as human beings?

Are we prepared to radically review and rewrite our theories of civilization, discarding outdated medieval political views in light of co-evolution and the latest scientific discoveries? How do science and technology—particularly genetics, informatics, and artificial intelligence—shape the behaviour, appearance, and thinking of the human species? How will they influence our responses to new needs and our way of life?

What will the new economy look like? What is the trajectory of creation and evolution? What is the purpose behind the birth, growth, and death of the universe and individuals? Ultimately, what is the future of humanity?

Hindu seers have addressed these questions. By understanding the core concepts of karma, dharma, yoga, and moksha (true freedom), individuals can navigate life's challenges with greater wisdom and purpose and build newer advanced societies and civilization. Bhagavad Gita has answers to many of our current-day anomalies. Irish poet and futurist George Russell observed:

> Goethe, Wordsworth, Emerson, Thoreau, among moderns have something of this vitality and wisdom, but we can find all they have said and much more in the grand sacred books of the East. The Bhagavad Gita and the Upanishads contain such God-like fullness of wisdom on all things, that I feel the authors must have looked with calm remembrance through a thousand passionate lives full of feverish strife ere they could have written with such certainty of things which the soul feels to be sure.(Egliton 1937, 20)

In *The Descent of the Supermind* (1939), Sri Aurobindo wrote, 'The evolutionary progression will continue till Super Mind, the original creative medium of the divine and the triune glory of Sat-Chit-Ananda stand evolved here in material Universe.'[21] He further stated, 'What we want is to hasten the advent of the supramental, not at all to fall into the ugly condition of humanity full of desires and low impulses.'[22]

Sri Aurobindo also envisioned humanity's spiritual evolution in his epic poem 'Savitri'[23]:

Our early approaches to the Infinite
Are sunrise splendours on a marvellous verge
While lingers yet unseen the glorious sun.
What now we see is a shadow of what must come.[24]

It is now up to Hindus, Indians, and forward-thinking individuals worldwide to recognize the invaluable treasures that India offers and to share them with humanity, viewing the world as 'one large family'.

Today's Framework of 'Hinduism'

First, let us look at the modern framework of religion: A prophet, a sacred book, a theology, designated places of worship, specific do's and don'ts, daily practices, celebrations, and festivals.

Now, let us examine the modern framework of so-called Hinduism: Mandirs, pilgrimages, poojas, and festivals. Additionally, there is an emphasis on classical dance and Sanskrit programmes. Increasingly, there is also the concept of a 'retributive god' within the framework—a deity who rewards or punishes based on the degree of one's devotion and faith, a notion closely resembling the Abrahamic ideas of religion.

Today, what is often referred to as Hinduism is striving to be on par with other 'religions'. The external world has crafted its own definition of religious identity, and many Hindus fear that if they don't conform to this definition and narrative, they will be excluded. However, the reality is that in the Middle East, the practice of other religions, including Hinduism, is largely prohibited, except in a few countries. Even carrying the Bible or the Gita to Saudi Arabia is considered a criminal act.

In the West, thanks to the significant presence of Hindus, particularly in the UK, Canada, and the US, there is some recognition of Hinduism. Elsewhere, however, it often remains a marginal narrative. This raises a crucial question: Should Hindus strive for a Hindu religious identity, or should they focus on a Hindu civilizational identity as a people?

It's a tough issue because there are benefits to being labelled a 'religion', but this comes at the cost of undermining dharma's true purpose. Legally speaking, you may lose out if you don't have a religious identity in your own country, given the current state of affairs.

Under pressure from the Abrahamic faiths and Western theologians, some Hindus have sought to demonstrate that they are not 'polytheists', but rather 'monotheist'. Others might label them 'pantheists' because they revere divinity in its many forms.

All these terminologies, however, were created by Western 'theology'. In the usual portrayal of Hindus 'worshipping millions of gods', we have lost the original pluralistic view of divinity. The common saying, '33 crores of dev devis' reflect this.

Vivekananda promoted the idea of *swadharma*, a personal divine entity or deity to follow. According to this concept, every individual can follow their own *swadharma*, a personal 'religious' or *adhyatmic* path or practice. However, most Hindus are unaware of this process, as the natural Hindu system has been subdued for a long time. The pluralistic practice of invoking the divine in various forms and objects, anywhere, has become anathema, leading Hindus to struggle and adopt a defensive stance.

Sanatani Adhyatma or the Science of the Higher or Inner Self

Let us, once again, review some fundamental concepts in the Hindu system related to creation and its cause. At times, various *darshanas*, including the six prominent ones, and *shastras* such as the Vedas, Upanishads, and *Yoga Sutras*, may seem to contradict each other. However, this is the beauty of the Hindu system: The sages examined various aspects from different perspectives and expressed their insights in multiple ways, as reflected in the phrase: '*Ekam Sat Viprah Vahuda Vadanti*' ('Truth is one; the wise call it by different names'). Despite these apparent differences, unity is preserved at the deepest level. They may not use the same name for the ultimate reality, or may even refrain from naming it altogether, but they do not deny any part of reality, regardless of the diverse ways in which it is perceived.

Let us now recap and attempt to understand a few key terms related to creation and the creator: Brahma, Brahman, Bhagwan, and Ishwara.

The all-pervasive Ishwara is omnipresent. To make this concept practical and less abstract, Hindus assert that if divinity is all-pervasive, it can be found in whatever form and wherever one chooses. In this sense, it is the most rational and scientific way to approach creation.

The *Isha Upanishad* says:[25]

ईशा वास्यमिदं सर्वं यत्किञ्च जगत्यां जगत्।

īśā vāsyamidaṁ sarvaṁ yatkiñca jagatyāṁ jagat |

(The whole of creation is permeated by Ishwara, and everything in creation is part of one complete whole that is inseparable from Ishwara.)

This means that Ishwara envelops everything in the entire universe—the cause of creation itself. Any motion or change occurring in the individual universe also affects the entire universe. The first part of the verse asserts that the entire universe is pervaded by Ishwara, the infinite universal knowledge and consciousness, which is present and connected throughout all creation.

The second part of the verse reflects a concept akin to the language of quantum physics. Einstein stated, 'For us believing physicists, the distinction between past, present and future is only a stubborn illusion.'[26] This can be summarized as 'reality is merely an illusion' (*maya* or apparent; *maya* is often generally translated as 'illusion', but its true meaning is 'apparent', which may not reflect the 'absolute nature or reality). Quantum theory has taken this idea further, aligning closely with the Upanishadic understanding of the universe. When we measure a particle, the apparent properties observed are not necessarily the complete reality. Physicists often consider these as 'secondary qualities' that exist in our measuring devices, sense organs, and the physical tools available to us. This suggests that quantum particles can be ascribed only as empirical realities, dependent on the method, condition, and tools of observation.

For instance, when a tree falls in a deep forest, is it true that nobody hears it and nothing happens to the universe?

Quantum physicists would argue that without a measurement tool, quantum particles do not exist in a defined state, and the properties of particles, such as electrons, remain undefined. Similarly, even if the tree falls and no one is around to hear it, it may have no observable effect on the rest of the world. Yet, according to quantum theory, it is still true that this simple act of nature impacts the whole universe.

We need to keep in mind though that the connection between quantum theory and *Isha Upanishad* is philosophical and metaphorical, not literal.

Another important description of creation is found in the *Chandogya Upanishad*:[27]

सर्वं खल्विदं ब्रह्म तज्जलानिति शान्त उपासीत ।

sarvaṃ khalvidaṃ brahma tajjalāniti śānta

(All this [creation] is Brahman. Everything comes from Brahman, everything returns to Brahman, and Brahman sustains everything.)

What differentiates Hindus from others is the emphasis on the karmic law governing everything. Our karma determines our future; not even the *devas* have control over it. The concepts of reward and punishment, as seen in later-day Islam and Christianity, were influenced by such ideas. In the Abrahamic religions, it is emphasized that there will be a final judgement day in the future when each person will be answerable for their 'religiosity', meaning how well they followed their books and prophet. If it is satisfactory, they will get to go to eternal heaven and meet the creator; otherwise, they will be thrown into an eternal hell.

A Hindu is meant to be tolerant, forgiving, and compassionate. This is the ideal of *ahimsa* (non-violence) for all of humanity. However, when threatened and attacked, Hindus have also taken up weapons and fought. Compassion and *ahimsa* apply in peaceful situations and peacetime, but not necessarily during harsh periods of survival and struggle.

A Return to the Original Ideas

One must work hard to generate wealth in order to live a good life, but we must keep two things in mind: the actions and results must be sustainable. However, remember that life is about more than just wealth and enjoyment; this is the path of detachment or *nivritti*. There may come a time when name, fame, wealth, and enjoyment will have less meaning. One will reflect on life, on what has been accomplished, and consider why people should remember them long after they are gone. In this light, one sustainable karma is *seva*, which means serving and giving. *Seva* can take the form of physical, mental, or financial support to anyone in need.

That concept of *seva* is deeply intertwined with *adhyatma*—the interconnectedness of all living and non-living beings. This understanding arises from a greater sense of self, which can be expanded to infinity. Ishwara is that which is present everywhere and in everything: that which cannot be described, felt, or touched. However, it is challenging to conceive of the abstract, which is why divine entities called deva and devi were created as reflections of the eternal sustaining source—Ishwara, Vishnu or Narayana, along with Brahma and Maheshwara.

Do I have to accept 'gods' or 'goddesses' to be a Hindu? Not necessarily. Bhakti (devotion) is one path, karma (action) is another, and jnana (knowledge) is yet another. You can choose one or follow all of these paths. A Hindu 'god' neither punishes nor rewards based on whether or not one follows them; such ideas belong to the beginner's level of *adhyatma* (spiritual knowledge). On the other hand, your fate is determined by your own karma. Others may say that you should act and leave the result at the feet of the lord, '*Karmanyeva adhikaraste ma falesu kadachana*', meaning that you should accept the result as the *prasad* (blessing) of your offering, viewing both your action and its outcome as sacred.

However, all the tools discovered and used in *adhyatmic sadhana* are equally useful on the material plane. Pooja, japa, mantra, yantra, tantra, and other practices are powerful methods that help prepare one for better outcomes in their actions, bringing peace and enhancing inner strength. At the same time, Patanjali's *Yoga Sutra* says, '*Yoga chittavritti nirodhah*', broadly meaning, managing your thoughts and emotions by calming you mind, enabling better focus on both adhyatmic activities and material pursuits. On the other hand, yoga is also described as '*karmashu kaushalam*', perfecting the actions for the optimum outcome towards a goal. Yoga empowers us in the material world and helps us discover the supreme infinite by inquiring within through *dhyana* (meditation), while harnessing the energy stored within us, such as the chakras.

Murti puja appears to be the primary path for millions of Hindus today, serving as a chance and means to connect with the divine. *Bhajan* and *kirtan* are powerful tools for this. However, these practices are still subsets of the larger dharmic and yogic system. In the Vedic era, or during the Satya Yuga, such forms were unnecessary because people were naturally 'Ishwara *pranidhana*' (aligned with divinity). They lived in pure *sat* (truth) in a state of *sattva* (purity).

As civilization progressed through the yugas, from Satya to Kali, materialism (represented by *rajas* and *tamas*) began to influence human behaviour. This shift diminished people's capacity to comprehend the finer aspects of *adhyatma.* As a result, more tools and methods were introduced. First came the symbols (such as *yantras*) and sounds (*mantras*), and eventually *vigrahas* and *murtis*—powerful ways for the average person to imagine, connect with, and experience the same divinity.

The Abrahamic religions attempted to view the Hindu system through their own prism and framework. They tried to fit various individuals, sages, *mathas*, and temple *sampradayas* of Hindus into their theology in order to understand divinity. However, they were puzzled and could not fully comprehend its vast scope. In the end, they resolved their confusion by simply grouping these practices under the labels of Hinduism, Jainism, Buddhism, and Sikhism.

Many Hindus, in their efforts to combat the Abrahamic faiths, often forget that even the Supreme Court of India recognizes that all the indigenous traditions mentioned above fall under the definition of Hinduism.

Hindu Rashtra

The Bharatiya concept of Rashtra (राष्ट्र) is a natural and organic construct rooted in a rich heritage of shared memories and a deep desire to live together. Rashtra is founded on dharma and is bound by spiritual laws of connectedness and oneness, coexisting with both visible and invisible boundaries. In this system, the identity of the people is also natural, and there is no struggle for the collective identity of all people within a Rashtra.

In contrast, a 'nation' is more rooted in materialism, focusing more on rights and less on dharma and associated duties, which are inherent to all. The concept of a nation tends to emphasize 'selfishness', whereas a dharmic Rashtra fosters 'selflessness'. Rashtra includes elements of self-sufficiency and self-fulfilment, whereas a nation is more dependent on systems like government, bureaucracy, and welfare. In modern nations, boundaries are often defined by religion and language, rather than by a shared history, and territorial struggles between them are common.

A nation can constantly evolve according to its needs and circumstances, as it is essentially a power structure based on expansionary measures such as territory, language, or religion. Rashtra is a sociocultural construct rooted in a rich heritage of memories and a shared desire to live together.

French philosopher Ernest Renan once pointed out that people form a nation because they choose to, describing it as 'a soul, a spiritual principle'. Here, he is actually referring to Rashtra, not a nation in the traditional sense. Speaking the same language or belonging to the same ethnic group does not constitute a nation (Rashtra). What truly defines it is having accomplished great things in the past and desiring to achieve them again in the future.

First, Bharat placed less emphasis on land defined by political identities and borders. While there were kings, empires, and emperors, Bharat's ancient Vedic culture extended far beyond its geographical boundaries, influencing regions across the Middle East, parts of Europe, Southeast Asia, and even China and Russia. As we move beyond the mythical and racial Aryan Invasion Theory, we increasingly discover that the people of Bharat spread their knowledge and scientific understanding across the world.

In his famous Uttarpara speech, Sri Aurobindo outlined the essence and goal of India's nationalist movement:

> I say no longer that nationalism is a creed, a religion, a faith; I say that it is the Sanatan Dharma which for us is nationalism. This Hindu nation was born with the Sanatan Dharma; with it, it moves, and with it, it grows. When the Sanatan Dharma declines, then the nation declines, and if the Sanatan Dharma were capable of perishing, with the Sanatan Dharma it would perish.[28]
>
> [...]
>
> This is the one religion that can triumph over materialism by including and anticipating the discoveries of science and the speculations of philosophy.[29]

Though Gandhi never called himself a 'Hindu nationalist', he believed in and propagated concepts such as dharma and 'Rama Rajya' (rule of Lord Rama) as part of his social and political philosophy. He said:

> By political independence, I do not mean an imitation to the British House of Commons or the Soviet rule of Russia or the Fascist rule of Italy or the Nazi rule of Germany. They have systems suited to their genius. We must have ours suited to ourselves. What that can be is more than I can tell. I have described it as Ramarajya i.e., the sovereignty of the people based on pure moral authority.[30]

He emphasized that 'Rama Rajya' meant peace and justice to him, 'Whether Rama of my imagination ever lived or not on this earth, the ancient ideal of Ramarajya is undoubtedly one of true democracy in which the meanest citizen could be sure of swift justice without an elaborate and costly procedure.' He also stressed that it meant respect for all religions: 'My Hinduism teaches me to respect all religions. In this lies the secret of Ramarajya.' Although Gandhi's practice and understanding of 'Hinduism' did not align with a broader interpretation of the dharmic system, in this case, his statement holds true within his personal understanding of religion, as it is again juxtaposed with dharma.

Apart from Gandhi, revolutionary leader Netaji Subhas Chandra Bose referred to Vedanta and the Bhagavad Gita as sources of inspiration in the struggle against the British.[31] Swami Vivekananda's teachings on universalism, his nationalist ideas, and his emphasis on social service and reform inspired Bose from his youth. The fresh interpretation of Bharat's ancient scriptures resonated deeply with him. Hindu spirituality formed a crucial part of his political and social thought throughout his adult life, though it was free from any sense of bigotry or orthodoxy. Bose, who called himself a socialist, believed that socialism in India had its origins in Swami Vivekananda's ideas. As historian Leonard Gordan explains, 'Inner religious explorations continued to be a part of his adult life. This set him apart from the slowly growing number of atheistic socialists and communists who dotted the Indian landscape ... Hinduism was an essential part of his Indianess.'[32] His strategy against the British also involved using Hindu symbols and festivals. In 1925, while in Mandalay jail, he went on a hunger strike when the prison authorities did not support the celebration of Durga Puja.

However, eminent figures like Gandhi and Dr S. Radhakrishnan have repeatedly made it clear that dharma does not denote a religion but refers to an 'eternal culture'. Gandhi's idea of 'Rama Rajya' is not very different from the concept of Hindu Rashtra, which is loosely translated as a Hindu nation due to the lack of an exact equivalent.

When someone uses the term Hindu Rashtra, does it imply a nation for Hindus only? That could have been the case during the independence struggle and the horrific partition, involving population exchange. However, India chose to be a democratic, secular state. This is the essence of Indian history. Except for Emperor Ashoka (who did not impose Buddhism on others but encouraged Buddhist ideals among his subjects), no king or Hindu ruler ever imposed a particular path on others. In that context, dharma is both sacred and secular (non-religious); it is not a theocracy (like an Islamic state) but a land of dharma that seeks to create a free society for all people.

India has always been a nation of and built by the Hindus. The vast length of its history and antiquity has been shaped by fertile ideas, such as '*Krinavantu Vishwam Aryam*', which calls for making the world noble. This Arya is noble, dharmic. If there were a 'Hindu Nation', it would still be pluralistic, just as it has been in the past and continues to be today, unlike over sixty Islamic theocratic states or, for that matter, dictatorial communist regimes. Hindu ideals of pluralism and freedom can only be upheld if Hindus are in the majority. We know what has happened in Afghanistan and Pakistan, and we can see what is happening in Bangladesh today.

The following is an excerpt from an article on Sri Aurobindo's view of the Bharatiya system in this regard:

> Ancient India considered individuals not as social, but as spiritual beings undergoing an evolutionary process. This is the key to that dharma-based society, for which its unique form of democracy streamed from the high planes of the intuitive mind.
>
> [...]
>
> The decline of a society that had lost the thread of life—and with it, of renewal—had commenced. Intellectual and artistic pursuit, the scientific and critical intelligence, creativity and

> intuition were numbed. Social functions became artificial, and the dharma so strict that it hampered the freedom of the spiritual quest; moksha [liberation] was sought in opposition to the sacredness of life. Partial truths were enhanced, others denied, the grand spiritual synthesis waned. When the British Empire took over not much was left of a society run for two millennia on the basis of intuitive democracy and self-government as dharma, intended as the quest for self-perfection of all the classes of society. The gates to foreign invasion were fully open.[33]

Bharat will remain pluralistic as long as Hindus are the majority, for they have been chanting for thousands of years—'*sarve bhavantu sukhina*' (may all be happy)—not just the Hindus, but all people. Additionally, '*vasudhaiva kutumbakam*' (the entire world, nay, the entire creation, is our family).

Many have searched for the true origins of democracy. We, as a people, are accustomed to Eurocentric and colonial-era narratives in which European civilization is depicted in a positive light, while the rest of the world is portrayed as being in the dark ages.

Western scholars suggest that democracy as a form of government originated in ancient Athens in 508 BCE. However, some historians also indicate that a democratic form of governance existed in other parts of the world, possibly before Greece, including in India.[34]

The ancient Greek historian Diodorus Siculus, in the 1st century BCE, wrote the universal history *Bibliotheca Historica* across forty books. In Book 2, Paragraph 39, he writes about India: 'Most of the cities had received a democratic form of government, although among certain tribes the kingship endured until the time when Alexander crossed over into Asia (326–327 BCE).'[35]

Since ancient times, India has had many forms of government, such as *janapad*, *saṅghas*, and *gaṇas*. Netaji Subhas Chandra spoke about this. In 1907, Sri Aurobindo expressed the following in his *Bande Mataram* magazine: 'Asia is not Europe and never will be Europe. The political ideals of the West are not the mainspring of the political movements in the East, and those who do not realize this great truth are mistaken.'[36]

Swami Vivekananda also spoke about modern democracy approximately 150 years ago:

> In every country, the means is the same after all, that is, whatever only a handful of powerful men dictate becomes the fait accompli; the rest of the men only follow like a flock of sheep, that's all. I have seen your Parliament, your Senate, your vote, majority, ballot; it is the same thing everywhere, my friend. The powerful men in every country are moving society in whatever way they like, and the rest are only like a flock of sheep. Now the question is this, who are these men of power in India? They who are giants in religion. It is they who lead our society, and it is they again who change our social laws and usages when necessity demands: and we listen to them silently and do what they command. The only difference with ours is that we have not that superfluous fuss and bustle of the majority, the vote, ballot, and similar concomitant tugs-of-war as in other countries. That is all.[37]

Sri Aurobindo hoped: 'Now that democracy has returned to Asia, its cradle and home, it will be purged of its foreign elements and restored to its original purity.'[38]

Therefore, the democracy we have in India today faces many problems. Democracy in the US also has its share of issues. Even twenty-five years ago, an average, ordinary person could become a congressman and genuinely represent the people. Today, however, one must have both money and connections to become part of the 'club'. On top of that, they are often surrounded by special interest groups and lobbyists.

According to Prof. Arvind Sharma, the development of 'religious nationalism' and the demand by Muslim leaders on the Indian subcontinent for the partition of British India into Muslim and non-Muslim nations during the first half of the 20th century confirmed the narrative of geographical and cultural nationalism based on Indian culture and religions.[39]

The idea of a sovereign nation-state is a recent development that came into existence after the Treaties of Westphalia[40] in 1648 in Europe. A state can be defined as a construct of a political system that comprises people, land, and a government bound by a set of directives known as the Constitution. Historically, when the modern concept of a nation-state, as mentioned earlier, did not yet exist, the idea of a Rashtra or a Hindu Rashtra was present from time immemorial. From Kashmir to Kanyakumari, and from Gandhara (in present-day Afghanistan) to Brahma-desh (modern-day Myanmar), the cultural thread kept millions of people united in the Rashtra.

As mentioned earlier, Hinduism and religion are not synonymous with dharma. Western and Marxist thinkers struggle to fit 'Hindu' into a geo-cultural identity because they cannot think beyond the confines of the concept of 'religion'. Savarkar viewed Rashtra as a political entity or 'Hindu polity' that protects the people and culture of the land. He suggested that the entire political and economic system of the land should be based not on Western constructs but on ancient, yet most appropriate, indigenous ideals.

In the book, *The RSS: Roadmaps for the 21st Century*, RSS leader Sunil Ambekar defined it as a sociocultural and civilizational construct, stating: 'Hindu Rāṣṭra is a result of thousands of years of experiential living and history. It is not an 'ism' propelled by any political or economic motivation. It is a comprehensive conception of civilization developed through the observance of certain values and cultural ways of life.'[41]

The second head (sarsanghchalak) of the RSS, M.S. Golwalkar, objected to the Western idea of nationalism. He said, 'Pseudo-secularism is the inevitable product of the foreign concept of nationalism that we wove into our constitutional fabric.'[42] He further explained, 'This is the real and abiding cornerstone of national harmony and integration, subscribing to common national ideals irrespective of personal religious creeds. And it is this concept, as applied to our country, that we call Hindu Rāṣṭra, the only rational, practical, and right concept.'[43]

He elaborated that 'being part of the "Hindu Rāṣṭra" means you are committed to the motherland, follow your duties, and aspire for your rights'. There is no religion involved here; it is akin to patriotism.

Some people refer to these ideas as Hindu nationalism, while others call it Hindu revivalism or absolutism. Some label it extreme conservatism, and some even call it fascism, which is often associated with a 'homogenized majority'.

First, what is nationalism? It is the love for the nation or state by its people. Nationalism is not only important but essential for the existence of a nation-state. Yes, in the name of nationalism, cultural, political, and military invasions and subjugations are possible. However, as long as there are borders, nationalism will endure, for it is human nature to love one's place of birth and have duties towards one's home and land.

The second point is whether there is such a thing as so-called Hindu nationalism. In reality, nationalism based on religious identity is not feasible in a pluralistic society. When a Hindu views the land as a mother or devi, atheists, communists, and those opposed to idolatry may feel threatened. However, that does not mean the Hindu majority should abandon their emotional connection to their land.

Let's examine conservatism, as some people claim it will take India back to the medieval age. Realistically, Hindus are the last group to move backward! Abrahamic religions do have a problem with science, and Hindus do not.

As for homogeneity, Hindus do not insist that everyone practise their religious rituals, which are themselves diverse. Therefore, the talk of homogeneity is absurd. It is the proselytizing religious evangelists and communist ideologues who struggle to impose their views on Indians through the process of conversion, using techniques of punishment and reward.

The Bogey of Fascism

If we examine the history of the early usage of the term 'fascism', we see that it was not necessarily seen as a monstrous idea. According to historian Stanley G. Payne, an authority on this subject, fascism has three key features:[44]

- Fascist negations: Anti-liberalism, anti-communism, and anti-conservatism.
- Fascist goals: The creation of a nationalist dictatorship to regulate economic structure and transform social relations within a modern, self-determined culture, as well as the expansion of the nation into an empire.
- Fascist style: A political aesthetic of romantic symbolism, mass mobilization, a positive view of violence, and the promotion of masculinity, youth, and charismatic authoritarian leadership.

In reality, fascism was a reaction to socialism and communism, which advocated for the abolition of private property. Fascists opposed this communist idea while promoting nationalism with capitalist elements, 'developing a distinct ideological framework that prioritizes the state and national identity over individual economic freedoms'.

Fascism earned a bad reputation after communists defined it as an 'extreme phase of capitalism' or 'a reaction to the capitalist crisis in the stage of imperialism'[45]. Over time, however, they struggled to explain Nazism as a class struggle and thus resorted to describing it as a dictatorship in any context. Some define fascism as ultra-nationalism, dictatorship, lack of freedom, societal regimentation, and so on, usually based on a superiority complex. Ironically, communist states today exhibit many symptoms of a fascist system, with government regulation of everything from production to consumption, imports to exports, and total government/party control of business, finance, and the economy.

Communists in India have used the term fascism to describe any Hindu unity movement or social movement. Since current nationalists in India advocate for the Hindutva ideology, they too are often equated with fascism. Savarkar referred to the land of the 'Aryan' race as Hindu. They equated Savarkar's assertions with fascism, in the same way they attributed it to Hitler. In ancient times, much of Bharat was known as Aryavarta, and the people greeted each other as 'Aryaputra', with Arya meaning 'noble'.

There was a time when many 'nationalists' around the world admired Germany, including Churchill and Roosevelt. Little did they know about the dark side of Hitler's Nazism at the time; this lack of awareness of Hitler's atrocities extended to some leaders in India as well.

But the communists would like to deceive us and deny the fact that the rise of fascism was, in a way, a reaction to Stalin's purging of millions of his people in the Gulags in the name of communism. Germany, and later many parts of Europe, found the Nazis to be a lesser evil compared to the enormous brutality of Stalin's regime, which has not been adequately publicized in the modern world. Thus, in horrific fear of communists, the Germans slowly embraced the Nazis. Of course, Hitler had to propagate the 'pure Aryan race' theory, find a common enemy in the Jews, and we know the devastating consequences for millions of Jews. And, if that was not enough, the communists made sincere attempts to deny the Holocaust![46]

Another fact is that Hitler drew inspiration from the precedent set by Turkish Muslim jihadi forces who killed millions of Armenians, with no punishment for the perpetrators.[47] Similarly, both the West and the communists remain silent about the Hindu genocides in Pakistan (which continue to this day) and, more prominently, in East Pakistan—first at the hands of Pakistani forces (supported by America) and later by jihadi forces, with similar atrocities continuing in Bangladesh as I write this![48]

The so-called left-liberals in India are, in reality, communists. Many were, and still are, involved in organizing a violent 'revolution' known as the Maoist movement, and they are sometimes referred to as 'urban Naxalites'. In every Indian state where they have held power, such as West Bengal and Kerala, violence and regular political killings have become the norm.

On the other hand, today's real fascists are the communists themselves. Communist regimes have stolen the freedom of millions, killed countless people, and decimated numerous cultures and traditions. This is evident in all communist-ruled countries, including China and Russia. If communists were ever to seize power in Delhi, they would likely replicate the 'long march', 'cultural revolution', and the systematic destruction of religions and religious communities, as Lenin once described religion as 'opium'!

What is understand in the West as left-liberal is not the same in India. In India, they pose as liberals only when fighting for power; once in power, a totalitarian regime inevitably takes over. They exploit the issues of 'Dalits and Muslim minorities' to sustain their 'revolution'. Hatred towards nationalists, portrayed as 'casteists' or 'communalists', is their primary propaganda weapon. Without such narratives, funding would cease, and their 'revolution' would collapse.

On the other hand, consider the Islamic countries. There is little to no freedom, especially for women. People are often beheaded for criticizing their leaders. Non-Muslims in most of these countries virtually have no rights, reflecting a different kind of fascism.

In contrast, India has a vibrant democracy, an independent judicial system, and a truly pluralistic society, largely due to the openness of the Hindus. The ideals of democracy, justice, and pluralism have completely disappeared in Afghanistan. Pakistan and Bangladesh seem to be following a similar path, and it may only be a matter of time before Islamists eradicate any remaining non-Muslim people or cultures in these nations.

This could happen to India as well, perhaps even within our lifetime, as Islamist movements like the Taliban promoted pan-Islamism. Groups such as ISIS, often collaborating with communists and NeoCols, pose a significant threat. Communists, much like theocrats, adhere to their doctrines rooted in Marx and Lenin, proclaiming slogans like 'Chairman of China is our chairman' while systematically destroying Indigenous cultures. Many in India recognize this danger, leading to a phase of strong assertion and demonstration by Hindus today.

A Hindu, if dharmic, by definition, cannot be a fascist and will not destroy lives or property due to theological belief. If such actions occur, they are solely for survival. True dharma embodies true freedom. A dharmic Hindu who asserts themselves brings only positive contributions to the world.

Hinduphobia is on the rise globally. This was not the case even ten years ago in modern times. However, Hinduphobia is not a new phenomenon—it began with the Islamic invasions and rulers, who were motivated by conquest and destruction. Later came the missionaries, followed by Marxists, beginning with Karl Marx himself. Figures like Churchill were also noted Hindu-haters.

The current rise of Hinduphobia indicates that assertive Hindus are at work and that Hindutva is making progress. Hindus must educate themselves and unite to demonstrate the transformative power of dharma to the world.

Psychology and Epigenetics of Trauma

Bharat lost thousands of books of knowledge from renowned institutions like Nalanda and Vikramsila, immense wealth from its temples, and its rich tradition of arts and architecture. Then came the British, who claimed that 'a single shelf of a good European library was worth the whole native literature of India and Arabia'.[49]

NeoCols continue to perpetuate the belief that Bharat is merely a land of foreign invasions and rulers, leaving Indians with nothing to take pride in. Colonial Britain systematically destroyed the native education system, eradicated indigenous industries, and was responsible for the death of millions. They contributed to the rigidity of today's caste system, established slaughterhouses for the mass killing of cows, and plundered Bharat of every conceivable resource and wealth.

The most critical impact of centuries of invasions and colonization has been the epigenetic changes that have influenced the psychology and national character of the people. Those who once built nearly all the foundational pillars of modern civilization—including mathematics, grammar, metallurgy, health sciences, educational methods, and more—were reduced to paupers in just 1,200 years. This is despite the Indian civilization spending millennia offering some of the world's greatest contributions.

Both Hindu men and women were historically renowned for their prowess on the battlefield, while Indian merchants travelled the world with unparalleled products that were unmatched elsewhere. However, after enduring centuries of trauma, the same people became subdued and docile. It seems that 1,200 years of historical experiences may have altered the epigenetics of Hindus, trapping them in a mental state characterized by slumber and self-pity—traits of once-dominant but now subdued people. This transformation could be attributed to the dominance of the freeze (surrender) and fawn (appeasement) responses from the 'Flight, Flight, Freeze and Fawn' syndrome.

The psychology of trauma is deeply embedded within the masses of India, manifesting in various stages: 1) denial, 2) protest/anger, 3) sadness/mourning, 4) fear/terror/panic, 5) rationalization, 6) acceptance, 7) new attachment/renewal, 8) forgiveness, and 9) gratitude.[50] However, the majority of the population remains far from reaching the final four stages.

If you're wondering what epigenetics is, it refers to the processes that influence how our genes and their basic component, DNA, function as the critical determinants of our physical and mental development from the embryonic stage to a fully developed human being. Think of the seed of a banyan tree: although tiny, the seed contains all the 'instructions' or codes necessary to grow into a massive tree. Similarly, in humans, genes play a vital role in the development of the entire body, including the brain. For instance, if a gene carries disease-related information, such as predisposition to diabetes, and this gene is 'expressed' or activated, we may develop the condition.

However, genes do not operate with complete autonomy. The epigenome is a chemical process that regulates genes, instructing them on what to activate or suppress. The study of this regulatory system is called epigenetics. Scientists today assert that every action we perform—whether consciously or unconsciously—affects our epigenetics. This involves switching certain traits on or off, which ultimately shapes our future behaviour as well as our physical and psychological functions.

Environmental factors like air, soil, water, chemicals, toxins and pathogens, along with lifestyle choices such as diet, stress, and daily events, significantly influence our epigenetics. Inputs from our sensory organs, thoughts, and actions first impact our brain cells—neurons that form circuits of experiences. Over time, some of these behaviours leave lasting imprints on our epigenome, traits that can then be passed down through generations.

One notable example is the 'eat as much as you can' trait, which developed during the hunter-gatherer era or periods of famine. This survival-driven trait was encoded into our genes to prepare for times of scarcity. The Hindus refer to the deep imprints left on our epigenome and brain as *samskara*.

The profound impact of prolonged subjugation is both physical and psychological, affecting personal and group behaviour. Psychological inhibitions prevent individuals from calling a spade a spade for many reasons—psychological, political, and more. 'Denial' or 'rationalization' can function as a form of generational post-traumatic stress disorder (PTSD). Depression often stems from dwelling on past challenges, anxiety arises from the fear of a perceived failed future, and stress is generated as a result. When these conditions engulf an entire society, it may behave erratically, which could explain phenomena like lynching mobs. However, a more significant impact occurs on the psyche of individuals, especially among the majority of Hindus in India.

A study on the victims of the Rwanda genocide revealed that their genes were altered to such an extent that their stress response became muted or shut off due to the severity of the trauma. As a result, when faced with new dangers, they were unable to fight or flee; instead, they froze. This phenomenon, known as 'gene silencing', can be passed down from one generation to the next.[51]

One study on aggressive behaviour and genetic correlation demonstrates:

> Behavioral genetics showed that distinct polymorphisms of genes that code for proteins that control neurotransmitter metabolic and synaptic function are associated with individual vulnerability to aversive experiences, such as stressful and traumatic life events, and may result in an increased risk of developing psychopathologies associated with violence … experiencing adversities during periods of maximal sensitivity to the environment, such as prenatal life, infancy, and early adolescence, may introduce lasting epigenetic marks in genes that affect maturational processes in the brain, thus favoring the emergence of dysfunctional behaviors, including exaggerated aggression in adulthood.[52]

Similarly, a future study may reveal that prolonged exposure to an environment and culture that promotes hatred towards others (e.g., kafirs) and regular experiences of violence (including animal slaughter and infliction of pain) in the family and society could not only alter an individual's psyche but also change their epigenome—effects that could be passed down through generations. The behaviours of terrorists, for example, can be seen in how they torture and kill non-Muslims. The actions of individuals converted under duress—through violence such as rape—may also have altered their epigenome, fostering hate and violence.

Hindutva and Hinduism

So, what is Hindutva, according to its followers? Hinduness is about feeling proud of being part of an open, scientific, and pluralistic system, heritage, and culture. Followers take pride in it, aiming to protect and sustain this system to safeguard freedom and knowledge.

Few Hindus have fully realized the harsh reality of Hindu subjugation and its long-lasting consequences. If someone expresses sadness about their past and current condition, and desires to restore self-glory, they too are Hindus. When Swami Vivekananda attended the British education system, he saw through their design to create 'brown sahibs' and boldly called for freedom. Such acts are part of 'political Hinduism', as defined by NeoCol in the context of Hindutva.

NeoCols and communists claim that if you perform your puja, bhajan, and kirtan, you are a 'good Hindu'. They define 'Hinduism' for you, asserting that only their version represents true Hinduism, and if you follow it, you are a good or 'true' Hindu. Any other activity—such as reorganizing or cleansing Hindu society of wrong practices or protecting Hindu assets—is dismissed as 'Political Hinduism', which they equate with 'Hindutva' according to their definition. Why should Hindus accept these convoluted definitions and conform to their design?

There are great devotees who follow the true path of Bhakti, but they are rare. Finding a Meera Bai or a Sant Kabir today is nearly impossible. Most Hindus, however, are content with *bhajans* and *kirtans*. Tears flow as they sing the praises of Ram and Krishna. Yet, an hour later, the same person who was so moved may walk past someone in need and pretend not to notice. The same individual, in an 'ecstatic' state just moments ago, might attack you if you displease them. Those who are so 'religious' often contribute to the pollution of rivers, including the Ganga, the most sacred of all. Today, such hypocrisies have taken root in the Hindu psyche.

Singing the names or praises of the divine is sacred and empowering. From a biological and psychological perspective, we release dopamine when we experience pleasure, and most *bhaktas* enjoy this sense of joy. There is nothing wrong with this; in fact, it is an essential part of life. However, many people envision Krishna with his flute, engaging in love affairs with Radha and the gopis, which is often presented as bhakti. What a misguided understanding of bhakti this is! Bollywood and our society are full of such romanticized love stories.

How old was Krishna when he was in Vrindavan? He wasn't even a teenager, yet gullible Hindus have taken the story literally as a series of love affairs, conveniently adding 'divinity' to justify the belief. Realistically speaking, Krishna should not be worshipped for his flute-holding image, but for his image holding the Sudarshan chakra. From early childhood, he fought demon after demon to protect society, and in the end, he fought the Mahabharata war to protect dharma.

The same applies to Sri Ram. He was called by the sages when he was very young to protect them from the *rakshashas*. He too fought on the battlefield to defeat Ravana. But pacifists often interpret these acts as mere metaphors, rather than seeking to emulate his life and fight the injustice we face every day. They either hope that some future Ram or Krishna will come to save them or claim that the Ramayana and Mahabharata carry higher meanings (and are not actual historical events)—arguing that it is all a matter of interpretation.

Let's call it the 'Gandhi Syndrome'. First and foremost, you must survive! So, when chanting 'Jai Sri Ram' or 'Jai Sri Krishna', it is a way to express reverence for the grand characteristics of Maryada Purushottam Sri Ram and the Purnavatar Sri Krishna. Anyone is free to chant these names, and it is absolutely fine to invoke them both during peacetime and when fighting against injustice, atrocities, and anti-national activities. Hindus have remembered Ram and Krishna for thousands of years not for their romanticism, but for their virtues and valour.

During the horrendous and helpless centuries of subjugation under Muslim rule in India, only Bhakti saved us. It was an internal practice, making it difficult to strip the names of the divine from our hearts. For millions of Hindus, it was the only option during such a crisis. The same was true for the Hindus who were transported as indentured labourers to the Caribbean and other nations by the British. They clung to their dharma, often only able to whisper the names of the divine.

Today, there are barely any Hindu-Sikhs left in Afghanistan. Hindus, Buddhists, and Sikhs in Pakistan and Bangladesh face regular hatred and violence, and their numbers are dwindling rapidly. Unfortunately, no amount of *bhajan* or *kirtan* has saved their lives, though these practices provided some solace during the hardest times.

Many of today's gurus in West Bengal, along with many politicians—especially communists—had fled East Pakistan due to the fear of religious persecution. Yet, they now preach the same pacifist religious sermons they once espoused while fleeing in the dead of night, sometimes wearing nothing more than a single piece of cloth. When a Hindu addresses these issues, leftists immediately accuse them of not following Hinduism, but Hindutva, which, according to them, is not the same as Hinduism. Every Hindu must take note of this and move beyond the concept of 'Hinduism' to embrace dharma. Only then will all scriptures, temples, and sermons hold true meaning; otherwise, they must be prepared to face a fate similar to Gandhar becoming Kandahar.

You may be kind-hearted and compassionate, perhaps even cowardly, and you may feel afraid to discuss these matters. You might say, 'The past is past; bury it and move on!' But it is not the past we are concerned with—it is the burning present. The days of being politically correct are over. The time has come to confront historical truths head-on and address issues vital to our civilization's survival.

Hindus are not advocating aggression. They are calling for course correction. Hindus never say: 'And kill them wherever you find them and expel them from wherever they have expelled you, and fitnah [persecution] is worse than killing. And do not fight them at al-Masjid al-Haram until they fight you there. But if they fight you, then kill them. Such is the recompense of the disbelievers.'[53] 'So whoever has assaulted you, then assault him in the same way that he has assaulted you.'[54] Is Islamism equivalent to fascism? Is that the reason communists in Bharat have been supporting Islamism, just as Britain, America, and France have supported it for short-term geopolitical gains?

Hindus do not persecute their neighbours for not following their path, nor do they label them as infidels, insisting they must either be converted or killed. They don't attack other people's religious or ideological institutions (e.g., communist offices), nor do they claim that others have no place in their country. Just seventy-five years ago, Indian Muslims had the opportunity to claim a large part of India under the name of Pakistan. The Muslim leaders created an 'Islamic' nation, which later became two examples of the worldwide phenomenon known as the Islamic nation—a concept rooted in monoculture. In contrast, Hindus created a secular democratic state in India. Hindus are, by nature, democratic and pluralistic; they would never establish a theocratic state, as there is no historical precedent for it.

However, after valiantly fighting many wars and battles against aggressors, Hindus are now forced to confront modern deceptions in the name of freedom and secularism, as it is a question of their survival. It is also the survival of the knowledge and message of the Vedas and the Upanishads, which aim to enlighten humankind in the future and serve as the flag bearers of every type of freedom. For this to happen, Bharat must remain Hindu. Bad examples can be found next door—in Afghanistan, Pakistan, and Bangladesh.

There is a common pacifist notion circulating everywhere: most Muslims are peaceful people. I approve of this idea, as it is indeed true. However, when the call for jihad comes from the mullahs, the majority of them join the forces after overcoming their initial hesitation of leaving a peaceful life behind to go to war for Islam. This is part of history. I've witnessed it firsthand in relatively peaceful Bengal, where my Muslim friends suddenly stopped speaking to me or spoke in a different language and tone whenever a new maulvi visited the area.

I've seen with my own eyes how, in a conflict between the Hindu and Muslim localities, no friendship was strong enough to outlast the pull of religious zeal. Even a ten-year-old boy would shout 'Allah hu Akbar' with the leaders and carry weapons! When genocidal atrocities are committed against Hindus in Bangladesh and Pakistan, how many Muslims come to the aid of Hindus or other minorities? Few, if any. Otherwise, why would someone leave their birthplace, their home, simply for being a Hindu or Sikh?

Is it 'survival of the fittest'? If so, Hindus are at the risk of becoming extinct soon. We might read about them someday (but wait—who writes history?). A docile, cowardly people, called the Hindus (or perhaps Indians, since under the new rule, the country's name might be changed to some other 'stan', not India or Bharat). Alarmist? If you are smart, do the numbers or find someone to do the numbers for you.

Now, the battleground is in Bharat as well. Thousands of infiltrators from Bangladesh and Rohingya Muslims are causing trouble in many parts of Bengal, Assam, and several other states. The mastermind behind 2020 Delhi riots, Tahir Mohammed, is a prime example of the spread of jihadi-ISIS technology. As the Muslim population increases in many areas, attacks on Hindus, Hindu women, and temples have become regular, much like in Bangladesh. Hindus are being stopped from celebrating Saraswati Puja and Durga Puja in parts of Bengal. It may sound alarmist, but this was the reality in Bangladesh seventy-five years ago; Hindus and Buddhists never thought they would have to leave their homes forever simply because they were not Muslims. But that is the harsh reality, not a mirage! The real mirage is if people continue to follow the 'hear no evil, see no evil' policy.

While much of the world has discarded communism and Marxism, in India, remnants of these ideologies still persist in educational institutes like JNU, academia, and the media. These so-called 'revolutionaries', often disguised as 'Urban Naxals', have formed numerous outfits. They collaborate with global 'Break India' forces. They manipulate and misguide young students and tribals, continuing to dream of establishing a communist rule in India. However, their ultimate goal is to sever India from its past, from the identity of Bharatvarsha, and fragment it into small parts to control the land, society, and people. While they fight their last battle for existence, the good news is that the transition to a more 'Indic' society has begun. However, the people of India will have to endure their propaganda a little longer before it completely burns out.

Generally, when faced with threats to their lives, a person may either fight back as a natural reaction or surrender due to epigenetics. But typically, Hindus tend to look the other way when a neighbour is in trouble. Swami Vivekananda once said that the lack of organization faculty among Hindus has contributed to much of their misery. Hindutva represents the infusion of such organizational faculty.

Is Hindutva against anybody? Self-empowerment and self-assertion do not mean being against someone. Feeling good about oneself, taking pride in one's identity, and asserting that identity are all part of dharma, as previously explained. Without this, survival and sustenance would fail, since assertiveness is necessary for change. Rights are not always given to people; they must be earned through struggle, assertion, and negotiation. For the masses, movements are essential when these assertions are challenged by those who occupy advantageous positions or seek to do so at the expense of those who have lost their rights.

Today's forces that seek to rule India through money, power, violence, or by brainwashing the poor and Dalits to destroy the remnants of dharma are bound to oppose Hindutva. Communists often forget that true freedom in any country exists due to a dharmic and scientific culture, not a theocratic one where even communists have no place. A great example of this is Bangladesh, where a significant communist movement once existed, but the Islamists are now eliminating the communists there.

Vivekananda noted that true freedom should be universal, with no privilege granted to any group. This freedom follows two parallel paths. One is societal freedom, where both users and creators are free. This freedom is necessary for social opportunities, harmony, cooperation, and ultimate liberation—a collective dharma. The other is personal freedom through dharma and *sadhana*, leading to *moksha*. For India, many foreign ideas, including religious, social, and communist ideologies, are misfits, which explains the conflict and challenges we face daily. Without inner freedom, one cannot liberate others or society. Thoreau said about this: 'Free in this world as the birds in the air, disengaged from every kind of chains, those who practice the yoga gather in Brahma the certain fruits of their works.'[55]

As for ultimate freedom, Thoreau said: 'The yogi, absorbed in contemplation, contributes to his degree to creation; he breathes a divine perfume, he hears wonderful things. Divine forms traversed him without tearing him and united to nature which is proper to him; he goes, he acts as animating original matter.'[56]

The Confused Hindu

The new generation of Hindus in India is being influenced to distance themselves from their heritage and adopt the Western lifestyle, marked by rampant consumerism and little responsibility towards their family, neighbours, and society. Alcohol and drugs are increasingly infiltrating their lives. Their understanding of culture is reduced to merely celebrating a few festivals, with little appreciation for the deeper traditions and knowledge systems. These festivals are often marked by intoxication and vulgar dances, reflecting a growing attraction to Western forms of celebration and entertainment.

In previous generations, the urban elite was somewhat 'religious', though their focus was largely on their professions, leaving little time to pass on cultural values and essential *samskars* to their children. This responsibility was left to the children themselves and to the mandirs and priests, but often the latter failed to inspire deeper engagement with the culture due to their own lack of knowledge.

In rural India, people are still more connected to their ritualistic culture. Unfortunately, the urban-rural divide is gradually diminishing, and urban culture is slowly infiltrating rural areas as well.

The RSS and the Sangh Parivar

Some might claim that they are fundamentalist 'Hindu right' groups, the slogan of some of these NeoCols! The largest 'nationalist' volunteer force in the world, the RSS, reaches out to victims of natural disasters before the army and other aid agencies. While they do not discriminate based on the victims' religion or caste, this is problematic for the NeoCols because people appreciate their efforts. If they were the rightful force to defend the region when the Pakistani mujahids attacked Kashmir until the Indian forces arrived, they helped save at least part of Kashmir. This, however, was a significant setback for the NeoCols and the jihadists. Do some RSS members have apprehension towards Muslims? Yes, and why not? If you read the history of Islamic atrocities and understand their concerns about its potential recurrence, it is entirely possible that they would resist any glorification of this horrific past, especially when they fear it might repeat itself.

If the NeoCols have brainwashed you, you might think this is utterly communal and an act of inciting hatred and violence. But let me ask you: think of your ancestors who were brutally tortured and killed, your womenfolk who were raped and sold into global slave markets, your children made into slaves, and worse, coerced into becoming soldiers to kill Hindus and destroy their temples. It's only natural to feel this way! Reflect on every Hindu girl kidnapped, raped, and forced to convert to Islam in Pakistan and Bangladesh since the Partition of India in 1947. Consider living as a third-class citizen (after the mainstream Muslims, then the Ahmadis, and then you). Think of the daily persecution and destruction of your temples—not yesterday, but today, right now!

Nadia Murad Basee Taha, a Yazidi survivor and leader from Iraq, was awarded the Nobel Peace Prize in 2018! Like the Hindus in West and East Pakistan, and like the Armenians in Turkey, there was no one to shed tears for the Yazidis. Nadia was kidnapped and held by ISIS for three months as a sex slave. Her organization 'Nadia's Initiative',[57] which aims to help 'women and children victimized by genocide, mass atrocities, and human trafficking to heal and rebuild their lives and communities', has become a ray of hope for many minority communities worldwide, such as the people of Chitral, Pakistan, who are also threatened with extinction. How and when will the global community hear the voices of the Hindu-Buddhist genocide in Bangladesh and the Hindu-Sikh-Baluch genocide in Pakistan? Over three million Hindu and Buddhists were killed, mostly by Pakistani forces in East Pakistan, after the third President of Pakistan, General Yahya Khan, ordered his army to 'kill three million of them, and the rest will eat out of our hands'.[58]

It is also well known that the then US President, Richard Nixon, supported the Pakistanis, as evidenced by declassified documents from the US State Department:

> When the fighting developed, the Nixon administration 'tilted' toward Pakistan. The tilt involved the dispatch of the aircraft carrier *Enterprise* to the Bay of Bengal to try to intimidate the Indian Government. It also involved encouraging China to make military moves to achieve the same end, and an assurance to China that if China menaced India and the Soviet Union moved against China in support of India, the United States would protect China from the Soviet Union.
>
> [...]

In East Pakistan, the army began a brutal campaign of repression designed to cow the Bengali dissidents. The Consulate General's reports from Dacca were graphic and disturbing. On March 28, the report from Dacca began: 'Here in Dacca we are mute and horrified witnesses to a reign of terror by the Pak military.' During the following week, the Consulate General reported that the army was setting houses on fire and shooting people as they emerged from the burning buildings and that the army had killed a large number of unarmed students at Dacca University. On March 28, Nixon and recently dead Kissinger discussed the reports of atrocities in East Pakistan in a telephone conversation. Nixon said: 'I wouldn't put out a statement praising it, but we're not going to condemn it either.'[59]

The *New York Times* reported the following on 30 September 2013, in an article titled 'Nixon and Kissinger's Forgotten Shame': 'As recently declassified documents and White House tapes show, Nixon and Kissinger stood stoutly behind Pakistan's generals, supporting the murderous regime at many of the most crucial moments. This largely overlooked horror ranks among the darkest chapters in the entire cold war.'[60]

If you are a typical 'religious Hindu', you may perform all the rituals, *japam*, *kirtan*, and *puja*, and may believe that this is 'Hinduism'. However, it is only when you delve deeper into history that you will discover your dharma and be able to transcend your personal beliefs and practices of 'religion'.

Lessons from Chandranath Basu

Chandranath Basu, in his book *Hindutva*, wrote (translation by the author from the original Bengali):

It is not an exaggeration to say that the characteristics of a Hindu (described elsewhere) are original which represents the 'virat' [grand] human being ... Whatever a Hindu has in terms of spiritual and scientific knowledge, sociology, and worldview—all are his own

> and so unique that without significantly modifying, others cannot use Hindu ideas and practices properly. This all-encompassing and all-absorbing mind cannot be found anywhere. Whatever is found in this universe—tiny and infinite, living and inert, male and female, past and future—all are present in the Hindu mind. The world of undifferentiated, undivided are beautifully bound together—one with many and many with one—the Hindu mind is like that. The Hindu mind is molded according to the cosmically constituted mind.

He wrote that we had lost that 'mind'. Invasions, the subsequent loss of knowledge, and severe damage to the continuity of our civilization are the root causes. He recommended that each Hindu become a true Hindu in thought and action:

> In order to recover our lost grand mindset—we must work very hard and do sadhana. Being the heirs of that mind, we are today incapable of acquiring that mind, and we have become unfit to be called a Hindu. Some day in the past, we had a great mind and civilization—this pride won't take us anywhere; instead, it will render us as not a rightful heir of the name Hindu. To take pride in ancient greatness is not fitting for us; reclaiming and recovering it in our lives is real Hindutva or Hinduness. No other civilization has the excellence we have achieved in the past, hence, to regain that glory—no other nation has the enormous, urgent, and necessary effort required by us. We have a considerable amount of work before us. Until we fulfill that mission, we won't be worthy of our great past's glory. To accomplish that, we need great power, strong determination, and a good amount of time. We have arrived at a crucial juncture of our history; we must contemplate this idea. If we keep the above in mind and then take pride in our past, then only the love for the ideals we have received historically will increase and will help us not have false pride and arrogance. False pride will hinder us from achieving that great mindset and the civilizational greatness back. And, until we attain that great attitude, rituals, and celebrations—no matter what we do—we won't become a

true Hindu. There is no more difficult and yet more remarkable accomplishment than becoming a true Hindu.[61]

So, What Next?

What is 'next', then?

The battle is twofold: the first is with the NeoCols, and the second involves addressing the past. For the first part, there must be constant vigilance and proactive efforts by civil society and the government to counter their influence, particularly in academia and the news media.

What about the second part?

Revenge? No!

Justice? Yes.

Reconciliation? Yes.

Correcting Indian History? Yes.

Historic wrongs cannot be righted all at once. It is a gradual, long process of healing and reconciliation, where Muslims must acknowledge that the land belongs to them as much as it does to people of other faiths. They need to engage with their mullah leadership to reject separatist ideas and come to terms with the reality of their foreign ancestors' tragic historical infliction on Bharatiya *sabhyata* and its people. By doing so, they contribute to healing the wounds and scars of the past.

Both for Hindus and the rest of the world, the way out of the global downfall of civilization lies in understanding dharma alongside modern science.

Dharma is supreme, not religion.

The days of Muslim invaders, rulers, and their battles are gone. However, if forgotten, history has a tendency to repeat itself. For the sake of healing, forgiveness and forgetting can be simple yet profound acts of compassion to help heal the Hindu psyche.

What if Muslim leaders were to proclaim the following tomorrow?

- Do not kill cows where Hindus live. If Muslims feel that desecration of the Quran and disrespect towards their prophet are blasphemous, how about respecting the reverence Hindus have for cows?
- Lower the volume of mosque loudspeakers or remove amplifiers altogether in Hindu-majority neighbourhoods.
- Return Kashi Vishwanath Temple and Krishna Janmabhoomi to Hindus as an initial gesture to atone for past atrocities. Eventually, all temples upon which mosques or mausoleums (mostly unused) were built should be returned to the Hindu community.
- Be vigilant and inform authorities if anyone in the community becomes radicalized or begins supporting jihad.
- Unequivocally condemn all acts of jihad worldwide, especially in India.
- Encourage giving children Bharatiya names. This helps integrate communities rather than keeping them separate.
- Reduce the number of madrasas and enrol children in modern school systems enabling them to contribute significantly to nation-building and fostering modern, prosperous, happy families.
- Use more Indic words in languages spoken instead of introducing more Arabic vocabulary.

Bharat is the birthplace of Indian Muslims, not Saudi Arabia or Turkey. Indian Muslims may follow their religious faith but don't need to bow to Arab imperialism or a global Caliph. They don't need to embrace Arab or Turkish culture by undermining, hating, or abandoning the traditions of their ancestors, which they followed only a few generations ago.

However, a more significant responsibility lies with Hindus, the original inhabitants of the land. Hindus should initiate a movement and work alongside the government and Muslim leaders to achieve the following goals:

- Use existing organizations, mandirs, maths, and ashrams to foster a proper understanding of 'dharma', ensuring that every individual is educated and empowered.
- Educate everyone about the significance of the *rnas* (debts to ancestors, society, nature, etc.) and encourage diligent practice.
- Change the names of villages, towns, or localities back to their original names. For example, rename Hindukush to Hinduparvat and GT Road to its ancient name Uttarapath. Replace names connected to tyrannical British rulers, such as Victoria Memorial in Kolkata, with native names like Swatantra Bhavan.
- Address Islamic atrocities through a tribunal: rewrite textbooks to accurately reflect history; use legal means and negotiations to reclaim or restore occupied or destroyed places of worship and other structures.
- Support projects that aim to undo the whitewashing of Islamic atrocities and the destructions of Bharat's heritage.
- Establish a tribunal on British colonial atrocities: document the number of deaths caused by British rule and demand a formal apology, identify and trace all valuables taken from Bharat and publish the findings, explore legal avenues in international courts to reclaim stolen artifacts and treasures, including those held by private entities like the Rothschilds.
- Identify individuals who admire and support figures such as Stalin, Lenin, Mao, and Pol Pot as enemies of humanity and the nation. These individuals should not hold government jobs or positions in taxpayer-funded institutions.
- Correct historical narratives and revise textbooks to educate the public about the atrocities perpetrated by communism over the past 100 years. Raise awareness of the dangers communism poses to civilization.
- Make education value-based and dharma-centred, focusing on true heritage, history, and character-building.

- Create a uniform national education system and curriculum for all states and educational institutions in the country.
- Implement the Uniform Civil Code (UCC) and National Register of Citizens (NRC).

Finally, all citizens, regardless of their religious tradition or path of birth, must embrace and uphold the universal idea of dharma—not religion or any 'ism'. Each individual should respect and adhere to their own traditions, provided these do not cause harm to people of other faiths or traditions. This will usher in an extraordinary era of unity. Let communist leaders encourage Muslim leaders to take these steps, and let the communists and political parties follow suit as well.

In 1897, in Madras, Swami Vivekananda said: 'We want that education by which character is formed, strength of mind is increased, the intellect is expanded, and by which one can stand on one's own feet,'[62] and 'Education is not the amount of information that is put in your brain and runs riot there, undigested all your life. We must have life-building, man-making, character-building assimilation of ideas. If you have assimilated five ideas and made them your life and character, you have got more education than any man who has got by heart a whole library.'[63]

The era of Romila Thapar is coming to an end. She and her contemporaries have shaped a generation of NeoCols. But what comes next? In this information age, people no longer need to read their books except for academic purposes. Information about our past is now accessible from many sources, although a significant amount of misinformation also circulates. This makes it imperative for Hindus to work diligently to identify and support Hindu intellectuals, writers, teachers, and media professionals. These individuals can help expose the distortions propagated by the current NeoCols, uncover the conspiracies behind their actions, and present accurate facts to both the present and future generations. Rhetoric and emotional reactions will not yield long-term results. Instead, a fact-based re-evaluation of Bharat—its history and culture—must be the foundation for restoring Bharat to its status as a great and progressive nation.

Scholar Sitaram Goel issued a warning to Hindus:

> Hindu society owes it to its own survival in the present and to the prosperity of its future generations to repudiate this perverse version of India's history and to put the record straight so that no one dares divorce Hindu spirituality from Hindu heroism, Hindu nation from the Hindu homeland, and Hindu culture from the national culture of India. Hindu saints, sages and scholars in general and Hindu historians in particular must come forward to do their duty towards their society and culture and to pay homage to their ancient heritage. Hindu *Dharmashāstras* have enjoined upon every Hindu to repay according to his or her capacity the *rishi-rina*, that is, the debt we owe to our seers and sages, by passing on to the next generation the Veda and the Itihāsa-Purāna, that is, the spiritual and cultural vision of Sanatana Dharma and the historical tradition of Hindu heroism. In the present situation, that is perhaps the best way to repay the pitri-rina, the debt we owe to our forefathers for the protection, preservation and perpetuation of our great Hindu society and its continuously creative culture.
>
> For long, historians have emphasised merely the ultimate collapse of the Indians, ignoring completely the resistance offered by them. *It is a fact of history that such sustained resistance, as encountered by the Muslim arms in India, was not faced by them in any other land they conquered.* The Indian resistance had another facet, which was the outcome of the resolute determination of the Indians to preserve their religious and cultural identity. While country after country, from the straits of Gibraltar to the banks of the Indus, witnessed the rapid Islamization of their individual cultures, even Northern India managed to survive as a predominantly 'heathen' land even after five centuries of Muslim rule [emphasis added].[64]

Future Is Dharma

I know, O God, the day shall dawn at last
When man shall rise from playing with the mud
And taking in his hands the sun and stars
Remold appearance, law and process old.
Then, pain and discord vanished from the world,
Shall the dead wilderness accept the rose
And the hushed desert babble of its rills;
Man once more seem the image true of God.
—Sri Aurobindo[65]

In this era of technology, where AI, ML, gene modification, robots, and potential interplanetary migration are supposed to be our focus, we are still dragged back to stone-age battles and tribal warfare under the banner of jihad. Powerful nations continue their attempts to dominate others, whether through force or deception.

Vivekananda said, 'Mark me, then and then alone you are a Hindu when the very name sends through you a galvanic shock of strength.'[66] Why? For three reasons:

- The unmatched contribution of Hindus to the world, both in material science and adhyatmic knowledge
- The sacrifice they have made in the face of the most brutal invaders and oppressors in history to protect dharma
- There is much more that Hindus can offer to world culture, for peace, freedom, and harmony, both today and in the future

Remember, Bhakti was not as prevalent in Bharat before Muslim period. During that period, Hindus lost many of their institutions and had only one way to remember and protect their culture—through their homes and hearts: Bhakti. The Bhakti movement was both one of the most glorious and saddest chapters of Indian history; people endured horrific cultural decimation, clinging to Bhakti as their only means of survival. It was their solace and helped preserve much of their traditions.

Thanks to the Western rediscovery and enthusiasm for 'yoga'—particularly Bharatiya Hatha Yoga, which Bharat almost forgot—it is returning home. However, much like the popular understanding of yoga as merely postures, without comprehending the deeper aspects of the system, we are left with only one facet of the Hindu tradition: pooja, bhajan, and kirtan. But even this is not the full scope of Bhakti Yoga.

The time has come for Bhakti to find its rightful place in people's hearts. Without the balance of karmic and gyan power, emotional beings may inadvertently cause further harm to the culture of the country. Let them draw inspiration from the great patriotic song[67] by Atul Prasad of Bengal (1930s):

হও ধরমেতে ধীর

(Hao dharmeta dheer)
Be dheer (steadfast) in dharma
Be a veer (uncompromising hero) in karma.
There is nothing to fear—
Hold your head high!
Forget all differences,
Unite and march on.
Bhagawan is with us,
Victory is assured.
Varied are tongues,
And diverse each dress.
Yet amid it all, a unity—
What a great grace!
Seeing the rise of a *maha-jati,* (a great nation) within Bharat,
The world will be bewildered with wonder!
The world will be bewildered with wonder!

Hindu *asmita* (self-respect) and assertion are inevitable, but people must remain patient and strategic, avoiding a purely 'reactive' approach. Hindus need to broaden their lifestyle and scope of activities beyond Bhakti. They must focus on karma—through *seva* and self-preservation(both physical and intellectual strength)—and jnana, excelling in the realms of thought, creativity, and knowledge, where they have been lagging.

Even during the modern freedom struggle, luminaries like J.C. Bose, Meghnad Saha, C.V. Raman, and Satyen Bose made significant contributions to the world of science. However, there are far fewer such individuals today. Hindus need to recognize their inherent strength in knowledge and practice, avoiding over-reliance on the Western or communist world. Let Hindus embrace their true dharmic essence.

The age-old story of the bully and the bullied returns. When someone who has been bullied for a long time suddenly takes a stand, the bully reacts with shock: 'What? You dare stand up to me?' Hindus, who have endured nearly 1,200 years of suffering—first at the hands of Islamists, then the British and Portuguese, and now the communists and NeoCols—are finally saying, 'Enough is enough'. The bully is stunned, and this is rapidly becoming the new reality.

Some of the bullied, however, continue to side with the bullies out of fear, believing that by appeasing them, they can avoid being targeted. This is the fourth F—'fawn'—a response within the 'Fight or Flight' syndrome. The mindset of 'My prophet and my book are the only truth; all others are false. If you do not follow me, you are doomed to eternal hell, and it is my duty to send you there if you refuse to convert'—is a narrative the coming era will no longer accept.

This rejection also applies to the communists and their utopia of a 'rule of the proletariats'. Civilization has progressed enough to deny these extremist claims. If the sane ones, like the Hindus, remain in denial or passive, extinction will be their fate.

On the other hand, the best way for Bharat to remain dharmic is to invite and encourage Muslims and Christians to practise yoga alongside their Hindu brothers and sisters. This can help reset their epigenetics towards becoming a people of dharma—respecting the dharma, culture, and history of Bharat—and adhering to the principles of the land of dharma.

Let 'Hinduism' fade to bring forth true Hinduness or Hindutva by rediscovering dharma. Dharma is 'Sanatan'—ever-renewing, self-correcting, and everlasting. In Swami Vivekandanda's words:

> The Upanishads are the great mine of strength. Therein lies strength enough to invigorate the whole world; the whole world can be vivified, made strong, and energized through them. They will call with trumpet voice upon the weak, the miserable, and the downtrodden of all races, all creeds, and all sects, to stand on their feet and be free. Freedom, physical freedom, mental freedom, and spiritual freedom are watchwords of the Upanishads.[68]

And that is the role of a 'Vishwa Guru'—India, Bharat!

In 1893, Swami Vivekananda, during his speeches at the World Parliament of Religions, elaborated on the need to challenge blind faith, such as the Christian theologies concepts of 'you are sinners'. His message applies universally to all blind faiths, belief systems, 'isms', and rigid theories. One of the key teachings of the *Rigveda* emphasizes *'Amritasya Putra'* (children of immortality) and *'Amritasya Chetanam'* (consciousness of immortality):[69]

अरं कृण्वन्तु वेदिं समग्निमिन्धतां पुरः ।
तत्रामृतस्य चेतनं यज्ञं ते तनवावहै ॥

aram kṛṇvantu vedim sam agnim indhatām puraḥ
tatra amṛtasya cetanam yajñam te tanavāvahai //

(Let them make ready the altar, let them set Agni in a blaze
in front. It is there—the awakening of the consciousness to
immortality. Let us two extend for thee thy effective sacrifice.)

It essentially means that we are all 'children of immortality', and to achieve and honour that status, one must cultivate the 'consciousness of being immortal'. This idea of immortality is a central theme in the Vedas and the Upanishads, particularly in the *Shvetashvatara Upanishad*:[70]

युजे वां ब्रह्म पूर्व्यं नमोभिर्विश्लोक एतु पथ्येव सूरेः।
शृण्वन्तु विश्वे अमृतस्य पुत्रा आ ये धामानि दिव्यानि तस्थुः॥

yuje vāṃ brahma pūrvyaṃ namobhir vi śloka etu pathyeva sūreḥ
śṛṇvanti viśve amṛtasya putrā ā ye dhāmāni diviyāni tasthuḥ ||

(O senses and O deities who favour them! Through salutations, I unite myself with the eternal Brahman, your source. Let this prayer, sung by me who follow the right path of the Sun, go forth in all directions. May the children of the immortal, who occupy celestial positions, hear it!)

Swamiji said:[71]

> Children of immortal bliss—what a sweet, what a hopeful name! Allow me to call you, bretheren, by that sweet name—heirs of immortal bliss—yea, the Hindu refuses to call you sinners. Ye are the Children of God, 'let this truth be known to all the *amritasya putrah*, all the sons of immortality and spread in the four corners of the world; let this hymn in the form of prayer of what I have realized become intense and spread over the whole world'.

Let us meditate on what Sri Aurobindo envisioned about the mission of Bharat:

> Her mission is to point back humanity to the true source of human liberty, human equality, human brotherhood. When man is free in spirit, all other freedom is at his command; for the Free is the Lord who cannot be bound. When he is liberated from delusion, he perceives the divine equality of the world which fulfils itself through love and justice, and this perception transfuses itself into the law of government and society. When he has perceived this divine equality, he is brother to the whole world, and in whatever position he is placed he serves all men as his brothers by the law of love, by the law of justice. When this perception becomes the

> basis of religion, of philosophy, of social speculation and political aspiration, then will liberty, equality and fraternity take their place in the structure of society and the *satyayuga* return. This is the Asiatic reading of democracy which Bharat must rediscover for herself before she can give it to the world. It is the *dharma* of every man to be free in soul, bound to service not by compulsion but by love; to be equal in spirit, apportioned his place in society by his capacity to serve society, not by the interested selfishness of others; to be in harmonious relations with his brother men, linked to them by mutual love and service, not by shackles of servitude, or the relations of the exploiter and the exploited, the eater and the eaten. It has been said that democracy is based on the rights of man; it has been replied that it should rather take its stand on the duties of man; but both rights and duties are European ideas. *Dharma* is the Indian conception in which rights and duties lose the artificial antagonism created by a view of the world that makes selfishness the root of action and regain their deep and eternal unity. *Dharma* is the basis of democracy which Asia must recognize, for in this lies the distinction between the soul of Asia and the soul of Europe. Through *dharma* the Asiatic evolution fulfills itself; this is her secret.[72]

Let Bharatiyas in Bharat re-establish the foundational pillars of its *sabhyata*:

Rishi Sabhyata: A vision encompassing the past, present, and future.

Vedic Sabhyata: A knowledge-driven society rooted in wisdom.

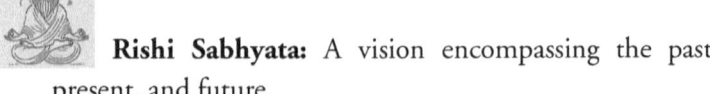

Dharmik Sabhyata: A consciousness of sustainability and sustenance.

 **Yogik Sabhyata:** A culture of unity and connectedness.

 **Sanskritik Sabhyata:** Renewal, refreshment, and reinvention of cultural identity.

 **Mukti Sabhyata:** A commitment to freedom, liberty, diversity, and pluralism.

The dark cloud hovering over the nation will slowly clear, and the land will once again become the true 'Bharat', shining brightly as the Vishwa Guru reemerges—not confined to hidden huts but spreading its light across the land and the world.

Let there be complete freedom and an environment conducive to the flourishing of countless unbiased and unattached creative truth-seekers in Bharat, who, in turn, will guide society towards a higher purpose. Let selfless individuals arise in abundance, protecting institutions and nurturing society with integrity. Let there be millions of ambitious individuals contributing to wealth generation without succumbing to animalist greed, creating a sound and ethical economy for the nation.

Utopia? Perhaps. Yet, we have lost our way—our social systems have been mutilated, corrupted, and diluted by cheap mimicry of the West. We remain distracted by residual communists, mongrelized Nehruvians, and the lingering influence of NeoCols. In this state, imagining a truly liberated India, grounded in authentic Indian ideas and ideals, feels distant.

Despite these challenges, there are heroes among Hindus because of how they live, but the nation needs many more. Hindus must free themselves from centuries of inhibitions, the baggage of the past, procrastination, and the deep-seated negative programming of their psyche and epigenetics. They must rediscover what it means to be authentically Hindus in thought and behaviour.

Every Hindu has the potential to become a *veer*—a protector of the land, its people, temples, culture, and heritage. That day is not far when every Hindu awakens to serve society, the nation, and the world with a sense of *dharmic* duty.

The world cannot afford to persist with battles and wars driven by 'isms', religions, intermediaries of 'God', and the business of divinity and its institutions. It is my fervent hope that the terms Hinduism and Hindu religion will soon be replaced by the universal idea of dharma, not just among Hindus but across all nations.

Dharma is the only universal principle that touches every aspect of life—a sustainable, progressive, and evolutionary way of living. It ensures a logical, scientific, and practical approach to life and to sustaining our planet. Coupled with a true understanding and application of the science of yoga, this universal idea can usher in a new renaissance, catalyzing a paradigm shift in human thoughts and action. It has the potential to elevate humanity to the next era of conscious and enlightened evolution, advancing human existence to a higher plane.

We cannot live even for a moment without practising some form of yoga. People of all races, religions, and sects unknowingly engage in yoga in its deeper sense. By practising it consciously, we can elevate our collective one-earth consciousness—transitioning from an animalistic existence to a human one, and eventually to the divine.

This transformation is the subject of our next exploration. When dharma and yoga work together, they simultaneously sustain and propel evolution. They hold the potential to address and overcome the fears of wars—be they physical, economic, or technological, including challenges posed by singularity.

Let dharma and yoga flourish everywhere, embraced by everyone, for the attainment of true freedom—*Mukti*.

Notes

Chapter 1: 'Amritasya Putrah': The Children of the Rishis and the Immortals

1 Vivekananda, Swami. *Lectures from Colombo to Almora: First Public Lecture in the East (Delivered in Colombo)*. Available online: https://en.wikisource.org/wiki/The_Complete_Works_of_Swami_Vivekananda/Volume_3/Lectures_from_Colombo_to_Almora/First_Public_Lecture_in_the_East_(Colombo)

2 Vivekananda, Swami. *Lectures from Colombo to Almora: The Common Bases of Hinduism*. Ramakrishna Mission Chandigarh. Available online: https://chandigarh.rkmm.org/AKAM/Books/Lectures_from_Colombo_To_Almora.pdf

3 https://frontline.thehindu.com/arts-and-culture/article25879760.ece; https://www.booksfact.com/religions/vedic-hinduism-influence-in-ancient-europe-italy-greece-russia.html

4 Suhas, H.K. 2004. *Consolation of Mind*, p. 111. iUniverse.

5 Deepak, B.R. 2020. *India and China: Beyond the Binary of Friendship and Enmity*, p. 6. Springer Nature.

6 Vivekananda, Swami. *Lectures from Colombo to Almora: The Common Bases of Hinduism*. Ramakrishna Mission Chandigarh. Available online: https://chandigarh.rkmm.org/AKAM/Books/Lectures_from_Colombo_To_Almora.pdf

7 Ibid.

8 Sharma, A. 2002. 'On Hindu, Hindustān, Hinduism and Hindutva'. *Numen*, 49 (1): 1–36.

9 Maclean, D.N. 1989. *Religion and Society in Arab Sind.* Available at: https://ia601408.us.archive.org/22/items/ReligionAndSocietyInArabSind/Religion%20and%20society%20in%20Arab%20Sind.pdf

10 https://courses.lumenlearning.com/atd-fscj-worldreligions/chapter/etymology-and-history/

11 Flood, G.D. 2008. *The Blackwell Companion to Hinduism*. John Wiley & Sons.

12 Flood, G.D. 1996. *An Introduction to Hinduism*. Cambridge University Press.
13 Ibid.
14 Ibid.
15 Mangalwadi, V. 1999. *The Legacy of William Carey: A Model for the Transformation of a Culture*, pp. 61–67.
16 https://www.academia.edu/33051482/DR_JOHN_THOMAS_THE_FIRST_BAPTIST_MISSIONARY_TO_BENGAL
17 Tomkins, S. 2007. *William Wilberforce: A Biography*, pp. 187–88. Oxford: Lion.
18 Ibid.
19 Altman, M.J. 2017. *Heathen, Hindoo, Hindu: American Representations of India, 1721–1893*, pp. 30–32. Oxford University Press.
20 http://www.columbia.edu/itc/mealac/pritchett/00generallinks/macaulay/txt_minute_education_1835.html
21 Kampfner, J. 2013. 'Macaulay by Zareer Masani: Review'. *Guardian*, 22 July.
22 Daughrity, D.B. 2005. 'Hinduisms, Christian Missions, and the Tinnevelly Shanars: A Study of Colonial Missions in 19th century India', pp. 4, 7. Alberta: University of Calgary.
23 Müller, F.M. 1860. *A History of Ancient Sanskrit Literature: The Primitive Religion of the Brahmanas*, p. 389.
24 'Chapter X', *The Life and Letters of the Right Honourable Friedrich Max Muller*, Vol. I. 1992.
25 Ibid., p. 328.
26 Ibid.
27 https://www.gutenberg.org/files/20847/20847-h/20847-h.htm
28 https://www.gutenberg.org/files/30269/30269-h/30269-h.htm
29 Oddie, G.A. 2008. *Imagined Hinduism: British Protestant Missionary Constructions of Hinduism 1793–1900*. New Delhi: Sage Publications.
30 *The Complete Works of Raja Ram Mohan Roy*, p. 3.
31 *The Works of Sir William Jones*, pp. 46, 374.
32 Morris, H. 1904. *The life of Charles Grant*, pp. 104–05. London: John Murray.
33 Ibid.
34 https://www.history.com/this-day-in-history/charter-granted-to-the-east-india-company
35 Ibid.
36 *The Life of John Thomas*, pp. 57, 58, 91. Macmillan, 1863.
37 Ibid.
38 Morris, L. 1904. *The Life of Charles Grant*, pp. 104–05. London: John Murray.

39 Ibid.
40 Ibid.

Chapter 2: Bharat and India

1 Dimmitt, C. and J.A.B. van Buitenen. 1978. *Classical Hindu Mythology: A Reader in the Sanskrit Puranas*. Temple University Press.
2 Rocher, L. 1986. *The Puranas*. Otto Harrassowitz Verlag.
3 Wilson, H.H. (trans.). 2018. *The Vishnu Purana*, edited by K.L. Joshi. Parimal Publication Pvt. Ltd.
4 Doniger, W. 2010. *The Hindus: An Alternative History*. Oxford University Press.
5 Vanita, R. 2005. *Love's Rite*. Palgrave Macmillan.
6 Gietz, K.P., et al. 1992. *Epic and Puranic Bibliography (Upto 1985)*. Otto Harrassowitz Verlag.
7 Bryant, E.F. 2007. *Krishna: A Sourcebook*, p. 112. Oxford University Press.
8 Ibid.
9 https://vedabase.io/en/library/sb/1/3/
10 Sangave, V.A. 2001. *Facets of Jainology: Selected Research Papers on Jain Society, Religion, and Culture*. Mumbai: Popular Prakashan; Zimmer, H. 1953. *Philosophies of India*, edited by Joseph Campbell. London: Routledge & Kegan Paul Ltd.
11 Jaini, P.S. 1977. 'Jina Rishabha as an avatar of Vishnu'. *Bulletin of the School of Oriental and African Studies*, XL (2): pp. 321–27.
12 https://www.srimadbhagavatam.org/canto5/chapter4.html
13 Radhakrishnan, S. 1923. *Indian Philosophy*, p. 287. Macmillan.
14 Bhargava, M.L. 1964. *Geography of Rigvedic India*, pp. 15–18, 46–49, 92–98, 100, 136.
15 Sircar, D. 1971. *Studies in the Geography of Ancient and Medieval India*, p. 3. Motilal Banarsidas; Apte, V.S. 1959. 'भरतः'. Poona: Prasad Prakashan.
16 Jain, C.R. 1929. *Risabha Deva—The Founder of Jainism*, p. 159. Allahabad: The Indian Press Limited; Shah, U.P. 1987. *Jaina-rūpa-maṇḍana: Jaina Iconography*, p. 72. Abhinav Publications.
17 https://archive.org/details/vp_vol1/page/n335/mode/1up?q=bharat; https://archive.org/details/vp_vol1/page/n337/mode/1up?q=bharat; *Vishnu Purana* (2.3.1, 2.3.8).
18 www.vcscsd.com › 18-PuranasPDF
19 Kipling, R. 1899. 'The White Man's Burden'. Published simultaneously in *The Times* (London), and *McClure's Magazine* (US), 12 February 1899.
20 Minute by the Hon'ble T.B. Macaulay, 2 February 1835.

21 Strachey, J. 1903. *India: Its Administration & Progress*, p. 5. London: MacMillan.
22 Schwanbeck, E.A. 1966. *Megasthenes' Indica*. Adolf M. Hakkert.
23 McCrindle, J.W. 1884. *Ancient India as Described by Ptolemy*, p. 33–189. Reprinted from the 'Indian Antiquary'.
24 Varahamihira. *Brihat Samhita*, XIV (1–31).
25 Jarrett, Colonel H.S. (trans.). 1894. *Ain-i-Akbari: Abul Fazl*, Volume III.
26 Athar Ali, M. 1995. 'The Evolution of the Perception of India — Akbar and Abu'l Fazl', *Proceedings of the Indian History Congress*, Volume 56, pp. 175–83. Indian History Congress. Available online: https://www.jstor.org/stable/44158617
27 Nora, P. 1989. 'Between Memory and History: Les Lieux de Mémoire', *Representations*, No. 26, Special Issue: Memory and Counter-Memory (Spring, 1989), pp. 7–24. University of California Press. Available online: https://www.jstor.org/stable/2928520
28 Vanamali. 2008. *Shakti: Realm of the Divine Mother*, pp. 83–84, 143–44. Inner Traditions.
29 Klostermaier, K. 2007. *A Survey of Hinduism*. State University of New York Press.

Chapter 3: Bharatiya Civilization or Sabhyata

1 Voltaire. 1777. *Lettres sur l'origine des sciences et sur celle des peuples de l'Asie*, Paris.
2 https://www.azquotes.com/quote/767404
3 Durant, W. and A. Durant. 1968. *The Lessons of History*, p. 101. Simon & Schuster.
4 https://en.wikipedia.org/wiki/Rishi#cite_note-Swami_Vivekananda_on_Rishis-9
5 *The Mundaka Upanishad with Shankara's Commentary*, Wisdom Library.
6 Vivekananda, Swami. 1897. *Lectures from Colombo to Almora*, Volume 3.
7 *Complete Works of Sri Aurobindo*, Volume 12, pp. 18–19.
8 https://www.goodreads.com/quotes/547244-civilization-begins-with-distillation
9 https://www.goodreads.com/quotes/44731-everything-that-is-really-great-and-inspiring-is-created-by
10 https://www.azquotes.com/quote/1337585
11 https://libquotes.com/thomas-sowell/quote/lbn2v0e
12 https://www.goodreads.com/quotes/7740111-violence-is-not-necessary-to-destroy-a-civilization-each-civilization

Chapter 4: Religion and Dharma

1 Scouteris, C.B. 1972. *The Meaning of the Terms 'Theology', 'to Theologize' and 'Theologian' in the Teaching of the Greek Fathers up to and Including the Cappadocians* (Greek), p. 187.

2 Adam, J. 1902. *The Republic of Plato*. Cambridge University Press.

3 The Vision of William concerning Piers Plowman, together with Vita de Dowel, Dobet, et Dobest, secundum Wit et Resoun, by William Langland. The 'Vernon' Text; or Text A. ix 136

4 Pattanaik, Devdutt. 2014. *Myth = Mithya: Decoding Hindu Mythology*. Penguin UK.

5 Ibid.

6 Harper, D. 2015. Etymology Dictionary.

7 Ibid.

8 Krishnan, K.S. 2019. *Origin of Vedas*. Notion Press; Boyce, M. 2001. *Zoroastrians: Their Religious Beliefs and Practices*, p.11. Psychology Press.

9 Migliore, D.L. 2004. *Faith Seeking Understanding: An Introduction to Christian Theology*, Second edition. Grand Rapids: Eerdmans; Kogan, M.S. 1995. 'Toward a Jewish Theology of Christianity'. *Journal of Ecumenical Studies,* 32 (1): 89–106.

10 https://www.giffordlectures.org/books/natural-religion-vol-1/lecture-2-definition-religion

11 https://www.giffordlectures.org/books/natural-religion-vol-1/lecture-2-definition-religion

12 Campbell, J. 2001. *Thou Art That: Transforming Religious Metaphor*, edited by Eugene Kennedy. New World Library.

13 Pattanaik, Devdutt. 2014. *Myth = Mithya: Decoding Hindu Mythology*. Penguin UK.

14 *Katha Upanishad* (1.1.21)

15 https://sanskritdocuments.org/doc_z_misc_vaakyasangraha/vaakyaexamples.html

16 'Karnaparva', Mahabharat (69.59).

17 Ramayana (2.21.42).

18 Ramayana (3.9.30).

19 *Vaisheshika Sutra* (1.1.2).

20 Sastri, A.M. (trans.) 1901. *The Bhagavat Gita with the Commentary of Sri Sankaracharya,* Second edition, p. 2.

21 Buddhadasa B. 1989. *Handbook for Mankind*, p. 128. Bangkok: White Lotus Press.

22 *Saman Suttam*, No. 83.

23 Sri Guru Granth Sahib, p. 196.

24 https://www.ttbook.org/interview/i-am-because-we-are-african-philosophy-ubuntu
25 https://classics.mit.edu/Confucius/learning.html
26 Analects (XII, 22).
27 Analects of Confucius, Analects VI, 28.
28 Covey, S. 1989. *The 7 Habits of Highly Effective People*. Free Press.
29 https://www.taoistic.com/taoteching-laotzu/taoteching-21.htm
30 'Bhisma Parva', Mahabharata (167.41); Hiltebeitel, A. 2011. *Dharma: Its Early History in Law, Religion, and Narrative*, p. 545–47. Oxford University Press.
31 *Manusmriti* (8.15).
32 'Karnaparva', Mahabharat (69:58).
33 *Dharma for All*. 1985. Sri Ramakrishna Math.
34 'Vanaparva', Mahabharat (313.117).
35 Swami Sastrananda. 1985. *Dharma for All*. Sri Ramakrishna Math.
36 Ibid.
37 Ibid.
38 Ibid.
39 Rangachari, R. 1985. *Dharma for All*. Sri Ramakrishna Math.
40 Swami Vivekananda. 1922. *The Complete Works of Swami Vivekananda*, Volume 3. Advaita Ashrama.
41 https://web.archive.org/web/20120330175816/http://www.belurmath.org/swamivivekananda.htm
42 *Manusmriti* (6.92).
43 Srimad Bhagavad Gita (16.2).
44 *Brihadaranyaka Upanishad* (1.4.14).
45 Rishi Aurobindo. August 1918–July 1919. 'Is India Civilised?', *A Philosophical Review*, Volume 5.
46 *Atharvaveda* (10.8.23).

Chapter 5: Samskriti and Culture

1 Huxley, Sir J. 1960. *Evolution after Darwin*, p. 17. Chicago University Press.
2 https://www.marxists.org/reference/archive/hegel/works/hl/hlprefac.htm
3 Huntington, S.P. 1997. *The Clash of Civilizations and the Remaking of World Order*. Penguin Books India.
4 Sastri, K.A.N. 1959. 'The Future for Traditional Cultures', *UNESCO Chronicle*.
5 Rishi Aurobindo. August 1918–July 1919. 'Is India Civilised?', *A Philosophical Review*, Volume 5.

6 Swami Prabhavananda. 1979. *The Spiritual Heritage of India: A Clear Summary of Indian Philosophy and Religion*; Arnold Toynbee in a private conversation with the author.

7 https://globaljournals.org/GJHSS_Volume14/E-Journal_GJHSS_(C)_Vol_14_Issue_1.pdf

8 https://katha.vkendra.org/2015/03/every-individual-had-equally-important.html?m=1

9 https://www.gutenberg.org/files/20847/20847-h/20847-h.htm

10 'Vanparva', Mahabharat (130.1.1).

11 Gandhi, M.K. *Young India*, January 1928.

12 Bentley, D. 1999. *The 99 Beautiful Names of God.* William Carey Library.

13 https://www.gandhipedia150.in/static/data/pdfs_with_letters/volume36_book_188.pdf

14 https://www.gandhiashramsevagram.org/gandhi-literature/mahatma-gandhi-collected-works-volume-41.pdf

15 *Ṛigveda* (1.164.46).

16 Burke, M.L. *Swami Vivekananda: Prophet of the Modern Age.* Calcutta: The Ramakrishna Mission Institute of Culture.

17 https://www.sacred-texts.com/aor/einstein/einsci.htm

18 Sri Aurobindo. *Essays Divine and Human*, p. 64.

19 https://ramakrishna.org/vivekanandaamerica.html

20 Sister Nivedita. 1966. *Notes of Some Wanderings with the Swami Vivekananda.*

21 Flew, A. (ed.). 1979. 'Golden Rule'. *A Dictionary of Philosophy*, p. 134. London: Pan Books in association with MacMillan Press.

22 Tullberg, J. 2012. 'The Golden Rule of Benevolence versus the Silver Rule of Reciprocity'. *Journal of Religion and Business Ethics*, 3 (2).

23 https://borgenproject.org/inspirational-quotes-on-education/

24 Dubuisson, D. 2003. *The Western Construction of Religion, Myths, Knowledge, and Ideology*, translated by William Sayers. Johns Hopkins University Press.

Chapter 6: Divinity in Vedic and Hindu System

1 https://upanishads.org.in/stories/the-light-of-the-lights

2 Halsey, W., Blackburn, R.H. and F. Francis. 1969. *Collier's Encyclopedia*, Volume 22, pp. 266–7, edited by Louis Shores. Crowell-Collier Educational Corporation.

3 'theism'. Dictionary.com; 'theism'. Merriam-Webster Online Dictionary.

4 Stevenson, A. 2010. *Oxford Dictionary of English*, Third edition, p. 461. New York: Oxford University Press.

5 'monotheism'. Cambridge Dictionary; Cross, F.L. and E.A. Livingstone (eds). 1974. 'Monotheism'. *The Oxford Dictionary of the Christian Church*, Second edition. Oxford University Press.
6 'Monotheism' and 'Polytheism'. 2014. *Encyclopædia Britannica.*
7 The term 'pantheist' designates one who holds both that everything constitutes a unity and that this unity is divine. *The New Oxford Dictionary of English*, p. 1341.
8 Wood, H. 2017. 'New Online Pantheism Community Seeks Common Ground'. *Pantheist Vision*, 34 (2): 5.
9 Noll, K.L. 2001. *Canaan and Israel in Antiquity: An Introduction*, p. 249. Sheffield Academic Press.
10 Heinrich, R.Z. 1953. *Philosophies of India*, p. 182, edited by Joseph Campbell.
11 Houlden, J.L. (ed.). 2005. *Jesus: The Complete Guide*, p. 390.
12 https://timesofindia.indiatimes.com/Now-meet-Ravan-the-saint/articleshow/6123749.cms
13 *Aitareya Brahmana* (7.15).
14 http://www.hindupedia.com/en/Jain_Dharm#Jainism_and_Vedic_scriptures
15 https://maithri.com/buddhist_chanting/maha-jayamangala-gatha/
16 https://dhammakami.org/2018/08/26/what-are-the-ten-questions-that-the-buddha-did-not-answer/
17 https://www.accesstoinsight.org/tipitaka/an/an11/an11.013.than.html
18 'Mahanama Sutta: To Mahanama' (AN 11.13), translated from the Pali by Thanissaro Bhikkhu, https://www.accesstoinsight.org/tipitaka/an/an11/an11.013.than.html
19 https://www.accesstoinsight.org/lib/authors/thanissaro/dhammapada.pdf
20 Davids, T.W.R. 2000. *Buddhism: Being a Sketch of the Life and Teachings of Gautama*, pp. 83–84. Asian Educational Services.
21 Ibid.
22 http://ramakrishnavivekananda.info
23 https://www.tehrantimes.com/news/464522/Inscriptions-in-Persepolis-palace-hold-clues-about-evolution
24 https://escholarship.org/content/qt0bh180f4/qt0bh180f4_noSplash_50ccdf784491b76f193dad213b917bb0.pdf
25 http://amara.aupasana.com/
26 *The Nighantu and the Nirukta Lakshman Sarup*, 1967. Motilal Banarsidass.
27 Mahabharata (13.308).
28 Bhagavad Gita (3.11).
29 *Brihadaranyaka Upanishad* (1.9.2).

30 *Vishnu Purana* (1.3; 6.3).
31 *The Practical Sanskrit-English Dictionary* and Cologne Digital Sanskrit Dictionaries: Shabda-Sagara Sanskrit-English Dictionary
32 Lonie, A.C.O. 1878. *Encyclopædia Britannica*. Volume 2, pp. 55–57, edited by T.S. Baynes.
33 Baumer, B. and K. Vatsyayan. 2001. *Kalatattvakosa*, Volume 1, p. 42. Indira Gandhi National Centre for the Arts.
34 *Rigveda* (10.97.11).
35 Ibid.
36 *Brihadaranyaka Upanishad* (4.5.6).
37 *Chandogya Upanishad* (7.25.2).
38 *Brihadaranyaka Upanishad* (11).
39 *Shvetashvatara Upanishad* (6.17.18).
40 https://www.christianity.com/wiki/salvation/difference-between-a-soul-and-a-spirit.html
41 Swami Vivekananda, 'Bhakti Yoga', p. 10.
42 *Bhāgavata Purāṇa* (1.1.1).
43 https://www.sadagopan.org/pdfuploads/Sri%20Bhashyam%20-%20Chapters%201%20and%202%20-%20Phala%20Adhyayam.pdf
44 *Mundaka Upanishad* (2.2.11).
45 *Chandogya Upanishad* (3.14.1).
46 Ibid. (6.9.4).
47 *Taittiriya Upanishad* (1.3).
48 *Aitareya Upanishad* (3.1.3).
49 *Chandogya Upanishad* (6.2.1).
50 *Chandogya Upanishad* (6.8.7).
51 *Mandukya Upanishad* (1.2).
52 *Isha Upanishad* (16).
53 *Brihadaranyaka Upanishad* (1.4.10).
54 Jones, S. (ed.). *The Mind of God and Other Musings* p. 44. Wisdom of Science.
55 Schrödinger, E. 1961. *'Meine Weltansicht': My View of the World.*
56 Schrödinger, E. 2012. *'What Is Life?'*, p. 129. Cambridge University Press.
57 Deluca, D. 2011. *Sacred Jewels of Yoga: Wisdom from India's Beloved Scriptures, Teachers, Masters, and Monks.*
58 *Mundaka Upanishad* (2.2.11).
59 Schrödinger, E. 2012. *'What Is Life?'*, p. 129. Cambridge University Press.
60 Ibid., p. 87.
61 Schrödinger, E. 1961. *Mein Leben, Meine Weltansicht: My Life, My World View.*

62 Interview of Fritjop Capra by Renee Weber. *The Holographic Paradigm*, pp. 217–18.
63 Ibid.
64 Ibid.
65 Prothero, S. 2010. *God Is Not One*, p. 144.
66 Pramhansa Yogananda. 2002. *God Talks with Arjuna: The Bhagavat Gita*, p. 125. Royal Science of God Realization.
67 Planck, M. 1932. 'Epilogue'. *Where Is Science Going*, p. 217.
68 Sri Aurobindo. *Essays Divine and Human*, p. 64.
69 *Shiva Purana* (16.99; 16.100).
70 https://www.britannica.com/topic/Samkhya
71 *Rigveda* (10.90).
72 *Shiva Purana* (16.96; 16.98).
73 *Shiva Purana* (2.1.6); *Rudra Saṃhitā* (1): *Sṛṣṭi khaṇḍa*, pp. 19–21. Wisdom Library; 'Chapter 6', Description of the nature of Mahāpralaya and the origin of Viṣṇu.
74 Macdonell, A.A. 2004. *A Practical Sanskrit Dictionary*, p. 47. Motilal Banarsidass; *The Practical Sanskrit-English Dictionary*, 1890.
75 Ibid., p. 270.
76 Swami Vivekananda, *The Complete Works of Swami Vivekananda*, Volume 3.
77 *Taittiriya Upanishad* (2.4.1).
78 *Isha Upanishad* (5–6).
79 *Patanjali Yoga Sutras* (1.24).
80 Nicholson, A.J. 2017. 'Refuting Vedantic Theism in the Samkhya-Sutra'. *The Oxford Handbook of Indian Philosophy*, edited by Jonardon Ganeri, pp. 598–622. Oxford University Press.
81 *Vishnu Purana* (6.5.78).
82 BAGA – *Encyclopaedia Iranica* (iranicaonline.org)
83 Duri, A.A. 2012. 'Bag̲h̲dād', *Encyclopaedia of Islam*, Second edition. Bearman, P., Bianquis, Th., Bosworth, C.E., van Donzel, E. and W.P. Heinrichs (eds.).
84 http://vedicsuktams.blogspot.com/2011/03/bhagya-suktam-rigved-7-41.html
85 *Mundaka Upanishad* (1.1.3).
86 *Kali-Saṇṭāraṇa Upaniṣhad* (1.1).
87 *Vishnu Purana* (6.5.74; 6.5.47).
88 *Vishnu Purana* (6.5.71; 6.5.72; 6.5.73).
89 Ibid. (6.5.76).
90 Ibid. (6.5.80).
91 *Rigveda* (6.50.12).
92 Ibid. (9.81.5).

93 *Manusmriti* (11.35).
94 Vaishnavism glossary, starting with 'v' (wisdomlib.org)
95 Theravada glossary, starting with 'v' (wisdomlib.org)
96 *A Sanskrit-English Dictionary*, p. 90. Oxford University Press.
97 Kapoor, S. and M.K. Kapoor. 2009. 'Bachitar Natak's Composition', Compositions 8, 9 and 10, pp. 16–17. *Dasam Granth*. Hemkunt.
98 Winternitz, M. and V.S. Srinivasa Sarma. 1981. *A History of Indian Literature*, Volume 1, pp. 543–44. Motilal Banarsidass.
99 Srimad Bhāgavatam (5.5.24).
100 https://prabhupada.io/books/sb/5/5/24
101 'Mysticism'. *Encyclopedia Britannica.*
102 https://www.washingtonpost.com/national/health-science/there-really-are-50-eskimo-words-for-snow/2013/01/14/e0e3f4e0-59a0-11e2-beee-6e38f5215402_story.html
103 https://www.speakingtree.in/blog/280-sanskrit-words-for-water

Chapter 7: The Hindu Dharmic System

1 de Zwart, F. 2000. 'The Logic of Affirmative Action: Caste, Class and Quotas in India'. *Acta Sociologica*, 43 (3): pp. 235–49.
2 https://knowindia.gov.in/my-india-my-pride/quotes-on-india.php
3 Eliade, M. 1960. *Myths, Dreams and Mysteries: The Encounter between Contemporary Faiths and Archaic Realities*, translated by P. Mairet, pp. 85–87, 207–09. London: Harvill Press.
4 Ibid.
5 Durant, W. 1935. *Our Oriental Heritage: The Story of Civilization*, Volume 1. Simon & Schuster.
6 Fowler, J.D. 1997. *Hinduism: Beliefs and Practices*. Sussex Academic Press; Kurien, P. 2006. 'Multiculturalism and American Religion: The Case of Hindu Indian Americans'. *Social Forces*, 85 (2): pp. 723–41.
7 Gough, A.E. 1882. *Philosophy of the Upanishads*, p. 48. Trubner & Co.
8 Bhishagratna, Kaviraj K.L. 1911. *An English Translation of the Sushruta Samhita in Three Volumes*, Volume 2.
9 Bely, P.Y., Christian, C. and J.R. Roy, March 2010. *A Question and Answer Guide to Astronomy*, p. 197. Cambridge University Press.
10 https://www.opindia.com/2020/08/american-astronomer-carl-sagan-hindu-cosmology-cosmos-universe/amp/
11 http://www.hinduwisdom.info/Advanced_Concepts.htm
12 Flood, G.D. 1996. *An Introduction to Hinduism*. Cambridge University Press.
13 https://www.pewforum.org/2012/12/18/global-religious-landscape-hindu/

14 https://www.pewforum.org/2015/04/02/religious-projection-table/2010/number/all/
15 https://www.speakingtree.in/blog/ekam-sat-vipra-bahuda-vadanti/
16 *Maha Upanishad* (6.71).
17 *Brihadaaranyaka Upanishad* (1.4.14).
18 'Yuddha Kanda', Valmiki Ramayana.
19 Hiriyanna, M. 2000. 'Philosophy of Values'. *Indian Philosophy: Theory of Value,* edited by Roy Perrett, pp. 1–10. Routledge.
20 https://www.esamskriti.com/e/Spirituality/Philosophy/What-does-DARSHANA-mean-1.aspx
21 Whicher, I. 1998. *The Integrity of the Yoga Darśana: A Reconsideration of Classical Yoga.* SUNY Press.
22 https://www.orientviews.wordpress.com/2011/11/16/varnashrama-dharma-is-not-totalatarian/amp/
23 https://www.theatlantic.com/amp/article/599728/; https://pubmed.ncbi.nlm.nih.gov/26780279/
24 Bharti, S.V. 2001. *Yoga Sutras of Patanjali: With the Exposition of Vyasa*, Appendix I, pp. 672–80. Motilal Banarsidas.
25 Pramhansa Yogananda. 2002. *God Talks with Arjuna: The Bhagavat Gita*. P. 489. Royal Science of God Realization.
26 Srimad Bhagvad Gita (4.27).
27 https://parliamentofreligions.org/programs/swastika-proclamation-swastika-is-different-from-hakenkreuz/
28 Whicher, I. 1999. *The Integrity of the Yoga Darsana: A Reconsideration of Classical Yoga*, pp. 99–102. SUNY Press.
29 http://www.garamchai.com/temples.htm
30 *Isha Upanishad* (1).
31 *Taittiriya Samhitā* (6.3.10.5).
32 *Satapatha Brāhmana* (1.7.2.11).
33 https://www.sambhashan.com/dharmo-rakshathi-rakshithaha/%3famp
34 http://www.vam.ac.uk/content/articles/j/jainism-today/#:~:text=Today%20there%20are%20some%20six,the%20community%20is%20around%2030%2C000
35 https://worldpopulationreview.com/country-rankings/buddhist-countries
36 https://www.britannica.com/topic/Sikhism
37 Bayly, S. 2001. *Caste, Society and Politics in India from the Eighteenth Century to the Modern Age*. Cambridge University Press.
38 Jaiswal, S. 1978. 'Some Recent Theories of the Origin of Untouchability; A Historiographical Assessment'. Proceedings of the Indian History Congress.

39 Macdonell, A.A. and K.A. Berriedale. 1912. *Vedic Index of Names and Subjects*, pp. 474–76. London: Murray.

40 https://www.orissapost.com/why-are-hindu-marriages-mostly-held-at-night/amp/

41 Brick, D. 2010. 'The Dharmasastric Debate on Widow Burning'. *Journal of the American Oriental Society*, 130 (2): pp. 203–23. Available online: https://www.jstor.org/stable/23044515?seq=1

42 Banerjee, P. 2003. *Burning Women Widows, Witches, and Early Modern European Travelers in India*. Palgrave Macmillan.

43 Eaton, R.M. 1996. *The Rise of Islam and the Bengal Frontier* (1204–1760), p. 166. University of California Press.

44 *Atharvaveda* (3.24.5).

45 Tengadi, D.B. 2014. *Pt Deendayal Upadhyay Ideology & Perception (Part 1): An Inquest*, p. 189. Suruchi Prakashan.

46 http://www.thoreau-online.org/walden-page154.html

47 Ibid. (7.42).

48 https://detechter.com/these-8-western-philosophers-were-influenced-by-hinduism/

49 Mishra, V. 1994. *The Gothic Sublime*, p. 249. SUNY Press.

50 https://quotes.yourdictionary.com/author/quote/608234

51 Oppenheimer, J.R. 2014. *Atom and Void: Essays on Science and Community*, p. 8. Princeton University Press.

52 https://www.brainyquote.com/quotes/j_robert_oppenheimer_386571

53 https://www.ece.lsu.edu/kak/quotes21_40.htm

54 https://www.goodreads.com/topic/show/75083-a-book-referred-to-by-the-greatest-minds

55 Yogananda Paramhansa. 2002. *God Talks with Arjuna: The Bhagavat Gita*, p. 125. Royal Science of God Realization.

56 Rao, S.R. 1999. *The Lost City of Dvaraka*, p. 2. Aditya Prakashan.

57 http://www.hinduwisdom.info/quotes251_270.htm

58 years (translated from German), Volume 2, p. 45.

Chapter 8: Bengal's Contribution to Modern Patriotism and Nationalism

1 Chakravarti, K. and S. Chakravarti. 2013. *Historical Dictionary of the Bengalis*, p. 18.

2 https://www.getbengal.com/details/did-you-know-a-muslim-hazrat-khan-jahan-ali-started-the-line-of-pirali-brahmins

3 Banerjee, H. 2016. *Rabindranath Tagore*, p. 2. Publications Division.

4 http://www.londoni.co/index.php/90-history-of-bangladesh/biography/ram-mohan-roy/541-raja-ram-mohan-roy-early-life-education-family-biography-of-muslim-and-bengali
5 https://www.thestatesman.com/opinion/the-lost-icon-of-modernism-143856.html
6 https://archive.org/details/theenglishworks01rammuoft/mode/2up
7 https://www.encyclopedia.com/environment/encyclopedias-almanacs-transcripts-and-maps/roy-ram-mohan
8 Richards, M. and P. Hughes. 2014. *Rammohun Roy*, Unitarian Universalist Historical Society.
9 Robertson, B.C. 2000. *Raja Rammohan Ray: The Father of Modern India*, p. 180. Oxford.
10 Thangamuthu, P. 2017. *Contribution of Raja Rammohan Roy's to The Indian Education*. p. 11.
11 *The Complete Works of Sri Aurobindo*, Volume 6, p. 173, Sri Aurobindo Ashram, 2002.
12 https://www.hindustantimes.com/inspiring-lives/raja-rammohan-roy-the-maker-of-modern-india/story-LheC0FfFDrZCGq70aNYuXN.html
13 *The Complete Works of Swami Vivekananda*, Volume 7, Inspired Talks.
14 Sister Nivedita. 1913. *Notes of Some Wanderings with Swami Vivekananda*.
15 https://indianexpress.com/article/who-is/who-is-raja-ram-mohan-roy-brahmo-samaj-5186268/ ; https://www.thebrahmosamaj.net/founders/rammohun.html
16 Speech delivered at Barisal, 14 October 1917. *Collected Works of Deshbandhu*.
17 Collet, S.D. 1914. *The Life and Letters of Raja Rammohun Roy*, p. iv.
18 Ibid., p. 240.
19 Ibid, p. 329.
20 Collet, S.D. 1914. *The Life and Letters of Raja Rammohun Roy*, p. ii.
21 Zastoupil, L. 2010. *Rammohun Roy and the Making of Victorian Britain*, pp. xiv, 262. New York: Basingtoke.
22 Ibid., p. 240.
23 Biswas, D.K. (ed.). 1992. *The Correspondence of Raja Rammohun Roy: 1809-1831*, Volume 1, p. 285. Calcutta: Saraswat Library.
24 Lavan, S. 1977. *Complete Works of Ram Mohan Roy*, p. 552; *Unitarians and India: A Study in Encounter and Response*, p. 41. Boston: Beacon, 1977.
25 Collet, P. 115
26 Sugirtharajah, R.S. 2019. *The Brahmin and His Bible: Rammohun Roy's Precepts of Jesus 200 Years on*, p. 37. Bloomsbury Publishing.

27 https://tagoreweb.in/Essays/charitro-puja-29/rammohan-ray-2461
28 Ibid.
29 Nag, K. and D. Burman (eds.). 1946. *English Works of Raja Rammohan Roy*, Part II, p. 50. Calcutta: Brahmo Samaj.
30 Roy, R.R. 1947. *English Works of Rammohan Roy*, Volume 2, p. 44.
31 Raychaudhuri, G. 2012. *Swami Vivekananda: O Bangali Unobinghsho Shatabdi*, p. 37. Kolkata: Aruna Prakashan.
32 Biswas, D.K. (ed.). 1992. *The Correspondence of Raja Rammohun Roy: 1809–1831*, Volume 1, p. 172. Calcutta: Saraswat Library.
33 Dasgupta, T. 1993. *Social Thought of Rabindranath Tagore: A Historical Analysis*, p. 7. Abhinav Prakashan.
34 Collet, S.D. 1914. *The Life and Letters of Raja Rammohun Roy*, pp. ii, iii.
35 Ibid., p. iii.
36 Ibid., p. xivii.
37 Hodder, A.D. 1988. 'Emerson, Rammohan Roy, and the Unitarians', p. 134. *Studies in the American Renaissance.*
38 Ibid., p. 135.
39 Ibid.
40 Zastoupil, 2002 p. 238.
41 Hodder, A.D. 1988. 'Emerson, Rammohan Roy, and the Unitarians', pp. 133–48. *Studies in the American Renaissance.*
42 Singh, B. 1991. 'Henry Willard French and India'. *The New England Quarterly*, 64 (4): p. 588. Available online: http://links.jstor.org/sici?sici=0028-4866%28199112%2964%3A4%3C574%3AHWFAI%3E2.0.CO%3B2-S
43 *The Harvard Theological Review*, 86 (4), p. 410, 1993; Jeswine. 'Apprentice to Hindu Sages', pp. 28–29; cited in *The New Thoreau Handbook*, 1994.
44 Ibid p.410: Thoreau, Original Source – Correspondence.
45 Hodder, A.D. 1993. 'Ex Oriente Lux: Thoreau's Ecstasies and the Hindu Texts'. *The Harvard Theological Review,* 86 (4): pp. 403–38.
46 Ibid., p. 494.
47 Ibid., pp. 403–38.
48 Singh, B. 1991. 'Henry Willard French and India'. *The New England Quarterly*, 64 (4): p. 588.
49 Rothbard, M. 1967. *Confessions of a Right-Wing Liberal.*
50 Maynard, W.B. 2005. *Walden Pond: A History*, p. 265. Oxford University Press.
51 Kifer, K. *Analysis and Notes on Walden: Henry Thoreau's Text with Adjacent Thoreauvian Commentary.*
52 Hendrick, G. and F. Oehlschlaeger (eds.). 1979. *Toward the Making of Thoreau's Modern Reputation*. University of Illinois Press.

53 Collet, S.D. 1914. *The Life and Letters of Raja Rammohun Roy*, pp. xivii, 188. Available online: http://ia800205.us.archive.org/5/items/lifelettersofraj00collrich/lifelettersofraj00collrich.pdf
54 Robertson, B.C. 2013. *Swami Vivekananda and Rajarshi Rammohan Ray: Two Views on Sacred Authority, Two Visions of Modern India*, p. 6. Nehru Memorial Museum and Library.
55 https://www.royalacademy.org.uk/art-artists/work-of-art/the-rajah-rammohan-roy
56 https://commons.wikimedia.org/wiki/File:Portrait_of_Raja_Ram_Mohun_Roy,_1833.jpg
57 Hodder, A.D. 1988. 'Emerson, Rammohan Roy, and the Unitarians', *Studies in the American Renaissance*, p. 146.
58 Kopf, D. 1979. *Brahmo Samaj and the Making of Modern India.* USA: Princeton University Press.
59 *Pakistan Journal of History and Culture*, Volume 11. p. 4. Pakistan: National Institute of Historical and Cultural Research.
60 Chattopadhyaya, R. 1999. *Swami Vivekananda in India: A Corrective Biography*. Motilal Banarsidass Publishers Private Limited.
61 https://vdocuments.in/en-wikipedia-org-wiki-sadharan-brahmo-samaj.html
62 Mittal, S.C. 1986. *Haryana: A Historical Perspective*, p. 80. Atlantic Publishers.
63 Collet, S.D. 1914. *The Life and Letters of Raja Rammohun Roy*, p. xivii.
64 Sharma, U. and K.S. Sharma. 1996. *Indian Political Thought*, p. 94.
65 Mitra, S.K. 2005. 'The centenary year of the war-cry: Vande Mataram', 21 August.
66 Pargiter, F.F. 1922. *Ancient Indian Historical Tradition*, p. 131. Delhi: Motilal Banarsidass.
67 *Manusmriti* (2.22).
68 *Varaha Purana* (75.11).
69 Tagore, Rabindranath. 1917. 'Nationalism in India'. *Nationalism.* Book Club of California.
70 https://archive.org/details/dli.bengal.10689.18434
71 https://soundcloud.com/ramakrishnamath/lecture-by-dr-s-radhakrishnan-on-swami-vivekanandas-centenary-1963
72 'Lectures from Colombo to Almora'. *The Complete Works of Swami Vivekananda*, Volume 3.
73 Ibid.
74 Ibid.
75 https://vivekavani.com/v-alasinga-letters-swami-vivekananda/

76 https://www.rediff.com/amp/news/interview/jana-gana-mana-was-not-sung-in-praise-of-the-english-king/20150717.htm
77 Bose, S. and I. Pande. 2011. 'Tagorean Universalism and Cosmopolitanism'. *India International Centre Quarterly*, 38 (1): pp. 2–17.
78 Paranjape. M.R. (ed.). 2015. *Swami Vivekananda: A Contemporary Reader*. Routledge.
79 Interview of Tagore in *The Times of India*, 18 April 1924.
80 'Letter to historian Dr Kalidas Nag by Rabindranath'. *Vishwa Bharti*, Volume 24, p. 375, 1982.
81 Ibid.
82 Tagore, R. 1926. 'Swamy Shraddananda'. *Kalantar*.
83 From the 'letter to Hemantabala Sarkar', 16 October 1933, quoted in *Swastika*.
84 'Samasya'. *Kalantar*, 1923.
85 https://www.researchgate.net/publication/331581549_Shivaji-Utsav_Shivaji_Festival_By_Rabindranath_Tagore_in_ArtsLiterature-by_Monish_R_Chatterjee/link/5c815c09299bf1268d449270/download?_tp=eyJjb250ZXh0Ijp7ImZpcnN0UGFnZSI6InB1YmxpY2F0aW9uIiwicGFnZSI6InB1YmxpY2F0aW9uIn19
86 Sen, N.B. *Glorious Thoughts of Tagore*, p. 165. New Book Society of India.
87 https://news.yahoo.com/news/hardlight-jana-gana-mana-adhinayaka-092007871.html
88 *Indian Express*, 3 June 1968.
89 Sen, P.C. 1939. 'Personal Letters'. *Our National Anthem*.
90 Ramaswami, S. 2010. *The Goddess and the Nation: Mapping Mother India*. Duke University Press.
91 'Shri Shri Pranavananda Upadesh', translated by Radhakrishna Pradhan.
92 Swami Vedananda. 'Sri Sri Yugacharya Jibancharit'. *The Biography of Prananbananda*.
93 https://www.caluniv.ac.in/about/vc.html
94 https://swarajyamag.com/magazine/a-death-in-kashmir-the-mystery-surrounding-syama-prasad-mookerjees-death; Roy, T. 2014. *The Life and Times of Shyama Prasad Mookerjee: A Complete Biography*. Prabhat Prakashan; https://m.hindustantimes.com/delhi/bjp-demands-inquiry-into-sp-mukherjee-s-death-claims-murder-conspiracy-by-sheikh-abdullah/story-8bQWp9xZwfZy0OYUY5FaZP.html

Chapter 9: Hindutva

1 https://www.speakingtree.in/allslides/2a-480499
2 http://www.valmikiramayan.net/yuddha/sarga124/yuddhaitrans124.htm#Verse17
3 'Hindutva'. Oxford English Dictionary Online, 2011.
4 Merriam-Webster, Inc; *Encyclopaedia Britannica*.1999. *Merriam-Webster's Encyclopedia of World Religions*. Merriam-Webster. p. 464.
5 *Shivaji and Swarajya, 1975*, p. 9. Orient Longman.
6 Setumadhava Rao, P. 1983. *Shivaji*, p. i. National Book Trust.
7 Banhatti, G.S. 1995. *Life and Philosophy of Swami Vivekananda*, p. 201. Atlantic Publishers.
8 Nanjunda Rao, Dr M.C. 1914–16. 'The Echoes of the Teachings of Vivekananda', p. 219. *Vedanta Kesari*. Available online: https://archive.org/details/Swami_Vivekananda_On_Sivaji_by_MC_Nanjunda_Rao_1916_Vedanta_Kesari
9 Ibid.
10 Black, J. 2006. *A Military History of Britain: From 1775 to the Present*. Greenwood Publishing Group.
11 Jordens, J.T.F. 1960. *Dayananda Sarasvati: His Life and Ideas*, pp. 77–78. Oxford University Press.
12 https://www.indiatoday.in/magazine/international/story/19890331-plaques-of-gandhi-patel-tilak-and-savarkar-put-up-in-london-815913-1989-03-
13 Ibid.
14 Sharma, A. 2002. 'On Hindu, Hindustān, Hinduism and Hindutva'. *Numen*, 49 (1): pp. 1-36.
15 'Swastika: SYMBOL'. *Encyclopædia Britannica*, 2017.
16 *Rigveda* (9.6.5).
17 https://aryasamajhouston.org/resources1/articles1/veda-sudha1/krinvanto-vishwamaryam1
18 Savarkar, V.D. *Essentials of Hindutva*, p. 6.
19 Savarkar, V.D. 1949. *Hindu Rāṣṭra Darshan*. Akhil Bharatiya Hindu Mahasabha.
20 Savarkar, V.D. *Essentials of Hindutva*, p. 4.
21 https://savarkar.org/en/pdfs/babarao-savarkar-v003.pdf
22 Savarkar, V.D. *Essentials of Hindutva*, p. 54.
23 Ibid.
24 Christophe, J. 1999. *The Hindu Nationalist Movement and Indian Politics (1925 to the 1990s): Strategies of Identity-building, Implantation and Mobilisation (with Special Reference to Central India)*, pp. 25–26. Penguin.

25 Kanungo, P. 2002. *RSS's Tryst with Politics: From Hedgewar to Sudarshan*. Manohar.
26 Chandra, B., Mukherjee, M. and A. Mukherjee. 2000. *India after Independence: 1947–2000*. New Delhi: Penguin Books.
27 https://indiankanoon.org/doc/631708/?__cf_chl_jschl_tk__=36acd65e357616e6d67ae3d70bcec16fad63aeb8-1604081795-0-AfMVp4ywmsIfuDrVngCBVaigRZJloT5vCf1DkaREGgFOj4U7TIa33S2MggA8dlL2-EhLRkKyhYQtbN4M6G8pSuTqJsGAS0gdLulpPu_jIeKypkH8wjFfENEmGMhLM1rUONrdz3ryl0ApZN4sM2i6lBAlGhSzwc5pYjsxoK5kmA9BDZlwb_cBPvHwi0fRLHCzNuZPFz-o108VeLOd5zG9UEaSlgGiTDOWKNd7nmpctVV2VDWjZKsnHoXY2l8JX3MrS3PubCbESZV0Gyec_rnsdvE7GZx_6RASEi4wBR_iLULIcuVr6RBmwlmGisbs_KIX48IicBxLcf87t44vIZsvMpZ7yA8k7aISccxNSBuW4DVm
28 https://indiankanoon.org/docfragment/925631/?big=0&formInput=sindhu
29 https://www.frontline.thehindu.com/the-nation/supreme-court-and-hindutva/article5596736.ece/amp/; https://academic.oup.com/book/11019/chapter-abstract/159365045?redirectedFrom=fulltext

Chapter 10: Nationalism: Meaning and Scope of Freedom

1 Berlin, I. 1958. *Two Concepts of Liberty*. Oxford University Press.
2 Cranston, M. 1954. *Freedom: A New Analysis*, Longmans Green.
3 Alder, J.M. 1958. *The Idea of Freedom*. p. 251 Greenwood Publishing Group.
4 Ibid.
5 Swami Vivekananda. 1919. *Complete Works of Swami Vivekananda*, Volume 4, p. 201. Advaita Ashrama.
6 Swami Vivekananda. 1919. *Complete Works of Swami Vivekananda*, Volume 5. Advaita Ashrama.
7 Sri Aurobindo. *The Ideal of Human Unity*, pp. 155–56.
8 Ibid.
9 Ibid., pp. 206–07.
10 Ibid., p. 513.
11 Tagore, R. 1917. *Nationalism*. Book Club of California.
12 Berlin, I. 1958. *Two Concepts of Liberty*. Oxford University Press.
13 Swami Vivekananda. 1947. *Complete Works of Swami Vivekananda*. Vedanta Press.
14 Ibid.
15 https://www.latimes.com/archives/la-xpm-2000-jul-04-me-47587-story.html%3f_amp=true

16 https://www.goodreads.com/quotes/143203-freedom-has-its-life-in-the-hearts-the-actions-the
17 https://belurmath.org/swami-vivekananda/
18 Chang, L. 2006. *Wisdom for the Soul: Five Millennia of Prescriptions for Spiritual Healing*. Gnosophia Publishers.
19 https://studylib.net/doc/5559592/the-role-of-hindu-dharma-and-our-role-in-hindu-dharma
20 https://www.ryandelaney.co/book-notes/the-7-habits-of-highly-effective-people-stephen-covey; https://www.franklincovey.co.uk/blog/2022/05/10/the-four-human-endowments/
21 Tagore, R. 1912. 'Poem No. 35'. *Gitanjali*. Indian Society of London.
22 https://www.forbes.com/quotes/3406/
23 Moore, S. (trans.). 1888. *Marx/Engels Selected Works*, Volume One. Moscow: Progress Publishers.
24 Tolstoy, L. 1901. *Patriotism and Government*. Free Age Press.
25 Harris, S.J. 1953. *Strictly Personal*. H. Regnery Company.
26 Phillips, T.C. 1850. *The Complete Poetical Works of Thomas Campbell*.
27 https://harpers.org/2008/07/mr-twain-offers-a-lesson-on-patriotism/
28 Hall, I. 2009. *British International Thinkers from Hobbes to Namier*, p. 172. Springer.
29 *Rigveda* (1.89.1).
30 Curtis, G.W. 1894. *On the Principles and Character of American Institutions, and the Duties of American Citizens 1856–1891*. Harper and Brothers.
31 Ghose, A. 1907. 'The Unhindu Spirit of Caste Rigidity'. *On Nationalism*, pp. 228–30. Rishi Aurobindo Ashram.
32 'Selected Speeches of Subhas Chandra Bose', p. 33. 1962. Ministry of Information and Broadcasting, Government of India.
33 *Rigveda* (10.192.2).
34 *Rigveda* (10.191.4).
35 *Rigveda* (8.32.16; 6.61.1).
36 *Taittiriya Samhitā* (6.3.10.5).
37 *Satapatha Brāhmana* (1.7.2.11).
38 Twain, M. 1889. *A Connecticut Yankee in King Arthur's Court*, pp.100–01. Harper and Brothers.
39 https://www.ushistory.org/paine/crisis/c-04.htm
40 https://documentaryheaven.com/we-arundhati-roy/#google_vignette
41 https://lskitka.people.uic.edu/flag.pdf

42 https://www.goodreads.com/quotes/147358-patriotism-means-to-stand-by-the-country-it-does-not
43 Tagore, R. 1917. 'Nationalism in India'. *Nationalism*. Book Club of California.
44 Bandopadhyaya, N.C. 1927. *Development of Hindu Polity and Political Theories*, p. 168. Calcutta: R. Cambray and Co.
45 Sri Aurobindo. *The Human Cycle: The Ideal of Human Unity War and Self-Determination*, p. 356.
46 https://mast.queensu.ca/~murty/Tagore-Nationalism-1915.pdf
47 Gide, A. 1930. *The Immoralist* (English). Alfred A. Knopf.

Chapter II: Misperceptions about the Hindu Dharmic System

1 https://www.opindia.com/2020/11/the-wire-rakes-up-manusmriti-to-demonise-hinduism-yet-again/
2 *Manusmriti* (3.55).
3 Ibid., (3.56).
4 Ibid., (3.57).
5 Ibid., (3.58).
6 *Rigveda* (10.90.11; 10.90.12).
7 Bhagavad Gita (4.13).
8 Srikantan, G. 2014. *Entanglements in Legal History*, p. 123. Germany: Max Planck Institute.
9 Sinha, J. 2014. *Psycho-Social Analysis of the Indian Mindest*, p. 5. Springer Academic.
10 https://www.mea.gov.in/Images/attach/amb/Volume_17_01.pdf
11 *Manusmriti* (10.64.65).
12 *Manusmriti* (8.337.338).
13 https://greenmesg.org/stotras/vedas/om_sarve_bhavantu_sukhinah.php
14 Sri Durga Saptasati, Chandi Path.
15 Watters, Th. 1904. *On Yuan Chwang's Travels in India, 629–45 AD*, Volume 1. London: Royal Asiatic Society..
16 Al-Biruni. 1887. *A Critical Study of What India Says, Whether Accepted by Reason or Refused* (Arabic), edited by E. Sachau, Trübner & Company (Originally Published in 1030).
17 de Zwart, F. 2000. 'The Logic of Affirmative Action: Caste, Class and Quotas in India'. *Acta Sociologica*, 43 (3): pp. 235–49.
18 https://voiceofindia.me/2017/06/22/logic-behind-the-perversion-of-caste-ram-swarup/amp/

19 Bayly, S. 2004. *Saints, Goddesses and Kings: Muslims and Christians in South Indian Society*. Cambridge University Press.

20 *Castes of Mind: Colonialism and the Making of Modern India*, 2001, p. 5. Princeton University Press.

21 https://originalpeople.org/casta/

22 https://socialsci.libretexts.org/Bookshelves/Sociology/Book%3A_Sociology_(Boundless)/08%3A_Global_Stratification_and_Inequality/8.01%3A_Systems_of_Stratification/8.1C%3A_Caste_Systems#:~:text=efforts%20for%20reform.-,Europe,clergy%2C%20bourgeoisie%2C%20and%20peasants

23 Dumont, L. 1970. *Homo Hieararchicus: The Caste System and Its Implications.*

24 Quigley, D. 1993. Reader in Social Anthropology Declan Quigley Clarendon Press. https://www.ece.lsu.edu/kak/caste3

25 https://archive.org/details/DharampalCollectedWritingsIn5Volumes/5DharampalJiCollectedWritings-essaysOnTraditionRecoveryAndFreedom/page/n225/mode/1up

26 https://bharatabharati.in/2012/08/30/caste-the-view-from-belgium-koenraad-elst/amp/

27 Swami Vivekananda in reply to the address of welcome from the Hindus of Jaffna, Sri Lanka. *Complete Works of Swami Vivekananda*. Advaita Ashrama.

28 *The Complete Works of Swami Vivekananda*, Volume 5.

29 Swarup, R. 'Logic behind perversion of caste'. *Indian Express*, 13 September 1996.

30 Lal, K.S. 1995. *Growth of Scheduled Tribes and Castes in Medieval India*. Aditya Prakashan.

31 Durkheim, E. 1997. *The Division of Labor in Society*, translated by W.D. Halls. New York: Free Press.

32 Fukuyama, F. 1996. *Trust: Human Nature and the Reconstitution of Social Order*. Simon & Schuster.

33 Kanagasabapathi, P. 2013. *Indian Models of Economy, Business and Management*, p. 135. PHI Learning Pvt. Ltd.

34 Swami Vivekananda. 1893. 'Lectures from Colombo to Almora'. *The Complete Works of Swami Vivekananda*, Volume 3.

35 https://esamskriti.com/e/History/Great-Indian-Leaders/My-beliefs-baaay-Swami-Dayanand-Saraswati-1.aspx

36 Ambedkar, B.R. 1936. *Annihilation of Caste*, Second edition, Appendix II. Available online: https://ccnmtl.columbia.edu/projects/mmt/ambedkar/web/appendix_2.html

37 Biswas, S. 'Gandhi's Approach to Caste and Untouchability'. *Social Scientist.*
38 https://auro-ebooks-in.s3.ap-south-1.amazonaws.com/book-uploads/Sri-Aurobindo-India-Rebirth.pdf
39 *Skanda Purana* (6.239.31).
40 Bhagavad Gita (4.13).
41 Letter of Swami Vivekananda to Khetri Maharaja Ajit Singh, 4 March 1895; https://www.rkmissionkhetri.org/news/?page_id=291
42 'Lectures from Colombo to Almore'. *The Complete Works of Swami Vivekananda*, Volume 3.
43 Swami Vivekananda on India and Her Problems, 1946, p. 78. Advaita Ashram.
44 Sri Aurobindo. 'Sapta Chatusthaya', *SABCL Supplement*, Volume 27.
45 http://www.kenwilber.com/home/landing/index.html
46 Sri Aurobindo. *Collected Works of Sri Aurobindo*, Volume 33, p. 46.

Chapter 12: Dharma Is the Future

1 Cadwalladr, C. 2014. 'Are the robots about to rise?', *Guardian*, 22 February. Available online: https://www.theguardian.com/technology/2014/feb/22/robots-google-ray-kurzweil-terminator-singularity-artificial-intelligence
2 Chalmers, D.J. 2010. 'The Singularity: A Philosophical Analysis'. *Journal of Consciousness Studies*, 17 (9–10): pp. 7–65. Available online: https://consc.net/papers/singularity.pdf
3 https://ourworldindata.org/child-mortality#:~:text=We%20are%20currently%20far%20away%20from%20the%20goal%20for%202030,15%2C000%20children%20die%20every%20day
4 https://www.who.int/news/item/18-06-2019-1-in-3-people-globally-do-not-have-access-to-safe-drinking-water-unicef-who
5 https://yaleglobal.yale.edu/content/cities-grow-so-do-numbers-homeless
6 https://www.macrotrends.net/countries/WLD/world/literacy-rate
7 https://www.independence.edu/blog/who-in-the-world-holds-a-college-degree; https://educateinspirechange.org/alternative-news/how-many-people-of-the-world-have-a-college-degree/
8 https://www.who.int/news/item/13-07-2020-as-more-go-hungry-and-malnutrition-persists-achieving-zero-hunger-by-2030-in-doubt-un-report-warns
9 https://www.who.int/news-room/fact-sheets/detail/sanitation
10 https://www.theguardian.com/inequality/2017/nov/14/worlds-richest-wealth-credit-suisse

11 https://www.unicef.org/press-releases/child-under-15-dies-every-five-seconds-around-world-un-report
12 https://newsinhealth.nih.gov/2014/02/stop-spread-superbugs
13 https://mom.com/momlife/staggering-sexual-assault-statistics-everyone-should-read/transgender-college-students-are-at-higher-risk
14 https://www.who.int/violence_injury_prevention/key_facts/en/
15 https://www.who.int/news-room/fact-sheets/detail/injuries-and-violence
16 https://www.cdc.gov/globalhealth/healthprotection/fetp/training_modules/2/ncd-burden-of-disease_ppt_final_09252013.pdf
17 https://ourworldindata.org/terrorism
18 Ehrlich, P.R. and A.H. Ehrlich. 2005. *One with Nineveh: Politics, Consumption, and the Human Future*. Island Press.
19 Huntington, S.P. 1996. *The Clash of Civilizations and the Remaking of World Order*. Simon and Schuster.
20 Fukuyama, F. 1992. *The End of History and the Last Man*. Free Press.
21 Doshi, N. 1976. *Guidance from Sri Aurobindo: Letters to a Young Disciple*. Shri Aurobindo Ashram.
22 *Collected Words of the Mothers*, 1978, Volume 13, p. 222. Sri Aurobindo Ashram. Available online: https://incarnateword.in/cwm/13/aims-and-principles
23 *Collected Works of Sri Aurobindo*, Volume 33, p. 46.
24 Ibid.
25 *Isha Upanishad* (1).
26 Shenker, I. 1972. 'Einstein Letters Show the Physicist as Person'. New York Times, 1 December.
27 *Chāndogya Upanishad* (3.14.1).
28 Kaiwar, V. and S. Mazumdar. 2003. 'Sri Aurobindo's Uttarpara Speech'. *Antinomies of Modernity: Essays on Race, Orient, Nation*. Duke University Press.
29 Paranjape, M.R. 2009. *Altered Destinations: Self, Society, and Nation in India*, p. 36. Anthem Press.
30 Prabhu, R.K. and U.R. Rao. 1960. *Mahatma Gandhi: The Mind of Mahatma Gandhi*, p. 374. Navajivan Mudranalaya, Navajivan Trust.
31 https://www.timesnownews.com/amp/spiritual/religion/article/independence-day-2020-influence-of-the-sacred-bhagavad-gita-on-the-freedom-fighters/637291
32 Gordon, L.A. 1990. *Brothers against the Raj: A Biography of Indian Nationalists Sarat and Subhas Chandra Bose*. Columbia University Press.
33 https://marketime.blogspot.com/2006/03/sri-aurobindo-on-nature-of-true.html

34 Robinson, E.W. 1997. *The First Democracies: Early Popular Government Outside Athens*, pp. 16–17. Franz Steiner Verla.
35 https://penelope.uchicago.edu/Thayer/E/Roman/Texts/Diodorus_Siculus/2B*.html#350
36 Grover, V. 1993. *Political Thinkers of Modern India: Sri Aurobindo Ghosh*, p. 30. Deep & Deep Publication; Sri Aurobindo. 1908. 'Bande Mataram', *Early Political Writings*.
37 https://shodhganga.inflibnet.ac.in/bitstream/10603/165186/8/08_chapter%205.pdf
38 Ibid.
39 Sharma, A. 2002. 'On Hindu, Hindustān, Hinduism and Hindutva'. *Numen*, 49 (1): pp. 1–36.
40 Lesaffer, R. 2014. 'Peace treaties from Lodi to Westphalia'. *Peace Treaties and International Law in European History: From the Late Middle Ages to World War One*. Cambridge.
41 Ambekar, S. 2019. *The RSS: Roadmaps for the 21st Century*. Rupa Publications.
42 Golwalkar, M.S. 1966. *Bunch of Thoughts*, p. 160. Bangalore: Vikram Prakashan.
43 Ibid., p. 150.
44 Griffin, R. and M. Feldman (eds). 2004. *The Nature of Fascism*, Volume 1, p. 9. Taylor & Francis; Ramswell, P.Q. 2017. *Euroscepticism and the Rising Threat from the Left and Right: The Concept of Millennial Fascism*, p. 258. Lexington Books.
45 https://www.historicalmaterialism.org/fascism-is-a-reaction-to-capitalist-crisis-in-the-stage-of-imperialism/
46 https://www.csmonitor.com/1985/0508/esov-f1.html
47 https://www.armenian-genocide.org/hitler.html; https://www.meforum.org/3434/armenian-genocide-hitler
48 https://www.smithsonianmag.com/history/genocide-us-cant-remember-bangladesh-cant-forget-180961490/
49 https://franpritchett.com/00generallinks/macaulay/txt_minute_education_1835.html
50 https://www.crosswalk.com/family/career/to-promote-positive-change-start-with-grief.html
51 https://neuroepic.mcdb.lsa.umich.edu/wp/5-genocide-genes/
52 https://www.ncbi.nlm.nih.gov/pmc/articles/PMC6008527/
53 Quran (2.191).
54 Quran (2.194).
55 Thoreau, H. 1849. Letter to H.G.O. Blake. Available online: https://yogainternational.com/article/view/why-did-thoreau-take-the-bhagavad-gita-to-walden-pond

56 Ibid.
57 www.nadiasinitiative.org
58 Hewitt, W.L. 2004. *Defining the Horrific: Readings on Genocide and Holocaust in the 20th Century*. P. 287. Pearson Education.
59 https://2001-2009.state.gov/r/pa/ho/frus/nixon/xi/45650.htm
60 https://www.nytimes.com/2013/09/30/opinion/nixon-and-kissingers-forgotten-shame.html
61 Bose, Ch. 1892. 'Hindutva: True History of Hindus', Calcutta: Gurudas Chattopadhyay, Medical Library.
62 https://vivekavani.com/plan-campaign-vivekananda/
63 https://vivekavani.com/education-manifestation-perfection-man/
64 http://voiceofdharma.org/books/hhrmi/ch2.htm
65 Sri Aurobindo. 1902–30. 'Collected Poems'. *SABCL*. Volume 5. The Meditations of Mandavya.
66 Swami Vivekananda. *The Complete Works of Swami Vivekananda*, Volume 3.
67 Sen, A.P. 1930. 'Utho Go Bharat Lakshmi' ('উঠ গো ভারত-লক্ষ্মী'). Hindusthan Record Company.
68 Swami Vivekananda. *The Complete Works of Swami Vivekananda*, Volume 3.
69 *Rigveda* (1.170.4).
70 *Shvetashvatara Upanishad* (2.5).
71 https://vivekavani.com/paper-on-hinduism-swami-vivekananda/
72 Grover, V. 1993. *Political Thinkers of Modern India: Sri Aurobindo Ghosh*, p. 30. Deep & Deep Publication.

About the Author

Kanchan Banerjee was born in a small village in West Bengal. He witnessed the rise of communist movements, including the Left Front and Naxalism, before moving to the US. He holds a bachelor's degree in biology from Bardhaman University, West Bengal, India, and a master's in computer science from Boston University, Massachusetts, US.

A thinker, researcher, and author, Kanchan is a prominent Hindu and Indian American social leader, actively supporting numerous Indian and Hindu organizations worldwide. He is also a dedicated yoga teacher. Kanchan has a keen interest in Indian history and its place in world history, which is driven by a desire to understand why Indians remain disconnected from their past and future.

His previous book, *The Crash of a Civilization*, received global recognition. *Amritasya Putrah* continues his quest to rediscover Bharat's rich heritage and chart a path forward.

www.ingramcontent.com/pod-product-compliance
Lightning Source LLC
Chambersburg PA
CBHW022132060526
44654CB00043B/521
9789365479508